Rhetoric in Civic Life

Catherine Helen Palczewski
University of Northern Iowa

Richard Ice
College of St. Benedict | St. John's University

John Fritch
University of Northern Iowa

Strata Publishing, Inc.
State College, Pennsylvania

9 8 7 6 5 4 3 2 1

Rhetoric in Civic Life

Strata Publishing, Inc.
P.O. 1303
State College, PA 16803
USA

Telephone: 814-234-8545
Fax: 814-238-7222

http://www.stratapub.com

Text and cover design by WhiteOak Creative.

Photo on front cover and pages ii, 1, 33, and 147, "Palm leaves woven together," © Caley Tse/Design Pics/Corbis.

Credits and acknowledgments appear on pages 271–272 and on this page by reference.

The URLs in this book were accurate as of the date cited or the date of publication. Neither the authors nor Strata guarantee the accuracy of information provided in websites listed.

Library of Congress Cataloging-in-Publication Data

Palczewski, Catherine Helen.
  Rhetoric in civic life / Catherine Helen Palczewski, Richard Ice, John Fritch.
    p. cm.
  Includes index.
  ISBN 978-1-891136-28-3 (pbk. : alk. paper)
  1. Rhetoric.   I. Ice, Richard, date. II. Fritch, John, date. III. Title.
P301.P23 2012
808–dc23
                      2011049565

ISBN: 978-1-891136-28-3

to Arnie, Jeanne, and Trudy
our partners in life
who enact with us the possibility of disagreeing
without being disagreeable

Brief Contents

Contents

Preface

The impetus for writing *Rhetoric in Civic Life* came from our desire for a textbook for our own courses that would approach rhetoric from a conceptual perspective, rather than unfolding chronologically or focusing on key theorists. We wanted to provide our students with a sense of the disciplinary evolution of rhetorical concepts, but with an emphasis on explicating the concepts, rather than on who said what and when.

This textbook is intended for introductory rhetorical theory courses; persuasion courses that adopt a rhetorical approach; courses on rhetoric, civic life, and civic engagement; and rhetorical criticism courses that approach criticism as an inventional practice. It could also be used for advanced rhetorical theory courses, perhaps supplemented with primary texts from core theorists.

Our goal was to provide an introduction that would help students understand how rhetoric shapes and creates meaning in the full range of civic life, from the instrumental rhetoric of deliberative and electoral politics to the constitutive rhetoric of public memory and identity formation. We wanted to write a textbook that students would find useful and engaging, and that also presented scholarship clearly and substantively, describing complex theories with the nuance and subtlety they deserve. We reference a range of classical and contemporary theories and theorists, comparing and interweaving ideas from the rise of ancient Greek democracy (Aristotle, Plato, and the Sophists), to twentieth-century theorists (including Kenneth Burke, Susanne K. Langer, Lucie Olbrechts-Tyteca, and Chaïm Perelman), to the most recent cutting-edge research appearing in the discipline's books and journals. We wrote this book from the perspective that rhetoric—whether verbal, visual, argumentative, or narrative—is symbolic action with consequences and, as such, deserves careful study.

We strove for writing that is clear and concise, but not oversimplified, providing extensive documentation through endnotes. We endeavored to define terms and concepts clearly and to provide an abundance of examples that would resonate with students. By including short texts and offering brief analyses that deploy the concepts covered, we attempted to show students how a rhetorical approach offers an enhanced understanding of how social reality is created, maintained, and challenged.

FEATURES OF THE BOOK

Emphasis on civic life: Although the book discusses rhetoric across its many theoretical, cultural, and practical contexts, the central emphasis is on rhetoric in civic life—not only the discourse of people in political power, but also deliberative debates about policy and cultural debates about civic identity. We wanted students to understand that all members of a public have a role to play in civic life, and to understand the range of, and limits on, each person's power. We wanted them to understand that rhetoric has consequences—particularly for identity, power, memory, and ideology—and, thus, shapes social reality.

Conceptual approach: We have attempted to provide a heuristic vocabulary that will help students make sense of rhetoric's forms, functions, and consequences. The textbook explores theories and theorists from an integrated, topical perspective. Thus, the contributions of some theorists appear in multiple chapters. We do not dictate a particular methodological approach, but rather offer a range of concepts that enable more subtle and nuanced analyses of symbolic action. The concepts should be generative; they should enable students to ask smarter questions about the symbolic actions they encounter.

Expansive range of rhetorical theories: The textbook grounds each chapter in traditional rhetorical theories, describing the core concept (rhetor, audience, argument, and so on), then extends the study of that concept by drawing from recent scholarship. For example, in the discussion of rhetors, we cover the classical conceptions of ethos, but also problematize the very notion of the rhetor with a careful consideration of identity as intersectional (rather than essential) and the possibilities of using strategic essentialism as a rhetorical resource. This approach enables the study of rhetorical forms from legislative debates and public address to body argument and visual rhetorics.

Detailed examples: Abundant historical and contemporary examples show how words, images, arguments, and stories have consequences. These examples include presidential speeches in times of crisis, a city council meeting about whether to protect local merchants or permit "big box" stores, abolitionist speakers who caused northerners to think of slaves as suffering human beings, image events and street theatre in political protest, political campaigns, national monuments that celebrate a shared history and reinforce a shared set of values, public debates over issues such as health care and immigration, and events and issues in students' personal and campus lives.

ORGANIZATION OF THE BOOK

Rhetoric in Civic Life is composed of nine chapters, organized into three parts. The chapters are organized around the central facets of rhetoric's form and function. The organization of chapters is flexible; however, we believe instructors can teach the chapters in any order they wish, according to their own needs.

Part I, "Introduction," consists of a single chapter.

Chapter 1, "Rhetoric as Symbolic Action," defines rhetoric and explains its historical foundation in democratic traditions. It explains rhetoric as a form of symbolic *action*, as a central means of enacting civic engagement, and as both a creator and practice of ideology, public memory, and power.

Part II, "Forms of Symbolic Action," includes four chapters.

Chapter 2, "Language," introduces language as symbolic action, a novel idea for many students. Drawing on theories of linguistic relativity, semiotics, and dramatism, the chapter shows that language is not merely a means by which humans transmit information; it also constitutes social reality. The chapter explores the ways that a public vocabulary forms social reality (through characterizations, metaphors, and ideographs), as well as the possibilities of resignification.

Chapter 3, "Visual Rhetoric," encourages students to ask not just "What does an image mean?" but also "What does an image do?" The chapter examines the power of four categories of visual rhetoric: iconic photographs, monuments, bodies, and image events.

Chapter 4, "Argument," describes the role of argument in civic life, the classical concept of *logos*, and approaches to analyzing an argument. It explores argument as a thing and as an interactional process, drawing on the Toulmin model and on theory about spheres of argument (technical, personal, and public).

Chapter 5, "Narrative," is informed by Walter Fisher's narrative paradigm and by Kenneth Burke's representative anecdote and comic/tragic frames, providing students with a critical approach to understanding narrative.

Part III, "Components of Symbolic Action," includes four chapters.

Chapter 6, "Rhetors," explores the concept of the rhetor as both producing and produced by rhetorical action. The chapter introduces students to the idea of persona and its various facets. It explains identity as a social construction and as intersectional. It emphasizes the ways in which personae create constraints on and opportunities for rhetorical action, and considers strategic essentialism as a rhetorical technique.

Chapter 7, "Audiences," revisits the basic premise that rhetoric is, at its core, *addressed*, and that the audience is both the receiver and the product of rhetorical action. The chapter shows how when one audience is created (a second persona), another may be denied existence (a third persona), and yet another may emerge as eavesdropping or silently complicit (a fourth persona). Pathos, values, and audience agency also are explained.

Chapter 8, "Rhetorical Situations," takes a synergistic approach, drawing on Bitzer's discussion of the basic components of the rhetorical situation, on his argument that rhetoric is situational, and on Vatz's critique that argues that situations are rhetorical. The chapter also explores Branham and Pearce's discussion of the various ways that a rhetor may react to a situation.

Chapter 9, "Publics and Counterpublics," introduces students to current theories of public sphere discourse, beginning with Habermas's basic model and incorporating current theories that recognize the possibility and productivity of multiple publics, as well as ways in which digital technologies have complicated traditional understandings of what constitutes a public and how publics emerge.

PEDAGOGICAL RESOURCES

Key Concepts: Every chapter opens with a list of key concepts, each of which is highlighted and defined within the chapter. The chapter itself offers definitions of each term, followed by examples.

Discussion Questions: Each chapter ends with a series of questions to guide student discussion and encourage students to apply the chapter concepts to the use of rhetoric in civic life.

Recommended Readings: Every chapter ends with a short list of recommended readings that students can use to explore the foundational literature of the field.

Instructor's Manual: The manual contains a variety of ancillary materials, including sample syllabi, discussion guides, and selected bibliographies for each concept from which additional readings can be assigned.

ACKNOWLEDGEMENTS

Scholarship is never an isolated endeavor. We are not, and should not be, confined to an ivory tower. Conversations with colleagues, fellow scholars, and friends always enliven our writing and thinking. Many of the examples and felicitous phrasings come from conversations with members of our intellectual family. In particular, we want to thank Robert Asen and Daniel Brouwer for help with all things public and counterpublic; G. Thomas Goodnight for help with all things rhetoric; Donn Parson, Arnie Madsen, and David Williams for help with all things Burke; Bettina Fabos for help with all things visual; Damien Pfister for help with all things blogosphere; Francesca Soans for help with obscure yet perfectly apt examples; Christopher Martin for conversations about current events; and Terence Check and Jeanmarie Cook for their conversations about pedagogy. Richard thanks the College of St. Benedict and St. John's University for a generous sabbatical leave that enabled him to work on this book. Richard and John also would like to thank their children (Hannah, Noah, Garrett, and Byron) for being tolerant and supportive throughout this process and willing to sacrifice evenings or weekends with their dads, who were working on this book.

The book was transformed throughout the writing process as a result of feedback from numerous reviewers: Lin Allen, University of Northern Colorado; Jennifer Asenas, California State University, Long Beach; Linda Czuba Brigance, State University of New York, Fredonia; Bonnie Dow, Vanderbilt University; Janis L. Edwards, University of Alabama; Pat J. Gehrke, University of South Carolina; Zac Gershberg, Keene State College; Ron Greene, University of Minnesota; Judith Hendry, University of New Mexico; Jim A. Kuypers, Virginia Polytechnic Institute and State University; Lenore Langsdorf, Southern Illinois University; Noemi Marin, Florida Atlantic University; Michael McFarland, Stetson University; Jerry Miller, Ohio University; Emily Plec, Western Oregon University; Lawrence Prelli, University of New Hampshire; Jennifer Reem, Nova Southeastern University; Steven Schwarze, University of Montana; John M. Sloop, Vanderbilt University; Matthew J. Sobnosky, Hofstra University; Stacey K. Sowards, University of Texas at El Paso; Nathan Stormer, University of Maine; Richard Vatz, Towson University; and Dylan Wolfe, Clemson University. Their challenges, corrections, and questions made the book immeasurably better. Any errors that remain are ours, not theirs.

We also thank our editor and publisher, Kathleen Domenig, for her patience and guidance throughout the writing of this book. We are sure that working with an authorial triumvirate is an editorial nightmare. We hope the end result made the hundreds, if not thousands, of e-mails worth it.

PART I

Introduction

Chapter 1

Rhetoric as Symbolic Action

Key Concepts

civic engagement	power
collective memory	public memory
constitutive rhetoric	rhetor
culture	rhetoric
ethos	rhetorical agency
hegemony	social reality
identification	symbol
ideology	symbolic action
logos	verbal symbols
pathos	visual symbols

Human beings make sense of their interactions with the world and with each other through the symbols (the words and images) they attach to their experiences. Words (language) and images (icons, pictures, photos, bodies, architectural structures) are not merely a means to transmit information, they are the grounds for the judgments people make about things, events, and other people. Quite simply, symbols matter.

How many people you know ever went home from grade school crying because of something another person said or a mean picture another person drew? Even if some children shouted, "Sticks and stones may break my bones, but words will never hurt me" through tear-stained faces, they recognized the immense power of words and symbols to hurt.

Columnist Kathleen Parker wrote a column called "Google Bombs Can Ruin Your Reputation,"[1] demonstrating how the words of one person in the many-to-many space of the Internet can have real effects on the reputations and livelihoods of other persons. The things people say (and the photos they post on social networking sites) matter.

Symbols matter. Your professional self-image is influenced by how others describe you. If you have received a positive job review, you know the power of words to make you feel better about yourself. People's symbol use makes a difference in interpersonal relationships, too. If you grew up in the United States and have ever been in a serious relationship, you know the power of the words "I love you" or the symbolic significance of a gold band worn on the ring finger. Most people do not speak the words lightly. The symbolism of a ring extends far beyond the typical meaning of an expensive gift of jewelry. People's symbol use also makes a difference in public communication. The words of public figures and symbols of citizenship possess the power to inspire, calm, reassure, enrage, provoke, challenge, and change the world.

Words inspired a nation to reach for the stars when, in 1962, President John F. Kennedy said: "We choose to go to the moon in this decade and do the other things, not because they are easy, but because they are hard, because that goal will serve to organize and measure the best of our energies and skills."[2]

Words calmed a nation faced with uncertainties when, from 1933 to the 1940s, President Franklin Delano Roosevelt delivered "fireside chats" to a nation buffeted by the Great Depression.

Words reassured the country of a person's fitness to serve when, in 1984, seventy-three-year-old President Ronald Reagan was running for reelection against the fifty-six-year-old former vice-president, Walter Mondale. When age became a campaign issue, President Reagan said, during a debate with Mondale, "I want you to know that also I will not make age an issue of this campaign. I am not going to exploit for political purposes my opponent's youth and inexperience."[3]

Visual symbols can enrage and provoke, as when leaders are burned in effigy, the US flag is burned in protest, or crosses are burned on homeowners' lawns to terrorize them out of living in a community.

Words and images also can be used to challenge, as when antiwar and free speech protestors at the 1968 Democratic Convention challenged Chicago police's repressive tactics by yelling at the cameras, "The whole world is watching."[4]

Because symbols matter, people debate the appropriateness of visual representations. After Olympic alpine skier Lindsey Vonn appeared on the cover of *Sports Illustrated*,[5] commentators discussed whether the image of her in a skiing tuck was sexist or sporty.[6] Given that women appear on only 4 percent of *SI* covers (including the yearly swimsuit edition), people began to consider what perception of women in general, and women athletes in particular, the cover generated.

What people communicate, and how they communicate it, has real effects on others and their perceptions. People cannot know what things or events mean until they have the symbols to attach meaning to them.

Because symbols have power, people can use them to induce others to take ethical, as well as unethical, actions. During World War II, Winston Churchill, considered one of the greatest English-speaking orators, delivered speeches to the British people to rally them to defend democracy and to US audiences to encourage them to become involved in the war. In the wake of British Prime Minister Neville Chamberlain's appeasement of Adolf Hitler on September 30, 1938, and German troops' occupation of the Sudetenland on October 15, Churchill, who at that time served no official role in the British government, sought to persuade the United States to defend democracy. On October 16 he warned, "The lights are going out. . . . We need the swift gathering of forces to confront not only military but moral aggression." He appealed to "English-speaking peoples" and "all the nations, great and small, who wish to walk with them. Their faithful and zealous comradeship would almost between night and morning clear the path of progress and banish from all our lives the fear which already darkens the sunlight to hundreds of millions of men."[7] He painted Hitler's forces as a darkness, smothering the lights of freedom; only the help of the United States could guarantee that Europeans would again see the sunlight of living in a free land. Churchill's speeches would help frame understandings of what the war in Europe meant to people living in the United States.

At the same time, Adolph Hitler was deftly persuading the German people to engage in horrific crimes against humanity and to wage total war. Using the metaphor of disease, Hitler explained on April 1, 1939: "Only when this Jewish bacillus infecting the life of peoples has been removed can one hope to establish a cooperation amongst the nations which shall be built up on a lasting understanding."[8] The vileness of this metaphor becomes clear in Hitler's call for an absolute eradication of the "Jewish bacillus" in order to save the German fatherland from disease. Infection can only be stopped when all the infection is removed. His use of language was dastardly as it sought the "perfection" of an Aryan nation. For Hitler, the Aryan race could only be saved if all Jewish people were eradicated.

These examples illustrate why rhetoric is profoundly important to civic society. **Rhetoric** is *the use of symbolic action by human beings to share ideas, enabling them to work together to make decisions about matters of common concern and to construct social reality.* Rhetoric is the means by which people make meaning of and affect the world in which they live.

Rhetoric can enlighten and confuse, reveal and hide. Churchill and Hitler both used rhetoric, but for very different purposes. Accordingly, the study of rhetoric involves not only an assessment of its effectiveness (both Churchill and Hitler were effective) but also of its ethics. (Churchill sought to defend freedom; Hitler sought the genocidal destruction of an entire people.)

In this book, we introduce you to concepts that will help you understand rhetoric and civic life. This chapter offers a foundational vocabulary you will need to understand, analyze, and creatively and ethically use rhetoric. We began by defining rhetoric as symbolic action that constructs reality. We will now explore rhetoric as the central means by which you engage in action in civil society, where you participate in public decision-making and culture formation. Finally, we will outline some constraints on and resources for rhetoric.

SYMBOLIC ACTION AND SOCIAL REALITY

To break down our definition of rhetoric, we look at each of its component parts: symbols and action. We then discuss how rhetoric actively constructs social reality.

Symbols

A **symbol** is *an arbitrary representation of something else, a word or an image that represents a thing, thought, or action.* The symbol $ represents the US dollar, although the symbol ∂ could just have easily been used. The symbol π represents pi, the ratio of any circle's circumference to its diameter, which roughly equals 3.141593. The US flag represents the nation and its values; a cross belief in a Christian faith; a Star of David in Judaism; and a crescent moon in Islam.

Symbols can be either verbal or visual. **Verbal symbols** are *symbols found in language* (whether spoken or written). Every word is a symbol insofar as it stands for something other than itself. When you use the term "dog," the word stands for an animal in the canine family. Other languages also have words for "dog" (perro/perra, suka, псина, 狗, chien, cane, hund, سگ), so symbols are by nature human constructions rather than innate to the things symbolized. Although people often think of symbols as abstractions, they may not think of words as symbolic. Yet, language is inherently a symbol system, both with written languages' use of alphabets and spoken languages' use of sounds to name and represent things, ideas, and people. Every word you use is a symbol.

Visual symbols are *symbols such as pictures, images, objects, and actions.* Examples of visual symbols include religious icons, photographs, tattoos, desktop icons, statues, flags, bodies, movies, and the act of bowing or saluting. For example, the US flag is just three colors of cloth sewn together, yet when people look at it, they think of it as the symbol of a nation. US citizens often have an emotional response to the flag because of what it symbolizes: such as democratic values. The key function of any symbol is that it conveys meaning. Although scholars for many years confined the study of rhetoric to the study of verbal symbols, they have recently recognized the importance of visual symbols.[9]

The meaning of a symbol is not the same for everyone. The fluidity of meaning is clear even when you consider language-based symbols. For example, "cat" refers to the scientific classification of the small carnivorous mammal *Felis catus* or *F. domesticus*. However, if a particular cat prowls around your life, the symbol "cat" may trigger thoughts of that particular cat, who symbolizes a warm, comforting, companion animal. On the other hand, if you have been scratched by a cat, you might have a different emotional response to the word. You might feel fear or distaste.

Although we describe verbal and visual symbols separately, almost all symbolic action is a mix of verbal and visual symbols. People listen to—and watch—speeches. People read—and look at—magazines and websites. People hear—and gaze at—movies.

Symbolic Action

When people use symbols, they engage in action. Our definition of rhetoric as symbolic action makes clear that humans use symbols to engage in actions with consequences. For example, when people exchange marriage vows and rings in a wedding ceremony, their actions create a new social relationship. The symbolic actions that compose a marriage ceremony (clothing, ring, vows, witnesses) create meaning beyond the wedding license the couple signs.

Things around you engage in motion: trees are moved by the wind, water by the tide, and earth by quakes. What distinguishes human action from these motions is that human action involves some level of intent and can be communicated about and reflected upon.[10] Human beings act on their environment in a variety of ways, such as walking, driving, planting a garden, and eating food. All these actions are instrumental—specific actions taken in order to cause an effect. Human action almost always is more than instrumental, however; it also is expressive and meaning-making.

Symbolic action is *expressive human action, the rhetorical mobilization of symbols to act in the world.* Symbolic actions include, but are not limited to, speeches, silent marches, movies, documentaries, plays, newspaper articles, advertisements, photographs, sit-ins, personal testimony, monuments, YouTube videos, and street theatre. People act in the world through symbol use that induces cooperation, generates identification, produces division, enables persuasion, and constitutes identity.

Rhetoric is constitutive, not just a tool of persuasion. Literary and legal scholar James Boyd White defines **constitutive rhetoric** as *the "art of constituting character, community, and culture in language."*[11] Rhetorical acts constitute character, community, and culture, as James Jasinski writes, by "invit[ing] their audience to experience the world in certain ways."[12] This understanding of symbolic action encourages thinking about how rhetoric constitutes people's understanding of themselves, their relations to each other, and the world; on the effects of rhetoric "beyond a narrow causal model of influence."[13]

The power of rhetoric to shape people's ideas of themselves, each other, and the world around them inspired rhetorical critic Kenneth Burke, an influential twentieth-century US scholar, to define human beings as the "symbol-using (symbol-making, symbol-misusing) animal."[14] Thus, the study of rhetoric provides insights into what it means to be human. For Burke, rhetoric is rooted in *"the use of language as a symbolic means of inducing cooperation in beings that by nature respond to symbols."*[15] Humans use symbols to interact with one another in order to work together to make decisions about matters of common concern.

Identification. For Burke, the primary aspect of rhetoric as symbolic action is **identification,** *a communicative process through which people are unified on the basis of common interests or characteristics.*[16] To make decisions about matters of common concern, people need to be able to identify what they have in common. Although attention to persuasion long dominated studies of rhetoric, "identification" now functions as a key term for what is known as "the new rhetoric."[17] With identification, the focus is less on how one person can "deliberate[ly] design" symbolic action to persuade other people, and more on how symbolic actions "spontaneously, intuitively, and often unconsciously act upon" people to create a sense of collective identity between them.[18] Identification does not automatically exist; it is created through symbolic action.

Identification can be created on the basis of characteristics over which a person has limited control (such as sex, race, class, sexual orientation, or nationality) or common interests (such as improving elementary and secondary education, lowering college tuition, or ending discrimination; or political party affiliation). Although Burke notes that "in forming ideas of our personal identity, we spontaneously identify ourselves with family, nation, political or cultural cause, church and so on," he also recognizes that rhetors induce listeners to feel identification with them;[19] the rhetor and audience become "consubstantial," or symbolically one.[20]

For Burke, the creation of identification is an essential characteristic of rhetoric and an integral element of persuasion. He writes: "there is no chance of keeping apart the meaning of persuasion, identification ('consubstantiality') and communication (the nature of rhetoric as 'addressed')."[21]

Rhetors can most effectively communicate and persuade when their audiences identify with them. For example, nineteenth-century abolitionist Angelina Grimké Weld used identification when she faced mob violence in Philadelphia on May 16, 1838, as she delivered a speech to an antislavery convention. Her challenge to the audience was to consider whether they wanted to identify with her and the slaves, or with the angry mob outside. Historian Gerda Lerner reports that while Grimké Weld was being introduced to the audience of three thousand men and women, "bricks crashed through the windows and glass fell to the floor."[22] As she spoke, the mob outside Pennsylvania Hall grew increasingly agitated, throwing stones and screaming during her hour-long speech. Although the people inside the hall were receptive to her message because they already opposed slavery, the mob outside the hall felt threatened by her argument that slavery was not an objective fact, but an immoral choice. Not wanting the mob to weaken her audience's resolve, Grimké Weld artistically turned the mob response into proof of the need to oppose slavery. She challenged the audience to use their fear of the mob as a basis for identifying with slaves' fear of violence from their masters:

> What is a mob? What would the breaking of every window be? What would the levelling of this Hall be? Any evidence that we are wrong, or that slavery is a good and wholesome institution? What if the mob should now burst in upon us, break up our meeting and commit violence upon our persons—would this be anything compared with what the slaves endure? No, no: and we do not remember them "as bound with them" [Heb. 13:3], if we shrink in the time of peril, or feel unwilling to sacrifice ourselves, if need be, for their sake. (*Great noise.*) I thank the Lord that there is yet life left enough to feel the truth, even though it rages at it—that conscience is not so completely seared as to be unmoved by the truth of the living God.[23]

She compared the threat of mob violence to the constant threat of violence under which slaves lived. She used the moment to induce her audience to identify with the slaves.[24]

Identification can bring people together to address and solve common concerns. Identification can also separate people by constructing "us" versus "them" social realities. For instance, Adolf Hitler induced non-Jewish German people to identify themselves as members of a superior race, an Aryan nation, which divided them from Jewish people. Identification can function for good or ill, unity or division. It can be used to recognize common concerns or disguise them, to solve common concerns or create new concerns.

Agency. Because rhetoric is an action, people exert some control over their messages. People possess rhetorical agency. Communication scholar Karlyn Kohrs Campbell explains that **rhetorical agency** is *"the capacity to act, that is, to have the competence to speak or write in a way that will be recognized or heeded by others in one's community."*[25] Because rhetoric involves both verbal and visual symbols, we extend her definition to include competence in visual rhetoric. Regardless of the medium, "agency" does not mean a person totally controls the meaning of a message. Instead, the term indicates some degree of control is available, that an individual is capable of symbolic action, not just motion.

In an autocratic or closed society, rhetoric plays a limited role because people lack agency. They have minimal control over what is said; people have to speak the party line or face punishment. In a democratic or open society, rhetoric plays a more significant role. People can form their opinions through the process of communication, and they have some degree of agency over what they communicate.

Social Reality

Rhetoric is more than a means to transmit information or persuade. When people engage in symbolic action, they participate in the construction of social reality. Saying that rhetoric "constructs social reality" does not mean that people and things do not pre-exist human symbolic action. Rather, we are saying that the *meaning* people ascribe to the things in their world is not predetermined, but created by symbolic action. Although people may know things exist apart from their symbol systems, they cannot know what those things mean or how to react to them except through the symbol system. Thus, reality is constructed—meaning that it is made and not given. It is social—meaning that it is created interactively.

Sociologist Peter Berger explains how, through language, humans impose order on reality.[26] People have individual experiences, but they classify those experiences in social terms. For example, a culture might have a sacred tree. The physical reality is that a plant exists, but the sacredness of the tree is socially constructed; members of the society agree that the tree is sacred and, through the use of symbols, communicate the importance of the tree to others in that society. The use of language orders (makes sense of) the physical reality.

Social reality is *reality as understood through the symbols humans use to represent it.* People create social reality as they name objects, actions, and each other. Although a material world exists from which human beings receive sensory data, they do not know how to interact with that world until symbolic action gives meaning to their sense data. Human beings' only access to reality is through symbols. Communication scholar Barry Brummett argues that "experience is sensation plus meaning" and "reality is meaning."[27] For example, the way you react to a dog named Cujo likely will be different from how you react to a dog named Puddles, even though they are the same breed.

Visual communication scholar Kevin DeLuca argues that people should understand rhetoric as "discerning [studying] and deploying [using] the available contingent means of constructing, maintaining, and transforming social reality in a particular context."[28] In other words, symbolic action—words and images—construct, maintain, and transform social reality. Imagine if you lived in a world devoid of symbolic action. You could not speak, take photos, upload video on YouTube, draw, pray, or engage in any action with symbolic importance. You also could not read, listen to music, watch videos, or receive others' symbolic actions. This world would not be total sensory deprivation, but it would be deprivation of all stimuli related to communication. Would you still feel human? Would you still possess the characteristics that make you human? Would you know how to act in the world or react to others? Symbolic action is not just an instrumental means to transmit information, it is central to making meaning of, and in, the world.

RHETORIC AS CIVIC ENGAGEMENT

Our definition of rhetoric focuses on the use of symbolic action to identify and solve issues of common concern and to construct social reality. A key aspect of that definition is that rhetoric is a social activity, meaning that it occurs among people. Thus, rhetoric has always been linked to social action and civic engagement.

Classical Origins

The word "rhetoric" comes from the ancient Greek word *rhetor*, which meant "public speaker." Thus, historically the term "rhetoric" referred to the art of public speaking.[29] Classicist George A. Kennedy explains that rhetoric was a civic art in ancient Greece and is a phenomenon of all human cultures; and that every communicative act is rhetorical in that it attempts to persuade someone.[30] Expanding on the original Greek definition, we use the term **rhetor** to mean *anyone or any institution that uses symbolic action.*

The academic study of rhetoric can be traced back to ancient Athens, where many of the most prominent thinkers and educators focused on it because citizens (adult males who were not slaves and whose parents were both Athenian) needed to know rhetoric to participate in political, economic, social, and legal structures. Athens's political system of direct democracy allowed male citizens the right to engage in civic discussion. When the Assembly met to discuss laws or issues of war, every citizen who had completed his military training was a voting member and had the right to speak and vote. All male citizens needed to be prepared to speak as members of the legislative body. Economically, business relied on a system of negotiation and bartering. Socially, male citizens spent leisurely afternoons at the gymnasium, a facility devoted not only to athletics, but also to discussions of art, poetry, politics, and gossip. Citizens spent evenings at dinner parties called *symposia*, where a man could be selected by lot to serve as the toastmaster for the evening, or be called on to deliver toasts or tell stories.

The legal system of Athens required rhetorical skill because it used juries, usually comprised of 201 to 501 citizens (but sometimes up to 2,001), depending on the importance of the case.[31] The legal system did not include lawyers; if someone was wronged or accused of wrongdoing, he spoke to the jury directly. (If a female of the citizen class was accused of wrongdoing, her closest male relative spoke for her.)[32] All citizens had to be able to speak effectively in front of the court.

The prominent role that rhetoric played in Athens generated disagreement, as represented by two groups: the Sophists and the Platonists. Sophists defended rhetoric, while Platonists were extremely skeptical of it.

Given the centrality of public speaking to Athenian politics and culture, when a man prepared to speak in public he either hired a speechwriter and then memorized the speech for presentation, or sought training in the art of rhetoric from Sophists.[33] In assessing the Sophistic tradition, communication scholar John Poulakos summarizes their definition of rhetoric: "Rhetoric is the art which seeks to capture in opportune moments that which is appropriate and attempts to suggest that which is possible."[34] Sophists, such as Protagoras and Isocrates, believed rhetoric was an art that could both delight and induce belief. The right thing spoken at the right time could entertain, even as it formed people's knowledge.

In contrast, Plato and Socrates believed knowledge could not be determined with the exchange of ideas, through rhetoric, but could only be known through philosophically understanding the existence of true and unchanging forms. Socrates argued that the Sophists' teaching of rhetoric made the weaker argument seem the stronger and, thus, worked against the truth. Plato used the trial of Socrates, who was convicted and sentenced to death for corrupting Athenian youth and not believing in the gods of the state, to demonstrate how rhetoric can be abused when it appeals to the baser instincts of majority rule.[35] In response to the injustice of this trial, Plato wrote several dialogues attacking rhetoric as a false art and a dangerous form of manipulation.

In one of these dialogues, the *Gorgias*, Plato recounted a debate between Socrates and the Sophist Gorgias about the ethics of rhetoric. Socrates warned that rhetoric is flattery and that people would misuse rhetoric for selfish or corrupt ends. In response, Gorgias argued that rhetoric was not to blame for these problems, any more than the maker of a knife or the knife itself was to blame for someone stabbing another person. Unconvinced by the Sophists, Plato distrusted rhetoric as a means of facilitating decision making, leading him to argue that democracy was not the best form of government. Good ideas were known only by the wisest, and not through public deliberations. He maintained that rhetoric could be used to deceive the masses within a democracy, and that it failed to teach virtue.

Despite Plato's criticisms, the study of rhetoric flourished in ancient Athens because of its role in legal, political, and social institutions. History demonstrates that where democracy is strong, the study of rhetoric is vibrant. Where nondemocratic government prevails, the study of rhetoric either disappears or is taught as merely a form of entertainment.

The disagreement between the Sophists and Platonists persists. Even in contemporary times, you probably have heard someone refer to an argument as "sophistry" or "mere rhetoric." Although Plato's dismissal gave Sophists a bad name, contemporary understandings of rhetoric are closer to the Sophistic tradition than to the Platonic tradition. We find ourselves more aligned with the Sophistic definition of rhetoric as the art of capturing the right thing to say in the right moment, of determining what is appropriate and possible; and opposed to the Platonic belief in fixed and immutable big-T Truths.

Because rhetoric had utility, Aristotle, a student of Plato's, systematized it. Aristotle, an extremely influential philosopher and scientist, is considered one of the founders of Western philosophy. One of the most influential writings on rhetoric in ancient Greece was his fourth-century BCE treatise, *On Rhetoric.*[36]

Aristotle defined rhetoric as "an ability in each [particular] case, to see the available means of persuasion."[37] Notice that the definition says that rhetoric is an *ability to see.* Thus, the use of rhetoric requires analysis of a situation in order to determine how to persuade. For Aristotle, a rhetorical situation "consists of three things: a speaker and a subject on which he [or she] speaks and someone addressed, and the objective of the speech relates to the last."[38] Rhetoric is addressed to particular people, on particular occasions, in particular times and cultures, about particular issues. Because rhetoric is specific to each particular situation, it is distinct from philosophy, which studies universals.

Persuasion plays a prominent role in Aristotle's definition insofar as a rhetor uses rhetorical proofs to persuade an audience. Aristotle identified three types of artistic proofs used in persuasion: **ethos**—*that which is "in the character of the speaker"* (we will define ethos more fully in Chapter 6); **pathos**—*that which leads the audience "to feel emotion"*; and **logos**—*that which relies on "argument itself, by showing or seeming to show something."*[39] Although Aristotle noted the importance of the reasoned appeals of logos, he also made clear the importance of ethos and pathos. He argued that ethos was the most effective form of proof because an audience who trusted the rhetor would be more receptive to her or his message. Conversely, if an audience did not trust the rhetor, then the rhetor's use of logos and pathos would be ineffective. Aristotle also pointed out that audiences make decisions based on their state of mind, not only on the basis of reasoned appeals. Because emotions play a significant role in the human experience, pathos appeals are an important part of rhetoric. Many decisions people make are based on emotions, taste, and individual preferences. These decisions are not necessarily irrational. A person's favorite color is based on personal preference. All the logical arguments in the world may not change that preference, but that does not make the preference wrong.

Much has changed since Aristotle wrote—for example, photography, mass media, the Internet, and changing societal norms have altered the ways rhetoric is understood—but his concepts remain useful to understanding contemporary rhetoric. A recent newswire story about online product testimonials explains their power as stemming from "easy anonymity and participatory, peer-to-peer ethos."[40] A recent news article quotes political communication professor Joseph Tuman on the 2010 California gubernatorial primary candidates: "So they're waging classic pathos arguments. They're not designed to make you think; they're designed to make you feel."[41] A *Washington Post* article, shortly before Barack Obama's inaugural address, commented that Obama "hasn't needed logos much because he's usually preaching to the choir."[42] People still use Aristotle's terms to make sense of rhetoric.

Rhetoric as Addressed

For Aristotle, the audience determines the objective of rhetoric. For Burke, rhetoric's "nature as addressed" to others is one of its definitive characteristics (in addition to identification).[43] Humans engage in symbolic action in order to communicate with one another. Rhetoric always involves an audience, even if that audience is not immediately present. Thus, the making of meaning is interactive and intersubjective. To construct, maintain, and transform reality requires the existence of others, of audiences.

Given that rhetors and audiences coproduce meaning, agency belongs not only to rhetors, but also to audiences. Agency includes the ability to construct and interpret symbolic actions, and to take action in response to those interpretations. Campbell describes agency as "communal, social, cooperative, and participatory and, simultaneously, constituted and constrained by the material and symbolic elements of context and culture."[44] In other words, we make meaning through a social, and not just individual, process. When you interpret messages or decode images you do not do so only with resources you alone innately possess. Instead, you rely on a complex set of contextual and cultural symbols.

Rhetoric is an action that creates meaning, informing how human beings understand and react to the world. It is not merely a mechanism of information transmission, but a means by which human beings construct social reality. The political, personal, and meaning-creating functions highlight how rhetoric affects what laws are passed, how people see themselves, and what people think they know. Rhetoric is essential to a democratic society.

Civic Engagement

Civic engagement is *people's participation in individual or collective action to develop solutions to social, economic, and political challenges in their communities, states, nations, and world.* Examples of how people engage in civic engagement include talking with others about ballot initiatives or pending legislation, using social networking sites for activism, volunteering with community organizations, participating in parades (whether celebratory or protest), working for electoral campaigns, signing petitions, voting, writing letters to the editor, and posting to blogs. Change (and maintenance) of social, political, and economic structures is accomplished through civic engagement, and civic engagement is accomplished through rhetoric.

Rhetoric scholar Gerard A. Hauser reviewed the scholarly research on why citizens engage in civic action in their communities, and concluded that the absolutely necessary requirement for "a well-functioning civic community is engagement in the . . . rhetoric of civil society."[45] In any democracy, whether it is direct (like Athens) or representative (like the United States), rhetors must understand how to frame ethical and effective appeals, and audiences need to understand how to see through manipulative appeals.

The use of rhetoric is not confined to people campaigning for office; nor are citizens' roles in rhetorical action confined to membership in audiences. Civic engagement helps each person understand who she or he is. Rhetoric scholar Bruce Gronbeck argues that "Civic engagement . . . is as much a matter of understanding the building and maintenance of political identity . . . as it is about getting legislation passed."[46] People use rhetoric as they develop identity (as individuals and citizens) and determine what should be done (by them as individuals and for them through legislation). They use rhetoric as they develop conceptions of themselves as individuals, group members, and citizens, all of whom can make a claim on others and on the government to act legislatively.

Rhetoric scholar Robert Asen points out that civic engagement was long defined in terms of what people did when participating in civil society. Citizenship was defined narrowly in terms of the specific acts of voting and civic organization membership.[47] Research using this *what* approach tends to see civic engagement as on the decline, as fewer people vote or belong to civic organizations. Asen is not so pessimistic. He advocates a different perspective, arguing that analysis of citizenship should focus on the *how*—not on citizenship as an act, but as a process of action. Thus, the question is: how do people enact citizenship and civic engagement? The answer is: through rhetoric. Civic engagement as a process, a "mode of public engagement," means participation in society has many different forms, all of which involve symbolic action.[48]

Asen argues that rhetoric is central to civic engagement because, in addressing other people in ways that seek identification, it is an act of interacting and engaging with others: "Engagement positions people as rhetorical agents hoping to persuade and/or seek recognition from others of their views, even as it recognizes that others hope to do the same. Commitment thus extends to a commitment to interaction itself."[49] When you engage in rhetoric, you necessarily commit yourself to an interaction. Thus, to understand citizenship, Asen examines the processes by which people engage and interact with each other. He explores how people come to understand themselves—through rhetoric—as members of groups and as individuals, and how "actions that begin on a small scale may spread across social, cultural, and political sites."[50] For Asen, engagement occurs when human communication generates new areas for discussion, when people are willing to accept the risk of being wrong (and accept correction of their views), when people affirm a commitment to engage one another in discourse, and when creative forms of communication create social connections among individuals.

Rhetorical citizenship in a democratic society is essential to the process of decision making in situations as mundane as a group of people deciding where to eat dinner (at a national chain or at a restaurant that supports local farmers) to situations as serious as you determining whether you want to join a national service organization (the armed services, Americorp, or the Peace Corps). Although people's reasons for doing things can be personal, those reasons can be expressed and contested. To truly enter the realm of rhetoric, people must be open to having their minds changed and to providing the reasons for their beliefs. They must be willing to continually provide reasons, listen, and modify their positions. This process of interaction and modification of positions is essential to decision making in an open society.

For example, if members of a campus group disagreed about how to spend a thousand dollars, it would not be productive if each person simply stated: I want the money spent *this* way, period. Instead, for the group to decide collectively what to do, each person would have to articulate the reason the money should be spent as she or he wanted. As people gave their reasons, some shared interests might become clear, at which point each person could see the merits in others' ideas. As the discussion proceeded, agreement might emerge. Or, it might become clear that the group members had totally competing interests, so that agreement could never be reached. At that point, they may find that the disagreement is less about what to do with the money (policy) and more about what it means to be a member of the group (identity).

Unfortunately, modern society increasingly allows people to refuse such interactions. The fragmentation of media enables you to seek out and listen only to those with whom you agree. When exchanges of diverse opinions do occur, it is becoming more common to hear people refuse to participate. You probably have heard comments such as "we'll just have to agree to disagree," or "it works for me," or "I don't have time to get involved," or even just "whatever." These comments are a way of ending discussion about differing opinions and ideas, rather than actually engaging people in discussion. They are antithetical to decision making based on the principles of rhetoric. Agreeing to disagree is not always a viable option. Oftentimes, decisions must be made between competing options and ideas.

What differentiates an open and free society from a closed, fascist, and dictatorial society is its willingness to tolerate the open expression of differing ideas and beliefs. In an open society, communication serves personal, epistemological, and political functions. It serves a personal function when it enables people to express themselves, both communicating and developing their sense of self. It serves an epistemological function when it enables people to test their ideas and to develop knowledge. It serves a political function when it enables people to participate in the processes of governance. President Abraham Lincoln's ideal of a "government of the people, by the people, for the people" cannot be realized if the people do not participate in those processes.[51] Additionally, a free press and its ability to report on public issues fulfills a political function when it serves as a check on government abuses. Your own rhetoric and your ability to listen to the rhetoric of others are essential to an open society.

For these reasons, the United States has a long tradition of protecting open communication, which it codified in the First Amendment to the Constitution.

Supreme Court Justice Holmes articulated this trust in freely exchanged ideas in 1919:

> [T]he ultimate good desired is better reached by free trade in ideas—
> that the best test of truth is the power of the thought to get itself accepted
> in the competition of the market, and that truth is the only ground
> upon which their wishes safely can be carried out. That, at any rate,
> is the theory of our Constitution. It is an experiment, as all life is an
> experiment. Every year, if not every day, we have to wager our salvation
> upon some prophecy based upon imperfect knowledge. While that
> experiment is part of our system, I think that we should be eternally
> vigilant against attempts to check the expression of opinions that we
> loathe and believe to be fraught with death, unless they so imminently
> threaten immediate interference with the lawful and pressing purposes
> of the law that an immediate check is required to save the country.[52]

Open communication is not to be feared. Ideas with which you disagree should not be avoided or suppressed. Instead, all people should develop the critical faculties that enable them to judge which ideas in the marketplace they should "buy," which expressions are worthy of assent, and which ideas should define their characters. People not only need the right to express their opinions, but also the skills and knowledge with which to do so, as well as a government and society willing to consider and respond to those opinions.

CONSTRAINTS ON AND RESOURCES FOR SYMBOLIC ACTION

When you engage in rhetorical action, you are constrained by social factors. Not every symbolic action will be completely and immediately understood by everyone hearing or seeing it, or accepted even if it is understood. You also possess resources for rhetorical action: stories, images, memories, and cultural values that are generally shared and can be used to communicate your message. In this section we discuss some of the limits on and resources for rhetoric: (1) the persuasive continuum, (2) culture, (3) public memory, and (4) power, ideology, and hegemony. This list is not exhaustive; other resources and constraints will be discussed throughout the text. However, this list constitutes overarching constraints and resources that influence most aspects of rhetorical engagement in civic life.

Persuasive Continuum

Because of limits on persuasion stemming from an audience, a topic, or even the rhetor, seldom is persuasion absolutely achieved or arguments completely dismissed. An audience is not totally persuaded or completely unconvinced by a single rhetorical action. When people think of persuasion, they often think of it as intentionally trying to change another person's actions or beliefs (sometimes against the other person's will), but such goals are not descriptive of all rhetoric.

Communication scholar Karlyn Kohrs Campbell describes persuasive purposes in terms of a persuasive continuum:[53]

create virtual experience	alter perception	explain	formulate belief	initiate action	maintain action

In many cases, changing a person's mind is not possible. Beliefs can be so deeply ingrained that an audience may not even recognize alternative meanings are possible. For this reason, a rhetor's goal may be to create a virtual experience for the audience members, so they come to feel they have experienced something they never thought possible. For example, when African-American activist Mary Church Terrell spoke about the effect of Jim Crow segregation laws in her 1906 speech "What It Means to Be Colored in the Capital of the United States,"[54] she *created a virtual experience*. When speaking to her primarily white, Northern audience, she had to make clear the effects of segregation. She provided example after example of the segregation African Americans faced in what was thought to be the cradle of liberty and equality: Washington, DC. Moving from finding shelter; to finding food; to finding a place to worship, work, and be entertained and educated, her speech created for her white audience the virtual experience of being "colored in the capital of the United States" and enabled them to identify with African Americans.

If a rhetor can create a virtual experience for audience members, s/he might be able to *alter their perception*, or at least introduce them to a new perspective. Ida B. Wells, journalist and long-time activist for African-American rights, fought against lynching. In her 1892 essay (also delivered as a speech), "Southern Horrors: Lynch Law in All Its Phases," she attempted to alter audience members' perception that black men were lynched because they were accused of raping white women.[55] She made clear that, as reported by white sources, the real reason that white people lynched black people was economic. White business people resented black people's economic success. She also pointed out that black children and black women had been murdered by white lynch mobs, but no white man had ever been lynched for raping a black woman, or even a black eight-year-old child, making clear that the fear of rape was an inadequate explanation for lynching. Although she may not have been able to convince her audience that all lynching was wrong, she at least opened their minds to an alternative perspective on lynching—that it was an economically and racially motivated crime of hate, rather than an act defending fragile white women's honor. Wells sought to create divisions between white people who lynched and those who would oppose lynching, and to foster identification between white people and black people.

If audience members are willing to entertain the possibility of an alternative perception, a speaker can then *explain* reasons behind that perception. Wells explained the reasons for her opposition to lynching, her demand that northerners condemn the act, and her call to African Americans to arm themselves in self-defense. She ended by explaining: "Of the many inhuman outrages of this present year, the only case where the proposed lynching did *not* occur, was where the men armed themselves in Jacksonville, Fla., and Paducah, Ky[*sic*], and prevented it. The only times an Afro-American who was assaulted got away has been when he had a gun and used it in self-defense."[56]

A more recent illustration of explanation is found in a speech George W. Bush delivered to the National Association for the Advancement of Colored People (NAACP) Convention when he was running for president in 2000. Going into the speech, he was aware that members of the NAACP tended to support Democratic candidates. Instead of going into the convention to tell them they were wrong, he took the approach of simply explaining his policies and why they would benefit the communities for which the organization worked. He opened the speech by recognizing that the relationship between the Republican Party and the NAACP had "not been one of regular partnership," so he asked them simply to give him "the chance to tell you what is in my heart." He sought to explain his own position, rather than to change the NAACP's. He described the central part of his education agenda as being "to challenge and change Title I, to make sure we close the achievement gap, to make sure that children are not forgotten and simply shuffled through the system." He explained that testing would be used to identify low-performing schools, which would then have three years to improve. If they failed to improve, he explained, "the resources must go to the parents so the parents can make a different choice."[57]

Once audience members are willing to alter their perception of an issue and listen to an alternative explanation, a rhetor might be able to *formulate beliefs*. As a result of speeches and essays such as Ida B. Wells's, she and other rhetors were able to begin formulating a belief in audience members' minds that lynching was a criminal act that violated black people's rights and that lynchers should face the most severe legal punishments possible. It took time to formulate that belief: a federal antilynching law was not even proposed until 1900 (and then received only three votes), and lynching persisted well into the 1950s. In fact, no federal antilynching law was ever passed, an oversight for which the US Senate apologized in 2005.[58]

Formulating belief is not the only possible goal for a rhetorician. In many cases, audience members seek out speakers in order to reaffirm their own beliefs. For example, people attend religious services to have their beliefs reaffirmed and attend political rallies for candidates they already support in order to maintain (and demonstrate) their belief in a candidate. In such cases, persuasion can maintain belief as well as formulate it.

Having a belief does not necessarily mean one acts on it. People often have good intentions but fail to turn those beliefs into lived realities. Most public service announcements (PSAs) attempt to *initiate action*. People may know that smoking is bad and that reading is good, but PSAs reminding people of these beliefs encourage them to turn those beliefs into action. The Rock the Vote campaign seeks to initiate action each election, as do on-campus alcohol awareness campaigns each term.

Social movements also employ rhetoric aimed at initiating or *maintaining action.* When a movement or campaign achieves success, members must be reminded that more work is yet to come. Thus, in the wake of the passage of the Civil Rights Act of 1964, which outlawed racial segregation in schools, public places, and employment, the civil rights movement did not stop. Instead, it maintained its members' actions for social equality, leading to the Civil Rights Act of 1968, which sought to end discrimination in housing. Conversely, when a movement faces a defeat, the members must be rallied in order to keep the movement going. During the struggle for women's right to vote, which lasted from the 1848 Seneca Falls Convention until the 1920 ratification of the Nineteenth Amendment, woman suffrage advocates had to work to maintain the activism of the movement's members. The period from 1896 to 1907 came to be known as "the doldrums" because of the number of defeats the activists faced: a total of 164 referendum defeats, an average of one every 27 days. In response, movement leaders had to develop rhetorical appeals that maintained the activists' prosuffrage activities.[59]

Culture

Rhetoric and civic engagement occur within particular cultures. According to anthropologist Clifford Geertz, **culture** is the *"historically transmitted pattern of meanings embodied in symbols, a system of inherited conceptions expressed in symbolic forms by means of which men [and women] communicate, perpetuate, and develop their knowledge about and attitudes toward life."*[60] Culture is composed of knowledge, experiences, beliefs, values, attitudes, meanings, hierarchies, religions, conceptions of time, social roles, worldviews, myths, and even the material possessions or artifacts acquired by a group of people, the meanings of which are transmitted through symbols. Your culture frames how you interpret rhetorical messages.

For example, in an individualist culture, appeals to each person's individual rights may carry more weight than in a more communitarian culture that places the concerns of the group ahead of individuals' rights.[61] In their study of the famous image of the man standing in front of the tank during the 1989 Tiananmen Square protests, communication scholars Robert Hariman and John L. Lucaites argue that Western media sources made that image emblematic of the event, rather than images of massive crowds, because the lone individual confronting the power of the state made sense to Western cultures that emphasize liberal individualism.[62]

Geertz uses the metaphor of a spider's web to explain the complex relationship between culture and symbol use: he says that humans are "suspended in webs of significance" they themselves "have spun."[63] For Geertz, symbols do not literally bring something into existence but locate a thing within systems of meaning. Patriotism, the love of or devotion to a country, is an example of a cultural system of meaning. In the US patriotic web of signification, key words such as "freedom," "equality," and "liberty;" visual symbols such as the US flag;

and icons such as Uncle Sam and the Statue of Liberty have come to symbolize the country. People who are citizens come to understand who they are because of their relationship to the United States, and pledge allegiance to it. Expressions of patriotism (as in Lee Greenwood's 1984 song "God Bless the USA," which played at the Republican National Convention that year, increased in popularity during Operation Desert Storm in 1991, and then regained popularity in the wake of the 9/11 attacks) create a sense of identification among many citizens. As that sense of belonging develops so, too, does a sense of differentiation and exclusion. Even as one creates identification (a sense of "us"), one also creates division (a sense of "them"). Identification is meant to counteract the feeling of division, but even as it does so it tends to recreate divisions along new lines. Patriotism normalizes the idea that some people deserve rights in a country because they "belong" while others do not because they do not belong. Patriotism also normalizes the idea that the loss of life of a fellow countryperson counts more than the death of an other.[64] Patriotism gives a particular meaning to being a citizen of a country. The words and symbols interweave so that to attack one (freedom) means you have attacked all (attacking freedom means you are attacking all the United States stands for). Sometimes dissent is called unpatriotic because it means one does not support the country unconditionally. Patriotism is a web of significance in which people are suspended and which they, themselves, have spun.

Geertz's definition of culture includes "a system of inherited conceptions expressed in symbolic forms,"[65] which means that the web of significance is learned. Communication scholars Judith Martin and Thomas Nakayama state that culture is comprised of "learned patterns of behavior and attitudes shared by a group of people."[66] The primary functions of culture are to teach shared meanings, shared views of the world, and a group identity. Through these functions, cultures also help reduce uncertainty and chaos, largely by socializing their members to behave in prescribed ways. Even as you are enmeshed in the web, however, you also help spin it.

Rhetoric is constrained by culture, but also constructs culture. Rhetoric is constrained by culture because people's interpretations of symbolic action depend on the culture in which they participate. What is persuasive to a rural, midwestern, US audience might not be persuasive to an audience in another nation, or even another part of the United States. Yet, rhetoric can be used to change culture. US culture has changed over time because of rhetoric. For example, women were once considered inferior and thus were systematically denied the right to vote. This state of affairs was considered "normal" in eighteenth- and nineteenth-century United States. Yet, in twenty-first-century United States, if someone advocated not allowing women the right to vote, you would probably think that person was crazy. Women achieved their current role through rhetoric and civic engagement that altered the culture.

Public and Collective Memory

Geertz points to the link between culture and memory, to the existence of cultural memory that resides in the web of significance, when he refers to historically transmitted meanings. If culture is learned patterns, where does one learn those patterns? People do not inherit a chest of drawers that contains their culture. Instead, people develop their culture as they inherit symbol systems that contain memories.

Memories are maintained through symbolic actions. Sociologist Barry Schwartz makes clear how memory requires symbolic action: "Recollection of the past is an active, constructive process, not a simple matter of retrieving information. To remember is to place a part of the past in the service of conceptions and needs of the present."[67] Memories do not just exist; instead, to remember requires human symbols to re-present memory. Communication scholar Carole Blair explains: "memory is based on the capacity to *re-present* an event, a place, a person, or an idea that one has already encountered."[68] People engage in the act of remembering, and in doing so develop a sense of collective identity. Remembering requires symbolic action on the part of people.

Memory can exist at the personal level, as when family members recall past experiences with each other. It can also exist at the cultural level, when the members of a culture engage in the memory work that sustains them as a culture. **Public memory** is *a particular type of collective memory that combines the memories of the dominant culture and fragments of marginalized groups' memories, and enables a public to make sense of the past, present, and future.*[69] Public memory is a particular type of **collective memory,** *memory that is not simply an individualized process, but a shared and constructed creation of a group.*[70] Memory is the product of rhetorical action even as it constrains the rhetorical actions of those who would challenge the dominant memory.

For example, citizens of a nation maintain and construct public memory though the monuments and memorials they choose to erect, and in the process construct an identity for themselves. In the United States, the Lincoln Memorial, Washington Monument, Vietnam Veterans Memorial, National World War II Memorial, and Korean War Veterans Memorial all construct particular memories of the nation's past. Memorials and monuments are examples of shared resources, collective memory made public.

Although a person may have particular memories and families may have group memories, public memories are those memories that give identity to a particular society. You personally have no memory of national events such as the American Revolution, but through your education and your participation in Fourth of July celebrations, through national monuments and speeches, you participate in a public memory of the events of the American Revolution, memories the Tea Party movement seeks to revivify. Thus, an individual's memories do not really make sense unless situated within a larger collective. Communication scholar Iwona Irwin-Zarecka writes, "'Collective memory'—as a set of ideas, images, feelings about the past—is best located not in the minds of individuals, but in the resources they share."[71]

However, remembering always involves forgetting. Collective memory may be controversial. It can be a point of contestation, in part because collective remembering is always intimately linked to collective forgetting. No single version of the past exists, and dominant interpretations of past events can "wip[e] out many of the others."[72] Thus, the subject of rhetoric can be which things to remember and how to remember them. For example, memorial depictions of Christopher Columbus illustrate both the amount of work done to maintain collective memory and the way memory also always induces forgetting.

Symbols in the form of statues and images, poems, stories, and named holidays all sought to fix collective memory of Columbus as definitive of the US identity as a nation of explorers. He has been celebrated as an American mythic hero since the genesis of the nation. His emergence as one of the pantheon of heroes was due, in part, to the revolutionary leaders' reluctance to ascend the pedestal in a country that ostensibly was built on democratic principles.[73] Into this void people placed Columbus. In the years during and immediately following the Revolutionary War, a number of poetic histories and references to Columbus emerged, including Phillis Wheatley's 1775 innovation of the poetic device "Columbia" as a symbol of both Columbus and America.[74] In 1792, the new capitol in Washington was subtitled the District of Columbia. These are acts of rhetoric that participate in the creation and maintenance of public memory.

The original narrative of Columbus-the-discoverer was woven into and stabilized US public memory without opposition for many years, if not centuries. Regardless of whether he was the first to land in the Americas, his is the day celebrated, his is the image immortalized in the US capitol, and his is the story told in textbooks and movies. In other words, all available anchoring devices for collective memory have been used to fix Columbus-the-discoverer in US public memory. However, in the process of commemorating Columbus, much was forgotten.

The Columbian quincentenary in 1992 provided a unique moment to highlight the way collective forgetting was connected to collective remembering. Native American protests against Columbus Day parades offered a way to materialize grievances. Native Americans engaged in rhetorical action in order to challenge collective memory and public memorializing practices. A leading scholar on indigenous peoples of Latin America, José Barreiro, introduced the special issue of the *Northeast Indian Quarterly* that was dedicated to "American Indian Perspectives on the Quincentenary." He explained the rhetorical significance of the quincentenary: "To the degree that the Quincentenary spectacle exalts Columbus as a metaphor for the expansion of Western materialist culture[,] a debate is joined that focuses issues of cultural values survival, environmental ethics and practice and sustainability in economic activity."[75] The celebration of Columbus's memory provided a focal point through which to reframe the nation's understanding of discovery and settlement. The reframing was not to be achieved by a single protest or a single text. For Native Americans, the issue was not the accurate chronicling of history, although that was a part of it, but the effects of commemorative holidays and parades on memory of what was done to Native Americans as a result of Columbus's landfall. The point was that Columbus did not "discover" an empty land, but claimed a land populated by a number of different peoples. The memory of Columbus is rhetorical insofar as it exhorts people in the United States to perceive their identity as explorers. Native Americans countered that rhetorical exhortation by depicting Columbus not as an explorer but as a colonizer.

Memories, even those enshrined in memorials, monuments, parades, and holidays, do not proceed uncontested. Memory can be a site of rhetorical conflict precisely because of the necessary relationship between remembering and forgetting. Those with power tend to shape public memory; those with less power must contest the forgetfulness caused by the partial memory of the powerful.

Power, Ideology, and Hegemony

Power, as defined by feminist scholars Cheris Kramarae and Paula A. Triechler, is *"the ability to get things done."*[76] The concept is not innately troublesome. However, because power is a social phenomenon, people have power in relationship to others. Social power is embedded in the communicative negotiations of gender/sex, race, class, sexual orientation and other identity ingredients. Differences are rarely constructed equally. Rather, the groups with more say about the construction are privileged over others.

Power is central to the study of rhetoric because it delimits the agency of rhetors. Communication scholars John L. Lucaites and Celeste M. Condit point out that people who study rhetoric need to consider the "systems of social conditions and their impact on public discourse."[77] Not all people have equal access to the public podium, because rhetorical actions occur in culturally and historically specific contexts in which power is apportioned unequally. Class, sex, race, citizenship, political affiliation, education, sexuality, and religion all influence the cultural resources that rhetors may access. Thus, Lucaites and Condit posit a refined definition of rhetoric that "portrays significant rhetors as those able to realign material life experiences and cultural symbols through the artful use of the available means of persuasion."[78] When you study rhetoric, you need to judge the skill of a rhetor, not against some abstract list of available persuasive means, but within the range of means available at a time, in a culture, and to a person given the social barriers she or he may face. The means of persuasion available to a US president differ from those available to an unemployed steelworker or to an immigrant living and working in the United States illegally. When you are in an audience, you need to consider these things before you judge a rhetor to be a failure or success.

Power is also central to the study of rhetoric because rhetoric is, itself, a form of power. Philosopher Michel Foucault, who has written extensively about power, notes that "as history constantly teaches us, discourse is not simply that which translates struggles or systems of domination, but is the thing for which and by which there is struggle, discourse is the power which is to be seized."[79] Rhetoric is both the object of power over which people struggle and the means by which people engage in a struggle for power. This becomes clearer as you explore the way in which ideology is rhetorical.

Power manifests itself rhetorically through the creation of a dominant **ideology,** which can be defined as *the ideas, values, beliefs, perceptions, and understandings that are known to members of a society and that guide their behaviors.* In *Making Sense of Political Ideology,* communication scholars Bernard L. Brock, Mark E. Huglen, James F. Klumpp, and Sharon Howell define ideology as "typical ways of thinking about the world [that] help shape human action"[80] because it normalizes "day-to-day social, political, economic, and cultural structures" by making them appear natural and inevitable.[81] It is composed of a group's socially accepted knowledge that explains, justifies, and interprets the social order. In short, ideology is a symbol system that explains why society is the way it is. Geertz identifies ideology as one example of a web of significance, because "the inherent elusiveness of ideological thought" is "expressed as it is in intricate symbolic webs as vaguely defined as they are emotionally charged."[82] Ideology is created and maintained through symbol use, but the ideological content of symbols is often difficult to track.

Ideology becomes most powerful when humans forget it is socially constructed and give it "the status of objective reality."[83] For example, marriage ceremonies are socially constructed rituals, but people forget these ceremonies are choices and begin to think they must be performed a particular way in order to be real. Cultural ideology about marriage ceremonies explains why the average cost of a US wedding tops $21,000, a hefty sum for a couple starting out, which might be better spent to make a down payment on a house or to pay off debts. You might even hear someone complain at a nontraditional (or less expensive) wedding that it was "not right" or "unnatural." Such comments indicate the existence of cultural ideology.

British cultural studies scholar Stuart Hall argues that dominant cultural ideology influences how people come to perceive reality.[84] For example, capitalism is not only an economic system, but also a dominant ideology in the United States that undergirds the values and behaviors that support competition, individualism, and consumerism, and that enables money to determine status and power. This does not mean that every person in US culture embraces the ideology unquestioningly, but it does explain the predominant US culture.

Burke offers a metaphorical description of how words operate together to constitute an ideology, and how that ideology induces people to act in certain ways: "An 'ideology' is like a spirit taking up its abode in a body: it makes that body hop around in certain ways; and that same body would have hopped around in different ways had a different ideology [or set of terms] happened to inhabit it."[85] In the case of the mob violence targeted at abolitionists, white supremacist ideology made the mob hop in a particularly violent way, legitimating the violence of slavery and the violence targeted at those who would challenge slavery. Ideology is not neutral, but tends to normalize the possession of power by the "haves" and the denial of power to the "have-nots."

Ideology guides the way people evaluate (attach meaning and valuations to) the world. It makes sense of social knowledge and order, helps people in a culture explain the reasons for good and ill, and offers direction for social action.[86] Like culture, ideology is resistant to change, but, also like culture, it is not unchangeable. Because it is constructed and maintained by symbols, ideology can be challenged and altered through symbolic action.

Not all ideologies carry equal power. Some become dominant. **Hegemony** is *the dominant ideology of a society, exerting social control over people without the use of force.*[87] Philosopher Rosemary Hennessy explains that hegemony is not a form of power that controls through overt violence; rather, it subtly controls by determining what makes sense: "Hegemony is the process whereby the interests of a ruling group come to dominate by establishing the common sense, that is, those values, beliefs, and knowledges that go without saying."[88]

Hegemony is constructed and maintained by rhetorical actions. Communication scholars draw on Italian political theorist Antonio Gramsci's concept of hegemonic ideology.[89] Gramsci argues that social control is primarily accomplished through the control of ideas. People are encouraged to see an idea as common sense, even if it conflicts with their own experiences. By following the cultural norms that guide behaviors, members of the culture uphold the ideology. People willingly belong to cultures for the protection and order they provide, even though (and because) hegemonic cultural ideology may control (or strongly influence) their beliefs.

Hegemony reduces one's agency because it limits the choices that make sense to a rhetor or audience. For example, because capitalism is the hegemonic US ideology, most people in the United States believe in free and open markets and in the freedom of consumers to choose where to shop and what to buy. Recently, in a small town where two locally owned restaurants were located next to a park, a multinational fast-food restaurant offered to buy the park land and pay to relocate the park so it could build a restaurant on that location. The town council held an open meeting to discuss the proposal. Some members of the community opposed the fast-food restaurant, arguing that it would put the locally owned restaurants out of business and destroy the community by taking away a valuable central public meeting place. These community members were accused of being "antidevelopment" and "against the free enterprise system." One council member said, "If you do not like fast food, then don't eat there. The other restaurants need to learn to compete. It's a free country." These statements did not really answer the opponents' arguments, but sought to silence the opposition by making them seem un-American, opposed to competition and freedom.

Because hegemony is embedded within symbolic actions, rhetorical critics need to learn how to read through it. Media scholar Stuart Hall identifies three positions from which audiences can decode a text: dominant or preferred (hegemonic) reading, negotiated reading, and oppositional (counterhegemonic) reading.[90] Different people in any given time have different resources available for oppositional readings, and have to expend more or less effort to construct them. Communication scholar Bonnie Dow observes that it is easy to "acquire the codes necessary for preferred readings" while "the acquisition of codes for negotiated or oppositional readings is more difficult and less common."[91] This text should provide you with the code, or vocabulary, with which to critically and oppositionally understand rhetoric.

CONCLUSION

Rhetoric is the use of symbolic action by human beings to share ideas, enabling them to work together to make decisions about matters of common concern and to construct social reality. What this definition makes clear, and Aristotle's does not, is that rhetoric is much more than a tool of information transmission or persuasion. Through rhetoric, people constitute identity, construct culture, maintain and challenge memory, and develop and sustain ideology; and are able to identify, maintain, and counter hegemonic power.

Our goal in this book is to introduce you to some of the joys and responsibilities of rhetorical action. Democracy is not a spectator sport, nor is life. To be able to participate, you need to understand how rhetoric works, and that it is at work in a variety of places: politics, religion, family, sports, entertainment, small town life, and workplaces. The ability to self-reflexively attach meaning to the world and to make sense of what the world means requires an understanding of rhetoric.

When studying rhetoric, scholars do not really use a single approach or a preset step-by-step method. Instead, they use what communication scholars William L. Nothstine, Carole Blair, and Gary A. Copeland refer to as "conceptual heuristics or vocabularies."[92] Throughout the chapters that follow, we present a vocabulary that describes the forms, components, and functions of rhetoric, and that should enable you to explain rhetoric's power to liberate *and* subordinate. We introduce you to diverse forms of symbolic action, including language, visual rhetoric, argument, and narrative. We show you ways to analyze how rhetorical action is composed of rhetors, audiences, and situations that constrain rhetoric even as they, themselves, are rhetorically constructed. We end with a discussion of public rhetoric that shows how you can identify yourself as an agent of civic action.

Rhetoric is essential to the functioning of civic culture. Civic engagement in open societies exists so that citizens can challenge the actions of those in power and engage each other in discussions and debates over what is right—for individuals, communities, the nation, and the world. Civic engagement is much more than the act of voting. It necessitates that you engage with other people and participate in symbolic actions that constitute your identity as a person, a group member, and a citizen. An understanding of how culture, memory, power, and ideology are rhetorical is integral to a complete understanding of the full power of rhetoric and of the constraints on rhetorical action.

DISCUSSION QUESTIONS

1. The authors suggest that the study of rhetoric is tied to democratic societies. Think about how the study of rhetoric may have been helpful in the years preceding the rise of Hitler. How might a society with a stronger emphasis on rhetoric have better understood Hitler and the Nazis?
2. Can you provide examples of the power of rhetoric in politics, the law, and your own daily life?
3. What is your position on the debate between Socrates and the Sophists? Is rhetoric morally neutral, or is it to blame for human failures?
4. The text suggested some constraints and resources for rhetoric and civic engagement. Can you identify others?

RECOMMENDED READINGS

Aristotle. *On Rhetoric*. Translated by George A. Kennedy. New York: Oxford University Press, 1991.

Asen, Robert. "A Discourse Theory of Citizenship." *Quarterly Journal of Speech* 90, no. 2 (2004): 189–211.

Hauser, Gerard A. "Rhetorical Democracy and Civic Engagement." In *Rhetorical Democracy: Discursive Practices of Civic Engagement*. Edited by Gerard A. Hauser and Amy Grim, 1–16 (Mahwah, NJ: Lawrence Erlbaum Associates, 2004).

Kennedy, George A. *A New History of Classical Rhetoric*. Princeton, NJ: Princeton University Press, 1994.

Poulakos, John. "Toward a Sophistic Definition of Rhetoric." *Philosophy and Rhetoric* 16, no. 1 (1983): 35–48.

ENDNOTES

[1] Kathleen Parker, "Google Bombs Can Ruin your Reputation," *The (Waterloo/Cedar Falls) Courier*, September 6, 2009, F3.

[2] John F. Kennedy, "Address at Rice University on the Nation's Space Program," September 12, 1962, Rice Stadium, Houston, Texas, http://www.americanrhetoric.com/speeches/jfkriceuniversity.htm (accessed August 26, 2009).

[3] "Debating Our Destiny: The Second 1984 Presidential Debate," *PBS NewsHour*, http://www.pbs.org/newshour/debatingourdestiny/84debates/2prez2.html (accessed August 27, 2007).

[4] Todd Gitlin, *The Whole World Is Watching: Mass Media in the Making and Unmaking of the New Left*, 2nd ed. (Berkeley: University of California Press, 2003).

[5] *Sports Illustrated*, February 8, 2010.

[6] Kate Dailey, "Lindsey Vonn's *Sports Illustrated* Cover: Sexist or Sporty? Two *Newsweek* Writers Discuss," February 8, 2010, http://www.thedailybeast.com/newsweek/blogs/the-human-condition/2010/02/08/lindsey-vonn-s-sports-illustrated-cover-sexist-or-sporty-two-newsweek-writers-discuss.html (accessed October 12, 2011).

[7] Winston S. Churchill, "The Lights Are Going Out," *Never Give In: The Best of Winston Churchill's Speeches* (New York: Hyperion, 2003), 182–185.

[8] Adolf Hitler, *The Speeches of Adolf Hitler*, vol. 1, ed. N. H. Baynes (Oxford, UK: Oxford University Press, 1942), 743.

[9] Charles A. Hill and Marguerite Helmers, eds., *Defining Visual Rhetorics* (Mahwah, NJ: Lawrence Erlbaum Associates, 2004); Diane S. Hope, ed., *Visual Communication: Perception, Rhetoric, and Technology* (Cresskill, NJ: Hampton, 2006); Lawrence J. Prelli, ed., *Rhetorics of Display* (Columbia: University of South Carolina Press, 2006).

[10] Kenneth Burke, "Dramatism," in *International Encyclopedia of the Social Sciences*, vol. 7, ed. David L. Sills, 445–452 (New York: Macmillan and Free Press, 1968), 447.

[11] James Boyd White, *Heracles' Bow: Essays on the Rhetoric and Poetics of Law* (Madison: University of Wisconsin Press, 1989), x.

[12] James Jasinski, "A Constitutive Framework for Rhetorical Historiography: Toward an Understanding of the Discursive (Re)Constitution of 'Constitution' in

The Federalist Papers," in *Doing Rhetorical History: Cases and Concepts*, ed. Kathleen J. Turner (Tuscaloosa: University of Alabama Press, 1998), 74–75.

[13] James Jasinski, *Sourcebook on Rhetoric* (Thousand Oaks, CA: Sage, 2001), 106.

[14] Kenneth Burke, *Language as Symbolic Action* (Berkeley: University of California Press, 1966), 16. Original is in italics.

[15] Kenneth Burke, *A Rhetoric of Motives* (Berkeley: University of California Press, 1969), 43.

[16] Burke, *A Rhetoric*, 20.

[17] Jasinski, *Sourcebook*, 305.

[18] Kenneth Burke, *Development and Design* (Worcester, MA: Clark University Press, 1972), 27–28.

[19] Burke, *Language*, 301.

[20] Burke, *A Rhetoric*, 21.

[21] Burke, *A Rhetoric*, 46.

[22] Gerda Lerner, *The Grimké Sisters from South Carolina* (New York: Schocken, 1967), 245.

[23] Angelina Grimké [Weld], "Address at Pennsylvania Hall," 1838, in Karlyn Kohrs Campbell, ed., *Man Cannot Speak for Her*, vol. 2 (New York: Praeger, 1989), 27.

[24] Karlyn Kohrs Campbell, *Man Cannot Speak for Her*, vol. 1 (New York: Praeger, 1989) 30. See also Stephen H. Browne, "Encountering Angelina Grimké: Violence, Identity, and the Creation of Radical Community," *Quarterly Journal of Speech* 82, no. 1 (February 1996), 55–73, for a discussion of how Grimké saw in violent reactions to abolitionists "not the repression of public discourse but an opportunity for it" (p. 70).

[25] Karlyn Kohrs Campbell, "Agency: Promiscuous and Protean," *Communication and Critical/Cultural Studies* 2 (2005): 3, italics added.

[26] Peter L. Berger, *The Sacred Canopy: Elements of a Sociological Theory of Religion* (New York: Anchor, 1967), 20.

[27] Barry Brummett, "Some Implications of 'Process' or 'Intersubjectivity': Postmodern Rhetoric," *Philosophy and Rhetoric* 9, no. 1 (1976): 21–53, 28–29.

[28] Kevin Michael DeLuca, "The Speed of Immanent Images: The Dangers of Reading Photographs," in Hope, *Visual Communication*, 79–90, 81.

[29] George A. Kennedy, *A New History of Classical Rhetoric* (Princeton, NJ: Princeton University Press, 1994), 7.

[30] George A. Kennedy, *Classical Rhetoric and Its Christian and Secular Tradition*, 2nd ed. (Chapel Hill: University of North Carolina Press, 1999), 1–2; George A. Kennedy, *Comparative Rhetoric: A Historical and Cross-Cultural Introduction* (New York: Oxford University Press, 1998), 1–28.

[31] David Phillips, *Athenian Political Oratory: Sixteen Key Speeches* (New York: Routledge, 2004), 6.

[32] Eric W. Robinson, *Ancient Greek Democracy: Readings and Sources* (Malden, MA: Wiley-Blackwell, 2004).

[33] Kennedy, *Classical Rhetoric*, 1–5, 29–30.

[34] John Poulakos, "Toward a Sophistic Definition of Rhetoric," *Philosophy and Rhetoric* 16, no. 1 (1983): 35–48, 37.

[35] I. F. Stone, *The Trial of Socrates* (New York: Anchor, 1989); Plato, *The Apology of Socrates*.

[36] Aristotle, *On Rhetoric*, trans. George A. Kennedy (New York: Oxford University Press, 1991). See Kennedy's "Prooemion," x–xi.

[37] Aristotle, *On Rhetoric*, 1.2.1 [1355].

[38] Aristotle, *On Rhetoric*, 1.3 [1358b].

[39] Aristotle, *On Rhetoric*, 1.2 [1356a–60], italics added.

[40] Jennifer Peltz, "Whose 5 Stars? Online 'User' Reviews Get Scrutiny," *The Associated Press*, July 29, 2009.

[41] Quoted in Steven Harmon, "GOP Candidates Polluting Airwaves," *San Jose Mercury News*, May 23, 2010.

[42] Henry Allen, "His Way with Words: Cadence and Credibility," *The Washington Post*, January 20, 2009, AA23.

[43] Burke, *A Rhetoric*, 37–46.

[44] Campbell, "Agency," 3.

[45] Gerard A. Hauser, "Rhetorical Democracy and Civic Engagement," in *Rhetorical Democracy: Discursive Practices of Civic Engagement*, ed. Gerard A. Hauser and Amy Grim, 1–16 (Mahwah, NJ: Lawrence Erlbaum Associates, 2004), 11.

[46] Bruce Gronbeck, "Citizen Voices in Cyberpolitical Culture," in Hauser and Grim, *Rhetorical Democracy*, 17–32, 28.

[47] Robert Asen, "A Discourse Theory of Citizenship," *Quarterly Journal of Speech* 90, no. 2 (2004): 189–211.

[48] Asen, "A Discourse Theory," 191.

[49] Asen, "A Discourse Theory," 201.

[50] Asen, "A Discourse Theory," 195.

[51] Abraham Lincoln, "Gettysburg Address," November 19, 1863, http://www.americanrhetoric.com/speeches/gettysburgaddress.htm (accessed September 1, 2009).

[52] Justice Oliver Wendell Holmes, *Abrams v. United States* 250 US 616, argued October 21–22, 1919, decided November 10, 1919, http://www.bc.edu/bc_org/avp/cas/comm/free_speech/abrams.html (accessed August 26, 2009).

[53] Karlyn Kohrs Campbell, *The Rhetorical Act*, 2nd ed. (Belmont, CA: Wadsworth, 1996), 9–17.

[54] Mary Church Terrell, "What It Means To Be Colored in the Capital of the United States," in Campbell, *Man Cannot*, vol. 2, 421–432.

[55] Ida B. Wells, "Southern Horrors: Lynch Law in All Its Phases," in Campbell, *Man Cannot*, vol. 2, 385–420.

[56] Wells, "Self Help," 1892, http://www.gutenberg.org/files/14975/14975-h/14975-h.htm (accessed June 10, 2010).

[57] George W. Bush, speech to the NAACP Annual Convention, Baltimore, Maryland, July 10, 2000, http://www.pbs.org/newshour/bb/politics/july-dec00/bush_7-10.html (accessed June 10, 2010).

[58] Avis Thomas-Lester, "A Senate Apology for History on Lynching," *Washington Post*, June 14, 2005, http://www.washingtonpost.com/wp-dyn/content/article/2005/06/13/AR2005061301720.html (accessed June 9, 2010).

[59] Campbell, *Man Cannot*, vol. 1, 157–179.

[60] Clifford Geertz, *The Interpretation of Cultures* (New York: Basic Books, 1973), 89, italics added.

[61] William B. Gudykunst, "Individualistic and Collectivistic Perspectives on Communication: An Introduction," *International Journal of Intercultural Relations*, 22 (1998): 107–134.

[62] Robert Hariman and John Louis Lucaites, "Liberal Representation and Global Order: The Iconic Photograph from Tiananmen Square," in Prelli *Rhetorics of Display*, 121–138. Image at http://www.sbs.com.au/news/article/1171447/-Tank-man-photo-on-Google-China.

[63] Geertz, *Interpretation*, 5.

[64] Judith Butler, *Precarious Life: The Power of Mourning and Violence* (New York: Verso, 2004) and Steven Johnston, *The Truth about Patriotism* (Durham, NC: Duke University Press, 2007).

[65] Geertz, *Interpretation*, 89.

[66] Judith N. Martin and Thomas K. Nakayama, *Intercultural Communication in Contexts*, 3rd ed., (Boston: McGraw-Hill, 2004), 3.

[67] Barry Schwartz, "The Social Context of Commemoration: A Study of Collective Memory," *Social Forces* 61 (1982): 374–402, 374.

[68] Carole Blair, "Communication as Collective Memory," in *Communication as . . . Perspectives on Theory*, ed. Gregory J. Shepherd, Jeffrey St. John, and Ted Striphas, 51–59 (Thousand Oaks, CA: Sage, 2006), 52.

[69] Richard Morris, *Sinners, Lovers, and Heroes* (Albany: State University of New York Press, 1997), 26, italics added.

[70] Maurice Halbwachs, *On Collective Memory* (Chicago, University of Chicago Press, 1992).

[71] Iwona Irwin-Zarecka, *Frames of Remembrance: The Dynamics of Collective Memory* (New Brunswick, NJ: Transaction, 1994), 4.

[72] Irwin-Zarecka, *Frames*, 217.

[73] Michael Kammen, *The Mystic Chords of Memory: The Transformation of Tradition in American Culture* (New York: Alfred A. Knopf, 1991), 27.

[74] Thomas J. Steele, S. J., "The Figure of Columbia: Phillis Wheatley Plus George Washington," *The New England Quarterly: A Historical Review of New England Life and Letters* 54, no. 2 (1981): 264–266.

[75] José Barreiro, ed., *Northeast Indian Quarterly: View from the Shore: American Indian Perspectives on the Quincentenary* 7 (Fall 1990), 2. See also José Barreiro, "What 1992 Means to American Indians," in *Without Discovery: A Native Response to Columbus*, ed. Ray Gonzales (Seattle: Broken Moon, 1992): 57–60.

[76] Cheris Kramarae and Paula A. Triechler, *Amazons, Bluestockings and Crones: A Feminist Dictionary*, 2nd ed. (London: Pandora, 1992), 351, italics added.

[77] John Louis Lucaites and Celeste Michelle Condit, "Reconstructing <Equality>: Culturetypal and Counter-Cultural Rhetorics in the Martyred Black Vision," *Communication Monographs* 57 (March 1990): 21n3.

[78] Lucaites and Condit, "Reconstructing," 6.

[79] Michel Foucault, "The Order of Discourse," in *Language and Politics*, ed. Michael J. Shapiro, 108–138 (New York: New York University Press, 1984), 110.

[80] Bernard L. Brock, Mark E. Huglen, James F. Klumpp, and Sharon Howell, *Making Sense of Political Ideology: The Power of Language in Democracy* (New York: Rowman and Littlefield, 2005), 39.

[81] Brock, et al., *Making Sense*, 39.

[82] Geertz, *Interpretation*, 195.

[83] Peter Berger defines legitimation in this way. We see ideology as legitimizing the social order. See Berger, *The Sacred Canopy*, 4, 9, 29.

[84] Stuart Hall, "Ideology and Communication Theory," in *Rethinking Communication Theory*, vol. 1, ed. Brenda Dervin, Larry Grossberg, Barbara O'Keefe, and Ellen Wartella, 40–52 (Newbury Park, CA: Sage, 1989).

[85] Burke, *Language*, 6.

[86] V. William Balthrop, "Culture, Myth, and Ideology as Public Argument: An Interpretation of the Ascent and Demise of 'Southern Culture,'" *Communication Monographs* 51 (December 1984), 343–344.

[87] Antonio Gramsci, Raymond Rosenthal, and Frank Rosengarten, *Letters from Prison* (New York: Columbia University Press, 1993).

[88] Rosemary Hennessy, "Subjects, Knowledges, ... and All the Rest: Speaking for What," *Who Can Speak? Authority and Critical Identity*, ed. Judith Roof and Robyn Weigman, 137–150 (Urbana: University of Illinois Press, 1995), 145–146.

[89] Joseph P. Zompetti, "Toward a Gramscian Critical Rhetoric," *Western Journal of Communication* 61, no. 1 (Winter 1997), 66–86, and John M. Murphy, "Domesticating Dissent: The Kennedys and the Freedom Rides," *Communication Monographs* 59, no. 1 (March 1992), 61–78.

[90] Stuart Hall, "Encoding, Decoding," *The Cultural Studies Reader*, ed. Simon During, 90–103 (London: Routledge, 1993), 98–102.

[91] Bonnie J. Dow, *Prime-Time Feminism* (Philadelphia: University of Pennsylvania Press, 1996), 13.

[92] William L. Nothstine, Carole Blair, and Gary A. Copeland, *Critical Questions: Invention, Creativity, and the Criticism of Discourse and Media* (New York: St. Martin's, 1994), 40.

PART II
Forms of Symbolic Action

Chapter 2

Language

Key Concepts

characterizations	inflated language
condensation symbol	metaphor
connotation	presentational symbolism
denotation	public vocabulary
discursive symbolism	resignification
doublespeak	semiotics
dramatism	terministic screen
euphemism	theory of linguistic relativity
gestalt	truncated passives
ideograph	

Language can elicit a complex range of responses in people: it can induce fear, it can awe, it can make people weep with sadness or with joy, it can motivate people to action, or it can bore them into a stupor. Language is a tool with which to transmit information, but it is also a rich, complex, transactional web that defines who you are and how you see the people, objects, and actions that enmesh you in daily life.

If you doubt the importance of language, think about times when disagreement arises over what word to use to name a particular individual or action. When Scott Roeder murdered Dr. George Tiller because he provided abortion services, when white supremacist James von Brunn opened fire in the US Holocaust Museum and murdered museum guard Stephen Johns, and when Joseph Stack flew his plane into the Austin IRS field office and murdered Vernon Hunter, debate ensued about whether their actions were simply *criminal* or qualified as *terrorism*.[1] Depending on how you name their actions, your reaction to the people and their actions shifts. A crime is viewed as worthy of punishment because it represents an instance in which one human being, motivated by personal gain or animosity, harmed another. An act of terrorism is viewed as worthy of even greater condemnation because it represents an instance in which one human being, motivated by hatred of a group, harmed another human being in order to terrorize all members of the group to which that person belonged. While a crime affects the person attacked (and that person's friends and family), terrorism also affects the larger social group to which the person belongs.

We open this chapter with a discussion of theories that describe how language constructs social reality. We will then identify four concepts that offer a vocabulary with which to describe how language functions as symbolic action:

terministic screens, public vocabulary, discursive and presentational forms, and resignification. Finally, we examine some ways in which language can be misused. This chapter demonstrates how language is more than a tool used to transmit information about the world in which you live; it is a way in which you make that world.

LANGUAGE AND THE CONSTRUCTION OF SOCIAL REALITY

Early studies of language relied on the correspondence theory, which assumes each word simply refers or corresponds to some thing in the world. For example, the word "dog" corresponds to a barking, wagging, furry member of the family *Canidae*. Understanding between people is based on each person's ability to know the meaning of the word "dog" and to what thing in the world it corresponds, but what interests us are the subtle differences in meaning that emerge for a word. Although it is useful to explain one of the basic functions of communication as information transmission, the correspondence theory fails to fully explain the power of language. Theorists now see language as much more than a tool used to reference some thing in the world. People use language to construct social reality, not just to refer to reality. In this section we discuss theories that explain how language makes meaning.

Semiotics

In the mid-1800s, US philosopher Charles Sanders Pierce coined the term **semiotics** to describe *the relationship among signs, meanings, and referents.* Around the same time, Swiss linguist Ferdinand de Saussure also pushed forcefully for a semiotic approach, arguing that a science that "studies the role of signs as part of social life" should be a part of psychology and linguistics.[2] Semiotics rejects the correspondence theory of language. It urges people to consider signifying practices—how language does not *have* meaning but, as a social practice, *makes* meaning.

Semiotics still recognizes a relationship between a sign and a referent, but that relationship is more complex. Semiotics defines a sign as composed of two parts: the signifier (the sound/image of the sign or the form it takes) and the signified (the concept referenced by the signifier).[3] A sign still refers to some thing in the world (the creature wagging its tail), but it is composed of the signifier (the word "dog") and the signified (the idea of what a dog is that never perfectly corresponds to the creature wagging its tail, otherwise how can a Great Dane and a teacup Chihuahua both be dogs?). What is signified influences how people understand the referent. In semiotics, people understand a sign's meaning by decoding the concept that is signified, and not just what the sign refers to.

The semiotic recognition of the signified enables a distinction to be made between the denotation of a word and its connotation. **Denotation** is *the literal, commonsense meaning of a sign, ostensibly value-free and objective.* "Dog" would denote a domesticated, carnivorous, four-legged, hair-covered mammal of the family *Canidae*. If this definition sounds like something you would find in a dictionary, it is because dictionary definitions attempt to provide the denotative meaning of a word. Denotation is where the correspondence theory of meaning stops in its explanation.

Connotation is *the emotional or cultural meaning attached to a sign; it is what is signified.* Connotative meanings are usage-specific. They emerge when the sign's denotative meaning is not sufficient to completely communicate a concept. Even though the same canine can serve as the referent for "dog," "cur," and "mutt," the change in what is signified influences your understanding of that canine. "Dog" likely induces a neutral or positive valuation, while "cur" and "mutt" would induce a negative valuation. The denotations of signs may be easily decoded, but their connotations require a more nuanced process of decoding.

The same term can have very different connotations in different contexts, because a sign does not correspond to a single concept or thing. For example, at a dog show, different categories of competition exist for each breed, including puppy dog, American-bred dog, open dog, puppy bitch, American-bred bitch, and open bitch. In that context, "bitch" has a very specific denotative meaning: a female canine. Because the word carries no negative connotation, it is common to hear a person comment to another: "Your Brittany bitch is gorgeous." In another context, "bitch" carries very negative connotations. When used as a derogatory term for a woman, it likens a human woman to a vicious and moody female dog.

Linguistic Relativity

Attention to the way language structures meaning led to the development of the Sapir-Whorf hypothesis, also known as the **theory of linguistic relativity,** *the idea that the structure of a language influences the way people perceive the world.* Anthropologist and linguist Edward Sapir explains that a person lives in both an objective reality and a social reality constructed through language. Thus, multiple social realities exist. Sapir explains:

> Human beings . . . are very much at the mercy of the particular language which has become the medium of expression for their society. It is quite an illusion to imagine . . . that language is merely an incidental means of solving specific problems of communication or reflection. The fact of the matter is that the "real world" is to a large extent unconsciously built upon the language habits of the group. . . . The worlds in which different societies live are distinct worlds, not merely the same world with different labels attached . . . . We see and hear and otherwise experience very largely as we do because the language habits of our community predispose certain choices of interpretation.[4]

Although people may know things exist apart from their language, they do not know what those things mean, or how they are to react to them, except through language. In other words, meanings are relative to the symbol system, or code, that produces them.

A number of studies on the linguistic relativity theory support the idea that people's language does, indeed, affect their perceptions. For example, the range of linguistic categories for color affect whether a person sees changes in hues.[5]

An example from the art community also illustrates the power of language to structure meaning. Artist Marcel Duchamp is credited with developing the form of art known as the "readymade," in which an artist elevates a found object to the highest levels of art "by the simple performative utterance of calling it 'art'."[6] In 1916, Duchamp became a member of the Society of Independent Artists, "founded in that year with the express purpose of holding exhibitions for any artist who cared to exhibit something. There were no juries, and no work would be refused."[7] To test the group's conception of art and its purpose, under a pseudonym Duchamp submitted an upended urinal he titled "Fountain." The committee rejected the piece. Duchamp resigned in protest because the group had violated its own commitment to accept all submissions.

This story illustrates the power of naming: a committee was given the power to determine what was, and was not, art. The example also raises the possibility that what people think of as a discarded urinal could be called art, and that as a result their reaction to that object—what it means to them—could change. In fact, even though "Fountain" originally was rejected as a work of art, its importance to contemporary art has attached both meaning and value to it. It is now recognized as a piece of art so important it sold in a 1997 Sotheby's auction for $1,762,500.[8] The performative utterance of Duchamp calling it "Fountain" and the controversy surrounding it made a discarded urinal into art.

People are capable of thinking beyond the limits set by language, but it takes effort. Sapir writes that "language is . . . a prepared road or groove."[9] Feminist lexicographer Julia Penelope explains that a person's language creates paths of least resistance through which she or he can understand the world. The more a person travels those paths, the deeper and more difficult it becomes to think outside the grooves, because "language focuses our attention on what we believe we know . . . and we neglect to glance aside at . . . the much larger, but apparently formless lands of all that we do not, but might know if we stepped outside the mainstream."[10] For example, even though language habits in the 1800s named black people as slaves, less than fully human, activists such as British parliamentarian William Wilberforce, the Quaker Grimké sisters, former slaves Sojourner Truth and Frederick Douglass, and US social reformer William Lloyd Garrison were able to see outside of the groove of white supremacy to name the immanent humanity of all people, regardless of color.

LANGUAGE AS SYMBOLIC ACTION

Kenneth Burke, one of the most significant rhetorical theorists of the twentieth century, described himself as a "word-man."[11] His theories about language continue to influence scholars in communication studies, English, philosophy, theatre, and sociology. Burke's theory is known as **dramatism,** *an idea that is premised on two interlocking assumptions: (1) "language is primarily a species of*

*action . . . rather than an instrument of definition," and (2) the best way to under-
stand human relations and motives is through an analysis of symbolic action.*[12]
When people use symbols, they engage in a form of human action that relies
on the mobilization of symbols, rather than physical force, to act in the world.
When using language, people *do* things; they induce cooperation, foment division, create identification, constitute identity, and shape social reality.

Burke's dramatistic approach offers many concepts to explain language's
power, and inspired scholars to develop even more. A few key concepts that
share Burke's basic assumption that language is a species of action include
terministic screens, public vocabulary, discursive and presentational form, and
resignification.

Terministic Screens

Words can shape human beings as much as human beings use words to shape the
world. Burke asks: "Do we simply use words, or do they not also use us?"[13] For
example, the English language describes the sexes of human beings in a binary
and dichotomous way: a human being is one of two sexes—male or female—and
those sexes are "opposite," as in the phrase "opposite sex." More than two sexes
exist, however. Many recent medical studies have determined that about one
in two thousand babies are born both/and or neither/nor, and that even more
people have more subtle sex anatomy variations that do not appear until later.[14]
This example makes clear how words begin to "use us" when you consider
what was done to babies who did not fit into the male/female binary. From the
1950s (when surgical intervention became a possibility) to the 1990s, doctors
embraced the concealment model, which calls for radical surgical intervention.
In many cases, doctors did not even consult the parents but simply made surgical
adjustments to make the baby's body fit the sex the doctor "assigned."[15] Literally,
babies' bodies were surgically altered to fit into the linguistic binary.[16] Since the
early 1990s, new language has emerged that makes space for sexually ambiguous
bodies, starting with biology professor Anne Fausto-Sterling's declaration that
at least five sexes exist along a continuum (male, merm, herm, ferm, female).[17]
In addition, activists embraced the term "intersex" to describe a person who
has ambiguous sex features. They also demanded a shift from a concealment
approach to a more patient-centered model. Language has power to reinforce
binaries that use us in real ways.

Language's ability to use us is explained by the way words operate as a
terministic screen, which Burke describes as *a screen composed of terms through
which humans perceive the world, and that direct attention away from some interpretations and toward others.* For Burke, language always acts to direct attention,
making all communication persuasive because "[e]ven if any given terminology
is a *reflection* of reality, by its very nature as a terminology it must be a *selection*
of reality; and to this extent it must function also as a *deflection* of reality."[18] Your
words screen what you see.

Every single time you think about something, the words you use to articulate your thoughts have directed your attention in one way rather than another.
The terms "male," "female," and "opposite sex" contribute to a terministic screen

that induces humans to see only males or females; without a term such as "intersex," the existence of sexually ambiguous people is deflected. Terms such as "natural resource" and "habitat" contribute to terministic screens that call for different reactions to a stand of trees, one screen inducing economic use and the other inducing protection.

Because US society has symbols that stand for money (currency), people tend to judge the quality of an item through its monetary value: attention is directed to a thing's cost, rather than its intrinsic characteristics. This monetary symbol system directs people's attention so powerfully, people judge the same thing to be of a higher quality when *only* the price assigned to it is changed. In a fascinating study that tested the power of marketing, researchers at the California Institute of Technology and Stanford University told volunteer subjects they would be tasting different wines sold at different prices, when in reality they were given the same wine over and over. Not only did the subjects indicate that the supposedly more expensive wine tasted better, their medial orbitofrontal cortexes (the part of the brain that processes feelings of pleasantness) reacted differently.[19] Because the dollar symbol directed their attention to read "more expensive" as "better quality," they were not able to see (or taste) what their own senses could have imparted—that all the wine was exactly the same.

Another example of the effect of terministic screens comes from the reproductive freedom and abortion controversy, a rhetorically charged issue in the contemporary United States. Two main sides have long dominated the controversy: pro-life and pro-choice. People who are pro-life tend to refer to the reality as a "baby" while those who are pro-choice tend to refer to the reality as a "fetus." Each term selects, deflects, and reflects reality in a particular way, and calls forth different clusters of terms that flesh out the contours of the screen.[20]

"Baby" accurately reflects reality insofar as people often ask "when is the baby due?" and feel pain at miscarriages as the loss of a baby. The term also selects a particular aspect of reality to highlight: it focuses your attention on the idea that the reality is a fully formed human being, separable from its gestational location. A person could leave a baby in a room unattended (but of course safely ensconced in a crib). However, when the baby is in the womb, it cannot be separated from its location. The term also selects a particular type of relationship to other human beings: "babies" have mothers and fathers, not women and men. "Baby" also calls forth positive associations because US culture is pro-natal—it celebrates the arrival of babies—and perceives babies as innocent and pure. Once people think of the reality as a separate and distinct human being, to terminate its existence means that someone has murdered the baby. Babies can be murdered; people do not talk about "terminating" babies.

In the process of selecting some parts of reality to highlight, the term "baby" also deflects part of reality. It deflects that the reality is located within a woman's body and it deflects the possibility that women can be anything more than mothers. It also deflects the fact that recognized development stages exist in the human as it undergoes gestation: from zygote, to blastocyst, to embryo, to fetus.

In the same way that "baby" reflects, deflects, and selects parts of reality, so too does the term "fetus," which selects those parts of reality that "baby" deflects. "Fetus" notes that the reality is described in medical and scientific terms, that gestational stages exist through which the fetus eventually becomes a complete human being, and that a fetus cannot exist without a woman to carry it. In fact, "fetus" reverses the order of the relationship created by "baby": babies have mothers, while women carry fetuses. With "baby," the baby is the entity that has agency and rights—a baby has a mother, and focus literally is on the baby first. With "fetus," the woman is the entity that has agency and rights—she carries the fetus, and focus is on her first.

In selecting the medical reality of the fetus, the term highlights that the fetus is not a complete human being. Although people may think fondly of sitting in a rocking chair and cuddling with a baby, the image of cuddling with a fetus is not quite the same.

In the process of selecting, "fetus" also deflects attention away from things the term "baby" selects. "Fetus" deflects the emotional attachments people have to small human forms, as well as the possibility that the fetus can be murdered. Fetuses are not murdered; instead, pregnancies are terminated.

The clusters of terms around "baby" and "fetus" form terministic screens through which individuals construct and view reality. Those screens form a context that infuses the terms with particular connotations, even though each term ostensibly refers to the same referent. As terms direct people's attention in one way rather than another, they "affect the nature of our observations." Burke posits that "much that we take as observations about 'reality' may be but the spinning out of possibilities implicit in our particular choice of terms."[21]

Public Vocabulary

Because rhetoric constructs, maintains, and transforms your understanding of reality, to understand some event in the world or some policy enacted by the government, you must ask not just "What is it?" but also "How do we talk about it?" Communication scholar Celeste Condit argues that the "process of convincing" involves more than just acceptance of a particular policy; it also requires "that a given vocabulary (or set of understandings) be integrated into the public repertoire."[22] John L. Lucaites and Celeste Condit describe this **public vocabulary** as the *"culturally established and sanctioned" terms that compose people's taken-for-granted understanding of the world.*[23] A public vocabulary forms a society's terministic screen. In debates about civil rights, the public vocabulary includes words such as "equality" and "justice," stories of racism such as Rosa Parks being forced to sit at the back of the bus and the murder of Emmet Till, and characterizations of the United States as a place that must "let freedom ring." Daily, people in a community call upon this vocabulary to justify social actions, but when conditions call for social change, "the public vocabulary needs to be managed and reconstituted in ways that require" rhetorical skill.[24] Rhetors can try to "rearrange and revivify" the existing vocabulary, or they can introduce new vocabulary.[25] Ideographs, characterizations, narratives, and metaphors are key elements of the public vocabulary.

Ideographs. Michael Calvin McGee, a noted communication scholar, coined the term **ideograph** to describe

> *an ordinary language term found in political discourse. It is a high-order abstraction representing collective commitment to a particular but equivocal and ill-defined normative goal. It warrants the use of power, excuses behavior and belief which might otherwise be perceived as eccentric or antisocial, and guides behavior and belief into channels easily recognized by a community as acceptable or laudable.*[26]

Words such as "freedom" and "security" are examples of ideographs: they are abstract words, used in ordinary language, that warrant the use of power. People cannot point at freedom or security, yet US troops are ready to give their lives to defend them. On September 11, 2001, when physical structures (the World Trade Center and the Pentagon) had been attacked, President George W. Bush used abstract language to declare: "our very freedom came under attack."[27] Because freedom was under attack and US security was undermined, Bush called for a collective commitment to the War on Terror. Such a call was a clear attempt to warrant the use of presidential power, both in the invasion of Afghanistan and the later attack against Iraq.

It may seem strange to think of military action as antisocial, but consider this: typically, we do not condone one person taking the life of another and, hence, name it "murder." However, in a time of war, people do condone the taking of life, and tend to speak of it as killing (the enemy), rather than as murder. Killing in the name of freedom is not murder. An antisocial behavior is condoned, in part because the abstraction calls for the people to condone the use of that power. The ideograph of "freedom" warrants the use of deadly force.

Scholars have studied a range of ideographs, including family values,[28] equality,[29] choice, and life.[30] In each case, the word offers a way to track ideology as expressed through language.

Characterizations and Narratives. Characterizations are *the labels and descriptions attached to acts, agencies, agents, scenes, and purposes.* These five terms constitute what Burke calls the dramatistic pentad. An *act* is "what took place, in thought or deed"; *scene* is "the background of the act, the situation in which it occurred"; *agent* is the "person or kind of person" who "performed the act"; *agency* is the means by which the act was accomplished; and *purpose* is the justification for the act.[31] Whenever you analyze a rhetorical act, you should be able to identify the way a rhetor characterizes each of these elements.

By exploring where differences arise between rhetor's characterizations of these elements, you can identify motives and reasons for disagreement. As Burke explains, "Men [and women] may violently disagree about the purposes behind a given act, or about the character of the person who did it, or how he [or she] did it, or in what kind of situation he [or she] acted; or they may even insist upon totally different words to name the act itself."[32] Thus, to understand human communication, you need to understand the stories told and the way in which the elements of the stories are characterized. Characterizations are never neutral but, according to Lucaites and Condit, "integrate cultural connotations and denotations while ascribing a typical and pervasive nature to the entity described."[33] These labels guide the way a society attaches values to people or actions. Depending on how an agent, scene, or act is characterized, your reactions to that agent, scene, or act may change.

For example, when the "Don't tase me, bro!" video went viral on YouTube in September 2007, characterizations influenced people's reactions.[34] The video was made when US Senator John Kerry addressed a Constitution Day Forum at the University of Florida. Andrew Meyer, a senior telecommunication major, asked why Kerry had conceded the 2004 presidential election and whether Kerry was a member of the Yale secret society Skull and Bones. As Meyer's questions exceeded the time allowed, university police officers attempted to escort Meyer out of the lecture hall. Meyer insisted he had done nothing wrong and declared his right to stay in front of the microphone. His microphone was turned off. The officers began to forcibly escort him outside. When he resisted, the officers drew a taser. Meyer screamed: "Don't tase me, bro!" as one of the officers fired the taser at him.

Initially, serious questions arose about an apparent use of excessive force against a college student. The act of tasing was characterized as unwarranted; the officers as out of line. As descriptions of Meyer emerged, however, the focus shifted from the officers' (agent) unwarranted (purpose) excessive use of force (act) and to Meyer as the agent. Media outlets described Meyer's purpose not as the exercise of free speech, but as attention seeking. One day after the incident, CNN reported that Meyer had brought his own camera and had a friend videotape him.[35] The *International Herald Tribune* reported that Meyer had begun his question only after he confirmed the other student had started videotaping, and noted that Meyer had a "penchant for practical jokes."[36] ABC's *Good Morning America* reported that Meyer "has a reputation for practical jokes, and stars in short comedy films he posts on the Internet."[37]

As this incident demonstrates, the same act and person can be characterized in very different ways. In one version, the officers acted in an unnecessarily violent way against an innocent college student exercising his free speech rights. In another version, an obnoxious practical joker pushed the officers to an extreme reaction by abusing the decorum of a public forum. Once the event became characterized by the juvenile request of "Don't tase me, bro," the focus firmly shifted to Meyer, and characterizations of Meyer affected the way people interpreted the tasing incident. It became a laughable practical joke, rather than an excessive use of state power.

Characterizations are the building blocks of narratives, or stories. Narratives direct people to see particular relationships between characterizations and, thus, offer explanations about how reality makes sense and works.[38] You tell stories about family members, daily events, classroom incidents, and yourself; and to explain why others should (or should not) take a specific course or professor. People's reliance on stories to better understand the world in which they live led moral philosopher Alasdair MacIntyre to describe the human being as "a story-telling animal."[39] (Chapter 5 explores narratives in more depth.)

Narratives play a significant role in public communication. They form and maintain public memory and teach cultural values. Communication scholar Walter Fisher identifies the way narratives offer good reasons in public deliberation and help people make sense of the world.[40] The dominant social narrative that informs the US public vocabulary is the American Dream, most vividly illustrated by Horatio Alger's stories. Alger wrote hundreds of books in the 1800s about young working-class men pulling themselves up by their boot-straps in order to improve their positions in life and achieving rags-to-riches success. These stories embodied the US ideal that regardless of where people start out, if they work hard enough, they can achieve success. Rhetorical critics Robert C. Rowland and John M. Jones suggest that when public figures refer to the "American Dream," they tap into this narrative and its characterization of the people in the United States as being "on a progressive journey to a better society."[41]

Metaphors. A metaphor is *a figure of speech in which two dissimilar things are said to be similar, offering a new perspective on a known issue.* For example, when Plato's *Republic* refers to government as the ship of state,[42] "ship" is a metaphor for government. Most people define government as the administrative arm of a state, but the power of government to direct the future of a state is not really made clear in that definition.

Burke explains that metaphor provides "perspective" insofar as it is "a device for seeing something *in terms of* something else. It brings out the thisness of a that, or the thatness of a this."[43] In Plato's metaphor, people learn something about government by looking at it as a ship; they gain perspective on the ship-ness of government. By thinking about government as a ship, one begins to think about government as having a direction, navigating through troubled waters, and needing a captain.

Insofar as metaphors enable you to see one thing in terms of something else, linguistics professor George Lakoff and philosophy professor Mark Johnson believe they enable a person to "elaborate a concept . . . in considerable detail" and also "find appropriate means for highlighting some aspects of it and hiding others."[44] Burke's observation that language selects and deflects is echoed by Lakoff and Johnson's description of how metaphors function.

A range of metaphors populates language ("range" and "populate" both being metaphors themselves). Lakoff and Johnson argue that metaphor is not only a "device of the poetic imagination" but a matter of "ordinary language."[45] They believe people's "ordinary conceptual system is metaphorical in nature,"[46] which means you cannot understand language unless you understand metaphor. Every sentence you use contains metaphors. In the previous sentence, "contains" is a metaphor. Sentences are words, and cannot really contain anything; but if you think of a sentence as a structure with sides, it can hold other things ("structure," "sides," and "hold" all being extensions of the metaphor "contains").

The power of metaphor resides in its ability to structure thought. Metaphors help people make sense of the world. Lakoff explores the use of the metaphor of "tax relief" and "tax burden" to demonstrate. According to Lakoff, "relief" implies that one has some affliction. In this case taxes are a burden, from which people need to be relieved. Within this metaphor, the person who relieves another of a burden is a hero, while anyone who would interfere with relief is a villain. What if, instead, people think of taxes as a patriotic obligation for living in the United States and reaping the benefits of its infrastructure? Lakoff points out:

> As Oliver Wendell Holmes famously said, taxes are the price of civilization. They are what you pay to live in America—your dues—to have democracy, opportunity and access to all the infrastructure that previous taxpayers have built up and made available to you: highways, the Internet, weather reports, parks, the stock market, scientific research, Social Security, rural electrification, communications satellites, and on and on. If you belong to America, you pay a membership fee and you get all that infrastructure plus government services: flood control, air-traffic control, the Food and Drug Administration, the Centers for Disease Control and so on. . . . It is an issue of patriotism! Are you paying your dues, or are you trying to get something for free at the expense of your country? It's about being a member.[47]

The metaphors of "dues" and "burden" structure your understanding of taxes in different ways.

Metaphors are ubiquitous and inconspicuous at the same time. They populate language, yet few people are aware of their presence. Metaphor's stealth nature is part of its power to structure thought. Finnish political scientist Riikka Kuusisto warns that if people do not recognize that metaphors express a particular and necessarily limited perspective, the implications of these metaphors may be heard as "objective factual descriptions and come to define the only way of seeing and doing things in a specific situation."[48] Instead of offering *a* perspective, the metaphor comes to be *the* perspective. If you do not hear how metaphors direct your attention, you will begin to accept a metaphorical interpretation of the world as fixed and objective reality.

In her analysis of Western metaphors concerning the war in Kosovo, Kuusisto identifies the ways US President Bill Clinton, British Prime Minister Tony Blair, and French President Jacques Chirac described the conflict through the metaphors of heroic fairy tale, athletic game, and business deal. All these metaphors operated in subtle ways to structure people's understanding of the conflict: "they made participation in the conflict chivalrous and reassuring (heroic tales), exciting and fun (games), and profitable and rational (trading)."[49] In the process, the metaphors downplayed "the misery, pain, and turbulence often associated with deadly quarrels."[50] Kuusisto concludes the metaphors "brought the complicated and destructive conflict into the sphere of the well-known and harmless."[51] The metaphors enabled people who lived outside the conflict zone and had no direct experience of the horrors of war to understand the war, but also provided a very particular understanding, one that "tied the progression of the events to a logic of responding and accepting the challenge, a logic that could not easily be reversed into negotiating or giving the enemy a second chance."[52] The metaphors of war as fairy tale, game, and trading directed attention toward reassurance, fun, and rationality, and deflected attention away from the horror of war.

Discursive and Presentational Forms

Susanne Langer, a prominent US philosopher, significantly contributed to understanding the primary role symbols play in constructing meaning within cultures and individuals, and how rhetors and audiences achieve meaning collaboratively.[53] Langer explored all forms of symbol use, including those related to art, myth, ritual, and science. To highlight the diverse functions that symbols perform, she advanced an important distinction between two types of symbols: discursive and presentational.

Discursive symbolism is *language use with a linear structure that operates through reason and not intuition*—for example, deliberative discourse. Discursive form breaks down complex relationships into an easy-to-follow linear structure, such as problem/cause/solution. In contrast, **presentational symbolism** is *"a direct presentation of an individual object"* that *"widens our conception of rationality far beyond the traditional boundaries, yet never breaks faith with logic in the strictest sense."*[54] Art and music are Langer's primary examples of presentational symbolism, but she also highlighted how some uses of language participated in presentational form. Langer uses the metaphor of clothing to explain the differences between the two forms:

> All language has a form which requires us to string out our ideas even though their objects rest one within the other; as pieces of clothing that are actually worn one over the other have to be strung side by side on the clothesline. This property of verbal symbolism is known as *discursiveness*: by reason of it, only thoughts which can be arranged in this peculiar order can be spoken at all; any idea which does not lend itself to this "projection" is ineffable, incommunicable by means of words.[55]

If you wanted to share your experience of seeing a moose in the wild, you could do so discursively or presentationally. Discursively, you would articulate what you saw in a linear format, word after word, breaking down the experience into a description of the time, the place, the sounds, the smells, and your emotions. The experience would unfold bit by bit. In contrast, presentationally, you could offer a painting or a photograph; or you could create a virtual experience of the moose all at once, the time, place, sounds, and your emotions all contained in the presentational form, taken in by your audience not over time as your words unfold, but all at once as they look at the image. You also could use a metaphor and say seeing the moose was a "thrill ride." The concept of presentational form shows us that meaning is not limited to denotations.

Metaphors are examples of verbal symbolic acts that function on a level beyond the discursive and, thus, are presentational. Even though verbal metaphors are presented in discursive form (through language), they operate presentationally. In fact, Langer argues, "Metaphor is our most striking evidence of *abstractive seeing,* of the power of human minds to use presentational symbols."[56] Metaphors encourage people to see one thing in terms of something else. In so doing, they collapse, rather than string out on a line, all the points made about the thing. A metaphor takes a complex subject with many components (say, war) and collapses them into a single easy-to-grasp concept (say, fairy tale). Langer's main argument is that discursive action is not the only form of "articulate symbolism."[57] Presentational symbols that operate on the level of intuition and the gestalt can be articulate and reasonable as well.

The German word "Gestalt" refers to a shape or form. In contemporary usage, **gestalt** is *a pattern or structure whose parts are so integrated that one cannot really describe the pattern simply by referring to the parts.* Langer explains, "The symbolic materials given to our senses, the *Gestalten* or fundamental perceptual forms which invite us to construe the pandemonium of sheer impression into a world of things and occasions, belong to the 'presentational' order."[58] An example often used to illustrate how human beings make sense of random impression is the "dog picture" attributed to R. C. James.[59] At first glance, the picture appears to be a random series of dots, but because the human brain possesses the perceptual form of "dog," the image of a Dalmatian emerges.

Gestalt explains how metaphors condense a series of impressions into a single understandable thing. For example, the metaphor of a computer virus uses the existing understanding of "virus" (a microscopic infectious agent that replicates inside living cells) to make sense of the pandemonium that happens when a software program is introduced into your computer to make it do something you do not want, often causing harm to your computer and your data and, in the process, replicating itself so that it can be transferred to other computers. Many things happen when you execute a software program on your computer, but the key thing on which the metaphor of "virus" focuses your attention is the idea of replication causing harm.

Presentational form helps people make sense of a barrage of impressions by ordering them into a form, but a form that is more than just the sum of its parts. Just as language can name and condense a large category of things into a single term, presentational symbolism can "telescope" many concepts into a single image that psychoanalysts call a condensation symbol.[60] In psychology, a condensation symbol is a single symbol that represents multiple emotions, ideas, feelings, memories, or impulses. In relation to civic discourse, political science scholar Doris Graber defines a **condensation symbol** as *"a name, word, phrase, or maxim which stirs vivid impressions involving the listener's most basic values" and readies the listener for action.*[61]

Within rhetoric, scholars study ideographs, as well as god and devil terms, as the primary forms of condensation symbols.[62] Rhetoric scholar Richard Weaver describes *god term* as an "expression about which all other expressions are ranked as subordinate," and which has the "capacity to demand sacrifice."[63] In contrast, *devil terms* are "terms of repulsion."[64]

Condensation symbols, including ideographs and god and devil terms, whether verbal or visual, operate presentationally because they do not lay out a series of ideas side by side, but instead condense them into an inseparable whole. "My country," "Old Glory," "American Dream," "un-American," and "family values" are examples of presentational form because they create a picture of the referent that possesses intense emotional or affective power. Langer's emphasis on these symbols reflects her interest in how symbolic action always involves emotional appeals and not merely rational claims. Groups often try to use these forms to advance a cause. For example, the Human Rights Campaign, the largest national lesbian, gay, bisexual, and transgender (LGBT) civil rights organization, uses the verbal condensation symbols of "Human Rights" and "Equal Rights" in its campaigns.[65] Those who oppose extending legal protections to LGBT people often refer to those legal protections as "special rights."[66] To counter the idea that those rights are special, the Human Rights Campaign highlights that the rights it fights for are human rights and *equal* rights. It supplements these powerful terms with a mathematical symbol that condenses their meaning into a symbolic form: the "=" symbol, which the campaign hopes will appeal to the United States's historic commitment to equality.

We end our discussion of discursive and presentational symbolism with an example that highlights the difference between them: the "Million Voices for Darfur" postcard campaign first launched by the Save Darfur Coalition in 2006. The Coalition asked people to send a postcard to then-President George W. Bush that discursively argued for humanitarian intervention in the Darfur region of western Sudan by calling on the president to act on his convictions:

> Dear President Bush,
>
> During your first year in the White House, you wrote in the margins of a report on the Rwandan genocide, "Not on my watch." I urge you to live up to those words by using the power of your office to support a stronger multinational force to protect the civilians of Darfur.[67]

Each single postcard contained a discursive argument, but the presentational element of the postcards lies in the metaphor used and in the sheer volume of postcards sent. The metaphor of being on "watch" in a condensed moment paints a picture of Bush as a soldier with the responsibility to protect others from harm. In addition, the collective mass of one million postcards, according to the Coalition, "communicated the will and resolve of the American people to see our government take action to end the Darfur genocide."[68] A single postcard could request action through the language it contained; a million postcards demanded action with their mass.

Resignification

Terministic screens, public vocabulary, and discursive and presentational form explain how language constructs social meaning and effects social change. Language itself can also be the focus of change—where the meanings of words, as words, are challenged and transformed. Burke noted this possibility when he wrote "a Dramatistic approach to the analysis of language starts with problems of terministic catharsis," which he describes as "when a major term is found somehow to have moved on, and thus to have in effect changed its nature either by adding new meanings to its old nature, or by yielding place to some other term that henceforth takes over its functions wholly or in part."[69] A term might be "moved on" when its connotations are challenged. **Resignification** is *a process in which people reject the connotation of a symbol, expose how the meaning of the symbol is constructed, and attempt to change its connotation.*

If a group is labeled with a particular word, it can reject the sign, saying "That word does not accurately denote us," or resignify the sign, saying "That word does denote our group, but its connotation is one we reject." Words with an intense connotation, words many are loathe to utter, are words that demand resignifying. If a term is so powerful it can do damage to a person labeled with it, then its power should be challenged. In some cases, the challenge takes the form of resignification. If a term is mild and noncontroversial, the group would not need to resignify it; thus, the examples to follow are trigger words or loaded terms.

Lawyer and civic activist Urvashi Vaid, in her analysis of lesbian and gay rights, finds that gay men originally used "queer" as a form of self-naming. By the 1920s, men who thought of themselves as different because of their homosexual attraction to other men called themselves "queer."[70] The term later developed the negative connotation it has when used as an epithet in playgrounds and streets. This connotation did not develop overnight. As rhetoric scholar Judith Butler explains, "'Queer' derives its force precisely through the repeated invocation by which it has become linked to accusation, pathologization, insult."[71] The connotation of a term is not an inherent or fixed part of it: what is signified develops over time, as people repeatedly use the term in contexts that infuse it with negative (or positive) meaning.

The fact that terms have histories explains the difficulty involved in resignifying them. People cannot simply decree that the connotation of a term change. If a connotation develops as the result of repeated usage in contexts that derogate, it can only change as the result of repeated usage in contexts that infuse the term with new, positive connotations. Resignification requires the repeated invocation of a term, linking it to praise, normalization, and celebration. The meaning of "queer" has altered with the emergence of queer theory and queer studies in the academy, Queer Nation's chant "We're here! We're queer! Get used to it!" and queer theory scholars such as Vaid reclaiming the term. Unfortunately, even when a term is resignified within a group, its new meaning may not carry beyond that group, which is why "queer" is still used as an epithet against people. Even though resignification is possible, it is difficult.

Another example is the word "black." Michael Osborn, a professor of communication studies, explores metaphors in the "dark-light family."[72] Particularly in the West, dark is associated with evil, light with good and godliness. The repetition and cultural embeddedness of these metaphors direct attention so that people see white as good, black as bad. People talk about "white knights," "black marks," and "white or black magic." Civil rights activists in the 1960s recognized that "black" had negative connotations. As part of their struggle for legal change, they also sought cultural change by resignifying the term. "Black is Beautiful" became a cultural slogan in the 1960s; it showed up on T-shirts and pinback buttons. As part of the critique of norms of beauty based on a European, white, thin, blue-eyed, and blond-haired ideal, activists attempted to resignify the term "black" to remove its negative connotations. "Black" did not mean dirty, evil, dark, and menacing; it could also mean kind, humorous, and beautiful.[73] This resignification finds its extension with the contemporary fashion and beauty industry's embrace of wider parameters for what is considered beautiful.[74]

THE MISUSE OF LANGUAGE

When Burke describes human beings as "symbol-making, symbol-using, symbol-misusing,"[75] he means that symbol use is not neutral. Symbols can be used to create differences among people, or to denigrate groups or individuals. They can be used to damage people, ideas, or institutions. In this section, we discuss some misuses of language and ways to identify them. We do not provide an exhaustive list of ethically questionable rhetoric, but introduce you to some of the unscrupulous ways that language can be used: doublespeak, truncated passives, and people/places/topics of silence. Most of this book celebrates the positive uses of rhetoric as symbolic action, but language can also be used to deceive and silence people.

Doublespeak

In his insightful novel *1984* (written in 1949), George Orwell depicted a society misled by language. Orwell's fictional society developed a new form of English, "Newspeak." In the novel, dictionaries were rewritten and words changed to alter people's thinking. You might notice that Orwell's conception of language is similar to the one we have laid out in this chapter; language and thought are linked, so the way to manipulate thought is to manipulate language. Orwell described this new language in the appendix of the novel: "The purpose of Newspeak was not only to provide a medium of expression for the world-view and mental habits proper . . . [for society], but to make all other modes of thought impossible."[76] Through the use of Newspeak's deliberately ambiguous language, it became possible to hold views that were otherwise contradictory, enabling the ruling party of the state to have as the state slogan: "War is peace; freedom is slavery; ignorance is strength."

Unfortunately, Newspeak is not limited to the fictional world. Hitler's concentration camps used the slogan "work will set you free," even though no one was freed and the work was slave labor. A more recent example of Newspeak comes from the US Pentagon. During the Vietnam War, the Pentagon referred to the containers used to send the bodies of dead soldiers back to the United States as "body bags." Then, during the first Gulf War, it renamed the containers "human remains pouches." The Pentagon's most recent term is "transfer tubes."[77] You would be hard pressed to know exactly what a transfer tube is because death has been removed from the discussion. At least the term "body bag" identified the purpose of the container, even though the term was less attractive.

Taking his cue from Orwell, English professor William Lutz wrote about **doublespeak,** *language used in the real world to confuse or deliberately distort its actual meaning rather than to achieve understanding.* Lutz explained doublespeak this way:

> Doublespeak is language that pretends to communicate but really doesn't. It is language that makes the bad seem good, the negative appear positive, the unpleasant appear attractive or at least tolerable. Doublespeak is language that avoids or shifts responsibility, language that is at variance with its real or purported meaning. It is language that conceals or prevents thought; rather than extending thought, doublespeak limits it.[78]

Lutz identifies two types of doublespeak: euphemism and inflated language.

A **euphemism** is *a word used to denote a thing in a way that avoids connotations of harshness or unpleasantness,* as when people refer to someone having "passed on" rather than "died." Another example can be found in how people talk about lying. A plethora of words are available in English to describe dishonesty or degrees of lying, most of which enable people to avoid saying that they lied: "white lie," "deception," "dishonesty," "untruth," "evasion," "falsehood," "fib," "fiction," "conceal," "hyperbole," "guile," "prevarication," "tall tale," "misstatement," "omission," "misleading," and so on. However, very few words exist for honesty; the main examples are "blunt," "candid," and "frank."[79] Euphemisms can be unethical because they tend to lessen the harshness of something that probably should be judged harshly, as in the example of transfer tubes. In public discourse, governments have used euphemisms to distort military action. In October 1983, the Pentagon did not use the more straightforward "invasion," but described the US invasion of Grenada using the more obscure phrase "predawn vertical insertion."[80]

Inflated language, Lutz explains, is *"language designed to make the ordinary seem extraordinary; to make everyday things seem impressive; to give an air of importance to people, situations, or things that would not normally be considered important; to make the simple seem complex."*[81] Inflated language is clearly evident in advertising. For instance, if you go to the store and see food labeled as "home-style," the language seems to suggest a type of food preparation. In reality the term is meaningless because it does not have a denotative meaning; it can be used to mean various things.[82] When television channels declare they are about to air a "special encore presentation," they really are just using inflated language to describe a rerun. People sometimes use inflated language on résumés when they try to make their jobs sound more impressive; for example, if you say you were a cleaning specialist instead of a janitor, or a special administrative assistant instead of a work-study student worker. (Just to be clear: you should not use inflated language on your résumé. Employers are very critical of inflated language.)

Truncated Passives

Language is much more than the words we use. Its power resides in the grammatical structure of language as well as in the individual words. Julia Penelope, a linguist who focuses on language's structures, reminds people "languages are much more than the words in their vocabularies. They are systems of rules. . . ."[83] Those rules, themselves, contain political consequences. In particular, she encourages people to watch out for **truncated passives,** *sentences that use a passive verb in order to delete the agent of action.* A sentence uses passive voice when it combines some "to be" verb with another verb and no do-er of the action appears in the sentence. Instead of active voice "I broke the toy," the passive voice "The toy was broken . . ." enables the speaker to leave out the phrase ". . . by me."

Individuals who attempt to avoid explicit responsibility for the consequences of the power they exercise often use truncated passives. When a communicator deletes the agent of action, then only the object on which the agent acted is present in the sentence. In this way, Penelope says, "Passives without agents foreground the objects (victims) in our minds so that we tend to forget that some human agent is responsible for performing the action,"[84] as in "mistakes were made" or "Hanoi was bombed."[85]

President Ronald Reagan introduced the passive phrase "mistakes were made" into public dialogue about presidential scandal, in response to the 1986–1987 Iran-Contra investigation. This phrase begged the question: mistakes were made *by whom?* Instead of saying "I made mistakes," or "This person made a mistake," the phrase made it seem as though the mistakes happened outside of human control. The phrase "mistakes were made" was resuscitated in 2007 by then–Attorney General Alberto Gonzales when he explained why eight federal district attorneys had been fired, apparently for politically motivated reasons.[86]

Penelope explains, "Agentless passives conceal and deceive when it doesn't suit speakers' or writers' purposes to make agency explicit. . . . This makes it easy to suppress responsibility" and, thus, results in "protection of the guilty and denial of responsibility, . . . the pretense of objectivity, . . . and trivialization."[87] Identifying truncated passives is one way to identify hidden power. Once you identify a truncated passive, you begin to ask who had the power to do this thing that happened. When someone says "mistakes were made," ask "by whom?"

People, Places, and Topics of Silence

Language is not only a collection of words, but a system of rules that has political consequences. Language rules influence who can speak, about what, and where. French philosopher Michel Foucault believed one could trace power by analyzing language. To truly understand language, people need to understand that it is a form of power and a place where power is contested. He wrote about language rules governing people, places, and topics in his essay, "The Discourse on Language," in which he outlined "rules of exclusion" that control people's use of language:

> We know perfectly well that we are not free to say just anything, that we cannot simply speak of anything, when we like or where we like; not just anyone, finally, may speak of just anything. We have three types of prohibition, covering objects, ritual with its surrounding circumstances, the privileged or exclusive right to speak of a particular subject; these prohibitions interrelate, reinforce and complement each other, forming a complex web, continually subject to modification.[88]

Foucault recognized that there are certain topics about which people are not allowed to speak, that certain cultural practices limit what people speak about and how they can speak, and that certain topics may only be addressed by particular people (such as experts). The three prohibitions also interact to create additional constraints. Who speaks, where, and about what is governed by rules of discourse. If you analyze language, then, you can discover people, places, and topics of silence.

Think about how these rules govern language use in a classroom. If a class is discussing a particular topic and a class member starts talking about something that goes beyond that topic, the other students might experience discomfort or irritation. Constraints on whose speech matters in the classroom make the power dynamics visible. For example, students rarely take notes when other students speak, nor do they direct their comments to other students, but instead funnel them through the instructor. In the classroom, the teacher is accorded credibility to speak. When students do formal presentations, they often move to the podium. People in the United States have been acculturated to the rules of discourse to recognize that the podium is a location that accords a person more power.

The rules governing people, places, and topics are in constant flux. A significant revision of the rules of discourse in the public sphere occurred as part of the US struggle to abolish slavery during the 1800s. Initially, slavery was viewed as a private economic matter, not an issue of public concern. The language of the time reflected this view. Additionally, when it came to debating issues in the public sphere, women and African Americans were not granted access. Thus, women and African Americans who were abolitionists had to justify their right to speak even before broaching the topic of slavery. They challenged the rules about who was allowed to speak. Only after they were allowed to speak were they able to demonstrate they were intellectually capable of being full citizens of the country. Their eloquence and rational argument made clear their brains were not inferior. Women's and African Americans' struggle for the podium (for the right to speak) was a challenge to the rules that governed communication in the public sphere.

The first US-born woman known to speak in public to a mixed-sex audience was African-American Maria Miller Stewart, who addressed Boston's African-American abolitionist community between 1831 and 1833.[89] Later, white Quaker sisters Sarah and Angelina Grimké spoke against slavery and argued that the era's dictates on womanhood were contradictory. Historian Barbara Welter, in her influential book *Dimity Convictions*, notes that during this time period, women were expected to be pure, pious, domestic, and submissive.[90] If a woman believed slavery was an affront to piety, however, then she had to leave the domestic sphere to agitate against it. Ultimately, the rules governing discourse in the public sphere shifted. Slavery became a topic open to debate; women and African Americans were slowly recognized as legitimate participants in this debate; and the evidence they brought from their own experience began to count.

CONCLUSION

Language is messy, unpredictable, and fascinating. Despite its messiness and unpredictability, people use it to make sense of their world. Language is a symbol system through which human beings construct, maintain, and transform social reality. It forms the terministic screens through which people observe and understand reality, and composes the public vocabulary central to public policy and identity formation. The role language plays in symbolic action is complex because language can operate both discursively and presentationally. Because it can operate presentationally—through metaphors and condensation symbols—it can become emotionally charged. Language is so central to reality that words, themselves, become a site for struggle, as in the case of resignification.

Language defines what people know. Human beings are both suspended in a web of signification and the spinners of the web. Language both enables and restrains; it makes sense of the world and imposes a particular sense on the world. It limits what you know, but also provides the possibility of seeing beyond the limits. Understanding that language does more than correspond to reality allows human beings to imagine a reality that may not yet exist. Language allows human beings to imagine, hope, and hypothesize.

Even though we tend to think public deliberation is at its best when purely logical and rational, in reality, the artistry of language affects its persuasiveness. Public discourse occurs within a larger cultural and symbolic context, or public vocabulary, and calls on the taken-for-granted assumptions about the world. Thus, to convince another person of an idea, purely rational and objective argument is not enough because communication occurs through language that has judgments embedded within it. To convince people, you need to think about your vocabulary as much as your goal.

When responding to rhetoric and formulating rhetorical messages, people need to understand, analyze, critique, and consider the language choices involved. The use of language to communicate is a symbolic action; consequently, individuals exercise choice about the nature of that action and about whether to use or misuse it.

The analysis of language requires nuanced thinking and facile imaginations. People need to think not only about what was said, but what else could have been said. Why was one word chosen, and how did it direct your attention differently from the way another word that could have been used? Identifying the difference between what was said and what could have been said will help identify the subtle ways in which rhetoric is at work. Identifying silences (of people, about topics, and in places) also enables you to identify the way language and power interact. Because language is a way to exercise power, and because power resides in language, understanding locations of silence is necessary.

DISCUSSION QUESTIONS

1. Can you think of an example where two different terms for the same thing direct your attention in different ways, selecting, reflecting, or deflecting different aspects of "reality"?
2. Can you think of examples of metaphors that have become so ingrained in the English language that people do not even think of them as metaphors?
3. Identify an example of a metaphor. Play out all the ways that metaphor is extended and how that extension structures the way people talk about the concept.
4. Find an advertisement and analyze the language of the ad. Can you identify a metaphor, a narrative, a characterization, an ideograph, and/or doublespeak? How does the ad use (or misuse) language?
5. Identify an example of a term undergoing resignification. How has its connotation changed? Has its denotation changed?

RECOMMENDED READINGS

Burke, Kenneth. "Dramatism." In *International Encyclopedia of the Social Sciences*, vol. 7. Edited by David L. Sills, 445–452. New York: Macmillan and Free Press, 1968.

Burke, Kenneth. "Terministic Screens." In *Language as Symbolic Action*, 44–62. Berkeley: University of California Press, 1966.

Fisher, Walter R. "Narration as a Human Communication Paradigm: The Case of Public Moral Argument." *Communication Monographs* 51, no. 1 (March 1984): 1–22.

Lakoff, George, and Mark Johnson. *Metaphors We Live By*. Chicago: University of Chicago Press.

McGee, Michael Calvin. "The 'Ideograph': A Link between Rhetoric and Ideology." *Quarterly Journal of Speech* 66, no. 1 (February 1980): 1–16.

ENDNOTES

1 Jonathan Turley, "They're Not 'Terrorists,'" *USA Today*, June 17, 2009,
  9A; Alan Levin, Thomas Frank, and Sharon Jayson, "In Austin
  Plane Crash, an Echo of Terrorism," *USA Today*, February 18, 2010,
  http://www.usatoday.com/news/nation/2010-02-18-plane-crash-building_N.htm;
  "Austin Man with Grudge against IRS Crashes Plane, Leaves behind Internet
  Suicide Note," *Los Angeles Times*, February 18, 2010, http://latimesblogs.latimes
  .com/comments_blog/2010/02/austin-man-with-grudge-against-irs-crashes-plane
  -leaves-behind-internet-suicide-note.html.
2 Saussure, quoted in Daniel Chandler, *Semiotics: The Basics* (New York: Routledge,
  2007), 2–4.
3 Sonya Andermahr, Terry Lovell, and Carol Wolkowitz, *A Glossary of Feminist Theory*
  (New York: Oxford University Press, 2000), 240.
4 Edward Sapir, "The Status of Linguistics as a Science," *Language* 5, no. 4 (1929):
  207–214, 209–210.
5 Julia M. Penn, *Linguistic Relativity versus Innate Ideas* (Paris: Mouton, 1972), 39.
6 Michael Mackenzie, "Marcel Duchamp and the Antimonies of Art Historical and
  Art Critical Discourse" [review essay], *Modernism/Modernity* 7, no. 11 (2000):
  153–163, 154.
7 Mackenzie, "Marcel Duchamp," 154.
8 Francis M. Naumann, "The Art of Defying the Art Market," *Tout-Fait:
  The Marcel Duchamp Studies Online Journal* 2, no. 5 (April 2003),
  http://www.toutfait.com/issues/volume2/issue_5/news/naumann/naumann1.htm
  (accessed May 5, 2009).
9 Edward Sapir, *Language: An Introduction to the Study of Speech* (New York:
  BiblioBazaar, 1921/1939/2007), 23.
10 Julia Penelope, *Speaking Freely* (New York: Pergamon, 1990), 203.
11 David Blakesley, "Introduction: Kenneth Burke, Word-Man," in Kenneth Burke, *Late
  Poems, 1968–1993: Attitudinizing Verse-Wise, While Fending for One's Selph,
  And in a Style Somewhat Artificially Colloquial* (Columbia: University of South
  Carolina Press, 2005), xvii.
12 Kenneth Burke, "Dramatism," in *International Encyclopedia of the Social Sciences*,
  vol. 7, ed. David L. Sills, 445–452 (New York: Macmillan and Free Press, 1968),
  447, italics added.
13 Kenneth Burke, "Definition of Man," in *Language as Symbolic Action*, 3–24
  (Berkeley: University of California Press, 1966), 6.
14 Melanie Blackless, Anthony Charuvastra, Amanda Derryck, Anne Fausto-Sterling,
  Karl Lauzanne, and Ellen Lee, "How Sexually Dimorphic Are We? Review and
  Synthesis," *American Journal of Human Biology*, 12 (2000), 151–166. See also
  Julie A. Greenberg, "Defining Male and Female: Intersexuality and the Collision
  between Law and Biology," *Arizona Law Review* 41 (Summer 1999), 265–328,
  267–268.
15 Anne Tamar-Mattis, "Medical Decision Making and the Child with
  a DSD," *Endocrine Today* (November 10, 2008), available at
  http://endocrinetoday.com/view.aspx?rid=32542 (accessed October 15, 2011).
16 Suzanne J. Kessler, "The Medical Construction of Gender: Case Management of
  Intersexed Infants," *Signs* 16, no. 1 (Autumn 1990), 3–26.
17 Anne Fausto-Sterling, "The Five Sexes," *The Sciences* 33, no. 2 (March/April 1993),
  20–24.

[18] Burke, "Terministic Screens," in *Language*, 45.

[19] Hilke Plassmann, John O'Doherty, Baba Shiv, and Antonio Rangel, "Marketing Actions Can Modulate Neural Representations of Experienced Pleasantness," *Proceedings of the National Academy of Sciences* 105, no. 3 (January 22, 2008), 1050–1054, doi:10.1073/pnas.0706929105.

[20] The description of "fetus" and "baby" as illustrations of terministic screens first appeared in Victoria DeFrancisco and Catherine H. Palczewski, *Communicating Gender Diversity* (Thousand Oaks, CA: Sage, 2007), pp. 110–111.

[21] Burke, "Terministic," 46.

[22] Celeste M. Condit, *Decoding Abortion Rhetoric: Communicating Social Change* (Urbana: University of Illinois Press, 1990), 6.

[23] John Louis Lucaites and Celeste Michelle Condit, "Reconstructing <Equality>: Culturetypal and Counter-Cultural Rhetorics in the Martyred Black Vision," *Communication Monographs* 57 (March 1990): 8.

[24] Lucaites and Condit, "Reconstructing," 8.

[25] Lucaites and Condit, "Reconstructing," 8.

[26] Michael Calvin McGee, "The 'Ideograph': A Link between Rhetoric and Ideology," *Quarterly Journal of Speech* 66 (February 1980): 15, italics added.

[27] George W. Bush, "Address to the Nation by President George W. Bush regarding Terrorist Attacks on the World Trade Centers and the Pentagon," Federal News Service, September 11, 2001, LexisNexis.

[28] Dana L. Cloud, "The Rhetoric of <Family Values>: Scapegoating, Utopia, and the Privatization of Social Responsibility," *Western Journal of Communication* 62, no. 4 (Fall 1998): 387–419.

[29] Celeste Michelle Condit and John Louis Lucaites, *Crafting Equality: America's Anglo-African Word* (Chicago: University of Chicago Press, 1993).

[30] Celeste Condit Railsback, "The Contemporary American Abortion Controversy: Stages in the Argument," *Quarterly Journal of Speech* 70, no. 4 (November 1984): 410–424.

[31] Kenneth Burke, *A Grammar of Motives* (Berkeley: University of California Press, 1969), xv.

[32] Burke, *Grammar*, xv.

[33] Lucaites and Condit, "Reconstructing," 7.

[34] "University of Florida Student Tasered at Kerry Forum," YouTube.com, November 15, 2007, http://www.youtube.com/watch?v=6bVa6jn4rpE&feature=related (accessed January 27, 2009). The authors want to thank Kaori Yamada for her research assistance with this example.

[35] "Cops on Leave after Taser Incident, Student's Behavior under Scrutiny," *CNN.com/US*, September 18, 2007, http://www.cnn.com/2007/US/09/18/student.tasered/index.html (accessed February 17, 2009).

[36] "Florida Student Arrested, Tasered at Kerry Forum Has a Penchant for Practical Jokes," *International Herald Tribune*, September 17, 2007, http://www.iht.com /articles/ ap/2007/09/18/america/NA-GEN-US-StudentTasered.php (accessed February 17, 2009).

[37] ABC, "Taser Attack: Is Taser Use Out of Control?" *Good Morning America*, September 19, 2007, http://www.lexisnexis.com/us.

[38] Lucaites and Condit, "Reconstructing," 8.

[39] Alasdair MacIntyre, *After Virtue: A Study in Moral Theory*, 3rd Ed. (Notre Dame, IN: University of Notre Dame Press, 2007), 216.

[40] Walter Fisher, "Narration as a Human Communication Paradigm: The Case of Public Moral Argument," *Communication Monographs* 51, no. 1 (March 1984): 1–22.

[41] Robert C. Rowland and John M. Jones, "Recasting the American Dream and American Politics: Barack Obama's Keynote Address to the 2004 Democratic National Convention," *Quarterly Journal of Speech* 93, no. 4 (November 2007): 425–448, 430.

[42] Plato, *The Republic*, trans. Benjamin Jowett, book vi, http://classics.mit.edu/Plato/republic.7.vi.html (accessed May 2, 2009).

[43] Burke, *Grammar*, 503.

[44] George Lakoff and Mark Johnson, *Metaphors We Live By* (Chicago: University of Chicago Press, 1980), 61.

[45] Lakoff and Johnson, *Metaphors*, 3.

[46] Lakoff and Johnson, *Metaphors*, 4.

[47] George Lakoff, "Framing the Dems," *The American Prospect* 14, no. 8 (September 2003), http://www.prospect.org/cs/articles?article=framing_the_dems (accessed October 11, 2011).

[48] Riikka Kuusisto, "Heroic Tale, Game, and Business Deal? Western Metaphors in Action in Kosovo," *Quarterly Journal of Speech* 88, no. 1 (February 2002): 54.

[49] Kuusisto, "Heroic Tale," 62.

[50] Kuusisto, "Heroic Tale," 62.

[51] Kuusisto, "Heroic Tale," 62.

[52] Kuusisto, "Heroic Tale," 62.

[53] For more on Langer's contribution to rhetorical theory, see Arabella Lyon, "Susanne K. Langer, Mother and Midwife at the Rebirth of Rhetoric," in *Reclaiming Rhetorica: Women in the Rhetorical Tradition*, ed. Andrea A. Lunsford, 265–284 (Pittsburgh: University of Pittsburgh Press, 1995).

[54] Susanne K. Langer, *Philosophy in a New Key*, 3rd ed. (Cambridge, MA: Harvard University Press, 1957), 96–97, italics added.

[55] Langer, *Philosophy*, 81–82.

[56] Langer, *Philosophy*, 141.

[57] Langer, *Philosophy*, 88.

[58] Langer, *Philosophy*, 98.

[59] For an example of the image, see http://psychology.jrank.org/pages/1286/6-Some-principles-with-examples.html, or search "dalmation gestalt picture."

[60] Langer, *Philosophy*, 191.

[61] Doris Graber, *Verbal Behavior and Politics* (Urbana: University of Illinois Press, 1976), 289, italics added.

[62] Murray Edelman, *The Symbolic Uses of Politics* (Urbana: University of Illinois Press, 1972), 6. See also David S. Kaufer and Kathleen M. Carley, "Condensation Symbols: Their Variety and Rhetorical Function in Political Discourse," *Philosophy and Rhetoric* 26, no. 3 (1993): 201–226.

[63] Richard M. Weaver, *The Ethics of Rhetoric* (Davis, CA: Hermagoras, 1985), 212, 214. See also Randall A. Lake, "The Metaethical Framework of Anti-Abortion Rhetoric," *Signs* 11, no. 3 (Spring 1986): 478–499.

[64] Weaver, *The Ethics*, 222.

[65] Human Rights Campaign, http://www.hrc.org (accessed May 1, 2009).

[66] See, for example, *Gay Rights/Special Rights—Inside the Homosexual Agenda*, Jeremiah Films, 1993, uploaded July 26, 2006, http://video.google.com/videoplay?docid=7664929225320091404 (accessed May 1, 2009).

67 "Senators Frist and Clinton Sign One Millionth Postcard Urging President Bush to Advocate Multinational Peacekeeping Force to Stop Darfur Genocide," http://www.savedarfur.org/pages/press/senators_frist_and_clinton_sign_one _millionth_postcard (accessed August 7, 2009).

68 Be a Voice for Darfur, http://www.addyourvoice.org/pages/about (accessed August 7, 2009).

69 Burke, "What are the Signs of What?" in *Language*, 367.

70 Urvashi Vaid, *Virtual Equality* (New York: Anchor, 1995), 42.

71 Judith Butler, *Bodies That Matter: On the Discursive Limits of "Sex"* (New York: Routledge, 1993), 226.

72 Michael Osborn, "Archetypal Metaphor in Rhetoric: The Light-Dark Family," *Quarterly Journal of Speech* 53, no. 2 (April 1967): 115–126.

73 Lillian Roxon, "'Black is Beautiful'—At Last," *Evening News*, November 12, 1973, 2, http://library2.nalis.gov.tt/infofiles/collect/news3/index/assoc/HASH0159 /ab69e6f8.dir/165.jpg (accessed January 13, 2010).

74 Kendra Hamilton, "Embracing 'BLACK IS BEAUTIFUL'—African American Involvement in Fashion Industry, and Consumer Spending on Apparel and Beauty Care Products," *Black Issues in Higher Education*, January 4, 2001, http://findarticles.com/p/articles/mi_m0DXK/is_23_17 (accessed January 13, 2010).

75 Burke, "Definition," in *Language*, 16.

76 George Orwell, *1984*, ed. Irving Howe (New York: Harcourt, Brace, Jovanovich, 1982), appendix, 198.

77 See National Council of Teachers of English Doublespeak Award, http://www.ncte.org/library/NCTEFiles/Involved/Volunteer/Appointed%20Groups /Past_Recipients_Doublespeak_Award.pdf. The NCTE gives an annual award to the most outrageous example of doublespeak.

78 William Lutz, *Doublespeak* (New York: Harper and Row, 1989), 1.

79 Penelope, *Speaking Freely*, 47.

80 James Warren, "A Vertical Insertion of Doublespeak," *Chicago Tribune*, August 12, 1990, http://articles.chicagotribune.com/1990-08-12/features/9003070579_1 _double speak-award-committee-on-public-doublespeak-william-lutz (accessed September 3, 2010).

81 Lutz, *Doublespeak*, 6, italics added.

82 Lutz, *Doublespeak*, 2–7.

83 Penelope, *Speaking Freely*, xiii.

84 Penelope, *Speaking Freely*, 146.

85 The most recognized recent example may be Reagan's discussion of the events surrounding the Iran-Contra affair, when he remarked: "Mistakes were made." Commenting on a similar example, Penelope notes, "At a superficial level, the omission of direct and explicit reference to himself made the events seem far removed from our immediate experience, occurring in some abstract realm where human beings are not responsible for their actions" (Penelope, *Speaking Freely*, 145).

86 Sheryl Gay Stolberg and Jeff Zeleny, "Mistakes Made on Prosecutors, Gonzales Admits," *The New York Times*, March 14, 2007, A1.

87 Penelope, *Speaking Freely*, 149.

88 Michel Foucault, *The Archaeology of Knowledge and the Discourse on Language*, trans. R. Sawyer (New York: Pantheon, 1972), 216.

89 Laura R. Sells, "Maria W. Miller Stewart," in *Women Public Speakers in the United States, 1825–1900*, ed. Karlyn Kohrs Campbell, 339–349 (Westport, CT: Greenwood, 1993).

[90] Barbara Welter, *Dimity Convictions: The American Woman in the Nineteenth Century* (Athens: Ohio University Press, 1976).

Chapter 3

Visual Rhetoric

Key Concepts

body rhetoric

dominant reading

enactment

iconic photographs

image events

negotiated reading

oppositional reading

presence

visual culture

Visual symbols, as much as verbal symbols, are rhetorical. The US flag symbolizes the nation and its values. Its meaning is so clear, Supreme Court Justice John Paul Stevens once wrote: "The flag uniquely symbolizes the ideas of liberty, equality, and tolerance—ideas that Americans have passionately defended and debated throughout our history. The flag embodies the spirit of our national commitment to those ideals."[1] The visual symbol of the flag can unify people behind shared ideals.

Sometimes, however, people interpret visual symbols as merely representations of a reality, not an interpretation of it. People might uncritically see photographs, even photographs of the flag, as merely recording an objective event. However, the way an event is recorded can shape people's beliefs and attitudes about it. Images can be rhetorical, as well as reportorial.

An example shows that photographs are not just neutral records of reality. Since the Vietnam War, US government officials have been aware that images of coffins containing war dead returning home can affect public support of the war effort. Journalists coined a phrase to measure this effect: "the Dover Test." The test asks whether the US public will continue to support a war if it is faced with a stream of images of flag-draped coffins arriving at Dover Air Force base, through which, since 1955, the remains of all deceased armed forces personnel return from abroad.

The Dover Test achieved stark public awareness during President George H. W. Bush's term. In 1989, during the United States invasion of Panama, twenty-three service members died. As part of regular news coverage, televisions showed a split-screen image, one half depicting flag-draped coffins arriving at Dover and the other half showing President Bush bantering with reporters during a news conference. The image created the impression that he was not concerned about the loss of life. In response, President Bush banned media coverage of Dover arrivals during the Persian Gulf War in 1991.[2]

The ban remained in place until February 2009, when the Pentagon lifted the ban after President Obama asked Defense Secretary Robert Gates to review the policy.[3] Presidents' willingness to maintain the ban showed they understood the power of a photo to influence public perception of a war. More powerful than media commentary about war casualties, in this example, is a powerful image. Photos of flag-draped coffins arriving at Dover make present the cost of war.

One way to understand the power of visuals such as the Dover photos is to consider the way they make something present, or give presence to an event, person, or thing. Visuals possess the characteristic of **presence** because of their *immediacy, the creation of something in the front of an audience's conscious-ness*. This creation may "act directly on our sensibility."[4] Visuals are a powerful example of presentational symbolism because they create virtual experiences in a particularly intense way, by making audience members feel as though they were present to witness an event. They offer a direct presentation instead of a discursive description.[5]

Presence can make things distant in time or space feel current and close. For example, it might be difficult for people today to understand the true horror of the Nazi Holocaust because it is distant in time (having occurred over seventy years ago). Similarly, it might be difficult for people living in the United States to understand the horror of the genocide in Darfur because it is distant in space, thousands of miles away from you. For this reason, the United States Holocaust Memorial Museum, in partnership with Google Earth, initiated "Mapping Initiatives" that would "enable citizens to understand Holocaust history and to bear witness to current threats of genocide across the globe."[6] Animated maps and Google Earth enable people to see "the enormous scope and impact of the Holocaust" and real time images enable people to "witness the destruction in Darfur." Instead of having people just read about historically and spatially distant events, the Holocaust museum makes those events visually present.

Because images have symbolic power, visual rhetoric functions persua-sively; it can shift opinion and create meaning. It is increasingly important to be able to read visual rhetoric and understand how it functions persuasively, especially as visual forms of communication appear in more diverse spaces than they did a few decades ago (on iPhones, computers, moving billboards, people's clothing, and so on) and because more people are capable of producing images seen on public screens (television, newspapers, and computers).

The way in which a person can be both a producer and receiver of images is illustrated by the haunting pictures of the 2007 Virginia Tech massacre that were taken on students' cell phones and played on newscasts. People took it upon themselves to provide up-to-the-minute reporting, creating an entry on *Wikipedia* on April 16, 2007 (the day of the attacks) and modifying it 1860 times on that day alone.[7] The potential for anyone to visually record the news is formalized by sites such as CNN's I-Report (ireport@cnn.com), which asks: "Is news happening in front of your eyes? Pull out your camera and I-Report it for CNN."[8] CNN does not ask for a written story, but for images.

These examples illustrate cultural theorists Jessica Evans and Stuart Hall's description of contemporary culture as "pervaded at all levels by a host of cultural technologies designed to disseminate viewing and looking practices through primarily visually mediated forms."[9] You live and work in a culture permeated and defined by visuals.

Although scholars for many years confined the study of the available means of persuasion to the study of verbal symbols, within the last few years they have recognized the centrality of visuals to the study of rhetoric.[10] In this chapter, we explain what we mean by visual rhetoric and how audiences interact with it. We then outline four forms of visual rhetoric: bodies, photographs, memorials, and image events. These four forms do not exhaust the types of visual rhetoric, but we selected them because each illustrates something unique about visual rhetoric. We end with guidelines for analyzing visual rhetoric.

THE RISE OF VISUAL CULTURE

US and global culture are becoming, in the words of Evans and Hall, a **visual culture**—*a culture distinguished by the ubiquity of visual forms of communication that appear in multiple media outlets at the same time (such as television, the Internet, cell phones, and magazines).*[11] Think about how you spend your time. You do not just listen to music; you watch music videos. You do not just read a book; you watch a movie adaptation of it. You do not just phone a friend; you send text messages with photos embedded. You do not read or listen to a speech; you watch it on YouTube or television. Communication scholar Lawrence J. Prelli argues that such a "rhetoric of display," rhetoric that makes ideas present through visual display, has become the dominant mode of communication in visual culture.[12] Even highly verbal speeches become visual events, with lavish attention paid to backdrops, clothing color, and camera angle.

Evans and Hall argue that it is impossible to understand contemporary culture without analyzing visuals, because a study of any contemporary media product—any television show, movie, advertisement, web page, blog, or magazine—would be "incomplete" if you only analyzed the words, or if you interpreted the "images as if they only functioned as artifacts to be read rather than as sights and often exhibitionist performances to be looked at."[13] Could you really explain television's power to shape contemporary culture if you only analyzed the scripts? Could you really explain the power of fashion magazines by studying only the stories? No and no. Cultural norms of fashion and body image are influenced by the actors on the screen and by the images in the magazine, perhaps even more than by the scripts and stories. People in a visual culture not only read words, they look at and interpret images.

Evans and Hall note that recognition of the importance of symbolic action means that researchers now explore how "social practices and relations" also function as "signifying practices."[14] Their point is that as you move through the world and interact with other people (in person or in mediated forms), you impart meaning to the world and your relationships; you also interpret the world and your relationships through the symbols you use. Communication, verbal and visual, is more than a means to transmit information. Television and movies are more than mere entertainment. Visual rhetoric, like language-based rhetoric, is a signifying practice through which human beings make meaning and make sense of the world in which they live.

Words and images, often in conjunction, construct reality. Visual rhetoric scholars Kevin Michael DeLuca and Anne Teresa Demo note that images and visuals, just pictures, "are important not because they represent reality, but create it."[15] Thus, when people analyze visuals, the question "What do the images represent?" is insufficient. That question assumes an absolute correspondence between the image and reality. When studying visual rhetoric, people should also ask "What do the images do?" and "What do the images want?"—meaning what attitude toward the world do these images want the audience to assume, and in what ways do the images direct a person's attention in one way rather than another?[16] When an advertisement contains an image of a stylish person using a product, the image does not merely depict that person's use of the product. Instead, the image wants you to see yourself using the product in order to be like the stylish person in the ad.

Both visual and verbal aspects are almost always present in symbolic action, yet they operate in ways similar to and different from each other. As Evans and Hall note: "the differences between language and the visual remain significant and require further attention; that is, the different cultural technologies and industries built upon them, their characteristic forms and rhetorical devices, and the ways in which they are put to work, disseminated, and made sense of by readers and viewers."[17] You cannot explain fully the power of Dover photos by saying the photo depicts a historically real event. A Dover photo is powerful because it simultaneously captures a symbolic moment of ritual, a family's pure moment of grief, the honor of military service, a coffin containing a person, and the human costs of war. Imagine if we had started the chapter by reproducing a particular Dover photo, instead of only describing Dover photos in general. Would you have had the same reaction? If you have seen one of the Dover photos, did you have a different or more intense reaction than when you just read about them?

Visual rhetoric was not absent prior to the age of electronic media. In fact, most of the forms of visual rhetoric discussed in this chapter predate television and computers, although these forms have been adapted to mass media. People have been using their bodies to make arguments as long as parades have crowded streets; events using spectacle have been around as long as audiences have listened and watched. Because electronic media make it easier to transmit images, however, and because interactive media enable everyone to be a publicist, attention to visual forms has increased. Photography first emerged in the 1820s. It became widely accessible in the 1880s when George Eastman developed film technology that replaced cumbersome photographic plates. Public monuments have played a role in the United States since the country's inception, with monuments literally being built into the bricks and stones of the nation's Capitol building. Scenes commemorating Columbus's life as a discoverer appear in the massive bronze doors that lead into the Capitol rotunda. Reliefs depicting settler-Indian relations adorn the Rotunda walls.[18] The last few decades have seen a proliferation of museums, memorials, and other memory sites.[19]

The prominence of visuals in public discourse has also increased; they are now omnipresent.[20] Photographs populate computer-mediated spaces such as

Myspace, Facebook, Google Images, and Flickr. Visual rhetoric scholar Diane Hope concludes that visual communication is "a foundational core within the discipline of communication. Visual artifacts provoke intended and unintended meanings for individual and collective identity."[21]

The interaction between mediated messages and audience interpretations is in constant negotiation, with hegemonic powers dominating in some cases and audience resistance triumphing in others. The more skilled an audience is in analyzing visual and verbal messages, the more it is able to resist a hegemonic interpretation. Communication scholar Celeste Condit warns, "Audiences are not free to make meanings at will from mass mediated texts" because "the ability of audiences to shape their own readings . . . is constrained by a variety of factors in any given rhetorical situation," including "access to oppositional codes . . . the repertoire of available texts" and the historical context.[22] What you can say about a visual text depends on the vocabulary you have and the questions you have been trained to ask. If the only code you have to analyze a movie is "thumbs up" or "thumbs down," you have a limited ability to provide a detailed critical analysis of it. If you also have language to talk about race, gender, class, and nationality, you have a greater capacity to shape your own reading.

For any given text, Stuart Hall identifies three possible readings.[23] A **dominant reading** (of preferred, hegemonic meaning) is *a reading in which a reader (or viewer) takes the "connoted meaning . . . full and straight . . . the viewer is operating inside the dominant code."*[24] The viewer does not challenge the ideology behind the message or the way in which it maintains hegemonic power. A **negotiated reading** is *a reading in which the viewer accepts some of the hegemonic meanings, but also recognizes some exceptions.* In such a reading, the denotational meanings are understood, but some of the connotational meanings are challenged. An **oppositional reading** is *a reading in which the viewer correctly decodes the denotational and connotational meanings of a text, but challenges it from an oppositional perspective.*

Because of the possible levels of reading, we find persuasive Evans and Hall's description of how visual rhetoric generates meaning:

> [M]eaning is constituted not in the visual sign itself as a self-sufficient entity, nor exclusively in the sociological positions and identities of the audience, but in the articulation between viewer and viewed, between the power of the image to signify and the viewer's capacity to interpret meaning.[25]

The meaning of a text is not determined by its author, nor is the meaning solely contained in the text. Instead, audiences interpret meanings of visual texts in the process of looking. As a result, a single text or image may have multiple meanings, meanings influenced by the audience's culture and personal interpretations. For example, younger viewers may interpret Mountain Dew's high-octane advertisements for the high-caffeine drink as positive celebrations of life on the edge, while older viewers may interpret the advertisements as glamorizing an unnecessarily risk-taking youth culture. Thus, when people analyze visual

-is it limited to actual images?

rhetoric, it is important to take into consideration not only the image and its producer, but also the social context surrounding the audience's interpretation of that image.

Although audiences may have different interpretations of the same text, often interpretations are relatively consistent. Why? The culture that constitutes the audience influences its interpretations; hence, many audience interpretations reinforce the interpretation preferred by those in power. Both media and viewers participate in the hegemonic process whereby the predominant ideology uses noncoercive legal and political forms to generate consent in the dominated. Hegemonic institutions usually do influence audiences; that is what makes them hegemonic. For example, most people in the United States take the mere existence of commercial advertising in stride; the United States as a capitalist society sees encouragements to consume as a normal thing.

When critically analyzing visual rhetoric, consider the image, the viewer, and the other influences at work, some of which may increase the audience's ability to open up the interpretive process and some of which may limit it. Thus, when reading the passage from Evans and Hall, remember they are not talking about a single interaction between viewer and image, but multiple interactions that may, ultimately, seem to lead away from the image and the viewer, although they all lead back to the context understood as socioeconomic positions and identities.[26]

TYPES OF VISUAL RHETORIC

In the sections to follow, we outline four types of visual communication that have received substantial scholarly attention. They are not necessarily the most important forms of visual rhetoric (though important they are), but they offer illustrations of how visual communication operates presentationally and can create presence, thus directing attention to some things while deflecting it from others.[27]

Bodies

Research on body rhetoric and body argument shows that verbal messages do not exist free from a material body that creates those messages. *Who* says a message and *how* a body is made present communicate as much as *what* is said. **Body rhetoric,** then, is *rhetoric that foregrounds the body as part of the symbolic act.*

When we speak of bodies, we are not speaking of some biological entity, but of a social and individual creation, performance, and inscription. Gender, sex, race, class, sexual orientation, religion, ethnicity, ability, age, and a host of other identity ingredients enter the discussion. Additionally, body rhetoric is often used by those who are denied access to more traditional forms of verbal address and of proof. In some cases, your own body may be your only available proof for a point you want to make.

To understand the power of bodies as rhetoric, consider the technique of enactment. **Enactment** occurs when *the person engaging in symbolic action* *functions as proof of the argument s/he advances.*[28] As you read the following uses of enactment, think about how, if the same statement was presented by any other person, the argument would lose some of its power, even though the words might be identical. The power of the visual proof enhances the power of the words.

Barbara Jordan delivered the keynote address at the 1976 Democratic National Convention. Her main argument was that the Democratic Party was the party of inclusion and opportunity, regardless of one's race, sex, or class. She sought to answer the question: "What is it, what is it about the Democratic Party that makes it the instrument that people use when they search for ways to shape their future?" As proof of the claim that the Democratic Party was an instrument of positive change, she offered herself. She proclaimed from her black, female body: "But there is something different about tonight. There is something special about tonight. What is different? What is special? I, Barbara Jordan, am a keynote speaker. . . . And I feel that notwithstanding the past that my presence here is one additional bit of evidence that the American Dream need not forever be deferred."[29]

Mary Fisher (an artist and the daughter of a major Republican fundraiser) delivered a speech on AIDS at the 1992 Republic National Convention. Her main argument was "the AIDS virus is not a political creature. It does not care whether you are Democrat or Republican; it does not ask whether you are black or white, male or female, gay or straight, young or old." She believed everyone, Democrats and Republicans, should be concerned about AIDS because it affected everyone. She proclaimed from her Republican, white, non–drug using, heterosexual, economically privileged, married when infected, HIV+ body: "You are at risk."[30] She functioned as proof that everyone present at the convention was at risk.

In September 2010, in the wake of a number of bullying-induced suicides of LGBT youth, journalist and author Dan Savage launched the "It Gets Better Project," an online website on which adults can post videos in which they "show young LGBT people the levels of happiness, potential, and positivity their lives will reach—if they can just get through their teen years."[31] As of February 2011, the site contained ten thousand user-created videos and has had over thirty million views. Each video is an example of enactment. Savage and his husband Terry begin their eight-and-a-half-minute video by talking about the violence and harassment they experienced as gay youth. A little over a minute into the video, they declare: "It gets better." They spend most of the video talking about their loving parents, the beginning of their sixteen-year relationship, their thirteen-year-old son, their travels to Paris, and their skiing trips—basically describing how normal, loving, and happy their lives are. They are proof that "it gets better."

As these examples demonstrate, bodies can be rhetorically powerful as they function as evidence for a claim. However, not only may bodies function as a *part* of an argument in the form of data, they can also be the *complete* argument. Argument traditionalists often relegate the role of the body in argument to a means of capturing and holding attention, rather than as a central part of the substance of the argument, but their perspective lacks explanatory power

Figure 1
Madres de Plaza de Mayo
© *Horacio Villalobos/Corbis*

when applied to contemporary activism. For example, in his study of the rhetoric of groups such as Earth First!, ACT UP, and Queer Nation, Kevin Michael DeLuca highlighted that the activists' bodies are "not merely flags to attract attention for the argument but the site and substance of the argument itself."[32] In the case of ACT UP and Queer Nation, two groups that focus on AIDS policy, the presence of the body is the argument, "for it is the body that is at stake—its meanings, its possibilities, its care, and its freedoms. In their protest actions, the activists use their bodies to rewrite the homosexual body as already constructed by dominant mainstream discourses—diseased, contagious, deviant, invisible."[33] Instead of presenting their bodies as passive, diseased, and dying, the activists present their bodies as active, healing, and living. Activists present integrated verbal and visual arguments about what the body means, what the government does to it, and how it is affected by disease.

Sometimes, body rhetoric may be the only rhetorical option available. In societies where free speech is not sanctioned, an image (a photo) and a presence (a body) may be the only way to negate a government's denial of wrongdoing. Communication studies scholar Valeria Fabj's study of the Mothers of Plaza de Mayo is an excellent example of a situation in which discursive argument was not an option and a visual form was necessary.[34] The Mothers formed in

1977 in order to protest the "disappearance" of their children under the repressive military regime that ruled Argentina from 1976 to 1983. Wearing as headscarves their children's nappies (diapers embroidered with the children's names and dates of disappearance) and carrying pictures of their disappeared children, they marched around the Plaza at a time when public protest was prohibited. Fabj argues it was the very "myth of motherhood," the social beliefs attached to the women's bodies, that allowed them "to draw from their private experiences in order to gain a political voice, discover eloquent symbols, and yet remain relatively safe at a time when all political dissent was prohibited."[35]

Bodies offer a powerful rhetorical resource. They can function as proof of an argument; they can be the argument; and they can argue when speech has been restricted. To really understand a rhetorical action, you must consider the body that speaks it.

Photographs

Research on the rhetoric of photographs shows that images never represent a reality that is free from the influences of symbolic action. Instead, photographs direct attention to a particular reality. Although people often think of photographs (assuming they are not Photoshopped) as exact representations of reality, all visual technologies (such as cameras, video recorders, and cell phones with digital recording technology) "structure images of reality."[36] Visual communication scholar Diane Hope explains that: "what viewers see, what they do not see, and how they contextualize images depends on structural choices made by producers, and include editing, framing, sequencing, contrast, focus, illumination and grounding."[37]

An example of photographs that persuaded people to see the world in a particular way can be found in Carleton Watkins's 1860s photographs of Yosemite Valley. The California Geological Survey began to map the valley in 1863. As part of his appeal to have the valley declared a public park, survey head Josiah Dwight Whitney used twenty-eight of Watkins's original photographs to illustrate the Survey's report, an unprecedented use of photographs to illustrate a scientific survey. When a bill finally was written calling for President Abraham Lincoln to preserve Yosemite Valley, advocates attached some of Watkins's photographs to the bill. As the images circulated, they "became iconic of an American vision of nature itself."[38] They were central to the preservation of that area and influenced the focus of environmental movements for years to come. How?

The images are more than a simple reflection of the Yosemite Valley. They also select and highlight a particular understanding of nature even as they deflect other understandings. Kevin DeLuca and Anne Demo ask, in their analysis of these photos, "What vision of nature do the photographs authorize, warrant, and legitimate?"[39] For them, Watkins's images were not "merely evidence in a conventional political argument," nor were they "simply representing reality or making an argument about reality. Instead . . . the pictures are constituting the context within which a politics takes place—they are creating a reality."[40] These images influenced what it meant to be an environmentalist by reducing

Figure 2
Cathedral Rocks, Yosemite Valley
Carleton Watkins, Library of Congress

the environment to pristine, untouched lands, rather than including all the land, sky, and water in which beings live. They also reinforced the prevailing myth that Euro-American settlers were the only people to step foot into this pristine wilderness, wiping the presence of Native Americans from public awareness. These images induced people to accept a particular view of nature as untouched by human habitation. The framing of the photos (framing being a technique that directs attention) meant that Native Americans were not present within the frame of reference.

The centrality of photographic images to a people's understanding of their identity cannot be underestimated. Watkins's images reinforced the identity of Euro-Americans as explorers and discoverers. When you study photographs, the questions are not limited to what meaning the image maker wants to transmit; they also include what the image does, how audiences read images, and how the rhetor calls a particular audience into being. You live in a visual culture and are bombarded by rhetorics of display. How do you develop an awareness of what images are asking of you, instead of just doing what they ask?

In a world increasingly dominated by electronic media, visual rhetoric scholars Robert Hariman and John Louis Lucaites argue, commonly viewed images can provide a sense of "shared experience"; even as public life seems

Figure 3
Values.com billboard

impersonal, people develop a personal connection (an identification) with the people they see in pictures. In addition, "the daily stream of images in the public media . . . defines the public through an act of common spectatorship. All viewers *seem* to see the same thing."[41] The "Pass It On" public service billboard campaign, cosponsored by The Foundation for a Better Life and the Outdoor Advertising Association of America, relies on common spectatorship. The Foundation seeks to create a sense of community and identification by celebrating shared experiences of positive values, such as unity, dedication, strength, soul, vision, sacrifice, persistence, and commitment. Using celebrities (such as Michelle Kwan and Wayne Gretzky), historic figures (such as Gandhi, Lincoln, and Churchill), and less well-known individuals (such as Brooks Dame, a bone marrow donor; firefighters at Ground Zero; a Tiananmen Square protester; and Marlon Shirley), the campaign encourages identification with those who exhibit these values and creates a shared experience of those values. Shirley, two-time Paralympic 100-meter champion and the only amputee to break the eleven-second barrier in that race, demonstrates the value of overcoming adversity. Even if a viewer does not know he was abandoned by his mother at the age of five, lived on the streets until he was placed in an orphanage, lost his foot in a lawnmower accident and then the rest of his lower leg in a football accident, the image illustrates the value of determination and heart. He is clearly an athlete, resting his prosthetic leg in a starting block. In addition, the composition of the image gives a sense of vitality and forward movement.

Thus, when discussing public communication, one needs to consider the ways visuals form what is considered public and shared. For people in the United States, a few key photos inform how citizens see themselves. Lucaites and Hariman identify these images as **iconic photographs:**

photographic images produced in print, electronic, or digital media that are (1) recognized by everyone within a public culture, (2) understood to

Figure 4
US Marines raising flag over Iwo Jima
AP Photo/Joe Rosenthal.

> *be representations of historically significant events, (3) objects of strong*
> *emotional identification and response, and (4) regularly reproduced or*
> *copied across a range of media, genres, and topics.*[42]

Examples of iconic photographs include Joe Rosenthal's 1945 photo of the
flag raising on Iwo Jima,[43] John Filo's 1970 photo of the Ohio National Guard
shooting of a Kent State student,[44] and Nick Ut's 1972 Vietnam War photo of
accidental napalm.[45] Each of these photos contribute to the way US citizens
came to see themselves. For example, the Pulitzer-Prize winning photo of Iwo
Jima, published at the height of World War II, presents a particular understanding of citizenship and war. Taken by Associated Press photographer
Joe Rosenthal, it depicts the US military seizing a Japanese observation post on
the island.

This image fulfills all the elements of an iconic photo. Most people in the
United States would recognize it. It represents a historically significant event; in
fact, it has come to represent all of World War II for many people. It creates
a strong emotional identification, as citizens identify with the men pictured,
with their struggle and victory. It is regularly reproduced; in fact, it is the most

reproduced photograph in history.[46] What is most significant, however, is how the photo has come to form an understanding of US public culture.

Hariman and Lucaites argue that this photo presents two arguments about what distinguishes and defines US citizens. First, war is more an act of labor than an act of killing. The marines and Navy corpsman are not pictured firing weapons, but laboring to erect the flag. Second, even in an act of conquest (taking a strategic place), the soldiers work together, regardless of rank, thus enacting egalitarianism and civic pride. In depicting war and egalitarian cooperation, the photograph "reflect[s] social knowledge and dominant ideologies; . . . shape[s] understanding of specific events and periods; . . . influence[s] political action by modeling relationships between civic actors; and . . . provide[s] figural resources for subsequent communicative action."[47] As people in the United States look at this image, they come to a shared vision of who they are and why the nation fought. The photo reflects a particular image of US citizens as hardworking (not warlike), equal (rank is irrelevant, as all participants labor equally), and proud of their nation (the US flag is a primary indicator of civic pride).

Monuments, Memorials, and Museums

On family vacations, many people visit monuments and memorials, such as the Washington Monument and the Vietnam Veterans Memorial in Washington, DC. They often read these structures as neutral markers of historical figures and events, but monuments do more than simply record historic facts. They are epideictic: they direct people about how to think about those facts from the past, how to act in the present, and what possible futures to seek. It should not be surprising, therefore, that controversy often arises over monuments and memorials. Although they are inanimate objects, they are not just markers of famous locations or ways to memorialize the dead; they also direct people's views of themselves. For example, one controversy actually resulted in renaming a national monument and adding another memorial to its space.

Off I-90 in southern Montana sits the Crow Indian Reservation, the site of the most famous battle in the Indian Wars, remembered not because it was a great victory for the US Seventh Cavalry under the command of Lieutenant Colonel George Armstrong Custer, but because on June 25, 1876, the Cavalry was annihilated on this site by the superior might of Lakota (Sioux), Hinono'eino' (Arapaho) and Tsistsistas (Cheyenne) warriors. In 1879, the battlefield was dedicated as a national cemetery. In 1881, the Seventh Cavalry Memorial was erected, listing the names of all the Cavalry members and "Arikaree" (Arikara Indian, also known as Sahnish) scouts slain in the battle. In 1925, Mrs. Thomas Beaverheart (daughter of Chief Lame White Man, a Southern Cheyenne killed in the battle) initiated Native American demands for inclusion. In 1946, the Custer Battlefield National Monument was dedicated.

After years of protest by Native Americans, in 1991 the Custer Battlefield National Monument was *rededicated* as the Little Bighorn Battlefield National Monument. A national design competition was authorized for an Indian Memorial. When President George H. W. Bush signed the federal law declaring the name change, he explained: "The public interest will best be served by establishing a memorial . . . to honor and recognize the Indians who fought to preserve their land and culture."[48]

An advisory committee composed of members of all the Indian nations involved in the battle, historians, artists, and landscape architects selected the memorial's theme, "Peace through Unity," in response to the advice of elders Austin Two Moons (Northern Cheyenne) and Enos Poor Bear, Sr. (Oglala Lakota).[49] In 1997, the committee selected John R. Collins and Alison J. Towers's memorial design, which incorporated a sculpture of Spirit Warriors designed by Lakota artist Colleen "Sister Wolf" Cutschall. The Indian Memorial was dedicated on June 25, 2003.

The need for the Indian Memorial becomes clear when one considers the way Euro-Americans remembered the battle prior to the 1991 law. Not only were the sites where Native Americans died unmarked, a marker in the national cemetery that memorialized US officers who died in the Indian Wars told a distorted story, referring to "hostile Indians" without noting the reason for the hostility: for decades US troops had forcibly driven them from their homelands and onto reservations. Until the law changed the name of the battlefield and required the memorialization of Native Americans who fought, only the names of Custer's soldiers, civilians traveling with the cavalry, and the three Sahnish (Arikara) Indians who scouted for the Seventh Calvary were inscribed on the monument. The deeds of the triumphant Sioux Indian chiefs Crazy Horse and Sitting Bull were not remembered in the official space, even though Native Americans kept these deeds alive in oral histories.

The evolution of the Little Bighorn site illustrates that public memory is grounded in the present rather than the past and is continually (re)made to fit the needs of the public(s) it serves. Initially Custer Battlefield National Monument served the need to justify the westward expansion and to celebrate the actions of the military. It held Custer up as a hero who ostensibly served the cause of fighting "hostile Indians." As needs arose to account for the wrongs committed against Native Americans, the form, content, and name of the site had to change to encompass those needs.

The Little Bighorn Battlefield is a place where the US conception of citizenship and nationhood is developed and maintained, a conception that directly implicates a particular history of Native Americans. Communication scholar Richard Morris notes in another context, "the continuous struggle to gain access to and control of America's collective memory is hardly a benign process."[50] In other words, the national monument site initially argued that only Custer and his men should be remembered. As it constructed and maintained memory about Custer, it generated amnesia about Native Americans and why they fought. With the new monument, the location argues that both soldiers and warriors should be remembered, that all the lives lost are worthy of being mourned. The question of how, and whom, to mourn is not a simple one. The Freedom Tower at Ground Zero, now called One World Trade Center, still has not been built, in part because disagreement over the form of monumental structures at the site delayed construction until 2006.[51]

As memorials and monuments sustain public memory, they make arguments about how to think about the identities of particular groups of people. Thus monuments and memorials are rhetorical. As communication scholar Victoria J. Gallagher notes, they "perpetuate values, admonish as to future conduct, and affirm or challenge existing power relations."[52] There are two reasons why they are able to perform those functions: (1) what is remembered has less to do with what happened in the past than with the needs of the present, and (2) the process of remembering always involves an act of forgetting as well.

Memory, and thus the architecture of memorials, monuments, and museums, serve the needs of the present. Thus, when people discuss memorials and monuments, they should question which parts of history are selected for memory, and why those elements are selected when others are not. Historians Peter Grey and Kendrick Oliver suggest that not only can a nation-state seek to remember key points in its history, such as wars, but "diverse and competing interest groups" can "seek to use constructions of the past to advance their agendas in the present."[53] One vivid example is the Vietnam Veterans Memorial. After the Vietnam War ended in 1975, the US public was deeply divided over its meaning. Even though the selection committee of eight architects and sculptors unanimously selected Maya Lin's Wall from among 1,421 proposals in 1981, controversy continued. Construction proceeded only after an agreement was reached to add a flagpole and Frederick Hart's Three Servicemen Statue. The wall was unveiled in 1982, the statue in 1984. Communication scholars Carole Blair, Marsha S. Jeppeson, and Enrico Pucci, Jr., point out that the tension over the monument "designates the domestic conflict over the war itself."[54] Lin's wall questions whether the war was an event worthy of admiration, while Hart's statue resoundingly affirms that it was.

The controversy over memory did not end with those two parts of the memorial. As women increasingly called for the ability to serve in combat roles and their contributions as service members were increasingly recognized, calls for a Vietnam women's memorial grew. Grey and Oliver state that in 1993, the "sacrifices made and horrors witnessed by American women—particularly nurses—during the conflict in Vietnam" were recognized.[55] Even this historically accurate reintroduction of women into the memory of Vietnam was not without controversy. People reacted negatively to the statue partly because of "its representation of a wounded soldier, drawing attention to the harsh, immediate purpose of the war, and rejecting, in the forlorn, desperate expressions of the nurses, the conventional iconic languages of healing, sacrifice and redemption."[56] Although amnesia about women's role had been corrected, people did not agree about how women should be remembered.

Collective memory scholar Barry Schwartz argues: "While the object of commemoration is usually to be found in the past, the issue which motivates its selection and shaping is always to be found among the concerns of the present."[57] So what was happening in 1993? Although women had served as medical personnel and in support positions in every war, and were admitted to the military academies in 1976, not until the late 1980s did serious debate occur about women serving in combat positions. Advocates for allowing women in combat argued that women, even in noncombat positions, faced all the dangers of war. Even noncombat nurses serving on the front lines in MASH units often ended up serving *in* combat. Thus, a statue recognizing women's roles in Vietnam participated in the ongoing debate about women in combat.

Research on the rhetorical power of monuments and memorials shows that architecture, itself, positions those who view the monuments (audiences) in particular ways, inducing particular reactions and preserving particular memories. Gallagher is among the scholars who have come to recognize that "the symbolic, architectural, and/or textual aspects of artifacts . . . impact both people who come into contact with them and the larger society of which those people are members."[58] The preferred readings of memorials and monuments call people to remember some events, and remember them in particular ways. Because some events and people are remembered, others are not; they are deflected. As monuments participate in creating public memory, they also induce public forgetting.

Image Events

Kevin DeLuca opens his book, *Image Politics*, with a paradigm example. On June 27, 1975, 50 miles off the coast of California, sailed the 160-foot Russian whaling ship *Vlastny*, equipped with a 90-mm cannon that shot 160-pound exploding grenade harpoons. Six Greenpeace activists in three inflatable rubber dinghies pursued the *Vlastny*. One dinghy, carrying Bob Hunter and Paul Watson, positioned itself between the whaling ship and a fleeing whale, thinking the whalers would not fire and risk hitting humans. They thought wrong. The whalers on the *Vlastny* fired over the heads of the activists and hit the whale, with the harpoon's trajectory carrying it less than five feet from the dinghy and the people riding in it.[59]

The event was captured on tape by other Greenpeace members, and was televised on CBS, ABC, NBC and around the world during the International Whaling Commission's conference. Although it did not save this one whale, the video opened Greenpeace's "Save the Whales" campaign, which eventually led to bans on commercial whaling, saving many whales.[60] Paul Watson commented:

> That thirty-second film clip that Fred had captured would be our ticket to the hot media of television.
>
> Armed with the tempting media bait of dramatic visual documentation, we could now gain access to the doors of human

awareness through the avenue that only television could provide. For the first time, we had some hope of inciting public indignation against whaling.

> . . . our efforts in the past had been stymied by the fact that . . . if the public thought about whaling at all, it was the image of Moby Dick that came to mind, along with brave whaling men in puny longboats locked in a heroic struggle against a monstrous giant beast. Thanks to our activities that day, the media began to present a different image of whaling from here on in.[61]

The images created a virtual experience for people who had no understanding of whaling. They altered perceptions by challenging the norms and assumptions of the dominant public, making present the violence involved in whaling.

DeLuca labels Greenpeace's symbolic act an image event. **Image events** are *"staged acts . . . designed for media dissemination."*[62] They may be used for protest, for example, as "mind bombs," to explode the typical ways people think about a topic, such as their relationship to the environment.[63] Image events combine visual and verbal rhetorics in order to challenge the images people have of corporations and of protestors. They are structured to elicit the attention of media outlets, so that they appear on the public screen of television, computers, and newspapers.

Although at first glance, one might think the Greenpeace effort was a dangerous and crazy stunt (would *you* be willing to sail in a rubber dinghy between a whaling boat and a whale?), DeLuca argues that "far from being the desperate stunts of the disillusioned, image events are the central mode of public discourse both for conventional electoral politics and for alternative grassroots politics in an era dominated by a commercial televisual electronic public sphere."[64] DeLuca noted that although people today could probably name famous speakers from the civil rights era, many would be hard-pressed to name a famous environmental speaker or memorable environmental speech. Even Al Gore has gained his fame as an environmental speaker by using images to transmit his message in his 2006 movie on global warming, *An Inconvenient Truth.*[65]

DeLuca's description of image events challenges traditional notions of how rhetoric operates. When you acknowledge the power of visuals, he argues, you begin to question many assumptions of "traditional rhetorical theory and criticism, starting with the notion that rhetoric ideally is 'reasoned discourse,' with 'reasoned' connoting 'civil' or 'rational' and 'discourse' connoting 'words.'"[66] Although these assumptions might apply to the discourse at town hall meetings, and although there is little that is civil or reasoned about Greenpeace's image event, it is not irrational.[67] Image events, though often outrageous, should not be dismissed as "gimmicks or the antics of the unruly" or reduced to "flares sent out to gain attention."[68] They actually form the substance of contemporary activism in a world saturated by images. Radical environmental groups "are using image events to attempt both to deconstruct and articulate identities, ideologies, consciousnesses, communities, publics, and cultures in our modern industrial

Figure 5
Taxpayer March,
Washington, DC.

Roll Call/Getty Images

civilization."[69] Greenpeace's images of the dying whales and of Greenpeace activists' willingness to sacrifice themselves to save the whales generated questions about human beings' relationship to the natural world and the way human beings value it.

Image events are used by a wide range of rhetors. Any time an act of public communication is planned with the hope of media dissemination, people consider the way the event will play on public screens. Thus, one could examine all of the following as image events: Sarah Palin's 2009 book signing tour, Barack Obama's 2009 inaugural address, the 1999 protests at the World Trade Organization meeting in Seattle, and the 2009 Tea Party Taxpayer March on Washington. The meaning of each event is not contained solely in the verbal content of the messages; it is also contained in the visual images: Palin thronged by long lines of adoring fans, Obama as president speaking to a crowd that overflowed the National Mall, police using tear gas and riot batons on protesters, and tens of thousands of conservative protesters in Washington, DC. An image of the Taxpayer March, for example, shows the mass of bodies filling the frame and extending to the horizon as it proceeds down Pennsylvania Avenue towards the Capitol, a central symbol of US government power. (The Patriot Action Network estimated 1.7 million people were in attendance and provided time-lapse video of the crowd. The National Taxpayers Union, which co-organized the event, said 200,000 to 300,000 people attended.) The diverse signs make the protest seem spontaneous rather than orchestrated.

Research on image events shows that the ability of electronic media to transmit visual rhetoric to broad audiences is a central element of visual rhetoric. Visual rhetoric, in some cases, requires its audiences to come to it (one must intentionally seek out places such as the Little Bighorn Battlefield National Monument). In contrast, image events are structured in such a way that media are induced to take the event to the audience, to transmit it so that even those who are not seeking exposure to a group's rhetoric may see the event when it is broadcast across various media.

When studying image events, keep in mind that they do not always function the same way verbal rhetoric does. As presentational symbolism, they operate holistically and not in a sequentially logical manner. In addition, they sometimes challenge, rather than invite, identification. Although Kenneth Burke believes that identification is central to rhetoric, DeLuca notes "the rhetorical tactic of image events works not so much through identification as through disidentification, through the shock or laughter that shatters" the taken for granted, the commonplace, and the meanings of fundamental ideographs.[70] In the Greenpeace example, does the viewer identify with the Russian whalers, with the Greenpeace activists, or with the whales? Image events are not necessarily meant to make the audience feel similar to the rhetor. Instead, their purpose may be to alter perception, to explode the commonplace so that new ways of thinking emerge.

Instead of using identification with already formed identities, DeLuca says, image events can both reconstitute or re-form the identity of the protester and "the identity of the dominant culture by challenging and transforming mainstream society's key discourses and ideographs."[71] Civil rights activists had long faced violence, but not until the circulation of photos of civil rights marches in Birmingham in 1963 were white people's sense of themselves and the law challenged. In 1960, during lunch counter sit-ins at Woolworth's, college students faced violence from white onlookers. In 1961, angry mobs confronted the Freedom Riders as police stood by and watched. In 1962, President Kennedy had to send in federal troops when James Meredith became the first black student to enroll at the University of Mississippi and white people reacted violently. Yet, northern white people were slow to react. Then, in May of 1963, Birmingham happened.

As civil rights activists peacefully marched, Commissioner of Public Safety Eugene "Bull" Connor ordered the police to use dogs and fire hoses to disperse them. Images of police dogs and fire hoses turned against black protestors, widely televised and published in numerous print media, shook the conscience of the nation and made clear to moderate white people that racial equality would not be attained via a gradualist approach.[72] Communication scholar Davi Johnson argues that a photograph of officers with police dogs attacking unresisting black protestors constituted "a visual reversal where the traditional characteristic of

Figure 6
Firefighters turning hose on civil rights demonstrators
Charles Moore, Black Star

the uniformed authorities are transposed into their opposites: the protector of order becomes the oppressor who brings chaotic brutality into the scene of civilization."[73] Instead of white people identifying with the police and accepting the ideograph of "law and order," they were induced to break their traditional patterns of identification. The photos asked white people to identify with black protestors who were breaking (unjust) laws.

It is not just protest groups that use images. Most campaign events are image oriented, positioning candidates so they look good on the evening news. Corporations, establishment politicians, and radical political groups all use images.[74] Understanding the ability of image events to reorient public discourse is essential to understanding the role of rhetoric in contemporary society and how it constitutes citizenship, participation, and meaning.

VISUAL AESTHETICS AND THE ANALYSIS OF VISUAL RHETORIC

Visual rhetoric is complex, with multiple interpretations possible. How might you go about systematically figuring out your reactions to visual rhetoric? You can only determine how and why an image achieves its purpose and effect if you can figure out how the image works. Some of the aesthetic elements unique to visual forms can be helpful. Compositional interpretation[75] would have you examine:

1. Content: what is shown.
2. Color: hue (the actual colors), saturation (the purity of the color), and value (the lightness or darkness of the color); not only what the colors are, but also their effects in terms of what they stress and whether they are harmonious.
3. Spatial organization: form, shape, and geometrical perspective, all of which can create the impression of movement or direct the eye in one direction or another.
4. Light: the type of light present, as well as its source.
5. Expressive content: the feeling evoked by an image.

A compositional interpretation of Watkins's images would analyze content (sweeping vistas of natural spaces), color (black and white photos may lack the vibrancy of color photos, but Watkins was able to capture the stark beauty of the space with his use of contrast), spatial organization (Watkins's photos of Cathedral Rocks sweep the eye upward as the shapes reach for heaven; his photos of rivers draw the eye in, pulling the viewer even deeper into the wild space), light (only natural lighting is present, but the light creates a sense of depth), and expressive content (Watkins's photos are noted for their ability to induce a sense of the sublime—a reverent sense of awe). Although critics may pick apart an image to understand its purpose and aesthetics, much about visuals is difficult to analyze.

After reviewing the findings of neuroscience, visual communication scholar and documentary photographer Rick Williams concludes: "*visual intelligence* is the primary intuitive intelligence because the majority of information that the brain processes is visual and most other intelligences also employ significant visual cognition. This does not suggest that visual information cannot be used rationally, but that the initial, primary response to visual cognition is precon-scious."[76] The goal is to access these intuitive intelligences in the same way people access cognitive intelligences.

How does one come to understand the expressive content of an image and its overall effect on what we think? Williams offers seven steps of personal impact assessment (PIA) that can be used to assess intuitive intelligence. Because this is a *personal* impact assessment, each person's answers will be distinct. Select a photo from a news website, then:

1. Look at the photo for a few minutes, thinking about the feelings and reactions it engenders.
2. List primary words that describe key elements of the image on the left side of a blank piece of paper. Leave space after each word.
3. For each primary word, list associative words that it triggers when you think about it.
4. Select the most significant associative word for each group of words.

5. Relate associative words to an inner part of yourself (your trusting self, your vulnerable self, your strong self, your fantasy self, your feminine self, your athletic self, your racial self, and so on). Images resonate with a particular part of your self; they call forth inner symbols. Try to figure out which part of your self resonates with the key associative words. There is no right or wrong answer; you are looking to identify where your personal interpretation of and reaction to the image comes from.

6. Review the inner symbols that are called forward and consider whether a story arises about yourself. The story can, according to Williams, "reveal the inner conflicts, emotions, values, or feelings that are behind your personal, intuitive creation of or attraction to the image."

7. Write down the story. Consider how it explains your attraction or reaction to the image. In the case of an advertisement, consider how the product advertised may resolve some inner conflict or fulfill some inner need identified in the story.[77]

These techniques give you a way to organize your reactions to an image; they help you organize data so you can make an argument about how an image functions. Identifying the purpose and effect of an image, and how its composition induces a reaction in you, is not the conclusion of the analytic process, however. Instead, it is the beginning.

CONCLUSION

Our goal in this chapter is to assist you in becoming a critical viewer of visual rhetoric, so you can resist the hegemonic pull that many images may have on your intuitive intelligence. Because visual forms are rhetorical, and not just objective recorders of some fixed world, viewers of visual rhetoric should not ask "what do images represent?" but instead "what do the images do?" Images induce you to see the world one way rather than another. The more aware you are of the rhetorical aspects of images, the more you will be able to determine when you should assent to the arguments they advance.

In a visual culture, civic life is constituted, maintained, defined, and performed through visual rhetoric. Public bodies enact citizenship; civic identity is constituted through photographs; national memories are maintained in monuments; and image events use media outlets to call attention to issues for deliberation and action. Although people often think of civic life as occurring only through the medium of talk, language is only one form of symbolic action. Visual rhetoric is as important to civic life as language. Ignoring visual rhetoric in studies of civic life strips people of one of their core senses. People not only hear each others' appeals, they also see each other.

Visual communication scholar Diane Hope explains: "Viewing audiences are not necessarily passive. Viewers select, choose, and perceive images according to the context, knowledge, and life experience they bring to the act of viewing."[78]

DISCUSSION QUESTIONS

1. In what ways is contemporary US culture a visual culture?
2. While watching TV or reading a magazine, find an example of visual rhetoric. Identify what type it is (iconic photograph, body rhetoric, monumental rhetoric, image event, something else). Explore how the example of visual rhetoric induces you to accept a particular understanding of the world.
3. Find a visual image and, using the vocabulary of compositional analysis and the process of PIA, analyze your reaction to it.

RECOMMENDED READINGS

Birdsell, David S., and Leo Groarke, eds. "Toward a Theory of Visual Argument." Special Issue on Visual Argument, *Argumentation and Advocacy* 33 (Summer and Fall 1996): 1–10.

Delicath, John W., and Kevin Michael DeLuca. "Image Events, the Public Sphere, and Argumentative Practice: The Case of Radical Environmental Groups." *Argumentation* 17, no. 3 (September 2003): 315–333.

DeLuca, Kevin Michael. "Unruly Arguments: The Body Rhetoric of Earth First!, ACT UP, and Queer Nation." *Argumentation and Advocacy* 36 (Summer 1999): 9–21.

DeLuca, Kevin Michael, and Anne Teresa Demo. "Imaging Nature: Watkins, Yosemite, and the Birth of Environmentalism." *Critical Studies in Media Communication* 17, no. 3 (September 2000): 241–260.

Hariman, Robert, and John Louis Lucaites. "Performing Civic Identity: The Iconic Photograph of the Flag Raising on Iwo Jima." *Quarterly Journal of Speech* 88, no. 4 (November 2002): 363–392.

Palczewski, Catherine H. "The Male Madonna and the Feminine Uncle Sam: Visual Argument, Icons, and Ideographs in 1909 Anti–Woman Suffrage Postcards." *The Quarterly Journal of Speech* 91, no. 4 (November 2005): 365–394.

ENDNOTES

[1] Justice John Paul Stevens, dissent in *United States v. Eichman*, 496 U.S. 310 (1990), at 321.

[2] "Lift the Veil on the Return of the Nation's War Dead" [editorial], *USA Today*, February 23, 2009, 10A.

[3] "Official: Pentagon Allows Coverage of War Coffins," CNNPolitics, http://www.cnn.com/2009/POLITICS/02/26/pentagon.media.war.dead/index.html (accessed February 26, 2009); Andrea Stone, "Ban on Photographing U.S. Troops' Coffins Lifted," *USA Today*, February 27, 2009–March 1, 2009, 1A.

[4] Chaïm Perelman and Lucie Olbrechts-Tyteca, *The New Rhetoric: A Treatise on Argumentation* (Notre Dame, IN: University of Notre Dame Press, 1969), 116, italics added.

[5] Diane S. Hope, in the introduction to the edited collection of essays *Visual Communication*, describes the way in which presence functions in visual rhetoric, referencing the works of Chaïm Perelman and Lucie Olbrechts-Tyteca. Generally, the process of "selecting certain elements and presenting them to the audience" implies that they are pertinent and important and, thus, imbues them with presence. Diane S. Hope, ed., *Visual Communication: Perception, Rhetoric, and Technology* (Cresskill, NJ: Hampton, 2006), 116. See also Lawrence J. Prelli, ed., *Rhetorics of Display* (Columbia, SC: University of South Carolina Press, 2006), 7. Although Perelman and Olbrechts-Tyteca discuss presence as it relates to data selection in a verbal argument, they use examples that make clear presence's applicability to the study of visual rhetorics. Visuals and presence, alike, act "directly on our sensibility." Perelman and Olbrechts-Tyteca, p. 116. Although all things exist, they do not act on a person's thoughts unless the item is made present. The item need not be physically present. Instead, it can be rhetorically present, through the use of verbal or visual forms of communication.

[6] For more information, visit http://www.ushmm.org/maps.

[7] The history can be accessed at "Revision History of Virginia Tech Massacre," http://en.wikipedia.org/w/index.php?title=Virginia_Tech_massacre&action=history (accessed February 16, 2009).

[8] CNN.com I-Report homepage, http://www.cnn.com/exchange/ireports/topics/forms/breaking.news.html (accessed June 7, 2007).

[9] Jessica Evans and Stuart Hall, "What is Visual Culture?" in *Visual Culture: The Reader*, ed. Jessica Evans and Stuart Hall, 1–8 (London: Sage, 1999), 7.

[10] Charles A. Hill and Marguerite Helmers, eds., *Defining Visual Rhetorics* (Mahwah, NJ: Lawrence Erlbaum Associates, 2004); Diane S. Hope, ed., *Visual Communication*; and Prelli, *Rhetorics of Display*.

[11] Jessica Evans and Stuart Hall, eds., *Visual Culture: The Reader* (Thousand Oaks, CA: Sage, 1999).

[12] Prelli, *Rhetorics of Display*.

[13] Evans and Hall, *Visual Culture*, 7.

[14] Evans and Hall, *Visual Culture*, 2.

[15] Kevin Michael DeLuca and Anne Teresa Demo, "Imaging Nature: Watkins, Yosemite, and the Birth of Environmentalism," *Critical Studies in Media Communication* 17, no. 3 (September 2000): 244.

[16] DeLuca and Demo, *Imaging*, 244. See also W. J. T. Mitchell, *What do Pictures Want?* (Chicago: Chicago University Press, 2005), especially chapter 2.

[17] Evans and Hall, *Visual Culture*, 7.

[18] Barry Schwartz, "The Social Context of Commemoration: A Study of Collective Memory," *Social Forces* 61 (December 1982): 374–402.

[19] Victoria J. Gallagher, "Memory as Social Action: Cultural Projection and Generic Form in Civil Rights Memorials," in *New Approaches to Rhetoric*, ed. Patricia A. Sullivan and Steven R. Goldzwig, 149–171 (Thousand Oaks, CA: Sage, 2004), 149.

[20] Diane S. Hope, ed., "Introduction: Identity and Visual Communication," in *Visual Communication*, 4.

[21] Hope, "Introduction," 5.

[22] Celeste Michelle Condit, "The Rhetorical Limits of Polysemy," *Critical Studies in Mass Communication* 6, no. 2 (June 1989): 103–122, 103–104.

[23] Stuart Hall, "Encoding, Decoding," in *The Cultural Studies Reader*, ed. Simon During, 90–103 (London: Routledge, 1993), 98–102.

[24] Hall, "Encoding, Decoding," 101, italics added.

[25] Evans and Hall, *Visual Culture*, 4.

[26] The authors want to thank Nathan Epley for these valuable insights.

[27] Prelli, *Rhetorics of Display*, 11.

[28] Karlyn Kohrs Campbell, *The Rhetorical Act*, 2nd ed. (Belmont, CA: Wadsworth, 309–310.

[29] Barbara Jordan, "1976 Democratic Convention Keynote Address: Who Then Will Speak for the Common Good?" New York, NY, July 12, 1976, http://www.elf.net/bjordan/keynote.html (accessed October 25, 2000). For an analysis of enactment in this speech, see Karlyn Kohrs Campbell and Kathleen Hall Jamieson, "Form and Genre in Rhetorical Criticism: An Introduction," in *Form and Genre: Shaping Rhetorical Action*, eds. Karlyn Kohrs Campbell and Kathleen Hall Jamieson (Falls Church, VA: Speech Communication Association, 1978).

[30] Mary Fisher, "1992 Republican National Convention Address: A Whisper of AIDS," Houston, TX, https://www.americanrhetoric.com/speeches/maryfisher1992rnc.html (accessed January 15, 2004).

[31] It Gets Better Project, "About," http://www.itgetsbetter.org/pages/about-it-gets-better-project (accessed February 18, 2011).

[32] Kevin Michael DeLuca, *Image Politics* (New York: Guilford, 1999), 10.

[33] DeLuca, *Image Politics*, 17.

[34] Valeria Fabj, "Motherhood as Political Voice: The Rhetoric of the Mothers of Plaza de Mayo," *Communication Studies* 44 (Spring 1993): 1–18.

[35] Fabj, "Motherhood," 2.

[36] Hope, *Visual Communication*, 17.

[37] Hope, *Visual Communication*, 17.

[38] DeLuca and Demo, "Imaging," 242.

[39] DeLuca and Demo, "Imaging," 244.

[40] DeLuca and Demo, "Imaging," 242.

[41] Robert Hariman and John Louis Lucaites, "Performing Civic Identity: The Iconic Photograph of the Flag Raising on Iwo Jima," *Quarterly Journal of Speech* 88, no. 4 (November 2002): 365.

[42] John Louis Lucaites and Robert Hariman, "Visual Rhetoric, Photojournalism, and Democratic Public Culture," *Rhetoric Review* 20, nos. 1/2 (Spring 2001): 37, italics added.

[43] Hariman and Lucaites, "Performing Civic Identity," 363–392.

[44] Robert Hariman and John Louis Lucaites, "Dissent and Emotional Management in a Liberal-Democratic Society: The Kent State Iconic Photograph," *Rhetoric Society Quarterly* 31, no. 3 (Summer 2001): 4–31.

[45] Robert Hariman and John Louis Lucaites, "Public Identity and Collective Memory in U.S. Iconic Photography: The Image of 'Accidental Napalm,'" *Critical Studies in Media Communication* 20, no. 1 (March 2003): 35–66. Image available at http://digitaljournalist.org/issue0008/ng2.htm.

[46] Hariman and Lucaites, "Performing," 364.

[47] Hariman and Lucaites, "Performing," 366.

[48] Quoted on Friends of the Little Bighorn website, http://www.friendslittlebighorn.com/Indian%20Memorial.htm (accessed June 20, 2007).

[49] Western National Parks Association, *The Indian Memorial at Little Bighorn Battlefield National Monument: Peace through Unity* (Canada: Western National Parks Association, 2003).

[50] Richard Morris, *Sinners, Lovers, and Heroes* (Albany: State University of New York Press, 1997), 25.

[51] See letter to the editor in the *New York Times*, July 1, 2005, http://www.triroc.com/wtc/media/freedomtower/timesletters.htm (accessed October 15, 2011).

[52] Victoria J. Gallagher, "Remembering Together: Rhetorical Integration and the Case of the Martin Luther King Jr. Memorial," *The Southern Communication Journal* 60, no. 2 (Winter 1995): 109–119, 112.

[53] Peter Grey and Kendrick Oliver, "The Memory of Catastrophe," *History Today* 51, no. 2 (February 2001): 9–15.

[54] Carole Blair, Marsha S. Jeppeson, and Enrico Pucci, Jr., "Public Memorialization in Postmodernity: The Vietnam Veterans Memorial as Prototype," *Quarterly Journal of Speech* 77 (1991): 263–288, 277.

[55] Grey and Oliver, "Memory," 12.

[56] Grey and Oliver, "Memory," 12.

[57] Barry Schwartz, "The Social Context of Commemoration: A Study of Collective Memory," *Social Forces* 61 (December 1982): 374–402, 395.

[58] Gallagher, "Remembering," 109.

[59] For a first person account of this event, see Paul Watson, "One Day on the Water with Bob Hunter," Sea Shepherd Conservation Society web page, http://www.seashepherd.org/editorials/editorial_050510_1.html (accessed July 17, 2007). Footage of the event can be seen on National Geographic, *The Great Whales*, 1978.

[60] See also John W. Delicath and Kevin Michael DeLuca, "Image Events, the Public Sphere, and Argumentative Practice: The Case of Radical Environmental Groups," *Argumentation* 17, no. 3 (September 2003): 315–333.

[61] Watson, "One Day."

[62] Delicath and DeLuca, "Image Events," 315, italics added.

[63] Robert Hunter as quoted in Kevin Michael DeLuca, *Image Politics* (New York: Guilford, 1999), 1.

[64] DeLuca, *Image Politics*, 17.

[65] Davis Guggenheim (director), *An Inconvenient Truth* (Los Angeles: Paramount, 2006).

[66] DeLuca, *Image Politics*, 14.

[67] Traditional approaches to images events, such as Boorstin's influential book, which calls them "pseudo-events," fail to account for the full power of images. Daniel J. Boorstin, *The Image: A Guide to Pseudo-Events in America*, 25th anniversary ed. (New York: Athenaeum, 1987), 188–189.

[68] DeLuca, *Image Politics*, 17.

[69] DeLuca, *Image Politics*, 17.

[70] DeLuca, *Image Politics*, 52.

[71] DeLuca, *Image Politics*, 16.

[72] Meg Spratt, "When Police Dogs Attacked: Iconic News Photographs and Construction of History, Mythology, and Political Discourse," *American Journalism* 25, no. 2 (2008), 85–105.

[73] Davi Johnson, "Martin Luther King Jr.'s 1963 Birmingham Campaign as Image Event," *Rhetoric and Public Affairs* 10, no. 1, (2007), 1–26, 14.

[74] DeLuca, *Image Politics*, 21–22.

[75] Gillian Rose, *Visual Methodologies* (London: Sage, 2001), esp. chapter 2, "The Good Eye." The elements that follow are taken from her book.

[76] Rick Williams, "Theorizing Visual Intelligence: Practices, Development, and Methodologies for Visual Communication," in *Visual Communication: Perception, Rhetoric, and Technology*, ed. Diane S. Hope, 31–56 (Cresskill, NJ: Hampton, 2006), 35.

[77] This list is adapted from Williams, "Theorizing," 48–50.

[78] Hope, "Introduction," 17.

Chapter 4

Argument

Key Concepts

argument	data
argument field	enthymeme
argument$_1$	particular audiences
argument$_2$	personal sphere
backing	public sphere
burden of proof	presumption
claim	qualifiers
claim of definition	spheres of argument
claim of fact	syllogism
claim of policy	technical sphere
claim of value	universal audience
conditions of rebuttal	warrants

The cover of the July 2008 issue of *National Geographic* shows a close-up of the face of a gorilla, with the question superimposed: "Who murdered the mountain gorillas?"[1] Mark Jenkins's feature story opens by describing the conditions in central Africa's Virunga Park, the forests of which are stripped by charcoal producers and the borders of which are crowded by refugees from the conflict in the Democratic Republic of Congo. During the summer of 2007, seven mountain gorillas were killed in the park. The story describes the killing this way:

> On July 22 of last year unknown assailants crouched in the forest, preparing to execute a family of gorillas. . . . [A]rmed with automatic weapons, the killers had hunted down the twelve-member Rugendo family, well known among tourists and well loved by the rangers of Virunga National Park. . . . On foot patrol the next morning [park rangers] found three female gorillas—Mburanumwe, Neza, and Safari— shot to death, with Safari's infant cowering nearby. The following day Senkwekwe was found dead: blasted through the chest that same night. Three weeks later the body of another Rugendo female, Macibiri, would be discovered, her infant presumed dead.
>
> Just a month earlier, two females and an infant from another gorilla group had been attacked. The rangers had found one of the females, shot execution style in the back of the head; her infant, still

alive, was clinging to her dead mother's breast. The other female was never found.

All told, seven Virunga mountain gorillas had been killed in less than two months. Brent Stirton's photographs of the dead creatures being carried like royalty by weeping villagers ran in newspapers and magazines around the world. The murders of these intelligent, unassuming animals the park rangers refer to as "our brothers" ignited international outrage. . . .

One thing seemed certain from the moment the bodies of the gorillas were found last July: Poachers had not killed them. Poachers who prey on gorillas leave an unmistakable calling card: They kidnap the infants and cut off the heads and hands of the adults—to be sold on the black market. But these bodies were left to rot where they fell, and the motherless infants left to starve to death.[2]

Notice how the essay speaks of the gorillas in human terms, describing them as members of a family, calling them by name, explaining how an infant was found clinging to her dead mother, and referring to execution-style shootings. Additionally, the magazine cover is a commanding piece of visual rhetoric: it shows a close-up image of a gorilla, eyes staring directly back at the readers with a face much like their own. The essay proceeds to lay out a forensic argument about who was most likely guilty of the "murders."

In the magazine's November 2008 issue, debate emerged about this story. One letter disagreed with the use of term "murder," arguing "the word 'murder' (the unlawful premeditated killing of one human being by another) is and should be reserved for people."[3] The writer worried that not only would the term be redefined, its meaning would be minimized "by equating people to animals," which would further desensitize people to the murder of millions of people in Darfur. Another letter referred to the images of women begging for charcoal that accompanied the original story, and argued: "The plight of these human beings should be our very first concern."[4]

Which author is right? Either what was done to the gorillas constitutes murder and people should feel about and react to it the same way they would to the murder of a human family of seven, or the killing of animals is not murder even though it may be a cause for sadness and a reaction. Which position is most persuasive? Is it murder? Can a nonhuman be murdered? When a gorilla is murdered/killed, what should be the government response? What penalty is appropriate for the murderer/killer?

Many people might rightly say Jenkins and the letter writers all have a right to their own opinions, but that misses the point. You have been exposed to different opinions. Which makes the most sense to you? You cannot accept them both, even if you can see both sides. Either you agree it is murder, or you do not. Arguments require people not only to understand another person's point of view, and that person's reasons for that position, they also require them to choose between competing arguments.

THE PLACE OF ARGUMENT IN A CIVIL SOCIETY

Argument is not something to be avoided. The letter writers did not start a fight by disagreeing or attacking the *National Geographic* article's author. Instead, a reasoned exchange of arguments occurred. Such an exchange is something to encourage. Citizen participation in decision making distinguishes a democracy from all other forms of government. If that distinction is to be more than superficial, and if democracy is to remain vibrant, citizens must be trained in the skills that enable reasoned and reasonable decision making. Influential US political philosopher John Dewey explains:

> [T]he faith of democracy in the role of consultation, of conference, of persuasion, of discussion, in formation of public opinion . . . [is] faith in the capacity of the intelligence of the common man [and woman] to respond with commonsense to the free play of facts and ideas which are secured by effective guarantees of free inquiry, free assembly and free communication . . . [T]he heart and final guarantee of democracy is in free gatherings of neighbors on the street corner to discuss back and forth what is read in the uncensored news of the day, and in gatherings of friends in the living rooms of houses and apartments to converse freely with one another."[5]

Argumentation is a skill central to democracy. Thus, this section offers a definition of argument and an explanation of its role in decision making, then outlines argument as interactive, contingent and, at its best, cooperative.

Argument is a complex concept. It can be defined as *reasoned discourse that seeks to persuade by presenting support for a position.* As discussed in Chapter 1, Aristotle outlined three types of proof for an argument: ethos (proof from the character of the speaker), pathos ("disposing the listener in some way"), and "argument [logos] itself, by showing or seeming to show something."[6] Some have simplistically defined "logos" as "logic." However, the Greek term "logos," like "argument," is complex. Classical rhetoric scholar George Kennedy points out that "logos" can mean "anything that is 'said,' but that can be a word, a sentence, part of speech or of a written work, or a whole speech."[7] "Logos" refers to the content of persuasion, usually the reasoning, but it is a broad concept.

"Argument" refers both to a thing one makes and an exchange in which one engages. Communication scholar Daniel O'Keefe divides argument into two types, describing argument$_1$ as a "kind of utterance" and argument$_2$ "as a particular kind of interaction."[8]

Argument$_1$ is *argument as a thing, the particular speech act in which one presents a claim and provides sufficient reasons to warrant assent to that claim.* Jenkins's story about the gorillas advances a number of arguments$_1$, including the arguments that gorillas were murdered, that there were many suspects, and that the battle over charcoal provoked the attacks. The letters responding to the story also contain examples of argument$_1$, including the arguments that gorillas by definition cannot be murdered because they are not human and that people should be more worried about the refugees than the gorillas.

Argument₂ is *argument as a form of interaction, the way in which arguments-as-things and the people using them interact with each other.* The exchange between the feature story and letters constitutes an argument₂, in which differing points of view are represented and contrasted to one another. At its best, argument₂ highlights areas of agreement just as much as it might represent a disagreement. It can create the conditions where agreement can be reached, not just where disagreement is solidified. For example, these authors could decide that regardless of whether the killing of gorillas rises to the level of the murder of a human, it is still an egregious act that deserves prosecution. As this example demonstrates, argument₁ forms the *basis* on which decisions are made; argument₂ is the *process* through which they are made.

In democratic systems in which members participate in decision making (systems as small as a shared household and as large as a nation-state), argument is indispensable. It provides the means through which the relative benefits and costs of a proposal can be assessed. Roommates may consult each other about whether their pooled resources should be used to buy a stereo or a new outdoor grill. Residents of a city may discuss whether a 1 percent local option sales tax should be assessed to raise funds to improve local schools, as Waterloo, Iowa, did in 1992. Residents of a state may debate about whether to vote for a ballot initiative banning same-sex marriage, as California did in 2008 with Proposition 8. Residents of a nation may argue about whether to ban flag burning. In a representative democracy, such arguments may find their focus in debates conducted by legislators. Extensive debate occurred in Congress in 1989 as part of the decision to pass the "Flag Protection Act."[9] The location of the debate then moved to the Supreme Court, which heard arguments about whether a ban on flag burning was constitutional. The Court ultimately decided such a ban violated the First Amendment and voided the law.[10]

These examples highlight two important themes: (1) arguments are necessarily interactive and (2) all decisions based on argument are necessarily contingent.

First, let us consider how argument is interactive. An exchange of arguments₁ creates argument₂. In the debates over California's Proposition 8, people offered a number of arguments₁. After California's Supreme Court declared unconstitutional Proposition 22 (a 2000 initiative that altered the state Family Code to ban same-sex marriage), people opposed to same-sex marriage proposed an initiative to amend the state constitution to declare: "Only marriage between a man and a woman is valid or recognized in California."[11] Amending the state constitution, proponents of the initiative believed, would block the state Supreme Court from declaring a same-sex marriage ban unconstitutional.

The former Speaker of the US House of Representatives, Newt Gingrich, released a video in support of the initiative. In it, he argued,

> Throughout American history, the people have defeated the threat of judicial tyranny . . . Our courts have an important role to play in our govenment, but it is not their role to define American values. That right

belongs with the people. . . . On November 4, the people can overrule the judges and undo what they did. They can vote yes on Proposition 8 to restore California's long-standing history of protecting marriage. . . . I can't overstate the danger of tyranny from elitist judges who believe they have the right and the power to dictate their values to the American people. . . . keeping the courts in check is one of the most important issues of the 2008 election. It is central to the future of America. On November 4, overrule the judges. Vote yes on Proposition 8 to defend and protect marriage.[12]

Gingrich advanced two arguments in support of Proposition 8. First, he said, it would protect marriage. Second, he argued, a vote for Proposition 8 would check activist judges; and it is the people's duty to resist judicial tyranny. He heightened the importance of this issue by asserting that checking the threat of judicial tyranny was among "the most important issues" in this particular election.

The *Los Angeles Times*, as well as California's nine other largest newspapers, editorialized against the initiative, arguing:

[T]he California Supreme Court overturned Proposition 22 . . . and ruled that marriage was a fundamental right under the state Constitution. As such, it could not be denied to a protected group— in this case, gay and lesbian couples. . . . Proposition 8 seeks to embed wording in the Constitution that would eliminate the fundamental right to same-sex marriage.

It's a rare and drastic step, invoking the constitutional-amendment process to strip people of rights. Yet in California, it can be done with a simple majority vote. All the more reason for voters to weigh carefully what would be wrought by this measure. . . . [T]he very act of denying gay and lesbian couples the right to marry—traditionally the highest legal and societal recognition of a loving commitment—by definition relegates them and their relationships to second-class status, separate and not all that equal.

To be sure, the court overturned Proposition 22, a vote of the people. That is the court's duty when a law is unconstitutional, even if it is exceedingly popular. Civil rights are commonly hard-won, and not the result of widespread consensus. . . . Californians have accused the state Supreme Court of obstructing the people's will on marriage before—in 1948, when it struck down a ban on interracial marriages.

Fundamental rights are exactly that. They should neither wait for popular acceptance, nor be revoked because it is lacking.[13]

The newspaper advanced two arguments in opposition to Proposition 8: First, marriage is a fundamental right for Californians and, hence, cannot be denied to any group. Second, it is the courts' job to protect fundamental rights from the tyranny of the majority.

As citizens of California listened to this interplay of arguments, they were pushed to form their own conclusions about the law. Even though some voters may not have come to a firm conclusion, they still had to cast their vote on November 4, 2008. Decisions often are made before people have attained certainty, but a decision can be reconsidered. Proposition 8 passed, but the debates over it have not ceased. Opponents filed court cases to have the law over-turned. The California Supreme Court heard oral arguments on those cases on March 5, 2009.[14] An additional ballot initiative was also placed in circulation to replace the word "marriage" with the phrase "domestic partnership" throughout California law.[15]

This continuing argument$_2$ illustrates our second point: argument is contingent. Human beings must make decisions and act even when complete information is lacking. People had to vote on the proposition even though debate had not finished. Thus, people make decisions that are contingent, meaning the conclusions depend on the circumstances and information available at a particular point in time, information which necessarily deals in probabilities and not certainties. These decisions are useful for the time being, but if new information arises, or times change, the conclusions people reach through argument may change.

Even when humans believe they possess all possible information, they still lack certainty. Human beings are not perfect and always possess incomplete knowledge. They often only know what is probable, not certain. That is why the goal of argument is not to achieve absolute certainty about what is true, but to resolve what is probably right and, hence, what should be done. New facts can always emerge, general beliefs change; thus, conclusions can shift. Although arguments may be presented in absolute language, the decisions based on them are not necessarily absolute, final, or the only option. The domain of argument is the probable. Still, a decision reached through argument is better than a decision made randomly.

For example, when you considered which college to attend, you used arguments to make that decision. You gathered information from various schools, came up with reasons why each school was better or worse, and came to a decision based on those information-backed reasons. When people asked you why you chose a particular school, you offered reasons, such as: "the university has a good reputation," "the university is the most affordable," "the school has a good program in the area I want to study," or "the location of the college and the programs it offers suit my interests." All these are reasons why you chose the school, and evidence for your claim that a particular school is best for you. Even if you could never be 100 percent certain that you chose the best college, these reasons enabled you to make a decision that is better than one made randomly.

An example of how the conclusions of *all* arguments are contingent, even arguments about facts, can be found in the recent debates over Pluto. First discovered in 1930, Pluto was demoted from planet status in 2006 when the General Assembly of the International Astronomical Union (IAU) voted to accept a definition of "planet" that would exclude Pluto. Neil deGrasse Tyson, an astrophysicist at the American Museum of Natural History and director of the Hayden Planetarium, chronicles Pluto's rise to and fall from planet status.[16] When it was initially discovered, scientists declared the mass of rock and ice to be a planet. It was located where the scientists thought a planet should be, given the orbital path of other planets. However, Pluto was idiosyncratic: it was very small compared to the other planets; its orbit is eccentric (it crosses the orbit of Neptune) and tips more than seventeen degrees from the plane of orbit of other planets in the solar system; and other icy objects share its orbital space. Thus, the claim "Pluto is a planet" was contingent and open to revision as more information became available.

Knowing that even scientific knowledge is contingent, when they planned the new $230-million Rose Center for Earth and Space at the museum, Tyson and other exhibit planners made determinations of the "shelf life of various astrophysical subjects,"[17] in other words, of the degree of reservations attached to various scientific conclusions. Since the Copernican revolution, scientists have possessed a high degree of certainty that the earth revolves around the sun. The exhibit planners were willing to cut such claims into permanent metal displays at the museum,[18] knowing they would have a long shelf life. In the "moderate shelf-life category" resided claims about water on Mars, which were displayed with "replaceable rear-lit transparencies." For knowledge claims with a brief shelf life, the exhibit would show videos that could easily be swapped out.[19]

Given that the subject of argument is the contingent and probable, people need an attitude toward argument that induces a willingness to argue. Just because a conclusion has been reached does not mean it cannot be reconsidered. Thus, the process of argument₂ works best when it is a cooperative, rather than combative, process. People need to want to engage in argument, to test ideas, and to work through disagreements.

Unfortunately, argument seems to have been given a bad rap. If you ask someone "Do you want to have an argument?" the other person would probably look at you as if you were crazy. People tend to view arguments as harmful rather than productive. This view is based on misconceptions about argument. People often understand argument through a structural metaphor, which organizes the concept of argument in terms of war. Linguists George Lakoff and Mark Johnson believe this understanding has implications not only for how people talk about argument, but also how they engage in it, for people "conceive of arguments, and execute them, according to the ARGUMENT IS WAR metaphor because the metaphor is built into the conceptual system of the culture in which you live."[20] People involved in argument perceive themselves "as having something to win and something to lose, territory to establish and territory to defend. In a no-holds barred argument, you attack, defend, counterattack, etc."[21] Even in the most systematic, rational arguments, these parallels between war and argument prevail: "There is still a position to be established and defended, you can win or lose, you have an opponent whose position you attack and try to destroy and whose argument you try to shoot down. If you are completely successful, you can wipe him [or her] out."[22]

Unfortunately, the argument-is-war metaphor works against seeing argument as cooperative. If you think of those with whom you disagree as enemies, your goal is not to communicate with them, but to vanquish them. Concomitantly, they are unlikely to want to talk to you if they are beaten down by the end of every exchange. Argument-is-war induces a worldview in which people who disagree are vicious enemies, opponents are to be vanquished, and the outcome of a dispute is final, without any possibility (or desire) for reliving the fight. For example, is there a person in your life with whom you do not want to argue under any circumstances? That person may not view argument as a way to work through a disagreement, but as a way to emotionally and intellectually beat you down.

Fortunately, argument-is-war is not the only way to view argument. Consider how the way you think about argument would change if you instead used another metaphor: argument-is-play. Viewing argument as play allows you to see how it can be productive and enjoyable. Play is a way in which people learn, cooperate, and experiment. It can be quiet or raucous; a solitary enterprise or a team sport. The outcome is uncertain and the goal is indeterminate, but you'll probably have fun while playing. Just as in play, argument can be a contest with only one winner (as in organized sports) or a form of engagement in which the goal is not to win (as in role-playing or playing house). In play, the goal is not to chase others from the field (or to deter them from even entering the game), but to induce them to join the argument. In play, you do not want to completely defeat your opponent, because you want to play again. The play metaphor represents an attitude adjustment about argument, and can influence the way you engage in the process.

Using the play metaphor, people can frame the argumentative interaction differently. In contrast to a metaphor that uses combat terms, the play metaphor talks about argument in a way that encourages other people to participate. For example, when a difference of ideas occurs during a class, class members can play out an idea to see all its nuances. When a student group is debating what to do, its members can see themselves as all members of the same team, working together to reach a goal.

In a democratic society, participation in argument is essential. Without it, decision making is left in the hands of the few people who are in positions of power. Arguments occur about many topics, with greater or lesser degrees of importance. If the only disagreement that people had with others was about which movie to attend, the world would be a much simpler (and more boring) place, but arguments arise over much graver issues: war and peace, life and death, justice and equality. Aristotle recognized the importance of such topics when he wrote about the subjects of political oratory in his *Rhetoric*. To be equipped to make decisions about these issues, an understanding of argument is essential. The next sections review the parts of an argument₁ and introduce the concept of presumption. The final section explores the various ways in which argument₂, as an interactional process, occurs in various spheres of argument.

CLASSICAL CONCEPTIONS

Aristotle's approach to logic has long influenced argument studies. At the heart was the concept of the **syllogism,** *a statement in which a conclusion is inferred from the truth of two premises.* You may have heard of this process as deductive reasoning, which is composed of a major premise, a minor premise, and a conclusion. In a perfect syllogism, the major premise speaks to a universal truth.

The minor premise speaks to a specific example of the universal. The conclusion is the result of combining the two premises.

> Major premise: All human beings are mortal.
> Minor premise: John is a human being.
> Conclusion: John is mortal.

The conclusion of a formal syllogism is certain only if the premises are certain. Of course, because humans are fallible, virtually no premise can be absolutely certain.

An example of deductive reasoning can be found in congressional arguments that genocide was committed in Darfur, Sudan. In July 2004, the US House of Representatives considered Concurrent Resolution 467 "Declaring Genocide in Darfur, Sudan."[23] The Resolution opened by citing the first three Articles of the 1948 United Nations Convention on the Prevention and Punishment of the Crime of Genocide. In particular, it quoted the definition of genocide in Article 2:

> genocide means any of the following acts committed with the intent to destroy, in whole or in part, a national, ethnical, racial or religious group, as such: (a) killing members of the group; (b) causing serious bodily or mental harm to members of the group; (c) deliberately inflicting on the group conditions of life calculated to bring about its physical destruction in whole or in part; (d) imposing measures intended to prevent births within the group; and (e) forcibly transferring children of the group to another group.

The Resolution then cites evidence that "an estimated 30,000 innocent civilians have been brutally murdered, more than 130,000 people have been forced from their homes and have fled to neighboring Chad, and more than 1,000,000 people have been internally displaced," killing, causing harm, and inflicting destructive life conditions being elements of genocide. The conclusion of the Resolution "declares that the atrocities unfolding in Darfur, Sudan, are genocide." The Resolution passed in the House with a vote of 422-0 and in the Senate by a voice vote. Within a year, President George W. Bush would call the events in Darfur genocide, breaking with the United Nations, which considered the killings to be crimes against humanity but did not think they rose to the level of genocide.[24]

Notice how the Resolution uses deductive reasoning. It begins by establishing a major premise regarding actions that constitute genocide. Next it develops the minor premise by citing specific instances fitting within the definition of genocide. Finally, it concludes that these actions are genocidal. The argument moves from the general major premise, through the instances of the minor premise, to a conclusion.

Aristotle recognized that people typically do not speak in formal syllogisms, especially because human beings rarely can be certain of their premises. Thus, he developed the enthymeme, which he defined as a "rhetorical syllogism."[25] Although much scholarly debate exists over exactly what Aristotle meant by the term, the definition we find most helpful is offered by communication scholar Lloyd Bitzer, who says that an **enthymeme** is *"a syllogism based on probabilities, signs, and examples, whose function is rhetorical persuasion. Its successful construction is accomplished through the joint efforts of the speaker and audience, and this is its essential character."*[26] What most distinguishes the enthymeme is not its form or content, but the process through which it is constructed—jointly by the speaker and the audience. Often the speaker will leave some of the premises unspoken so that the audience fills them in. Bitzer argues the process of co-construction makes the enthymeme extremely persuasive because *"the audience itself helps construct the proofs by which it is persuaded."*[27] The concept of enthymeme also suggests that the distinction between argument$_1$ and argument$_2$ may be too rigid. The making of an argument$_1$ can also be interactive.

Enthymemes are widely used. Advertising slogans, political campaigns, and conversations with friends often rely on enthymemes. People do not systematically lay out every premise, but rely on shared beliefs and values to fill them in. An illustration of how the audience fills in reasoning can help to clarify how enthymemes function. In 1991, Gatorade developed a marketing campaign featuring Michael Jordan, arguably the greatest basketball player of all time. The slogan of the campaign is "Be Like Mike." The commercial features highlights of Jordan playing basketball and drinking Gatorade, interspersed with images of regular people playing basketball, while the "Be Like Mike" jingle plays in the background." The commercial ends with the slogan "Be Like Mike. Drink Gatorade."[28]

Given that the Gatorade marketing campaign was one of the most successful in history, it is reasonable to conclude that many members of the audience complete the reasoning by filling in the principle that, if you mimic the behavior of another person, you become more like that person.[29] The power of the campaign occurs largely because the reasoning is left for the audience to provide. If made explicit, the reasoning becomes suspect. If members of the audience were told that by drinking Gatorade, they would become better basketball players, they would obviously be skeptical. When allowed to fill in the reasoning on their own, they are more likely to accept it.

Enthymemes consistently appear in presidential campaign rhetoric, as candidates tap into beliefs shared by the people they see as their base.[30] During the 2007 primary for the Republican presidential nomination, Mitt Romney's campaign aired a sixty-second spot known as the "Ocean" advertisement.[31] Within the advertisement, Romney voices over the image of waves crashing on a beach as children play on the shoreline. He begins by referring to a *Wall Street Journal* editorial, penned by Reagan speechwriter Peggy Noonan in the wake of the 1999 Columbine shootings, in which she described contemporary culture as "the ocean in which our children swim" and a "culture of death," full of television, radio, magazines, and newspapers that bombard children with images of violence and sex, and said, "The boys who did the killing, the famous

Trench Coat Mafia, inhaled too deep the ocean in which they swam."[32] Extending Noonan's metaphor of ocean, Romney explains he wants to: "clean up the water" where people swim. He also wants to limit Internet pornography, drugs, and violence on TV and in video games. The advertisement concludes with the simple statement: "Mitt Romney. President."[33]

The unspoken part of the enthymeme—the part the audience is asked to fill in—is that any person who wants to clean up the culture should be supported in a bid for the presidency and that Romney is more committed to doing these things than any of the other Republican candidates. The advertisement also relies on the audience to fill in the premise that controlling pornography, drugs, sex, and violence on TV should be one of the primary goals of the president. The spoken part of the argument is that Mitt Romney would like to control pornography, drugs, and violence on TV. The main conclusion (contained in the slogan that ends the advertisement) is: you should vote for Mitt Romney for president of the United States.

The process of arguing can involve a variety of strategies. The central question is: how can you know when you have presented (or heard) a good argument? In order to present a coherent argument₁, you must be able to: (1) provide any parts of the argument for which other people ask or about which they are uncertain, and (2) understand what type of claim you are advancing and what type of data are needed to support that claim.

THE TOULMIN MODEL

Philosopher Stephen Toulmin was troubled by the inadequacy of the syllogism as a model for actual argument in which premises are never certain.[34] For instance, a person may understand the data offered and the conclusion advocated, but not *why* that particular data supports the conclusion. Toulmin believed an explanation of the relationship between the data and the conclusion was needed. He developed a description of argument patterns composed of the following parts: claim, data, warrant, qualifications, backing, and conditions for rebuttal. Based on Toulmin's work, argument scholars Wayne Brockriede and Douglas Ehninger developed a model that we adapt here:[35]

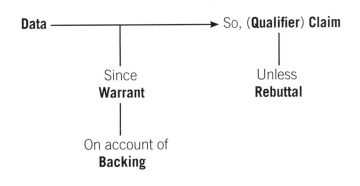

Parts of Argument₁

Toulmin defines the **claim** as *"the conclusion whose merits we are seeking to establish,"*[36] or what the rhetor is trying to persuade the audience to believe. For example, Mark Jenkins, the author of the article about the gorillas, claims "Poachers had not killed them."[37] Because neither he nor the readers were present when the gorillas were killed, he had to provide data for that claim.

Argumentation scholars distinguish between four types of claim: fact, definition, value, and policy. A **claim of fact** is what it sounds like, *a claim that advances an empirically verifiable statement.* Say, for example, Jo shot and killed Sam. In a courtroom, the claim of fact might be: "Jo ended Sam's life." Evidence to support such a claim likely would include Sam's body, the murder weapon, and testimony that Jo was the one to use the weapon against Sam. (Although the claim is called a claim of fact, it is possible that it will be disputed or controversial.)

A **claim of definition** is *a claim that identifies how a concept or term should be defined.* Definitions enable people to make distinctions among things that at first glance might appear quite similar. In the legal realm, various labels and definitions are applied to the act of one person taking the life of another. If Jo shot and killed Sam, the act could be defined as self-defense, manslaughter, first-degree murder, or second-degree murder. Courts establish criteria to determine when an act meets a particular definition, then apply them to the particular act to determine which crime, if any, was committed. For example, when a woman kills a boyfriend or husband who has battered her, it was once considered murder, and often first-degree murder, because her action was premeditated and with intent to cause death. As people better understood domestic abuse and accepted the concept of "battered-wife syndrome," they have come to see women who kill their abusers as acting in self-defense.[38] By definition, what these women did changed from murder to self-defense, although the act was factually the same.

A **claim of value** is *a claim that advances a statement about what is worthy.* A claim of value may be based on arguments about what is good or bad, just or unjust, right or wrong, or beautiful or ugly. Such claims are not empirically verifiable; instead, they are based on the judgments of the audience. People often assume that killing another person is wrong, but in some instances killing another person is generally considered acceptable. If Jo killed Sam in self-defense, it would not be considered wrong. Of course, what constitutes self-defense is not self-evident. The arguments about when taking another life should not be punished are arguments about claims of value.

Finally, a **claim of policy** is *a claim that addresses what should be done.* A claim of policy usually contains the words "should" or "ought to." It is up to legislators to determine what the appropriate punishment should be for each type of crime, although juries and judges have some discretion. For example, "The death penalty should be the punishment for first-degree murder" is a claim of policy. Embedded within a claim of policy is a complex series of related arguments, wherein the arguer establishes that a significant problem exists, the proposed policy can solve the problem, the benefits of the policy outweigh any potential costs, and the policy is necessary given the limits of alternative solutions.

Most extended arguments include all of these types of claims. Distinguishing between types of claims can help you figure out what is really at issue. For example, if you wanted to organize a debate about global warming on your campus, the first thing you would need to figure out is whether you want the debate to be about a question of fact (is human activity the primary cause of global warming?), a question of policy (should the federal government enact higher fuel efficiency standards for autos in order to reduce global warming?), or a claim of value (is stopping global warming more important than preserving our fossil fuel–based economy?).

The example that began this chapter is an illustration of claims of definition, which play a central role in debate. Before you could answer the question of fact, "who murdered the Virunga gorillas?" you would first need to answer the definitional question of whether killing a gorilla is murder. The way claims of definition complicate public debate is also illustrated by the controversy over regulating pornography and obscenity. Before you can debate a question of fact (does viewing pornography encourage men to accept rape myths?), a question of value (is pornography morally wrong?), or a question of policy (should pornography be regulated through civil or criminal law?), you need to first figure out what "pornography" is. Is "pornography" best defined by activist Andrea Dworkin and legal scholar Catharine MacKinnon as "the graphic sexually explicit subordination of women through pictures and/or words,"[39] or by the US Supreme Court as that which "the average person, applying contemporary community standards would find . . . taken as a whole, appeals to prurient interest";[40] or is it just speech like other speech? Depending on how you define the term, you would answer the questions of fact, value, and policy differently.

Toulmin describes **data** as the *"information on which the claim is based."*[41] Data are sometimes referred to as evidence or supporting materials. Jenkins's description of the gorillas provides data to support the claim that poachers were not at fault: infants were left clinging to their dead mothers; and the gorillas' bodies had not been cut up after death.

Supplying incorrect or insufficient data to support a claim is an example of bad argument. Improperly collected statistics, poorly chosen examples, or quotations that are taken out of context are some of the ways in which evidence can be incorrect. For instance, an argument may rely on a public opinion poll, but the statistics summarizing the poll may not be useful if the poll was not properly conducted. Many television news programs conduct call-in polls in which viewers are encouraged to call and vote. The results cannot be generalized to the entire public, because only those people watching that particular news show and sufficiently interested in the topic will participate.[42] The data generated is not necessarily representative of the entire population's opinions.

Someone might also present a bad argument by providing insufficient evidence to justify the claim. When you reason from example, you must provide a sufficient number of examples before you can warrant a generalization.

Almost everyone knows someone who has lived a long life in spite of a less-than-healthy lifestyle. If you were to justify smoking cigarettes and eating a poor diet on the basis of one person, you would be engaging in a hasty generalization. If Jenkins based his claim that poachers had not killed the gorillas on the data that only one of the seven gorillas was left unscathed, he would have provided insufficient data.

The need to guard against accepting a claim supported by insufficient data is demonstrated by social satirist Stephen Colbert's concept of *truthiness*. Selected by *Merriam-Webster's Dictionary* as the Word of the Year 2006, *truthiness* is defined as "1: 'truth that comes from the gut, not books' (Stephen Colbert, Comedy Central's *The Colbert Report*, October 2005) 2: 'the quality of preferring concepts or facts one wishes to be true, rather than concepts or facts known to be true' (American Dialect Society, January 2006)."[43] Colbert explains further: "It used to be, everyone was entitled to their own opinion, but not their own facts. But that's not the case anymore. Facts matter not at all. Perception is everything. It's certainty."[44] Colbert is being humorous, but he is also making a serious point. Too frequently, people jump to conclusions based on an impulsive reaction without researching the facts and sometimes, even despite facts.

To avoid this reliance on unjustified opinion, when presented with a claim, you need to ask: What data support this claim? Simply saying that you "feel" something is true is not sufficient. Why does Jenkins's description of the condition of the dead gorillas serve as data proving poachers were not involved?

Toulmin describes **warrants** as *bridges, or the generalizable "rules" and "principles" that link the data to the claim.*[45] Warrants show that the jump from the data to the conclusion is reasonable, that the conclusion is warranted. Jenkins uses empirical knowledge about poaching to connect his data to his claim: "Poachers who prey on gorillas leave an unmistakable calling card: They kidnap the infants and cut off the heads and hands of the adults—to be sold on the black market."[46] Thus, if the "calling card" was not present, the killers were not poachers.

Toulmin explains warrants are needed because a listener may not understand why the data provides proof of a claim. For example, last summer, John told his spouse, "I need new golf clubs (claim). The grooves on my irons are smooth (data)." To him, that was sufficient. However, his spouse did not understand the connection and asked, "What does that mean?" John then explained the warrant: grooves are what put spin on the golf ball, and the spin is what makes the ball stop on the green. Thus, when the grooves are smooth, it is time to get new clubs. Happily, John got his new golf clubs.

The rhetor provides the warrant by explaining why the data warrants the conclusion. Some warrants, however, are faulty. For example, people often assume that because one thing happened after another, the first thing caused the second. (This assumption is called the *post hoc ergo propter hoc* fallacy.) If you have a superstition, chances are it is based on this error in reasoning. If you claim you always do better on a test if you go to a movie the night before, you probably have based your claim on faulty reasoning. Just because the movie came before the successful test does not mean it caused the successful test. Thus, the warrant "when a thing happens after another, the thing is caused by the event preceding it" is flawed. This mistake is common because it is difficult to distinguish causation from correlation. Correlation is found when two events happen at about the same time, but one does not necessarily cause the other.

For Toulmin, **conditions of rebuttal** indicate *"circumstances in which the general authority of the warrant" should be set aside.*[47] Conditions of rebuttal provide reasons why the argument may not be correct and offer challenges to the data or the strength of the warrant. In the gorilla story, one condition of rebuttal might be that the poachers were interrupted before they could "kidnap" the infant or take the hands and feet. That condition seems unlikely, however, given that the killings happened over many days.

Toulmin defines **qualifiers** as *those statements indicating the "strength conferred by the warrant."*[48] Not all claims have the same level of certainty. The level is often determined by the strength of the conditions of rebuttal. Claims can be qualified with terms such as "usually," "possibly," "likely," "in all probability," "presumably," and "always." Notice that each qualifier represents different levels of certainty.

One of the best examples of using qualifiers in argument is a weather report. Meteorologists make an argument when forecasting tomorrow's weather. They claim the weather will be of a particular type, based on the data from weather stations, models, and radar. Usually, meteorologists will qualify a forecast with a probability; for example, "there is a 50 percent chance of rain tomorrow." We might say: "it will *probably* rain tomorrow." That is a different claim from "it will *certainly* rain tomorrow" (a claim few, if any, meteorologists would ever make).

Jenkins provides no qualifiers in his essay. He does not say: "Poachers probably had not killed the gorillas." Instead, his is an unequivocal statement: "Poachers had not killed them."

Finally, Toulmin describes **backing** as *assurances that the warrants are authoritative and/or current.* The backing says the warrant is supported. Usually, backing will provide an answer to the conditions of rebuttal. Although Jenkins provides no explicit backing for his description of poaching, if pressed he could likely point to studies and past experiences with poaching. In other words, his warrant is based on inductive reasoning, which is based on his accumulated experience of poaching.

In discursive form, an example of an argument₁ that contains all the parts of the Toulmin model would read as follows:

> The Smithsonian American Art Museum displays quilts as art (data),
> so a quilt is a form of art (claim) almost always (qualifier), unless the
> quilt is machine-made (conditions of rebuttal), given the Smithsonian
> Institute is a qualified arbiter of what constitutes art (warrant) because
> it is the nationally endowed museum of the United States (backing).

Just as most arguments are not formal syllogisms, arguments are not usually laid out following Toulmin's pattern. You will have to figure out the components. (As this example demonstrates, rigidly following the Toulmin model results in overly complex sentences.)

What would an argument containing the elements of the Toulmin model look like in prose form? What follows is an argument that Elizabeth Cady Stanton advanced in 1892 in a speech to the Committee of the Judiciary of the United States Congress. Her "Solitude of Self" speech is fascinating because it provides a philosophical foundation for granting women the right to vote.[49] As you read the following passage, which outlines her argument, notice how it fulfills each part of argument Toulmin identifies.

> The strongest reason for giving woman all the opportunities for higher education, for the full development of her faculties, forces of mind and body; for giving her the most enlarged freedom of thought and action; a complete emancipation from all forms of bondage, of custom, dependence, superstition; from all the crippling influences of fear, is the solitude and personal responsibility of her own individual life. The strongest reason why we ask for woman a voice in the government under which she lives; in the religion she is asked to believe; equality in social life, where she is the chief factor; a place in the trades and professions, where she may earn her bread, is because of her birthright to self-sovereignty; because, as an individual, she must rely on herself. No matter how much women prefer to lean, to be protected and supported, nor how much men desire to have them do so, they must make the voyage of life alone, and for safety in an emergency they must know something of the laws of navigation. To guide our own craft, we must be captain, pilot, engineer; with chart and compass to stand at the wheel; to match the wind and waves and know when to take in the sail, and to read the signs in the firmament over all. It matters not whether the solitary voyager is man or woman.[50]

Stanton's argument could be broken down as follows:

> *Qualifier, Claim:* "woman [should be given] all the opportunities for higher education . . . a complete emancipation from . . . all the crippling influences of fear." In this passage, "all . . . most enlarged . . . complete" make clear the claim is unqualified; Stanton does not recognize a less than exhaustive application.
>
> *Data:* "the solitude and personal responsibility of her own individual life"
>
> *Warrant:* each person has a "birthright to self-sovereignty"
>
> *Backing:* "as an individual, she must rely on herself"
>
> *Rebuttal:* Stanton anticipates that someone might argue "women prefer to lean" on men, so she says "No matter how much women prefer to lean" they ought to experience full freedom.

Because Stanton delivered this speech toward the end of her career, after decades of debate on the issue of woman suffrage, it makes sense that she would deliver the argument$_1$ in its most complete form. As people engage in argument$_2$ and are challenged to explain themselves, the various parts of an argument$_1$ are filled in. In other words, argument$_2$ usually is necessary to call forth a complete argument$_1$.

Knowing the parts of an argument$_1$ will help you understand what a person is arguing, become better at constructing an argument, and understand where you disagree with someone. For example, is the disagreement on the level of the data or the warrant? The answer allows you to locate the point of disagreement. Knowing the parts of an argument also helps you critique and analyze an argument. You can understand whether someone is making a warranted argument; that is, you can determine whether a rhetor's claim is supported by data and reasons, or parts of the argument are missing.

This knowledge also will help you understand when people introduce an argument that is irrelevant—that does not speak to the claim, data, or warrant, but introduces an irrelevant issue. For example, *ad hominem* attacks are arguments against the person making the claim that are irrelevant to the claim. The title of Al Franken's 1999 book, *Rush Limbaugh is a Big Fat Idiot*,[51] contains an ad hominem attack. Even if some of Limbaugh's arguments are wrong, Franken cannot demonstrate this by highlighting Limbaugh's girth or by calling him an idiot. If someone attacks you, rather than a part of your argument, you could point out that the attack is irrelevant: your claim is still warranted.

Ad hominem arguments are not always irrelevant. During the 2007 presidential primary campaign, they can be seen not only in verbal comments, but also in multimodal forms, such as YouTube videos. In what is considered the first video to go viral during that campaign, ParkRidge47 (Phillip de Vellis) posted an attack advertisement against Hillary Clinton and supporting Barack Obama, titled "Vote Different."[52] A mashup of the famous "Apple/1984" advertisement,[53] the "Vote Different" video replaces the original advertisement's image of a movie screen, showing a male face speaking to undifferentiated and gray-clad masses, with a screen showing Hillary Clinton's face.[54] In both advertisements, amid the wash of gray, sprints a woman in red and white running shorts and top. At the end of the ad, she flings a sledgehammer at the screen, smashing it and freeing the masses. The original commercial ended with the January launch date of the Macintosh computer and a hint that this is a reason why 1984 will differ from George Orwell's *1984*. The mashup remake ends with a reference to *1984*, then jumps to a simple graphic "BarackObama.com" accompanied by a mashup of the Apple and Obama logos.

The advertisement represents an ad hominem attack insofar as it does not offer an assessment of Hillary Clinton's policies, but instead creates a visual analogy between Clinton and the controlling face and voice of the Orwellian dystopia. The mashup wants you to see Clinton as controlling and dangerous.

When a question of character is at issue, or when arguers claim they should be believed because of their characters (in other words, their characters are what warrants their arguments), ad hominem arguments become relevant. Particularly in contemporary politics, when candidates run on their personalities and images as much as on their political positions, arguments concerning their characters become highly relevant.[55] To the extent that Hillary Clinton's campaign argued she was the better candidate because her experience formed her character as presidential, the advertisement had a point. It argued one could engage in politics as usual, voting for a person perceived to be part of the Washington establishment, or one could "vote different."

A statement that sounds as if it has all of the parts of a complete argument does not necessarily justify assent. It may provide bad data. A warrant may be nonsensical. A qualification may not be strong enough. The connections between the data, claim, and warrant may be weak. Not only must people be able to identify the parts of an argument, they also need to be able to assess the strength of those parts.

Argument Fields

Although a complete argument ought to contain all the component parts outlined by Toulmin, not all arguments sound alike. An argument between friends about what movie to see proceeds differently from an argument in a legislative hearing about what regulations ought to be placed on movies. In a debate between friends, the argument "It's my turn to pick," may be perfectly reasonable, but a legislator who said "It's my turn to have a law passed" would likely be laughed out of the assembly. The idea that the norms and rules of argument change from field to field was introduced most completely by Toulmin. He explains that an **argument field** is *an argument type in which the types of data used and conclusions reached are of the same logical type*. Arguments "come from different fields when the backing or the conclusions in . . . arguments are not of the same logical type."[56] The elements involved in argument (claim, data, warrant, and so on) do not change, regardless of the field in which the argument occurs, but the criteria for examining an argument do vary. As examples of field dependent argument, Toulmin points to argument in the fields of law, marine biology, and mathematics, which are field dependent because they each use different types of data and warrants to support claims. In law, citing previous court decisions as precedent is a central way to provide data, but court decisions would be unpersuasive at a presentation on marine biology. All fields require data and the other parts of the Toulmin model, but what counts as legitimate data, warrants, and so on, varies from field to field.

PRESUMPTION AND BURDEN OF PROOF

Regardless of the type of claim, your argument will not take place in a vacuum. All arguments have claims and data that precede them; thus, audience members are predisposed to believe one side more than the other. Presumption as a concept was developed in 1830 by Richard Whately, Anglican Archbishop of Dublin, in his book *Elements of Rhetoric*. Whately defines **presumption** as *a* *predisposition to believe that a claim is correct until overwhelming evidence proves otherwise.*[57] This definition makes clear that arguments do not occur in a political or social vacuum; instead, as rhetorical scholar Karen Whedbee explains, they are "'grounded' within a context of commonly accepted opinions, practices, and institutions."[58] Whately's view is that the most commonly and widely held ideas deserve presumption and should only be set aside if there is good reason to do so.

The Pluto controversy described earlier contains appeals to presumption, with defenders of Pluto arguing that until exploratory missions had flown to Pluto and "additional factual details" were uncovered, Pluto should remain a planet.[59] One Pluto defender articulated a particularly strong presumption for maintaining Pluto's planet status: "I believe that until we land on Pluto and find incontrovertible evidence that that world does not wish to be called a planet, that we should leave things as they are."[60] Despite substantial evidence that Pluto is not like other planets, Plutophiles argued that overwhelming evidence was necessary to overcome the presumption that Pluto was, indeed, a planet.

Whately also explained the relationship between presumption and the **burden of proof,** or *the obligation to offer reasons sufficient to overcome presumption.* Whately claimed that the burden of proof "lies on the side of him [or her] who would dispute" the claim presumed correct.[61] Burden of proof is an important concept for determining when you should assent to a claim that another person advances. The burden of proof lies on people who support ideas that lack presumption.

People most commonly hear of presumption and burden of proof in relation to courts of law. The accused are "presumed innocent." This does not mean they *are* innocent, or that they are more likely innocent than not. Instead, it means that before anyone concludes the accused is guilty, the prosecution must meet its burden to prove the accused is guilty. Presumption is almost always fixed and unchanging in a criminal court of law. Presumption can be overcome and the burden of proof fulfilled if the prosecution provides evidence proving guilt beyond a reasonable doubt, but it cannot shift (unless there is a defense such as insanity, in which case the defense bears the burden of proving insanity).

In other debates, presumption may not be predetermined. In fact, debate can begin with where presumption rests and who, then, carries the burden of proof. Often, arguers spend time establishing that presumption is on their side, and that if any doubt exists in the audience's mind, the audience should side with them. For example, people who oppose abortion often appeal to presumption about when life begins. In a 1988 speech, then-President Ronald W. Reagan advanced a presumption appeal when he said: "Isn't there enough evidence for even skeptics to admit that those who assert the personhood of the fetus may be right? And if we are to err, shouldn't it be on the side of life?"[62] In other words, President Reagan was arguing that unless overwhelming evidence is presented that proves otherwise, people must assume a fetus is a full person. This appeal does not prove abortion is wrong because the fetus is a person, but instead seeks to sway those who may be uncertain about the fetus's personhood.

Another example of a presumption appeal comes from the debates over the 2003 invasion of Iraq, which was justified by the claim that Saddam Hussein possessed weapons of mass destruction (WMDs). As time passed and no WMDs were found, administration officials were pressured to justify the invasion. On August 5, 2003, Secretary of Defense Donald Rumsfeld held a Pentagon press briefing. When asked why the United States had not yet found the weapons that were the reason for the war, he answered: "as we all know, the absence of evidence is not evidence of absence."[63] This statement clearly located presumption with those who believed Saddam Hussein possessed WMDs. According to Rumsfeld, the burden of proof was not on those who believed weapons existed, but on those who argued that they did not.

SPHERES OF ARGUMENT

Although many arguments in which you engage on a daily basis may be technical (such as the communication in a classroom as you discuss specialized scholarly articles) or personal (such as the interpersonal interactions you have with friends), one purpose of this book is to orient your thinking about communication toward a public sensibility. How can people resolve disagreements about public issues such as global warming, immigration, the war in Iraq, abortion, or desegregation? To understand the dynamics of public argument, it helps to understand the distinctions between the processes of public, personal, and technical argument.

Philosopher Chaïm Perelman emphasizes that arguments are always addressed to an audience.[64] Although people often think of the strength of an argument in terms of how well it will convince a **universal audience,** that is, *an audience composed of all reasonable and competent members of humanity,* the reality is that people address arguments to **particular audiences,** or *actual audiences.*[65] The debate between creationism/intelligent design and evolution provides an example. For scientists, only peer-reviewed scientific data count when determining which theories should be taught; thus, citing evidence from the Bible to explain creation would be unpersuasive to an audience of scientists. In contrast, evidence from the Bible might be sufficient to persuade a religious audience that data from nonscientists pointing to intelligent design should be taught as a theory. In each case, the arguers are addressing particular audiences. Arguments are different according to their audiences and purposes (resolving a technical dispute, working through a personal issue, or developing public policy.)

Communication scholar G. Thomas Goodnight recognizes that the persuasiveness of an argument and the form it takes depend on the sphere of argument in which it occurs.[66] According to Goodnight, **spheres of argument** are *"branches of activity—the grounds upon which arguments are built and the authorities to which arguers appeal."*[67] Goodnight recognizes that what is persuasive depends on the purpose of the argument. To explain how different grounds for argument emerge, Goodnight posits three spheres of argument: personal, technical, and public. He argues that particular warrants and data count differently depending on the sphere in which they are argued.

Think about the last time you and friends were talking. What did you talk about? Music? Your favorite TV show? The newest movie? What a friend should do about a family conflict? You and your friends may have covered a range of topics, from arts to interpersonal relations. It is doubtful that any of you declared another friend incapable of speaking about a topic because s/he was unqualified. The next day, probably no one in your group remembered the specific arguments. Your experience in this instance is an example of the **personal sphere**, *the place where the most informal arguments occur, among a small number of people, involving limited demands for proof, and often about private topics.*

Argument in the personal sphere tends to be ephemeral, meaning it is not preserved. No preparation is required. Many things count as evidence, which is pulled from memory. All topics are open to discussion even if the participants have no special knowledge about them. Expertise is not necessary; anyone can talk on any subject. The test of what constitutes a valid argument in the personal sphere is truthfulness: are the people with whom you disagree honestly representing their beliefs? The time limits imposed probably have nothing to do with the nature of the disagreement, and more to do with when people must leave. Ultimately, the relationships involved do not require agreement among everyone.

Contrast this to the **technical sphere**, *the argument sphere that has explicit rules for argument and is judged by those with specific expertise in the subject.* An example of a technical sphere argument occurs any time medical professionals try to publish their scholarship in a specialized journal such as *Journal of the American Medical Association* or *The Lancet*. Technical arguments are judged by referees, or peer reviewers, who have special expertise in the area being discussed. When the arguments are deemed valuable, they are preserved and published. Other members of the specialized medical community may then join the discussion.

The function of this type of argument is, as Goodnight states, to "advance a special kind of knowledge."[68] It takes special expertise to contribute to a technical dispute. It also takes special expertise to read or understand it. Terms, phrasings, and the complexity of the argument make it relatively inaccessible to anyone not trained in medicine. The argument in a medical essay may be difficult for you to follow because the data being used is unknown to you, or because the warrants were left unstated and you did not know how to provide them.

Another example of technical argument can be found in courts of law. Judges oversee disputes between trained lawyers and must themselves possess special expertise in order to apply the rules of argument fairly. Lawyers must not only have received training, they must also have passed a test (the bar exam) that deemed them competent to practice law. Very specific rules govern who may speak, when they may speak, and what they may say. The proceedings are recorded. Not all evidence counts. (For example, hearsay evidence is usually excluded in criminal cases.) The ultimate authority for determining punishment is the law; a jury may decide a case, but its decision is bound by the rules of law and the judge's instructions. Many times, the test of argument in the technical sphere is truth, either in terms of objective facts or in terms of which claim best approximates people's understanding of the world.

In many ways, the technical and personal spheres of argument represent two extremes. The **public sphere** is *the argument sphere that exists "to handle disagreements transcending personal and technical disputes."*[69] Ultimately, the issue at hand is broader than the needs of a group of friends or of a specialized technical community. For example, arguments about whether the university should raise tuition, a parking ramp is the best way to solve the parking problem downtown, or the local school bond referendum should be passed are all public sphere arguments. Generally, the issues affect a broad range of people and, hence, a broad range of people may speak to them. The demands of proof are not as rigid as in technical argument or as fluid as in personal argument. The test of validity for such an argument tends to be whether it is right, as in "just" (not as in "correct"). People, as members of a community, try to serve the community's interests with public argument and, thus, need to assess whether they can come to agreement about what is the right thing to do.

The Pluto controversy offers an example of the distinction among public, personal, and technical claims. In the February 1999 issue of *Natural History*, Tyson wrote an essay titled "Pluto's Honor." In it, he argued:

> As Citizen Tyson, I feel compelled to defend Pluto's honor. It lives deeply in our twentieth-century culture and consciousness and somehow rounds out the diversity of our family of planets, like the troubled sibling of a large family. Nearly every schoolchild thinks of Pluto as an old friend. And there was always something poetic about being number nine. As Professor Tyson, however, I must vote—with a heavy heart— for demotion. Pluto was always an enigma to teach.[70]

In other words, Tyson recognizes that arguments that might matter in a personal or public sphere (such as public perception, schoolchildren's beliefs, and the poetry of nine) are not relevant in the technical realm, where technical questions of how planets are grouped are the only criteria. Children's sadness at not finding Pluto along with the terrestrial and gas giant planets in the Scales of the Universe exhibit (which portrays the relative size of things in the solar system) simply does not count as relevant data in the debate.

Other scientists also recognized this distinction among argument spheres. In a debate Tyson organized at the American Museum of Natural History on the status of Pluto, Jane Luu, codiscoverer of the first actual Kuiper belt object (the belt in which Pluto resides), argued Pluto was not a planet and made clear that continuing to refer to it as a planet "would only be due to tradition and sentimental reasons. . . . So, in the end, the question goes back to this: Should science be a democratic process, or should logic have something to do with it?"[71] Luu was basically asking: Is this a technical or public sphere debate? Substantial public outcry arose over the IAU's vote to demote Pluto from planet status, but the data used by the scientific community was what mattered. As Tyson explains, "Science is not a democracy. As is often cited (and attributed to Galileo), the stated authority of a thousand is not worth the humble reasoning of a single individual."[72]

Just because an argument belongs in the public sphere does not mean technical arguments are irrelevant. In debates over what individuals and governments should do to combat global warming, technical debates about the causes and rate of warming, as well as about the effectiveness of solutions, play an important role. Other arguments might start in the technical sphere, but become public sphere arguments. Communication scholars Valeria Fabj and Matthew J. Sobnosky explore how HIV/AIDS activists challenged the medical establishment's drug-testing protocol (a technical issue) because it failed to serve public interests. The traditional requirements of double-blind studies to administer placebos to terminal patients seemed to magnify, rather than lessen, the public health crisis of HIV/AIDS.[73] Fabj and Sobnosky argue that public sphere deliberation was enhanced by activists' introduction of a personal and technical issue (individuals get diseases doctors treat) into the public sphere of deliberation. Activists trained themselves in the technical language of medicine so they could persuasively argue that public, and not just technical, concerns should govern drug-testing protocol.

Spheres of argument do not denote locations. The most technical arguments might occur in the most private locations: imagine two doctors debating the best treatment for a patient while in the restroom, or two lawyers having a heated personal discussion, while preparing for court, about where they should eat lunch. Spheres of argument do influence argumentative practices—the norms and rules that govern how the argument ought to proceed and that may influence who is allowed to speak, from what location, and on what topics.

The person, topic, or location does not determine the sphere; instead, the sphere influences who may speak on what topic and in what location.

CONCLUSION

"Argument" refers both to the complex relation of claim, data, warrant, backing, qualifications, and conditions for rebuttal and to the process by which people engage each other in the exchange of reasons. Most important, however, arguments are a central part of communication in a democratic society. The attitude people take into argument influences how they engage in argument. Believing argument is war induces you to treat people with whom you disagree as enemies to be vanquished. This perspective is not conducive to creating an environment that encourages open communication. In contrast, if you conceive of argument as play, you are likely to see debate as a cooperative enterprise. Argument only works in deliberation and judgment if people are willing to change their minds when they hear a sound argument. Interlocutors are not enemies, but fellow humans, vulnerable to the same dangers, injuries, and harms as other humans, and thus deserving of the full measure of respect due to people considered to be friends.

We do not mean to imply that argumentative processes are just play without real consequence. The outcomes of argument have real consequences to which campus project is funded, which job candidate is hired, which political candidate wins, whether or not a country is invaded, and so on. Our objective with this argrument-is-play metaphor is not to suggest the stakes involved in argument are less important, but to heighten our sense of responsibility to the people with whom we argue.

Deliberation, judgment, and decision making—all crucial elements of democracy—require that members of a community be able to explain and justify their positions. Deliberation also requires that people compare and contrast competing arguments so they can make decisions even when faced with incomplete information. Every person makes decisions every day; and it is always better to make a decision based on sound evidence, strong reasoning, and warranted conclusions. When argument is conceived of as a cooperative enterprise in decision making, its utility as a way to resolve differences, rather than magnify them, becomes clear.

You may have found that an argument that works for one audience is not persuasive to another. As you listen to public discussion of a policy, you realize the way that argument progresses is different from the way that you and a friend may resolve a disagreement. Argument is a process: the best argumentative engagements are those in which people engage with each other and are open to persuasion.

We think a good principle for arguing is as follows: you should be as open to persuasion and change as you hope the person with whom you are arguing is. When you walk into an argument$_2$, you should be willing to alter your position in the face of other arguments. The willingness to alter your own position is the basis of democratic government, the First Amendment, and the marketplace of ideas, all of which rely on the assumption that people will make reasoned decisions when presented with information and arguments. As an argument progresses, data is accepted and discarded, warrants are challenged and reinforced, qualifications and reservations are added to claims, and claims are rejected or accepted. Rejection of a claim influences the other arguments$_1$ offered, because that claim may actually function as backing or warrant for other arguments. As particular arguments are abandoned, the argument$_2$, itself, evolves.

DISCUSSION QUESTIONS

1. Read an article advocating a policy, a letter to the editor, or an editorial. Diagram one of the arguments in that essay, identifying as many components of the Toulmin model as you can.
2. Read a newspaper or magazine in which a public policy issue is discussed. Identify places where appeals to presumption are used.
3. Identify a topic about which much debate proceeds. Create examples of the four types of claims (fact, definition, value, policy) that could be made

in relation to that topic. In other words, craft four topics that people could debate, each topic focusing on a different type of claim.

4. Read an article advocating a policy, a letter to the editor, or an editorial. Identify examples of faulty or incomplete arguments. Are the data adequate? Is a warrant unclear? Are the examples too few from which to generalize? Can you construct an argument that advances the same claim, but without faulty reasoning?

RECOMMENDED READINGS

Fabj, Valeria, and Matthew J. Sobnosky. "AIDS Activism and the Rejuvenation of the Public Sphere." *Argumentation and Advocacy* 31 (Spring 1995): 163–184.

Goodnight, G. Thomas. "The Personal, Technical, and Public Spheres of Argument: A Speculative Inquiry into the Art of Public Deliberation." *Argumentation and Advocacy* 18 (Spring 1982): 214–227.

O'Keefe, Daniel J. "Two Concepts of Argument." *Journal of the American Forensic Association* 13 (1977): 121–128.

ENDNOTES

[1] Mark Jenkins, "Who Murdered the Virunga Gorillas," *National Geographic* 214, no. 1 (July 2008): 34–65. The full story is available online at http://ngm.nationalgeographic. com/2008/07/virunga/jenkins-text (accessed October 12, 2011). A video that accompanies the story is available at: http://ngm.nationalgeographic.com/2008/07/virunga/gorillas-video-interactive (accessed October 12, 2011).

[2] Jenkins, "Who Murdered," 39, 45.

[3] Chris Falzon, letter to the editor, *National Geographic* 214, no. 5 (November 2008), 8.

[4] Bryan Berry, letter to the editor, *National Geographic* 214, no. 5 (November 2008), 8.

[5] John Dewey, "Creative Democracy," *1939–1941/Essays, Reviews, and Miscellany*, vol. 14, *John Dewey: The Later Works, 1925–1953* (Carbondale: Southern Illinois University Press, 1988), 227.

[6] Aristotle, *On Rhetoric*, trans. George A. Kennedy (New York: Oxford University Press, 1991), 1.2 [1356a].

[7] George A. Kennedy, *A New History of Classical Rhetoric* (Princeton, NJ: Princeton University Press, 1994), 11.

[8] Daniel J. O'Keefe, "The Concepts of Argument and Arguing," *Advances in Argumentation Theory and Research*, ed. J. Robert Cox and Charles Arthur Willard (Carbondale: Southern Illinois University Press, 1982), 3–23, esp. 3–4, and "Two Concepts of Argument," *Journal of the American Forensic Association* 13 (1977): 121–128.

[9] For examples of the congressional debate, see *The Congressional Record*, September 12, 1989.

[10] *United States v. Eichman*, 496 U.S. 310 (1990).

[11] California Secretary of State, Elections and Voter Information, http://www.sos.ca.gov/elections/bp_11042008_pres_general/prop_8_text_law.pdf (accessed March 18, 2009).

12 Newt Gingrich, "Stop Imperial Judges . . . Support Proposition 8," YouTube, http://www.youtube.com/watch?v=73Q4V8WNF6k (accessed March 19, 2009).

13 "Reneging on a Right" [editorial], *Los Angeles Times*, August 8, 2008, http://www.latimes.com/news/opinion/la-ed-marriage8-2008aug08%2C0%2C1229155.story (accessed March 19, 2009).

14 All the legal briefs and filings concerning this case can be found at the California Supreme Court website: http://www.courtinfo.ca.gov/courts/supreme/highprofile/ prop8.htm (accessed March 19, 2009).

15 Initiative 1356 (09-0003), Substitutes Domestic Partnership for Marriage in California Law, Summary Date: 03/09/09, Circulation Deadline: 08/06/09, Signatures Required: 694,354, http://www.sos.ca.gov/elections/elections_j.htm#circ (accessed March 18, 2009).

16 Neil deGrasse Tyson, *The Pluto Files: The Rise and Fall of America's Favorite Planet*, (New York: Norton, 2009).

17 Tyson, *Pluto*, 63.

18 Tyson, *Pluto*, 64.

19 Tyson, *Pluto*, 64.

20 George Lakoff and Mark Johnson, *Metaphors We Live By* (Chicago: University of Chicago Press, 1980), 63–4.

21 Lakoff and Johnson, *Metaphors*, 62.

22 Lakoff and Johnson, *Metaphors*, 63.

23 US Congress. House., 108th Cong., 2d sess. H. Con. Res. 467.

24 Jim VandeHei, "In Break With U.N., Bush Calls Sudan Killings Genocide," *Washington Post*, June 2, 2005, http://www.washingtonpost.com/wp-dyn/content/article/2005/06/01/AR2005060101725.html (accessed February 22, 2011).

25 Aristotle, *On Rhetoric*, 1.2 [1356].

26 Lloyd F. Bitzer, "Aristotle's Enthymeme Revisited," *Quarterly Journal of Speech* 45, no. 4 (December 1959): 399–408, 408, italics added. See also Thomas M. Conley, "The Enthymeme in Perspective," *Quarterly Journal of Speech* 70 (1984): 168–187.

27 Bitzer, "Aristotle's Enthymeme," 408.

28 The full video is on YouTube at http://www.youtube.com/watch?v=b0AGiq9j_Ak (accessed October 12, 2011).

29 Darren Rovell, *First in Thirst: How Gatorade Turned the Science of Sweat into a Cultural Phenomenon* (New York: AMACOM, 2005).

30 Kathleen Hall Jamieson, Erika Falk, and Susan Sherr, "The Enthymeme Gap in the 1996 Presidential Campaign," *PS: Political Science and Politics* 32, no. 1 (March 1999): 12–16.

31 The spot can be viewed on YouTube, at http://www.youtube.com/watch?v=vFyDWjATbok (accessed November 7, 2007).

32 Peggy Noonan, "The Culture of Death," *Wall Street Journal* (April 22, 1999), http://peggynoonan.com/article.php?article=40 (accessed February 20, 2011).

33 Script for "Ocean," http://www.mittromney.com/News/Press-Releases/Ocean_Ad (accessed November 7, 2007).

34 Stephen Toulmin, *The Uses of Argument* (Cambridge, UK: Cambridge University Press, 1969), 130.

35 Wayne Brockriede and Douglas Ehninger, "Toulmin on Argument: An Interpretation and Application," *Quarterly Journal of Speech* 46, no. 1 (February 1960): 44–53.

36 Toulmin, *The Uses*, 97, italics added.

[37] Jenkins, "Who Murdered," 45.

[38] Lauren K. Fernandez, "Battered Woman Syndrome," *Georgetown Journal of Gender and the Law* 8 (2007): 235–250.

[39] Andrea Dworkin and Catharine A. MacKinnon, *Pornography & Civil Rights: A New Day for Women's Equality* (Minneapolis: Organizing Against Pornography, 1988), 138–139.

[40] U.S. Supreme Court, *Paris Adult Theatre I et al.* (413 U.S. 24) 1973.

[41] Toulmin, *The Uses*, 97, italics added.

[42] Muzzio, Doug, "The Savvy Voter: Analyze a Poll," PBS's *By The People: Election 2004*, http://www.pbs.org/elections/savvyanalyze.html (accessed January 22, 2009).

[43] "Truthiness," Merriam-Webster's Words of the Year 2006, http://www.merriam-webster.com/info/06words.htm (accessed January 22, 2009).

[44] Stephen Colbert, interview by Nathan Rabin, January 25, 2006, http://www.avclub.com/articles/stephen-colbert,13970 (accessed January 22, 2009).

[45] Toulmin, *The Uses*, 98, italics added.

[46] Jenkins, "Who Murdered," 45.

[47] Toulmin, *The Uses*, 101, italics added.

[48] Toulmin, *The Uses*, 101, italics added.

[49] For an analysis of the speech, see Karlyn Kohrs Campbell, "The Humanistic Underpinnings of Feminism: 'The Solitude of Self,'" *Man Cannot Speak for Her*, vol. 1 (New York: Praeger, 1989).

[50] Elizabeth Cady Stanton, "The Solitude of Self," *Man Cannot Speak for Her*, vol. 2, ed. Karlyn Kohrs Campbell (New York: Praeger, 1989), 373.

[51] Al Franken, *Rush Limbaugh Is a Big Fat Idiot* (New York: Dell, 1996).

[52] Chris Cillizza, "Creator of Hillary Attack Ad Speaks," washingtonpost.com Politics Blog, March 30, 2007, http://blog.washingtonpost.com/thefix/2007/03/author_of _hillary_attack_ad_sp.html (accessed November 21, 2007).

[53] "1984 Apple's Macintosh Commercial," YouTube video, http://www.youtube.com/watch?v=OYecfV3ubP8 (accessed November 21, 2007).

[54] "Vote Different," YouTube video, http://www.youtube.com/watch?v=6h3G-lMZxjo (accessed November 21, 2007).

[55] John F. Cragan and Craig W. Cutbirth, "A Revisionist Perspective on Political *Ad Hominem* Argument: A Case Study," *Central States Speech Journal* 35, no. 4 (Winter 1984): 228–237.

[56] Toulmin, *The Uses*, 14, italics added.

[57] Richard Whately, "From *Elements of Rhetoric, The Rhetorical Tradition*," in *The Rhetorical Tradition: Readings from Classical Times to the Present*, ed. Patricia Bizzell and Bruce Herzberg (Boston: Bedford, 1990), 846–847.

[58] Karen Whedbee, "Authority, Freedom and Liberal Judgment: The Presumptions and Presumptuousness of Whately, Mill and Tocqueville," *Quarterly Journal of Speech* 84 (1998): 176.

[59] Julian Kane, quoted in Tyson, *Pluto*, 66.

[60] David Levy, quoted in Tyson, *Pluto*, 100.

[61] Whately, "*Elements*," 847, italics added.

[62] Ronald W. Reagan, *Weekly Compilation of Presidential Documents* (Washington, DC: GAO, 1988), 74.

[63] Donald Rumsfeld, "DoD News Briefing—Secretary Rumsfeld and Gen. Myers," August 5, 2003, United States Department of Defense, http://www.defenselink.mil/transcripts/2003/tr20030805-secdef0525.html (accessed January 13, 2005).

[64] Chaïm Perelman, *The Realm of Rhetoric*, trans. William Kluback (Notre Dame, IN: University of Notre Dame Press, 1982), 9–20.

[65] Perelman, *The Realm*, 14.

[66] G. Thomas Goodnight, "The Personal, Technical, and Public Spheres of Argument: A Speculative Inquiry into the Art of Public Deliberation," *Argumentation and Advocacy* 18 (Spring 1982): 214–227.

[67] Goodnight, "The Personal," 216, italics added.

[68] Goodnight, "The Personal," 219.

[69] Goodnight, "The Personal," 219, italics added.

[70] Neil de Grasse Tyson, "Pluto's Honor," *Natural History* 108, no. 1 (February 1999): 82.

[71] Quoted in Tyson, *Pluto*, 71.

[72] Tyson, *Pluto*, 127.

[73] Valeria Fabj and Matthew J. Sobnosky, "AIDS Activism and the Rejuvenation of the Public Sphere," *Argumentation and Advocacy* 31 (Spring 1995): 163–184.

Chapter 5

Narrative

Key Concepts

character development	personification
comic frame	plot
myth	public memory
narrative	representative anecdote
narrative fidelity	social truth
narrative probability	tragic frame
personal memory	vivacity

If you type the phrase "American dream" into a LexisNexis search of major US and world publications, the phrase appears around one thousand times every six months. The "American dream" is an ideograph that encapsulates a central narrative about the US experience: hard work will lead to success regardless of a person's origins. Drawing on Horatio Alger's nineteenth-century rags-to-riches stories of young men pulling themselves up by their bootstraps, public discourse repeatedly taps into this narrative. In her 1984 address accepting the Democratic nomination for the vice presidency, Geraldine Ferraro said: "Our faith that we can shape a better future is what the American dream is all about. The promise of our country is that the rules are fair. If you work hard and play by the rules, you can earn your share of America's blessings."[1] Ronald W. Reagan's presidential rhetoric also called on the story of the American dream.[2] In his 1986 remarks before he signed a tax reform bill, he explained:

> And what of America's promise of hope and opportunity, that with hard work even the poorest among us can gain the security and happiness that is the due of all Americans? You can't put a price tag on the American dream. That dream is the heart and soul of America; it's the promise that keeps our nation forever good and generous, a model and hope to the world.[3]

In his 2007 presidential campaign, Barack Obama delivered a speech in Bettendorf, Iowa, in which he highlighted US citizens' shared values as defined by the American dream:

> In big cities and small towns; among men and women; young and old; black, white, and brown—Americans share a faith in simple dreams. A job with wages that can support a family. Health care that we can count on and afford. A retirement that is dignified and secure. Education and opportunity for our kids. Common hopes. American dreams.[4]

As these examples demonstrate, although the "American dream" story is called forth often, the story is not always told the same way. Communication scholars Robert C. Rowland and John M. Jones's comparative analysis of Reagan's presidential rhetoric and Obama's 2004 Democratic Convention address explores how the American dream was used to support both conservative and liberal agendas. Reagan focused on a personal agent in a scene of prosperity, while Obama discussed more communitarian values in a scene where limitless possibilities can only be realized in a society committed to the success of everyone.

Narratives are everywhere. Narratives, or stories, inform people's personal lives. Families tell stories about their pasts that affect the ways family members perceive their families. Most people can cite stories from books that have changed the way they live their lives. People who belong to a particular religious tradition possess identities grounded in that tradition's narratives. Christians, for instance, rely on the story of the birth, death, and resurrection of Jesus as the basis of their faith. Buddhists rely on the stories and teachings of Siddhartha Gautama's life.

Narratives also inform public life. Political views are shaped by the stories that politicians tell. People often vote for candidates who have life stories they find particularly appealing. Newspapers, TV news shows, and Internet sites are filled with narratives about the issues and personalities of the day. Often, when people think of stories in the news, they think of gossip about personalities such as Oprah Winfrey, Paris Hilton, Tiger Woods, Angelina Jolie, and Brad Pitt, but those stories are a small fraction of the stories in public discourse. People also tell stories about the effects of inadequate health care on individuals, the Bush administration's decision to wage a war in Iraq, Chilean and Haitian people's response to earthquakes, and the history of the nation. These stories play an important role in framing the way members of the public remember what has happened. Narratives are an important way to understand the world in which people reside.

Quite simply, narratives are rhetorical. In the next section, we describe the form and function of narrative. We then review criteria used to judge narratives: aesthetics, authorial intent, empirical truth, and social truth. Throughout the chapter, we examine narratives at the micro level of the individual story and the macro level of the overarching myth that structures a culture. Our goal is to help you understand how narratives function within all areas of civic life.

FORM AND FUNCTION OF NARRATIVES

Professor of romance languages Gerald Prince defines **narrative** as *"the representation of at least two real or fictive events or situations in a time sequence, neither of which presupposes or entails the other."*[5] As representations, narratives are a form of symbolic action. They are referential, meaning they depict or describe events; they are not the event themselves. Prince's reference to at least two events emphasizes the temporal component of narratives; a story moves across time as events relate to each other. The events do not presuppose or require one another: a causal or logical relationship is not necessary for the two events to exist. Instead, the narrative itself develops the relationship between them.

Obviously, not all communication is narrative. Statements such as "Two plus two equals four" or "A penny saved is a penny earned" fail to meet the definition of narrative. To be a narrative, a rhetorical action must organize people's experiences by identifying relationships among events and across time. Narratives have several important functions, including the formation of memory and the creation of a sense of cultural identity and community.

Forming Memory

Narratives form two types of memory: personal and public. They give people a personal sense of who they are as individuals with a history, as well as a public sense of who they are as members of a community that also has a history.

Personal memory is *the manner in which individuals remember their pasts.* People remember events through the narratives told about them. Individuals recollect events from their daily lives as stories that they keep in their own personal memories or share with others. The ability to remember narratives seems almost innate within humans. Think for a moment about what you did yesterday. The way you remember yesterday's events is most likely a narrative or a series of narratives. As you think about your more distant past, the memories become even more grounded in narratives. What do you remember from your grade school days? Probably all that you remember from that time are narratives: events that happened one day on the playground or on a particularly memorable birthday. However, these memories are based on the narrative you have created about that day. They certainly do not include everything from that day.

The narratives people remember are not mental videos of their pasts. They select which bits of information they will remember. Most people's daily experiences are rapidly forgotten. For instance, can you remember what you ate for lunch one month ago? Probably not—unless it becomes part of a narrative. One coauthor's brother, Mark, often tells the story of an elementary school cafeteria experience—a story of a lunch eaten decades ago, not just a month ago. Mark begins by saying he was in second grade and did not want to eat the school lunch, but the principal told him he must try everything on his plate. He told the principal that he did not like cheese potatoes, but the principal said Mark had to try them. Mark did, and then threw up his lunch. In Mark's story, the cheese potatoes are remembered out of all school lunches because they are incorporated into a story. His account is selective. He does not recall what he did at recess, what he learned at school, or whom he was sitting by in the classroom that day. Mark selectively remembers some of the events of the day because he places them in the context of a narrative. This story is, however, one of Mark's defining days in elementary school. For him, it is important because it says much about his character and his values: he obeyed the principal even when he did not want to do so. Many stories that you remember may tell a great deal about how you view yourself.

Narratives serve as retrospectives.[6] They make sense of events of your life by placing them in relation to one another, thus imbuing them with significance.[7] In rhetoric, narratives tap into what English professor Marshall Grossman describes as "an essential activity of the human mind."[8] Audience members are accustomed to narratives; they remember their own pasts as narratives that they tell to other people, so they understand narrative form easily.

Just as narratives can form and maintain individual memory so, too, can they form and maintain the memory of collectives of people. Collective memory occurs whenever people who compose a group share memories. For instance, the students, alumni, faculty, and surrounding community of a university often participate in retelling stories and developing a collective memory of the place. Students, alumni, and faculty of the University of Kansas can tell the story of why the school's colors are red and blue: Many of the original faculty received degrees from Harvard and Yale. The faculty from Harvard wanted the school color to be the crimson of Harvard. The faculty from Yale wanted it to be the blue of Yale. The story is important to KU students and faculty because it represents the prestigious lineage of the school. Students and faculty develop a collective memory of a university. Employees develop stories that constitute the collective memory of the company. People develop stories of why their community is the way it is.

Stories often provide a sense of positive identity, but not all stories are favorable. For example, part of the collective memory of students at Virginia Tech is the 2007 shooting by Seung-Hui Cho, who killed thirty-two people. Although most students now did not enroll in the school until after 2007, memories of that event still affect their experience as members of the Virginia Tech community.

Public memory is *a particular type of collective memory that combines the memories of the dominant culture and fragments of marginalized groups' memories, and enables a public to make sense of the past, present, and future.* Communication scholar Richard Morris explains that "public memory is perhaps best conceived as an *amalgam* of the current hegemonic bloc's cultural memory and bits and pieces of cultural memory that members of other cultures are able to preserve and protect."[9] Although a particular memory may become dominant (for example, the story of Columbus's arrival in the Americas), bits and pieces of marginalized stories persist and can be used as the basis to challenge the dominant public memory (for example, indigenous people's memories of colonization).

Another example of public memory that is driven by a dominant perspective, yet also contains bits and pieces of marginal memories, can be found by comparing the story told in the 1950 film *The Jackie Robinson Story* and the memorialization of Robinson at the Negro League Baseball Museum in Kansas City, Missouri. In dominant memory, as portrayed in the film, Robinson is an exceptional figure in Major League Baseball, which celebrates Jackie Robinson Day every April 15 and, in 1997, retired his jersey number 42, making it the first number retired from the entirety of a major US sports league. The dominant narrative in the film describes Robinson as an exceptional player who faced severe difficulties while playing in the majors (poor travel conditions, hotels that refused him entry, fans and other players who called him names).

In contrast, the Negro League Baseball Museum does not focus on the story of Robinson in the Major Leagues, or even on Robinson. Instead, it tells the story of Robinson's days as a player in the Negro Leagues, portraying him as an above average, but far from great, player who, like all black players, faced racism, including Jim Crow segregation laws. On the museum website, Robinson is not foregrounded. Instead, visitors can read about all the players, who are listed alphabetically. The first images a visitor sees are of John "Buck" O'Neil, Verdell Mathis, and the Hilldale Giants.

The difference between the two narratives is striking. In the dominant story, the white scene (Major League Baseball) is the dominant scene. The story dominating public memory focuses on the integration of Major League Baseball; the key actor is Robinson; the key event celebrated is the integration of the Major Leagues. In the museum, the African-American scene (the Negro Leagues) is the dominant scene; Robinson is only one figure among many; and the integration of the Major Leagues has a downside: "While this historic event was a key moment in baseball and civil rights history, it prompted the decline of the Negro Leagues," which had become "centerpieces for economic development in many black communities."[10] When Robinson's career is framed by his role in the Negro Leagues, it is a much different story. Through narratives, public memory is formed, but different publics have more or less power to have their version of events remembered.

Narratives are important to the creation of public memory because some narratives are held in common by a society and become the dominant narratives of a culture. They affect the way that members of a culture view the world in which they live, but they are not universally shared. There are variations of the dominant story. Some people may develop a narrative that runs counter to the dominant narrative.

One of the most important narratives for a group is its origin narrative, a story of the moment in which the group was formed. That story provides meaning for the group. In families, wedding anniversaries and birthdays are celebrated. In the United States, people celebrate the Fourth of July as the birthday of the nation. In each of these instances, part of the celebration involves telling an origin story. Fourth of July celebrations include the story of the colonies' small army taking on the superior armies of King George, which suggests to members of the culture that the United States and its people can overcome great difficulties when they work together.

Sociologist Barry Schwartz explains how origin stories function:

the magnetism of social origins resides not simply in their priority and ordering power, but in the *meaning* of this priority and ordering power, as defined by later generations and in light of their own experiences, problems, and needs. While the object of commemoration is usually to be found in the past, the issue which motivates its selection and shaping is always to be found among the concerns of the present.[11]

In other words, a public comes to understand itself in the present by telling stories of its historical past. Such stories form public memory.

In the United States, most citizens know the foundational narratives of the country, including Columbus's 1492 landing in the Americas, the Pilgrims' difficult first winter in 1620, and the 1773 throwing of tea into Boston Harbor to protest British taxation without representation. Many people also know the story of Patrick Henry justifying the Revolutionary War with a speech featuring the line: "Give me liberty or give me death."[12] Schoolchildren still learn stories about Abraham Lincoln, including the story that as a young store clerk, "Honest Abe" walked miles to return a penny to its rightful owner. Many citizens can recite stories of successes in World War II, such as those retold in the 1998 film *Saving Private Ryan* and the 2001 television miniseries *Band of Brothers*. Hollywood tells the story of the success of the 1980 US Olympic ice hockey team, in the 2004 movie *Miracle*. Each of these stories assists in creating US public memory.

Creating Culture and Community

Members of a society understand their nation and their place in it through the stories that are told about it. Political scientist Eloise Buker says that narratives, whether historical or imaginative, help "celebrate our great events, but they also allow us to explore new ways of living together."[13] Narratives create culture and community by teaching cultural values, explaining causality, and entertaining.

Teaching Cultural Values. Dominant narratives imbue a culture with a set of values. For example, people continue to tell stories about the D-Day invasion of Normandy on June 6, 1944. Filmmakers have produced more than twenty movies and documentaries about D-Day. Authors have written numerous books and articles about it. Very few of the books and movies stop with the end of the day. Instead, they move past the events of June 6 in order to give meaning to the day. The official home page of the US Army describes the impact of the invasion: "The D-Day cost was high—more than 9,000 Allied Soldiers were killed or wounded—but more than 100,000 Soldiers began the march across Europe."[14] At the top of the page, the words "Freedom Brotherhood Sacrifice Victory" make clear the lessons of D-Day.

Dominant US culture remembers and retells many stories that provide a basis for its values. Think of the narratives many schoolchildren read and the values that such stories teach. What value is taught in the story of "Honest Abe" returning a penny to its rightful owner? In the stories of the colonists' success in the Revolutionary War and US service members' success in the World Wars?

Even popular culture stories develop values. At the height of the Cold War, the US Olympic ice hockey team became a part of the US success story. The team, primarily comprised of college hockey players who were not good enough to play professionally, defeated the team from the Soviet Union, arguably the greatest Olympic hockey team in history. As the game ended, announcer Al Michaels shouted, "Do you believe in miracles?" Goalie Jim Craig wrapped the

US flag around his shoulders and skated around the rink. The story was told over and over again during the 2010 Olympics in Vancouver. According to the official web site of the Vancouver Olympics, the "Miracle on Ice" is the story of "a match which has acquired mythical status in America as an against-all-odds victory for wide-eyed, optimistic college kids over the iron-willed, passionless Russian sports machine."[15] Regardless of the venue in which the story is told, the lesson remains the same: college kids who believed in the American dream could defeat the greatest hockey team in the world, just as freedom and democracy could defeat communism. Mike Eruzione, who scored the winning goal, told the *Boston Globe*: "It was us against them. It was freedom versus communism. Nobody gave us a hope in hell of winning."[16]

A myth is a particular form of narrative that teaches cultural values as it structures how you think about yourself, other people, and the society. Communication scholar Martha Cooper defines **myth** as "*a dramatic vision that serves to organize everyday experience and give meaning to life.*"[17] According to feminist scholars Sonya Andermahr, Terry Lovell, and Carol Wolkowitz, myths are a dramatic vision because they contain a story of conflict that is not about an actual event, but is "*the imagined past of a culture*"[18] that guides future action. They organize life because they explain people's relations to one another. They justify particular actions and hierarchies. Rhetorical critic V. William Balthrop argues that myths give meaning because they provide a "cultural image of perfection."[19] They enable a culture to visualize and understand what is good or evil, right or wrong.

Yet myths are ethereal; we may not be aware of their presence. They may be taken for granted, as objective reality. If, as anthropologist Clifford Geertz argues, culture is a "system of inherited conceptions expressed in symbolic forms," then myths are one of the central symbolic forms because they "communicate, perpetuate, and develop knowledge about and attitudes toward life."[20] The meanings contained in myths constitute the essence of the culture and represent that which is taken for granted, the point at which one cannot further explain the reasons for an action or a belief.[21]

Myths help people learn values and form beliefs through the dramatic telling of social lessons. They impart an identity to people who identify with the story. Myth is not the only symbolic form that maintains culture, transmits ideology, and structures values, beliefs, and attitudes, but it is a central and distinctly symbolic one. Myth is a narrative form whose power does not rely on truth or falsity, but on its appeal to a sense of social truth.

The melting pot myth (and metaphor) has held particular power in the United States, where citizenship is defined by a series of rights and responsibilities rather than by a particular ethnicity or birthplace. The melting pot myth offers a story to explain who the US people are. It valorizes giving up a person's individual cultural identity for the good of the nation. Citizenship is open to people of all races, but the melting pot myth means that in becoming a US citizen, all vestiges of one's earlier culture melt away.

This story of immigration and assimilation came into general usage in 1908 with the publication of Israel Zangwill's play, *The Melting Pot*. The myth emerged during industrialization, when the form and function of a melting pot were widely understood. A melting pot is a vessel that can withstand extremely high temperatures and not lose its shape, even as its contents are melted into an indistinguishable and fluid mass. When various ores and metals are added to the pot and mixed together, they form a substance stronger than the individual ingredients. The United States was the vessel, impermeable to the high temperatures caused by the pressures of immigration; within the United States, diverse peoples represented the ores and metals that would be fused together into a homogenous and strong mass.

Historian Amy Maria Kenyon describes one particularly telling dramatization of this myth as a ritual enactment of the narrative of citizenship. Henry Ford, the founder of Ford Motor Company and the key developer of modern assembly-line techniques, sought to integrate his workers, many of whom were immigrants, into US culture. In 1914, he instituted English courses, in which the first thing workers learned to say was: "I am a good American." At the end of the course, workers would participate in a "melting pot" ceremony. Historian Robert Lacey provides a vivid description:

> "Across the back of the stage was shown the hull and deck of an ocean steamship at Ellis Island," described one eyewitness to the graduation ceremony. A gangway led down from this ship and, in the dim light, a "picturesque figure" appeared at the top of the gangway, dressed in foreign costume and carrying his possessions wrapped, Dick Whittington–like, in a bundle tied to a stick over his shoulder. It was the first graduate of the after-hours language classes, and one by one the other graduates followed him down the gangway into "an immense cauldron across which was painted the sign *Ford English School Melting Pot.*" Each successful graduate entered the Melting Pot in his foreign costume, carrying a sign indicating the country he had come from. But minutes later they all emerged from the great cauldron "dressed in American clothes, faces eager with the stimulus of new opportunities. . . . Each man carried a small American flag in his hand."[22]

Kenyon describes this myth as creating a "cultural image of perfection": "the melting pot is the 'cooking up' of social identities, a fictional process that closes the circle by constant reference back to utopia, or rather to the myth of the American people as 'colorless' (i.e., white) blend of once-present, but now mercifully absent (albeit nostalgia-laden), manifestations of ethnic difference."[23] When a single myth becomes dominant in a culture, it often defines and delimits that culture. The myth of the melting pot influences definitions of what it means to be American, declares it is the responsibility of immigrants to assimilate, and makes the predominance of white culture seem normal. Even if you do not overtly think of the melting pot, it may influence your attitudes toward and beliefs about immigration.

Implying Causation. Because a narrative relies on a chronological telling of events, the event that happened first is seen to be the cause of later events. Literary theorist Seymour Chatman maintains that all good narratives possess the elements of causality, or at least contingency.[24] If one event in the story did not cause another, then at least the events are related in such a way that they bring into being or evoke a particular situation.[25] Even when a narrative does not explicitly offer causal reasoning, the audience members will supply it as they listen to the story.

A story about the end of the Cold War exemplifies implicit causal reasoning. The National Museum of American History website describes the end of the Cold War this way:

> Throughout the 1980s, the Soviet Union fought an increasingly frustrating war in Afghanistan. At the same time, the Soviet economy faced the continuously escalating costs of the arms race. Dissent at home grew while the stagnant economy faltered under the combined burden. Attempted reforms at home left the Soviet Union unwilling to rebuff challenges to its control in Eastern Europe. During 1989 and 1990, the Berlin Wall came down, borders opened, and free elections ousted Communist regimes everywhere in eastern Europe. In late 1991 the Soviet Union itself dissolved into its component republics. With stunning speed, the Iron Curtain was lifted and the Cold War came to an end.[26]

Note how this narrative provides several sets of events (protracted war in Afghanistan, weakened economy, arms race, and attempted reforms) and implicitly links them to the end of the Cold War. Nowhere in the paragraph are these called "causes," but the suggestive power of the narrative format leads the reader to identify these events as causing the end of the Cold War. This is not to say the suggestion is wrong; indeed, most historians would agree that at least some of these events helped bring the Cold War to an end.

However, the causal relationship identified is not always accurate. The *post hoc ergo propter hoc* fallacy occurs when the reasoning takes the form of "after this therefore because of this." Narratives that imply causation without demonstrating it may well be subject to this criticism. Athletes' superstitions are examples. In baseball, many teams have adapted a rally cap as a superstition. The rally cap varies from team to team, but could involve putting caps on backwards or inside out. When a team is behind late in the game, the players on the bench may put on a rally cap when the team comes up to bat because they have heard stories of other teams wearing rally caps and coming from behind to win. If the team comes from behind, the rally cap is seen as a cause of the comeback. Obviously, the players on the bench wearing rally caps did not have a causal effect on batters hitting the ball, but the superstition is validated by the success. Students of rhetoric should scrutinize the reasons supporting the causal suggestions in the narrative.

Engaging Interest. Narratives are interesting and enjoyable, even when they are about painful events. Even the scariest or saddest narratives rivet audiences' attention because they allow people to learn about the human condition. By hearing about how other people experienced pain and how they responded in the face of overwhelming circumstances, people learn about their own limits and potentials. Holocaust survivors who recount their personal histories are often among the most popular guest speakers on college campuses.

Stories develop imagination and provide new perspectives while enlightening and educating listeners. For example, Upton Sinclair's *The Jungle* offered an exploration of meatpacking practices in the early 1900s. The novel was quite graphic, exploring the gruesome practices and working dangers:

> and as for the other men, who worked in tank-rooms full of steam, and in some of which there were open vats near the level of the floor, their peculiar trouble was that they fell into the vats; and when they were fished out, there was never enough of them left to be worth exhibiting, — sometimes they would be overlooked for days, till all but the bones of them had gone out to the world as Durham's Pure Leaf Lard![27]

Such passages caught the attention of audiences. Readers became interested in the meatpacking industry and its conditions. In part because of Sinclair's novel, the public pushed for greater regulation of the industry.

Listeners find narratives easier to follow than detailed observations or complex reasoning patterns. President Ronald Reagan made storytelling a central part of political rhetoric, consistently integrating narratives into his State of the Union addresses. Political communication scholar Kathleen Hall Jamieson argues that Reagan was not considered "the great communicator" because he was particularly eloquent, but because he understood the medium of television, which was uniquely suited to the use of memorable narratives and visual "vignettes that capture his central claims."[28]

The purpose of the State of the Union address is to "recommend to [Congress's] Consideration such Measures as he [the President] shall judge necessary and expedient."[29] Presidents realize a laundry list of initiatives does little to hold audience attention, so they often incorporate stories of US heroes into their speeches. It has become tradition since Reagan's time to seat the people about whom these stories are told near the First Lady. In his 2008 State of the Union Address, President George W. Bush told the following story:

> Dikembe Mutombo grew up in Africa, amid great poverty and disease. He came to Georgetown University on a scholarship to study medicine—but Coach John Thompson got a look at Dikembe and had a different idea. Dikembe became a star in the NBA, and a citizen of the United States. But he never forgot the land of his birth, or the duty to share his blessings with others. He built a brand new hospital in his old hometown. A friend has said of this good-hearted man: "Mutombo believes that God has given him this opportunity to do great things."

And we are proud to call this son of the Congo a citizen of the United States of America.[30]

Why would this story fit into a State of the Union address? This story, and others like it, can add interest to a speech when a recitation of the facts and explanations of the policy proposals are overly dry. As part of President Bush's claim that US foreign policy is about more than "war and diplomacy," that it also includes service and generosity, he told the story of Dikembe Mutombo. In the preceding paragraphs, he had listed the activities of the US armed forces, the UN, NATO, and detailed dollar amounts of US foreign aid, but his main argument was "The greatest strength we have is the heroic kindness, courage, and self-sacrifice of the American people."[31]

One reason the Mutombo story is engaging is that it adds vivacity and a sense of humanity to Bush's speech. **Vivacity** is *a sense of immediacy or presence created through the use of descriptions, imagery, and colorful language that make an idea come alive.*[32] Narratives with vivacity are more compelling because they are rhetorical acts that engage the imagination of the audience, which, in turn, allows the audience to see the humanity of the characters portrayed. The details in narratives help listeners understand the actions and reactions of the characters.

Another example of vivacity can be found in Holocaust survivor Elie Wiesel's autobiographical book *Night*, originally published in the United States in 1960. Scholars of Holocaust literature maintain that his book is powerful because it humanizes Holocaust victims and helps readers understand the life that people in Nazi concentration camps were forced to live. The book opens with the story of Moishe the Beadle, a poor immigrant who was in the first wave of Jewish people deported from Sighet, Wiesel's hometown. After surviving the Gestapo's mass murder of everyone else on the train, Moishe returned to Sighet. Wiesel's story makes real the suffering that Moishe had witnessed:

> Day after day, night after night, he went from one Jewish house to the next, telling his story and that of Malka, the young girl who lay dying for three days, and that of Tobie, the tailor who begged to die before his sons were killed.
>
> Moishe was not the same. The joy in his eyes was gone. He no longer sang. He no longer mentioned either God or Kabbalah. He spoke only of what he had seen.[33]

The power of this story comes not from statistics about train cars full of Jewish people murdered by the Nazis, but from the detailed telling of one person's story and the effect of witnessing the murders on that one person. The details engage the reader; the reader experiences the horrors of the events Moishe witnessed. The power also comes from the naming of each person—Moishe, Malka, Tobie—which helps personalize the event for the reader.

Narratives form personal and public memory. They create a sense of culture and community by teaching cultural values, implying causation, and engaging an audience. These functions are not neutral. Stories can be extremely entertaining yet contain questionable values, or inform public memory by creating a false causal relationship. Thus, it is important to develop skill in assessing narratives.

JUDGING NARRATIVES

If you are ill, a series of increasingly specialized doctors may conduct a battery of objective scientific tests to determine the cause of your illness. Blood tests, X-rays, MRIs, CT scans, ultrasounds, and biopsies should tell your doctors what ails you, but diagnosis is neither that easy nor that objective. Tests alone cannot tell those who treat you everything they need to know. For this reason, physician Rita Charon forcefully argues, doctors need to develop expertise in listening to their patients' stories. Realizing her medical training had not taught her to listen to her patients' stories, she returned to university to earn her PhD in English. She was convinced medical science had something to learn from the humanities. In her book, *Narrative Medicine*, she proposes that health care providers practice medicine using the "narrative skills of recognizing, absorbing, interpreting, and being moved by the stories of illness."[34]

As Charon explains, narratives have great power to create understanding and knowledge, even in the most scientifically dominated fields. Objective truth is not the only useful currency in human communication. According to Charon:

> A scientifically competent medicine alone cannot help a patient grapple with the loss of health and find meaning in illness and dying. Along with their growing scientific expertise, doctors need the expertise to listen to their patients, to understand as best they can the ordeals of illness, to honor the meanings of their patients' narratives of illness, and to be moved by what they behold so that they can act on their patients' behalf. Nurses and social workers have mastered these skills more fully than have physicians, but all can join in strengthening these capacities in health care.[35]

Charon's insights about the power of narratives compelled Columbia University's College of Physicians and Surgeons to call on her in 2000 to found and direct a Program in Narrative Medicine to "fortif[y] clinical practice with the narrative competence to recognize, absorb, metabolize, interpret, and be moved by the stories of illness."[36] The program seeks to help "doctors, nurses, social workers, and therapists to improve the effectiveness of care by developing the capacity for attention, reflection, representation, and affiliation with patients and colleagues."[37] The power of stories, just stories, to help in the provision of medical care has been so profound, the entire May 2009 issue of the *Journal of Applied Communication Research* devoted itself to narrative medicine.[38]

Excellent medical care and excellent assessment of public policy are not just achieved through skill in reading and interpreting empirical test results, but also through skill in hearing and interpreting narratives. Narratives can and should be judged on several levels: aesthetics, authorial intent, empirical truth, and social truth. Assessing narratives is not a simple process of awarding a thumbs-up or thumbs-down. It is a complex process.

Aesthetics

The narratives most capable of affecting people are typically developed in a particular way. They hold the attention of listeners through two common characteristics: (1) plot and (2) character development.[39]

Plot is *the "chain of causation" of events within a narrative.*[40] Plot is critical because it relates the meaning of the events in the narrative by laying out a story line, or the arc of the story. A good plot captures the audience's attention by providing a mechanism for understanding how the narrator selected the various events and related them to each other. Most narratives rely on a plot that reveals information in a chronological manner and provides the relevance or connectedness of the information as the narrative develops. Sometimes, a plot develops in a way so that the connection of the events may not be understood until the end of the narrative. Some plots use flashbacks, a technique that violates strict chronology, but most unfold chronologically to develop the connections as the story progresses. For example, a presidential candidate's biography video shown at the national convention will probably present a chain of events that makes the candidate seem destined for the presidency.

Character development, a second characteristic of good narratives, is *the process of describing the actions of and relationships among actors within the story.*[41] Characters in narratives should conform to the behaviors that the audience expects. If those behaviors are antithetical to audience expectations, the narrative is likely to be dismissed. Consider the way politicians attempt to portray themselves in political campaigns: they try to develop an image that corresponds to what voters desire. When John Kerry received the presidential nomination and introduced himself to the 2004 Democratic National Convention, he walked to the podium, saluted, and said, "I'm John Kerry and I'm reporting for duty."[42] He portrayed himself as a decorated war veteran ready to lead the nation in a time of war.

During the campaign, a group known as Swift Boat Veterans for Truth contested Kerry's self-portrayal, offering a counternarrative portraying him as a man who did not really deserve the Silver Star he had been awarded for actions during his tour of duty in Vietnam.[43] Much of the 2004 presidential campaign became a contest between these competing narratives.

Characters are often the human beings in the story, but they need not be. Aesop's fables, the *Star Wars* movies, and the Bible all contain numerous nonhuman characters. Nonhuman characters in other narratives include nations and the environment. Even nonhuman characters typically act in ways consistent with human activity, however. This *attribution of human characteristics to nonhuman characters in a narrative* is called **personification.** One primary way personification occurs is through nonhuman characters' use of symbols. In Aesop's fable of the tortoise and hare, the hare laughs when the tortoise challenges him to a race. Obviously, a tortoise cannot speak to a hare, nor can a hare laugh, but personification allows for the teaching of morals in fictional settings that can be applied to people's lives.

Within any narrative, plots and characters may be more or less complex. The complexity is somewhat related to the willingness of the audience to accept the story. People often reject simplistic accounts of complex events. On the evening of September 11, 2001, for example, a five-year-old commented that it was an "unlucky day." In one sense, the child's explanation was perfectly accurate: a day on which two planes had crashed into the two main buildings of the World Trade Center would have to be considered a bad day. But this narrative was not sufficiently complex to satisfy the need of most adults to understand that event. The collapse of the buildings was not the result of random motion (say, an earthquake) but human action.[44] While this is an extreme example, it demonstrates how narratives lacking in complexity may be rejected.

On the other hand, an audience may reject overly complex narratives. Conspiracy theories typically offer complex explanations for events by claiming that people worked together (conspired) to produce them.[45] Such theories seem to defy simpler explanations of events and are thus rejected by the vast majority of people. One conspiracy theory, for example, suggests that Charles Harrelson, father of the actor Woody Harrelson, assassinated President John F. Kennedy.[46] However, for the theory to be true: Charles Harrelson had to be in Dallas, be one of the three tramps found near the grassy knoll, and be one of the tramps pictured despite not strongly resembling the pictures of the tramps; the shot had to come from the grassy knoll; and Lee Harvey Oswald had to have not shot Kennedy. The conspiracy theory quickly becomes difficult to accept because of its overwhelming complexity.

We don't want to sound too much like Goldilocks, but we would suggest that narrators seek to find the "just right" level of plot and character development. Detail in character and plot development is necessary to create vivacity and audience engagement, but adding detail just to entertain may detract from the story's ability to transmit values and memory. It is also important to remember that just because you have told an aesthetically appealing story, you have not necessarily told a *good* story. Issues of truthfulness, truth, and social truth must be considered as well.

Authorial Intent

This judgment standard calls for a critic to determine whether the rhetor intends to make factual claims.[47] Authorial intent is not as easy to determine as it may first seem. Recent debates over the accuracy of memoirs such as James Frey's *A Million Little Pieces* (and whether there is such a thing as a semifictional memoir) highlight the challenges.

Still, we find there is utility in asking: Is the author attempting to tell a story grounded in events that have actually occurred? Critics should begin by determining whether rhetors claim to be reporting facts and which parts of the narrative they claim are factual. Then the audience can assess the narrative's empirical truth. When watching a news story on television, an audience believes the story is based on actual events. For example, during the summer of 2004, Dan Rather of CBS News reported that he had received a fax documenting that George W. Bush's service in the Alabama Air National Guard had been reduced through his father's influence. When Rather reported the story, he intended to report something that had happened, but it became increasingly apparent afterward that the fax had been forged.[48] Rather's story was called into question. Despite his attempts to defend the overall accuracy of the narrative, Rather ultimately stepped down as *CBS Evening News* anchor, partially in response to complaints about the inaccuracy of the facts of his story.

On the other hand, if one were to approach Stephen King about the movie based on his novel *The Shining* and say to him, "Excuse me, Mr. King. But Danny never said 'Red rum. Red rum,'" Stephen King would probably look at you as if you were deranged. The difference between Dan Rather and Stephen King as authors is that one is attempting to base a story on factual events while the other is not. The difficulty occurs when a rhetor mixes the factual and the invented within any given story or speech. When a rhetor attempts to make a factual claim, however, that claim may be judged from an empirical standpoint.

Empirical Truth

What is the relationship between narratives and empirical truth? On one level, audiences should be able to expect that a narrative meant to depict actual events reports the events as accurately as possible. Audiences should ask: did those events really happen? A paradigmatic case of how uncritical acceptance of a compelling personal narrative carries serious risks is the US Congress's acceptance of the October 1990 testimony of Nayirah, a Kuwaiti teen who claimed she witnessed Iraqi soldiers throwing babies out of incubators. Then-President George H. W. Bush repeated the story at least ten times in the weeks following her testimony, significantly contributing to Congress's willingness to go to war. Her story would later be determined to be false. Nayirah was a member of the Kuwaiti royal family; and her testimony was part of a well-funded PR campaign to induce the US government to fight on behalf of Kuwait. In a segment critical of the public relations campaign, *60 Minutes* noted that her powerful story had "mesmerized the nation and the world."[49]

Narratives based on facts, especially historical facts, can teach lessons. The 1986 movie *Hoosiers*, based on factual events, teaches much the same moral as Aesop's fable of the tortoise and the hare. The empirical truth of *Hoosiers* is that a basketball team from one of the smallest towns in Indiana can beat every team in the state if it works hard enough and has enough persistence. The 2007 movie *The Great Debaters* tells a similar story about a group of African-American debaters from Wiley College in Texas who defeated the national championship team from Harvard University by working hard, overcoming incredible racism, and speaking a truth learned not only from books but also from their own personal stories.[50] A song based in reality, such as "8th of November," by Big and Rich, can teach of the horrors and heroism of war. It tells the story of

Niles Harris, a nineteen-year-old boy who left his home in South Dakota to fight in Vietnam and was wounded in a battle in which most of his brothers-in-arms were killed. The song concludes by telling of the physical and emotional scars that Harris, now fifty-six, has carried throughout his life.[51]

A complication to the empirical truth test is that rhetors may be completely truthful, telling events as known through their subjective experience, yet not be telling the empirical truth. For example, witness misidentification in trials is the leading cause of wrongful conviction. Those testifying believe what they say and are trying to do the right thing, yet they still contribute to the incarceration of an innocent person.[52]

A second complication is that it is possible for a narrative to be based entirely on factual statements, and yet for the whole of the narrative to be false. When children, teens, and politicians are suspected of doing things they should not be doing, they often base the narratives explaining their actions on numerous factual statements. How can the narrative then be false? There are two main reasons. First, the narrative can omit significant details in its development. At some point, for example, someone may have asked you, "What did you do last night?" You may have given a complete account. If you omitted some events, the story you told was not exactly false, yet it was certainly not the most accurate account of what you did. Second, the narrative can incorporate the correct events and details, but fashion them in a way that leads to a false inference. For instance, in the early 2000s, debates and media coverage about the war in Iraq focused on the progress (or lack thereof) being made. Some argued that the situation was deteriorating, while others argued that the situation was improving on an almost daily basis. Both sides based their claims on the same facts, but their conclusions were very different.

This example points to an important conclusion about empirical truth. For any given set of facts, incompatible narratives may be created. Most historians recognize that evidence inconsistent with any given narrative will always exist. Philosopher Michael Krausz writes: "Yet, no matter how widely one might cast the evidential net—no matter how richly the evidence may be described—it may still underdetermine any one single interpretation."[53] Krausz's point is that the world is extremely complex. Narratives attempt to simplify that world so it can be understood, but the process of simplification means that any given narrative cannot account for all the empirical facts that might be relevant. Narratives about Christopher Columbus's discovery of the Americas exemplify how incompatible narratives can be based on the same evidence. No one disputes the evidence historians use when discussing Columbus's voyages, but assessments of Columbus vary, viewing him as the "first American" for his willingness to explore,[54] as a genocidal imperialist,[55] or as lucky in that he became famous for being so lost that he thought Cuba was Japan.[56]

Facts never fully determine the validity of a narrative. Incompatible narratives may be derived from the same facts. People may even believe a narrative when they are confronted with evidence that is incompatible with it. At this point, you may fear a form of total relativism in which no narrative can make claims to any type of truth and all narratives are equally true. Such a conclusion would be incorrect. In judging competing narratives, says historian Peter Stansky, a historian must "take all the available 'facts,' which are often contradictory, and judge which interpretation [or narrative] of them may seem the most [right and] 'truthful.'"[57] The same is true of audiences.

To say that many narratives are possible is not the same as claiming that every possible narrative is equally correct, nor that every possible narrative must be considered. Sometimes, writes historiographer Donald Spence, narratives are "just plain wrong."[58] Some, however, contain social truth. Narratives supporting the existence of the Easter Bunny, Santa Claus, and the Tooth Fairy lack an empirical basis. Most people over the age of ten know that they are just plain false, but the stories persist because of the social truths they possess. Young children who insist on the existence of Santa, the Easter Bunny, and the Tooth Fairy are being truthful.

One might argue that we should only believe stories if they are empirically true; if the events recounted in the story actually happened, in the order told; and if the actions were done by the people to whom they were attributed. This is the standard to which histories are held, but empirical truth as a standard for all stories, imaginative and historical, is not enough.

Social Truth

The relationship between narratives and truth is complex. Historians, literary critics, philosophers, and rhetoricians have argued about the connection between narratives and truth at least since the time of Aristotle. Mark Twain explained the relationship between imaginative fictional stories and historical stories: "Truth is stranger than fiction, but it is because Fiction is obliged to possibilities; Truth isn't."[59] Twain's point is that fictional stories must be consistent with listeners' expectations of the way the world works. By conforming to expectations, fictional narratives can be quite effective and speak to social, if not empirical, truths. Sinclair's *The Jungle* had a profound impact on readers. Aesop's fables teach audiences specific moral lessons.

The complexity of narratives lies in the different types of truth claims that they can advance. German sociologist Jürgen Habermas identified claims that can be made about three worlds: the objective world, the subjective world, and the intersubjective world. The test of the validity of a claim about the objective world is truth: can the claim be empirically verified? The test of a claim about the subjective world is truthfulness: does the person making the claim believe it to be true? The test of a claim about the intersubjective world is rightness: can reasonable people, through communication, reach agreement about what is right?[60]

We use the concept of **social truth** to refer to *those beliefs and values that do not refer to some objective reality, but to social reality—those beliefs about what is right that people have arrived at together.* An example of a social truth is that liberty is one of the US's highest values; that it is guaranteed and should be preserved. The Declaration of Independence declares "life, liberty, and the pursuit of happiness" are "unalienable rights." The story behind this declaration is that a creator endowed people with the right to liberty. The value of liberty is a social truth because it cannot be empirically proven or demonstrated. In fact, cultures that are more collectivist in nature are less likely to value liberty. The value of liberty is established primarily through communication, including the stories told within the culture that help to establish that value. Through communication, people can reach an intersubjective idea (neither fixed and objective, nor totally random or completely subjective) of what is right. The nature of that intersubjective social truth is complex.

Narratives play an important role in the formation of memory and values. The social truth of a narrative does not necessarily lie in the objective *truth* of the individual statements that compose the narrative, but in the *meaning* of the story. Professor of moral philosophy Jonathan L. Gorman notes: "Plots have a truth, but it is not a scientific one;" it is "not a truth about the subject the plot purports to be about."[61]

Examples of fictive narratives that teach social truth abound. The parables of the New Testament are not usually taken as historical events, even by many Christians who believe the Bible is the literal word of God. Jesus introduced or concluded some of the parables with the statement: "He who has ears to hear, let him hear."[62] His point was that the parables were stories whose truths would only be understood by believers. Many of the parables are understood as illustrative stories that teach the social truth about heaven even though their settings were the present locations of the listeners.[63] Aesop's fables are another example of fictive narratives. Animals do not really talk; hares and tortoises do not really race; foxes do not really reject unreachable grapes as sour; and wolves do not really don sheep's clothing; but the fables teach lessons such as "slow and steady wins the race" or "appearances are deceptive."

The narratives in popular music also often contain a type of truth even when the story is not based on empirical events. For instance, the Dixie Chicks' "Travelin' Soldier" tells the story of a high school band member who fell in love with a young man about to be deployed to Vietnam. He went to war and was killed. The song concludes with the young woman under the stands at a high school football game while her band is on the field and the public address announcer calls for a moment of silence for the young man.[64] The song is fictive, but it teaches an important lesson about the personal losses of war. It is a story about Vietnam, but the Dixie Chicks likely meant for it to speak to the losses of all wars.

As these examples show, the traditional distinction between fiction and nonfiction (or between historical and imaginative) stories is too simple. In fact, the relationship between the two is highly complex. Scholars of narrative typically maintain that fiction actually must be truer than nonfiction, in the sense that the events must be believable. Nonfiction, on the other hand, ultimately resorts to the claim that the events actually happened. If someone had created a fictive narrative a few years ago of a man who was born of a Kenyan father and a Kansan mother, grew up in Hawaii and Indonesia, went to college at Columbia and Harvard, was elected to the Senate from Illinois in 2004, was elected president of the United States in 2008, and won the Nobel Peace Prize in 2009, most people would have concluded that the story was fanciful and rejected it out of hand. However, these events comprise a portion of the narrative of Barack Obama.

Fictive narratives can be socially true, and stories based in facts always have elements of fiction because of the artistry inherent in the creation of stories: the rhetor creates the story. The events recounted in narratives have no necessary starting or ending point; narrators select the beginning and ending points according to the ideas they are trying to communicate. In addition, the rhetor determines what counts as facts.

A simple way to understand all this is to talk to fans of opposing sports teams after a game. Although the final score of the game may seem objectively true, listen to the various descriptions of the game. After the 2006 Super Bowl, Seattle Seahawks fans constructed a narrative in which bad calls of the referees, not the opposing team's superior play, determined the outcome of the game. Their team did not lose the game (despite what the score and their bare ring fingers might indicate). Instead, the referees stole the championships from them. This narrative began with a seemingly bad call in the first quarter of the Super Bowl and concluded with another questionable call early in the third quarter. After the same game, Pittsburgh Steelers fans constructed a narrative that claimed the Steelers overcame all adversity to win the Super Bowl. The Seahawks did not lose the game; the Steelers team won it. This narrative began with the Steelers's place as the sixth seed in the AFC playoffs and ended only with the Super Bowl parade. Both narratives are grounded in the same set of events, but the narrators select different events and interpret the same events in different ways. Even what counts as the key plays of the game differs in the narratives.

Another example of competing narratives grounded in the same set of historical events is the debate over the effect of the New Deal in the 1930s. Looking at the same set of historical events, narratives differ about the impact of President Franklin Delano Roosevelt's policies on the economy. Traditionally, historians have held that the New Deal stimulated the economy. William Edward Leuchtenburg, in his famous treatise on the New Deal, argues that FDR's decisive policies ended the Great Depression.[65] Historian Burton W. Folsom, Jr., however, argues that the New Deal actually exacerbated it.[66] Both narratives are grounded in historical evidence, but each emphasizes different aspects of the historical record. Readers must evaluate each narrative on the basis of the historical evidence, plot, and character development it presents.

A narrator tells the audience which events are important by placing them within the structure of a narrative and omitting those considered irrelevant. The narrator also helps direct the understanding of the events, by ordering and structuring them.

Sophisticated audiences evaluate the narratives they hear. As we discussed when we talked about social truth, audiences must be able to do two things. First, they must be able to assess which narratives are just plain wrong. Second, they must be able to employ standards that will assist them in determining which narratives are better, even in the face of multiple, incompatible narratives, all of which could be plausible.

Several aspects of narratives can help us assess their social truth claims. These aspects are not intended to be considered in evaluating the empirical or factual claims of the narrative, only in evaluating the social truth claims. They include narrative fidelity and narrative probability, the representative anecdote, and the comic frame.

Narrative Fidelity and Narrative Probability. These aspects of narratives are derived from rhetorical critic and theorist Walter Fisher's writing on the narrative paradigm. Fisher developed two standards for evaluating narratives: narrative fidelity and narrative probability. **Narrative fidelity** asks *whether the events included in the story correspond to the experiences and understanding of reality of the audience.*[67] This standard focuses on the external consistency of the story by asking people to look at "whether the stories they experience ring true with the stories they know to be true in their lives."[68] **Narrative probability** asks *the question "what constitutes a coherent story?"*[69] *or, more simply, does the story hang together?* This standard focuses on the internal consistency of the story, requiring people to look at the development of characters and plot, and asking whether the characters react the way we would expect people to react. Narrative probability and fidelity can be used to judge both fiction and nonfiction. Fisher writes, "Formal features are attributes of narrative probability: the consistency of characters and actions, the accommodation of auditors, and so on."[70]

A narrative should have both narrative fidelity and narrative probability, but it may have one of the two and lack the other, or it may lack both. Such narratives are relatively common. For example, if a student tells a story insisting s/he turned in a twenty-page research paper, a professor might not believe the story. It might lack fidelity because the student claims to have turned the paper in on a day when s/he was absent. It might lack probability because the student claims both to have spent the three hours immediately before class finishing the paper and to have not missed class because s/he attended another class in the adjacent room immediately before the professor's class. The coherence of the story is called into question because the student could not both be in a classroom and working on the paper at the same time. The professor doesn't know whether the student turned in the paper, but the story is so suspect the professor has no reason to believe it.

Certain types of narratives are, perhaps, more likely to exhibit strengths in either narrative fidelity or narrative probability than others. Narratives of trauma survivors, for instance, sometimes lack narrative probability (they might lack internal consistency because trauma, by definition, is unusual and extraordinary) while having a great deal of narrative fidelity (they report what actually happened). For example, one author of this book was once in a very bad van accident. His story about the accident is that he was sleeping, felt the van swerve, woke up, asked what was happening, was told a deer had run in front of the van, turned in his seat, and went back to sleep before being thrown from the van. Given the speed at which the accident happened, it does not seem likely that all those events took place in those few short seconds. The story lacked narrative probability, but the injuries and destroyed van give it narrative fidelity.

A story may be true and yet lack narrative fidelity. Invisible Children is an organization seeking to "end the use of child soldiers in Joseph Kony's rebel war and restore Northern Uganda to peace and prosperity."[71] One difficulty the organization faces is that the stories of children being abducted and forced to serve as soldiers, while empirically true, lack narrative fidelity for many people in the United States, who find it difficult to understand that anyone would force children to fight to the death in a war. Consequently, Invisible Children has relied on activism, peaceful protests including sit-ins, and videos. The videos, in particular, present stories with strong narrative probability.

Representative Anecdotes. A **representative anecdote** is *a narrative that summarizes a person, thing, or situation.* The concept, as developed by Kenneth Burke, helps critics better understand the appropriateness of the narrative.[72] If a narrative claims to speak to a social truth, then it should be representative of the social truth. Burke developed his notion of the representative anecdote as a response to the behaviorist argument, which dominated the first half of the twentieth century, that the world—even human behavior, as complex as it is—could eventually be understood through science and mathematics. Burke rejected such notions. His discussion of the representative anecdote borrows some of the language of the social sciences, but he redefines those terms for his own uses. Social scientists use the term "representative," for instance, to discuss how a sample should be drawn from a population. Burke writes of a representative anecdote: *"It must have scope. Yet it must also possess simplicity; in that it is broadly a reduction of the subject-matter."*[73] For Burke, the issue was not whether the anecdote was a statistically representative sample; rather, he believed that a single powerful anecdote could represent a complex human experience.

The representative anecdote is not subject to the tests of statistics and the social sciences. Rather than examining, for instance, the statistical accuracy of the sample, Burke argues that an appropriate representative anecdote will contain, in a nutshell, the essence of the item being represented. One way to think of Burke's representative anecdote is to think of your family or the household in which you grew up. If someone were to ask you about the way you were raised or your family life, you might tell a story that would summarize or encapsulate your experiences. You would not tell your entire life history, but you might pick a moment from when you were five years old, or ten, or fifteen, that would represent all that you are. It would not be representative from a social scientific perspective—indeed, the story might be about an atypical and unrepeated moment or event—but it would demonstrate to the listener the essence of your childhood.

This notion of the representative anecdote leads to two important ideas. First, the narrative must be relevant to the point being made. Sometimes, rhetors tell stories that are inherently interesting but do not relate to the point being made. Second, the narrative must capture or summarize the most important aspects of the subject it is meant to represent, even though it may not be typical of that subject. For instance, during the presidency of George W. Bush, *Late Show* host David Letterman had a recurring segment called "Great Moments in Presidential Speeches," in which he showed short video clips of Bush mis-pronouncing words.[74] These clips were not typical of Bush's speech; he said most words correctly. Still, the clips were intended to summarize Bush's public speaking skills in a way that a statistical analysis could not.

Burke's conception of the representative anecdote suggests that one way to test a narrative is by determining whether the narrative is representative. When Letterman showed those clips, he was claiming that they were representative of Bush's communication, regardless of how frequent the misstatements happened. When you are assessing public rhetoric, it is important to determine the repre-sentativeness of the narrative.

Comic and Tragic Frames. The final aspect of narrative that is useful in assessing its social truth claims is its frame or narrative worldview. We turn to Kenneth Burke's description of tragic and comic frames.[75] In general, a **comic frame** is *a viewpoint that would have you see others as mistaken rather than as evil*. If a person does something you perceive as wrong, then the solution is not to destroy the person, but to correct her or him. As part of recognizing the inherent falli-bility of humanity, a comic frame would also induce you to ask whether you are as mistaken as those with whom you disagree. The comic orientation ultimately asks for humility, not in the face of some higher power, but in the face of the human condition.

In contrast, the **tragic frame** is *a viewpoint that would have you see others as vicious and evil rather than as mistaken*. Because "evil" implies that a person has an inherent defect, correction is not possible as a solution. Destruction is the only solution to a wrong action, the only way to rid the world of evil. The tragic frame also induces humility, but only because if you become too arrogant, a higher power will put you in your place. As Burke explains, the tragic "frame of acceptance admonished one to 'resign' himself [or herself] to a sense of his [or her] limitations."[76]

Imagine, for example, that a friend passes you in the hallway but does not say "Hi." With friends, people tend to operate in a comic frame, creating a story to explain the event that assumes the best of them. You might construct a story containing the explanation that your friend was probably having a bad day, or was really busy and may not have seen you. Your friend did not intentionally snub you, but instead just made a mistake, a mistake you are just as likely to make in similar circumstances. In contrast, imagine that someone you do not really like passes you in the hallway and does not say "Hi." In this case, you might operate in a tragic frame and construct a story that attributes pernicious motives to the person. You might conclude that the person was being rude, snubbed you, intentionally ignored you, or was just being vicious. Your story assumes the worst of the person, even though the action was the same as your friend's. The point of the comic frame is to induce you to give people the benefit of the doubt, to think about the reasons they might take actions and not immediately attribute mali-cious motives to them. As Burke explains: "Like tragedy, comedy warns against the dangers of pride, but its emphasis shifts from *crime* to *stupidity*."[77]

In a passage that highlights the differences between meanings, attitude, and character in the comic and tragic frames, Burke concludes that a comic frame offers the most humane equipment for living: "The progress of humane enlightenment can go no further than in picturing people not as *vicious*, but as *mistaken*. When you add that people are *necessarily* mistaken, . . . you complete the comic circle, returning again to the lesson of humility that underlies great tragedy."[78] The comic frame is preferable because it "should enable people *to be observers of themselves, while acting*. Its ultimate would not be *passiveness*, but *maximum consciousness*. One would 'transcend' himself [or herself] by noting his [or her] own foibles."[79] In other words, a key characteristic of the comic frame is self-reflexivity, meaning that you would turn whatever criticism you lodge against someone else back against yourself to see how you engage in the same action or whether you had contributed to the other person's mistaken deeds.

Even though the comic frame might sound as though it involves frivolity or comedy, that is not the case. Do not think of the comic as less serious than the tragic. Religious studies professor John Morreall explains: "Comedy is not 'time out' from the world; rather it provides another perspective on the world, a perspective no less true than the tragic perspective."[80] Frames structure responses to events in the world. If you operate in the tragic frame, you would tend to construct stories about evil, which must be destroyed. If you operate in the comic frame, you tend to construct stories of mistakes from which everyone can learn. In a comic frame, disagreement is a sign that someone is mistaken, and you are just as likely as the other person to be mistaken. In a tragic frame, a disagreement is usually seen as evidence that another person is being vicious, if not evil. As Burke constantly reminds us, a name for something often contains within it an attitude toward that thing and, thus, also contains "cues of behavior."[81] Thus, it makes sense that how you name someone else is influenced by your frame, and that the name influences the actions toward the other person. As Burke explains, "Call a man [or woman] a villain, and you have the choice of either attacking or cringing. Call him [or her] mistaken, and you invite yourself to attempt setting him [or her] right. Contemporary exasperations make us prefer the tragic (sometimes melodramatic) names of 'villain' and 'hero' to the comic names of 'tricked' and 'intelligent.'"[82]

When Burke was writing, "contemporary" meant 1937. The preceding years had seen the United States emerging from the Great Depression; Japan leaving the League of Nations; Adolf Hitler coming to power in Germany, stripping German Jews of their citizenship rights, and creating with Mussolini the Rome-Berlin Axis; Italy invading Abyssinia (Ethiopia); the Spanish Civil War breaking out; and the abdication crisis rocking Great Britain. Still, Burke's comment remains apt over seventy years later.

The 1990s and 2000s saw a host of events that appear to be the handiwork of villains and that are often rhetorically presented as evidence of evil in the world. In US public discourse, "evil" was invoked to describe the two students who on April 20, 1999, killed twelve other students and one teacher at Columbine High School before committing suicide. News stories referred to "Columbine Evil Revisited."[83] One *New York Times* editorial concluded: "Columbine . . . was about evil."[84] The connection between school shootings and evil was revisited after the April 16, 2007, shootings at Virginia Tech, in which the shooter killed thirty-two people before committing suicide. Columnist Cal Thomas remarked, "My prayers are with the Virginia Tech community that had this evil unleashed upon them."[85]

Most recently, rhetoric about the war on terror has caused communication scholars to consider the invocation of evil. President George W. Bush's speech on the evening of September 11, 2001, described the acts of that day as evil, declaring: "Thousands of lives were suddenly ended by evil, despicable acts of terror. . . . Today our nation saw evil, the very worst of human nature. . . . The search is underway for those who were behind these evil acts."[86] From that evening on, every speech he gave about the events of September 11 would refer to "evil." Not only would the term "evil" be used to describe the actions (as in "evil, despicable acts of terror"), evil itself would become an entity. In his address from the Cabinet Room on September 12, Bush concluded, "This will be a monumental struggle of good versus evil, but good will prevail."[87] In his remarks on September 14, during a National Day of Prayer and Remembrance ceremony, he used the tragic frame, making clear that evil cannot be corrected, but must be obliterated: "Our responsibility to history is already clear: to answer these attacks and rid the world of evil."[88] He would eventually expand the descriptor of "evil" to apply to more than those who perpetrated 9/11. In his January 2002 State of the Union address, he declared that the countries of Iran, Iraq, and North Korea "constitute an axis of evil." Toward the conclusion of his speech, he declared: "We've come to know truths that we will never question: evil is real, and it must be opposed."[89]

Despite Bush's invocation of evil as a verifiable fact, the reality is that "evil" is an evaluative word, not a statement of fact.[90] A number of political science and communication scholars have offered commentary on Bush's use of the word. Journals in political science, such as *International Affairs*, and communication studies, such as *Rhetoric and Public Affairs*, published special issues exploring "how 'evil' is produced, deployed, used, and misused in public discourse."[91]

Discussions of the decision to launch the war in Iraq based on the belief that Iraq possessed weapons of mass destruction (WMDs) also provide an example of tragic and comic plot lines. Ultimately, no WMDs were found in Iraq.[92] Some commentators frame the decision to enter the war tragically. They maintain that the intelligence was intentionally manipulated to allow the Bush Administration to lead the US into war.[93] Other commentators place the decision in a comic frame, suggesting that the decision to attack Iraq was based on mistaken intelligence.[94] Burke would suggest that, in most cases, the comic frame of acceptance is superior because of the willingness to admit mistakes and acknowledge the humanity of the people on the other side of the issue.

Our point here is not that there are no tragedies. Tragedies do happen, in part because people operate in a tragic frame. Even in the face of tragedy, however, a comic frame may be more humane. When an act of violence occurs, do not assume that locking up the person who committed it will end all violence.

Instead, ask: what have I done to contribute to a world in which tragedies occur; and how can I change the world—the social structures, the culture, the rhetorical formations—so that such acts are less likely to happen again?

CONCLUSION

Narrative, in the most basic sense, is the placement of two or more events in a time sequence. The human instinct to structure thinking and communication sequentially has several ramifications for rhetoric. The narrative structure leads audiences to perceive causation, helps them to remember, and entertains them. Sometimes, because these functions of narratives are so powerful, audiences are more susceptible to accepting narratives that are wrong, in either the factual or ethical sense.

It is vital for members of an audience to understand the human side of the narrative by participating with the characters of the story, and to understand what the narrative is teaching about the nature of living through its character development and structure. As a member of an audience, however, you also must remain vigilant in applying the standards for evaluating narratives.

Narratives, the stories people tell each other, are central to civic life. They maintain public memory and teach cultural values. They are part of the warp and woof that holds the fabric of civic life together. They help place people in relation to one another, and to the history of the group, the nation, and the culture.

DISCUSSION QUESTIONS

1. List the things you did or that happened to you yesterday. Then tell a story that includes all those events, but not in the order in which they happened. Then ask whether the listener thinks one thing you did caused another.
2. Identify a story that members of your family tell over and over. Why is that story repeated? What does it tell you about your family's values?
3. Novels and songs often tell narratives that affect people's lives and values. Identify a novel or song that has affected you. Why did it have such an effect on you?
4. People often describe commercial TV news coverage and newspaper articles as "stories." Given the definition of narrative in this chapter, are such things stories? Why?
5. What does the melting pot mean to you? Has a different myth begun to replace it?

RECOMMENDED READINGS

Braden, Waldo W. "Myths in Rhetorical Context." *The Southern Speech Communication Journal* 40 (Winter 1975): 113–126.
Fisher, Walter R. "Narration as a Human Communication Paradigm: The Case of Public Moral Argument." *Communication Monographs* 51 (1984): 1–22.

Rowland, Robert C., and Kirsten Theye. "The Symbolic DNA of Terrorism." *Communication Monographs* 75, no. 1 (March 2008), 52–85.

ENDNOTES

[1] Geraldine Ferraro, "Vice Presidential Nomination Acceptance Address," July 19, 1984, http://www.americanrhetoric.com/speeches/gferraroacceptanceaddress.html (accessed May 12, 2009).

[2] Robert C. Rowland and John M. Jones, "Recasting the American Dream and American Politics: Barack Obama's Keynote Address to the 2004 Democratic National Convention," *Quarterly Journal of Speech* 93, no. 4 (November 2007): 425–448.

[3] Ronald Reagan, "Remarks before Signing the Tax Reform Act of 1986," October 22, 1986, http://www.americanrhetoric.com/speeches/ronaldreagantaxreformactof1986.html (accessed May 15, 2009).

[4] Barack Obama, "Obama's November 7, 2007, Speech on the 'American Dream'" CNNPolitics.com, http://www.cnn.com/2007/POLITICS/12/21/ obama.trans.americandream (accessed May 12, 2009).

[5] Gerald Prince, *Narratology: The Form and Functioning of Narrative* (New York: Mouton, 1982), 4, italics added.

[6] J. B. Schneewind, "Virtue, Narrative, and Community: MacIntyre and Morality," *Journal of Philosophy* 79 (1982): 659.

[7] Barbara DeConcini, *Narrative Remembering* (Lanham, MD: University Press of America, 1990), 112.

[8] Marshall Grossman, *The Story of All Things* (Durham, NC: Duke University Press, 1998), 34.

[9] Richard Morris, *Sinners, Lovers, and Heroes* (Albany: State University of New York Press, 1997), 26.

[10] "Negro Leagues History," http://www.nlbm.com/s/history.htm (2004) (accessed February 21, 2011).

[11] Barry Schwartz, "The Social Context of Commemoration: A Study in Collective Memory," *Social Forces* 61 (1982): 374–402, 395.

[12] Patrick Henry, "Give Me Liberty or Give Me Death," March 23, 1775, at Henrico Parish Church, Richmond, Virginia, Second Virginia Convention, http://www.americanrhetoric.com/speeches/patrickhenrygivemeliberty.html (accessed March 6, 2010).

[13] Eloise Buker, *Politics through a Looking-Glass: Understanding Political Cultures Through a Structuralist Interpretation of Narratives* (New York: Greenwood, 1987), 1.

[14] US Army, "D-Day: June 6, 1944," http://www.army.mil/d-day (accessed September 6, 2010).

[15] "Ice Hockey: After 30 years, Miracle on Ice Still Stirs Emotions," *With Glowing Hearts*, official website of the 2010 Vancouver Olympics, http://www .vancouver2010.com/olympic-news/n/news/afp-news/ice-hockey—after-30-years —miracle-on-ice-still-stirs-emotions_264698Mw.html (accessed March 6, 2010).

[16] Quoted in "Ice Hockey."

[17] Martha Cooper, *Analyzing Public Discourse* (Prospect Heights, IL: Waveland, 1989), 161.

18 Sonya Andermahr, Terry Lovell, and Carol Wolkowitz, *A Glossary of Feminist Theory* (New York: Oxford University Press, 2000), 174.

19 V. William Balthrop, "Culture, Myth, and Ideology as Public Argument: An Interpretation of the Ascent and Demise of 'Southern Culture,'" *Communication Monographs* 51 (December 1984), 341.

20 Clifford Geertz, *The Interpretation of Cultures* (New York: Basic Books, 1973), 48, 89.

21 Balthrop, "Culture," 342.

22 Robert Lacey, *Ford: The Men and the Machine* (New York: Little, Brown, 1986), 126.

23 Amy Maria Kenyon, *Dreaming Suburbia: Detroit and the Production of Postwar Space and Culture* (Detroit: Wayne State University Press, 2004), 126.

24 Seymour Chatman, "Towards a Theory of Narrative," *New Literary History* 6 (1975): 295–318, 318.

25 Seymour Chatman, *Coming to Terms: The Rhetoric of Narrative in Fiction and Film* (New York: Cornell University Press, 1990), 9.

26 National Museum of American History, "Cold War Timeline: The End of the Cold War," 2000, http://americanhistory.si.edu/subs/history/timeline/end (accessed February 26, 2010).

27 Upton Sinclair, *The Jungle* (Pasadena, CA: Upton Sinclair, 1920), 117.

28 Kathleen Hall Jamieson, *Eloquence in an Electronic Age: The Transformation of Political Speechmaking* (New York: Oxford University Press, 1988), 119.

29 US Constitution, Article II, Section 2.

30 George W. Bush, "2007 State of the Union Address," January 23, 2007, http://www.americanrhetoric.com/speeches/stateoftheunion2007.htm (accessed January 1, 2010).

31 Bush, "2007 State of the Union."

32 George Campbell, *The Philosophy of Rhetoric* (Edinburgh, Scotland: George Ramsey, 1808; Google Books), 163–165.

33 Elie Wiesel, *Night*, rev. ed. (New York: Hill and Wang, 2006), 7.

34 Rita Charon, *Narrative Medicine* (New York: Oxford University Press, 2006), 4.

35 Charon, *Narrative*, 3.

36 The Program in Narrative Medicine, College of Physicians and Surgeons, Columbia University, "Mission Statement," http://www.narrativemedicine.org/index.html (accessed March 6, 2010).

37 Program in Narrative Medicine, "Mission Statement."

38 Special issue on narrative medicine, *Journal of Applied Communication Research* 37 (May 2009).

39 Although most scholarly works devoted to narratives identify a number of other characteristics, such as narrator and setting, plot and character development are the two most important. See, for instance, Paul Cobley, *Narrative* (London: Routledge, 2001).

40 Cobley, *Narrative*, 239, italics added.

41 Ronald Jacobs, "Narrative, Civil Society and Public Sphere," in *Lines of Narrative: Psychological Perspectives*, ed. Molly Andrews, Shelley Day Sclater, Corinne Squire, and Amal Treacher, 18–35 (New York: Routledge, 2000).

42 John Kerry, "2004 Democratic National Convention Acceptance Address," Boston, July 29, 2004, http://www.americanrhetoric.com/speeches/convention2004/johnkerry2004dnc.htm (accessed August 27, 2010).

43 Swift Vets and POWs for Truth, http://www.swiftvets.com (accessed August 27, 2010).

[44] Robert C. Rowland and Kirsten Theye, "The Symbolic DNA of Terrorism," *Communication Monographs* 75, no. 1 (March 2008), 52–85.

[45] G. Thomas Goodnight and John Poulakos, "Conspiracy Rhetoric: From Pragmatism to Fantasy in Public Discourse," *Western Journal of Speech Communication* 45, no. 4 (Fall 1981): 299–316.

[46] John Harlow, "Secrets of Woody's Hitman Father," *Times Online*, April 8, 2007, (accessed February 25, 2010).

[47] This standard is derived partially from the work of John R. Searle, "The Logical Status of Fictional Discourse," *New Literary History* 6 (1975): 319–332.

[48] William Safire, "First, Find the Forger," *New York Times*, September 22, 2004, http://query.nytimes.com/gst/fullpage.html?res=9A02E5DE1339F931A1575AC0A9629C8B63 (accessed March 8, 2010).

[49] Morley Safer, "Iraqis Stealing Incubators from Babies May Have Been a Fraud," *60 Minutes*, January 19, 1992, LexisNexis: CBS News Transcripts.

[50] This movie illustrates how historical narratives can be changed to achieve narrative truth. Although the movie depicts a debate between Wiley and Harvard, the debate that actually occurred was between Wiley and the University of Southern California, the national championship team in 1930.

[51] For a video of "8th of November" visit http://www.youtube.com/watch?v=ozpdBvB0hek (accessed October 12, 2011).

[52] See Elizabeth Loftus and Katherine Ketcham, *Witness for the Defense* (New York: St. Martin's, 1991), reprinted at http://www.pbs.org/wgbh/pages/frontline/shows/ dna/photos/eye/text_06.html as part of *Frontline*, "What Jennifer Saw," 1997, http://www.pbs.org/wgbh/pages/frontline/shows/dna (accessed March 5, 2010).

[53] Michael Krausz, *Rightness and Reasons: Interpretation in Cultural Practices* (Ithaca, NY: Cornell University Press, 1993), 47.

[54] Samuel Eliot Morison, *Admiral of the Ocean Sea: A Life of Christopher Columbus* (Boston: Little, Brown, 1942).

[55] Noam Chomsky, *Year 501: The Conquest Continues* (Boston: South End, 1993).

[56] Helen Wallis, "What Columbus Knew," *History Today* (May 1992): 17–23.

[57] Peter Stansky, "The Crumbling Frontiers of History or History and Biography: Some Personal Remarks," *Pacific Historical Review* 59 (1990): 1–13, 6.

[58] Donald Spence, "Saying Good-Bye to Historical Truth," *Philosophy of the Social Sciences* 21 (1991): 245–252, 247.

[59] Mark Twain, *Following the Equator: A Journey around the World Part 2* (Hartford, CT: American, 1897), 156.

[60] Jürgen Habermas, *Reason and the Rationalization of Society*, vol. 1, *The Theory of Communicative Action* (Boston: Beacon, 1984).

[61] J. L. Gorman, review of *Writing History*, by Paul Veyne, *History and Theory* 26 (1987): 99–114, 110, 113.

[62] See, for instance, the parable of the sower in Luke 8.

[63] Simon Kistemaker, *The Parables of Jesus* (Grand Rapids, MI: Baker, 1987).

[64] Video of "Travelin' Soldier" at http://www.youtube.com/watch?v=nLBgmbXBOb8 (accessed October 12, 2011).

[65] William Edward Leuchtenburg, *Franklin D. Roosevelt and the New Deal, 1932–1940* (New York: Harper and Row, 1963).

[66] Burton W. Folsom, Jr., *New Deal or Raw Deal: How FDR's Economic Legacy Has Damaged America* (New York: Threshold, 2008).

[67] Walter Fisher, "Narration as a Human Communication Paradigm: The Case of Public Moral Argument," *Communication Monographs* 51 (1984): 1–22, 8.

[68] Fisher, "Narration," 8.

[69] Fisher, "Narration," 8, italics added.

[70] Fisher, "Narration," 16.

[71] Invisible Children, http://www.invisiblechildren.com/home.php (accessed August 27, 2010).

[72] Kenneth Burke, *Grammar of Motives*, rev. ed. (1945; Berkeley, CA: University of California Press, 1945 and 1969), esp. part 3. For a detailed description of this standard, see Arnie Madsen, "Burke's Representative Anecdote as a Critical Method," in *Extensions of the Burkeian System*, ed. James W. Chesebro, 208–229 (Tuscaloosa: University of Alabama Press, 1993).

[73] Burke, *Grammar*, 60.

[74] Huffington Post, "Letterman Presents Final 'Great Moments in Presidential Speeches'" (video) January 2009, 16, http://www.huffingtonpost.com/2009/01/16/letterman-presents-final_n_158705.html (accessed August 27, 2010).

[75] Kenneth Burke, *Attitudes toward History*, 3rd ed. (Berkeley: University of California Press, 1937 and 1984).

[76] Burke, *Attitudes*, 39.

[77] Burke, *Attitudes*, 41.

[78] Burke, *Attitudes*, 41.

[79] Burke, *Attitudes*, 171.

[80] John Morreall, *Comedy, Tragedy, and Religion* (Albany: State University of New York Press, 1999), 3.

[81] Burke, *Attitudes*, 4.

[82] Burke, *Attitudes*, 4–5.

[83] Austin Fenner and Corky Siemaszko, "Columbine Evil Revisited: Colo. Pauses, Honors Memory of Slain 13," *Daily News* (New York), April 21, 2000, 8.

[84] Alan Wolfe, "Littleton Takes the Blame," *New York Times*, May 2, 1999, 4:17.

[85] In Bob Beckel and Cal Thomas, "What about the Guns?" *USA Today*, April 19, 2007, 21A.

[86] George W. Bush, "9/11 Address to the Nation: A Great People Has Been Moved to Defend a Great Nation," September 11, 2001, http://www.americanrhetoric.com/ speeches/gwbush911addresstothenation.htm (accessed November 1, 2007).

[87] George W. Bush, "The Deliberate and Deadly Attacks . . . Were Acts of War," September 12, 2001, http://www.americanrhetoric.com/speeches/gwbush911cabinetroomaddress.htm (accessed November 1, 2007).

[88] George W. Bush, "Remarks at the National Day of Prayer and Remembrance," September 14, 2001, http://www.americanrhetoric.com/speeches/gwbush911prayer&memorialaddress.htm (accessed November 1, 2007).

[89] George W. Bush, "State of the Union Address," January 29, 2002, http://www.whitehouse.gov/news/releases/2002/01/20020129-11.html (accessed November 7, 2007).

[90] William Casebeer, "Knowing Evil when You See It: Uses for the Rhetoric of Evil in International Relations," *International Relations* 18, no. 4 (2004): 441–451.

[91] Dana L. Cloud, "Introduction: Evil in the Agora," *Rhetoric and Public Affairs* 6, no. 3 (2003), 509.

[92] Senate Committee on Intelligence, *Postwar Findings about Iraq's WMD Programs and Links to Terrorism and How They Compare with Prewar Assessments*, 109th Cong., 2d sess., September 8, 2006, http://intelligence.senate.gov/phaseiiaccuracy.pdf (accessed March 7, 2010).

[93] Cynthia Cotts, "Reason to Deceive: WMD Lies Could Be the New Watergate," *Village Voice*, June 17, 2003, http://intelligence.senate.gov/phaseiiaccuracy.pdf (accessed March 7, 2010).

[94] Richard Norton-Taylor, "We Got It Wrong on Iraq WMD, Intelligence Chiefs Finally Admit," *Guardian.co.uk*, April 8, 2005, http://www.guardian.co.uk/politics/2005/apr/08/uk.iraq (accessed March 7, 2010).

PART III

Components of Symbolic Action

Chapter 6

Rhetors

Key Concepts

authority	performance
ethos	persona
goodwill	practical wisdom
identity	social power
image	strategic essentialism
intersectionality	virtue
mystification	

Ronald Wilson Reagan, president of the United States from 1981 to 1989, is known as the "Great Communicator."[1] As president, his personal popularity was consistently high, averaging 61 percent (with a high of 81 percent), even though his job approval averaged 53 percent (with a low of 35 percent). During the 1982 recession, Gallup polls found that "when only about 4 in 10 Americans approved of the job Reagan was doing as president, 6 in 10 Americans rated him on the positive end of a 10-point rating scale."[2] This 20 percent gap between the public's assessment of his personal popularity and its approval of his policies was unprecedented and perplexed political observers.[3] Why did people who disagreed with what Reagan advocated still find him to be a credible and persuasive speaker?

One factor contributing to his persuasiveness was his ability to inhabit the role of the president. Not only was he the legally elected president of the United States, he acted the part. Communication scholar J. Jeffery Auer explains, "A president must project a positive public persona, an identifiable personality, character and image. . . . Ronald Reagan . . . [has] a clearly identifiable personality, and a steady image."[4] American studies professor James Nuechterlein argues that Reagan's "leadership was, above all, a triumph of personality. His eloquence, charm, courage . . . and remarkable sense of self revived Americans' pride in the presidential office and, by extension, in the nation itself."[5] English professor M. E. Bradford says that "in his virtues and personal style [Reagan] symbolized our national character, not necessarily as it is, but as we wish it to be."[6] As a former movie star, Reagan had played characters that possessed iron will, strong character, and perseverance. As president, Reagan performed the roles of president: commander-in-chief, legislative leader, and symbolic head of state.[7] He rhetorically constructed an image composed of interlocking performances of his trustworthy character, his identity as a proud American, and his authority as president. This image, as Auer writes, was "bigger than the man."[8]

In this chapter we discuss the rhetor as an essential part of any symbolic action. As rhetors produce symbolic action, they are also produced by it. To explore this process, we outline the general concept of "persona," then discuss its various facets: character, roles, identity, authority, and image. An analysis of Sojourner Truth's speech "Aren't I A Woman?" illustrates these concepts.

PERSONA AS PERFORMANCE

Historically, the term "persona" referred to the mask worn in theatrical performances. When playing a particular character or a particular mood, an actor would hold up the appropriate mask. Etymologically, the word means "to speak through," "per" meaning "through" and "sonare" meaning "sound." The mask was the image that the actor spoke through to amplify the character being played. Actors are not the only people who perform a persona, however. People perform a range of personae in everyday life. Psychologists use the term "persona" to refer to the façades people present to the world when portraying themselves in public differently from the ways they do in private. A person can also present different façades to various audiences or in various situations, but "façade" does not mean "fake." Just because a professor speaks one way when lecturing to a class, and another when talking to friends about kayaking, does not mean the professor is not really herself during those exchanges.

The rhetorical **persona** is *the character, role, identity, authority, and image a rhetor constructs and performs during a rhetorical act.* Central to this definition is an understanding that a persona is something a rhetor does, not something a rhetor innately has. A rhetor, through symbolic action, constructs and performs a persona, which the audience perceives to be the source of the symbolic action.

This definition is informed by English scholar Wayne Booth's examination of authorial persona. Booth drew a distinction between the identity of the actual author of a work of fiction and the identity that the author performed in that work. In *The Rhetoric of Fiction*, Booth refers to that performed identity as the author's "second self" or "implied author" who "chooses, consciously or unconsciously, what we read; we infer him [or her] as an ideal, literary, created version of the real man [or woman]; he [or she] is the sum of his [or her] own choices."[9] Booth sought to raise awareness of the fact that works of literature did not reflect of an authentic authorial self, but, instead, were rhetorical. An authorial persona is performed when a person presents particular elements to the world as definitive of who she or he is; it is not just a neutral reflection of the person.

Narratives, whether in a novel or in an explanation of why you need a homework extension, attempt to influence an audience to see an event in a particular way. Your narratives are told from a particular perspective—your persona. Personae appear not only in works of fiction, but also in every rhetorical action. Because every act of communication contains its own drama, every act of communication also contains characters, including the persona of the rhetor.

Sociologist Erving Goffman uses a drama metaphor to explain how people in social situations perform roles. He defines a **performance** as *"all the activity of* *a given participant on a given occasion which serves to influence in any way any of the other participants.*"[10] When you give a public presentation, you engage in a performance. You not only present your speech, you also enact a role. Your choice of what to wear, whether to speak from the front of the room or from your seat, what level of formality to display, what evidence to use, and what attitude to take toward the audience and topic all influence the way others perceive you and your message. Thus, in order to completely understand how rhetoric works, you must recognize how persona invites assent both to the request made and to the person making it. Communication scholar Randall Lake notes that "arguments seek assent not only to the claim stated but also to the claim enacted."[11] Your symbolic actions seek affirmation of what you say and as whom you say it.

When people think of a performance, they usually think of an actor who memorizes a script and performs it in front of an audience. A person's daily interactions with others, as well as the public interactions of a rhetor with an audience, are not scripted (although they might sometimes be rehearsed); however, they are still a performance. When you try to persuade your professor to give you an extension on a paper, you probably plan what you will say: you produce a loose script to respond in a way that is consistent with the professor's expectations and the image you wish to convey. A script is not written for you, but you may draft one in your head, rehearse it, edit it, and then finally perform it for its target audience. Why do you feel the need to rehearse? You want to perform a persona that enhances your persuasiveness by directing the audience's interpretation of the message. The message itself will also inform the audience's perception of you. Depending on how you make your request, your professor may perceive your character to be trustworthy because you displayed the identity of a hardworking student, or perceive your character to be lacking because you appear to be a procrastinator. The professor may grant your request because you played the role of student and asked politely, or refuse it because you played the role of superior and demanded an extension, thus assuming an authority you do not possess.

Although personae are rhetorically constructed, an archetypal form (or prototype) for the persona may preexist the rhetorical action in which it is performed. Returning to the theatre roots of the concept, communication scholars B. L. Ware and Wil A. Linkugel clarify that "*persona* does not refer to the personality" of the actor as a person, but to "the characteristics assumed by the actor when [she or] he dons the mask."[12] In plays a persona preexists; an actor steps into the role. Similarly, a rhetor does not create a persona out of nothing; rather, the persona can "reflect the aspirations and cultural visions of audiences."[13] For example, when you perform the role of good student, you do not create from scratch the characteristics and habits of a good student. Instead, a prototype of the good student already exists within the audience's cultural expectations. The university culture generally agrees that the qualities of a good student include being prepared, serious, engaged, focused, and interested, as well as being a critical thinker. You bring individual characteristics to the role, but the archetype existed prior to your performance of the persona.

FACETS OF PERSONA

To highlight the ways in which persona is performed and is itself a symbolic action, we describe the various facets of persona in the following sections. Character, roles, identity, authority, and image are interlocking parts of a person's persona. We use the metaphor of "facet" because these concepts are interconnected parts of a larger whole, yet each concept offers a distinct perspective. The distinctions among the facets are not absolute. Particular roles, such as firefighter, carry particular character elements, such as courage. When people seek to develop authority, they often seek to portray the image of a leader. In addition, people perceive particular identities to fit particular roles better. For example, people's perception of sex roles makes female nurses and elementary school teachers less remarkable than male nurses or teachers. All these facets of persona have two things in common: (1) skillful choices about each can enhance symbolic action and (2) each facet is produced by symbolic action.

Character

Imagine you are shopping for a new stereo. The salesperson cannot answer any of your questions about sound quality or features, and insists on steering you toward the most expensive equipment. You begin to question the character of a person who does not seem to have your best interests in mind, so you ask for help from someone else. The second salesperson is someone with whom you worked when you bought a television, and whose advice was helpful. This salesperson also provides complete answers to your questions and is willing to admit it when a cheaper model may be just as good as a more expensive one. You trust this person, both because of your previous experience but also because of the way the stereo discussion is handled. The second salesperson has ethos, while the first one lacks it.

In Chapter 1, we defined **ethos** as *that which is "in the character of the speaker"*; more completely, it is *the character of a rhetor performed in the rhetorical act and known by the audience because of prior interactions*. This understanding of ethos is informed by two classical scholars: Aristotle and Cicero. Aristotle defined ethos as an appeal based on a rhetor's "presentation of character" within a persuasive act.[14] Ethos, as an artistic proof, is created by the rhetor. Roman rhetorician and statesperson Cicero described it as composed of elements of character outside the rhetorical act.[15] He included "the customs, the deeds, and the life" of the rhetor of which the audience was already aware.[16] For Cicero, the rhetor's character known from previous acts was more important to demonstrating ethos than the appeals a rhetor made in the speech.

In our definition, ethos is developed both prior to and within a rhetorical act. For example, when Richard Nixon was president in the early 1970s, he normalized relations with "Red China." After World War II, the People's Republic of China became a communist country. The United States cut off all ties with it and viewed it as an enemy. In 1972, Nixon became the first US president to visit China and began developing diplomatic ties. The US people accepted Nixon doing this because of his ethos. He was known as a staunch anti-communist; if he thought it was acceptable to work with the Chinese, it must be. Nixon did not rely on his past character alone, however. In his messages to the US public, he explained and justified his foreign policy decision, using his authority as president and praising the virtue of closer US-PRC ties.

Because *ethos* is character existing prior to, and within, a rhetorical act, to understand it, one needs to understand the components of character. Aristotle's description is helpful. For Aristotle, character is comprised of three dimensions: practical wisdom (*phronesis*), virtue (*arête*), and goodwill (*eunoia*).[17]

Practical Wisdom. Rhetors demonstrate **practical wisdom** or prudence (phronesis) through the use of *common sense and sound reason*.[18] If a rhetor attempts to persuade with arguments the audience perceives to be irrational, unbelievable, or unrealistic, the rhetor's character is harmed and the audience will probably not be persuaded. Practical wisdom is conveyed by a rhetor's command of information and ability to make decisions based on sound reasons.

In a local campaign for school board that one of the authors witnessed, candidates participated in a forum. One candidate aggressively defended strong positions on the issues. He wanted to overhaul school financing, opposed the school funding referendum, and favored terminating the superintendent. On the surface, he seemed to have a clear agenda and advocate forceful action. As the forum progressed, however, he was unable to answer questions about the district's finances, how the district would function if the referendum failed, and his grievances against the superintendent.

The other candidates failed to take strong stands on issues, but appeared open to public concerns. One audience member said she wanted a board member who listened to her concerns, showed common sense, and gathered information before making decisions.

The first candidate lost the election by a wide margin. The results seemed to surprise his backers because the election results for the referendum were very close and he had been the only school board candidate to oppose it. Yet, he failed to gain the support of voters who shared his opinion because they did not believe he possessed practical wisdom. Even though many voters agreed with him on some fundamental issues, they perceived other candidates as possessing better practical wisdom.

Virtue. Rhetors are perceived to possess **virtue** (arête) if they seem to be *sharing the values the audience considers worthy of merit*. Aristotle, based on fourth century BCE Greek society's view of the world, said that virtue included "justice, manly courage, self-control, magnificence, magnanimity, liberality [generosity], gentleness, prudence, and wisdom."[19]

During election campaigns, candidates try to portray themselves as possessing the virtues of leadership. When former New York Mayor Rudolph Giuliani campaigned for president in 2007, he explained: "I'll set a course and stick with it. I'll be on offense on terrorism. I'll be a fiscal conservative. I'll lower taxes. I'll seek private market solutions to most problems."[20] In the first part of this statement, Giuliani attempted to portray himself as a decisive, unwavering, self-confident, and courageous leader. He stated his positions boldly to portray himself as a forceful defender of values consistent with the conservative agenda because he was attempting to persuade Republicans to support him for their party nomination: he portrayed himself as possessing the virtues he believed his audience valued. Additionally, his campaign website offered a biography that focused on his virtues of leadership as a crime fighter, reformer, fiscally responsible mayor, and courageous leader during the September 11, 2001, attacks on his city.[21]

Aristotle identified what he believed were ideal virtues; however, his ideals were limited by his culture. For example, he argued: "the virtues and actions of those who are superior by nature are more honorable, for example, those of a man more than those of a woman."[22] Today, although many of the values he identified might be considered virtuous, we hope people do not believe that a person's biology determines their ability to possess virtue. In addition, what a virtue means is open to contest. It is defined by the culture, the situation, and the audience. In some cultures the virtues of a good leader might be courage, conviction, and forcefulness, but in others they might be listening to others, seeking advice, and seeking understanding. Although a definitive set of values cannot be developed for what constitutes virtue for the ethos of a rhetor, the values that the audience esteems determine whether it perceives the rhetor to be virtuous.

Goodwill. A rhetor who possesses **goodwill** (eunoia) is perceived as having *the quality of being motivated by the audience's best interests, as putting the needs of the audience ahead of the rhetor's own interests and motives,* much as a friend would.[23] In order to have goodwill, Aristotle argues, the rhetor has to understand the frame of mind of the audience. When the rhetor assesses the audience and incorporates the appropriate appeals, s/he appears to be motivated by the audience's interests and needs. A rhetor who is perceived as having goodwill might propose a policy for the greater good that goes against the rhetor's self interest. For example, if you are working on a group project for a class, you hope the other group members possess goodwill. You most likely enjoy working with, and favorably assess, those people who are more concerned about the grade of the group than their own personal performances.

When Barack Obama announced his candidacy for the presidency on February 10, 2007, he attempted to demonstrate goodwill by explaining that his motives for running were not grounded in self-interest, but in the interest of the nation. In his speech, Obama talked of his motivation to move to Illinois after completing law school. He spoke of moving to a new city where he was offered a job by a church for a salary of $13,000. He took the job, he claimed, because of a "single, simple, powerful idea—that I might play a small part in building a better America." He then talked of encountering violence, visiting inadequate schools, and meeting unemployed people. He concluded that he "received the best education" he had ever had.[24] Obama portrayed himself as doing good things for others, not for himself. His demonstration of goodwill was part of his ethos because, through his work in Chicago, he stated he had become a better leader who understood the needs of people and the meaning of Christianity.

Ethos is a complex construction of a rhetor's character consisting of the audience's perceptions of a rhetor's practical wisdom (phronesis), virtue (arête), and goodwill (eunoia), a perception informed by the rhetorical act and by the rhetor's actions preceding the act. If the audience perceives a rhetor to be trust-worthy and to possess the character qualities the audience esteems, then the audience will be more open to the rhetor's message. For Aristotle, ethos was the most effective persuasive proof because when audiences trust rhetors, they are more receptive to their persuasive messages, including logos and pathos appeals.

Character is understood differently today. Aristotle wrote of rhetors possess-ing character; now, people consider character not as an innate possession, but as a rhetorical construction. Communication scholar Edwin Black notes, "We are more skeptical about the veracity of the representation; we are more conscious that there may be a disparity between the [person] and his [or her] image; we have, in a sense, less trust."[25] Inherent to this loss of trust is the recognition that ethos is not something that just is. Ethos is created; it is performed. As scholars become increasingly aware of the performative aspect of rhetoric, they develop additional ways to assess the rhetor's persona.

Roles

People perform various roles in their daily lives, as well as across their lifetimes. On any given day you probably assume several roles, each having particular functions, qualities, characteristics, and communication patterns. Suppose you make three requests during a day. You ask your professor to extend the deadline on a paper, your friend to let you borrow something, and your subordinate at work to perform a required task. In each of these situations, you play a different role: student, friend, or manager. You perform different personae, each calling for different attitudes toward the audience. As a student, you are a subordinate to the audience, as friend a peer, and as manager a superior. You are the same person, but the role you perform to make the request influences the request. At the same time, the nature of the request places you in a particular role. By becoming aware of social roles and the way they affect perceptions of the rhetor, you can become more aware of the factors that influence reception of rhetorical acts.

Social Roles. If the rhetor plays a role that is held in high regard and consis-tent with the values of the society, the audience can be more receptive to the message.[26] Goffman explains that during performances, individuals "tend to incorporate and exemplify the officially accredited values of the society."[27] People dress up for job interviews because US society equates professional dress with a professional work attitude. A potential employer can see you more easily in the role of worker if you perform the role of a worker. Thus, when you inter-view for a professional job, you likely dress in a way you think others perceive to be professional, rather than in blue jeans, flip-flops, and a ripped T-shirt; speak in a professional manner, using complete sentences and limited slang; and move in a professional way, sitting up in your chair rather than slouching with your feet on the table.

However, people also can perform roles in a way that challenges the society's values in order to highlight unspoken (and sometimes contradictory) norms attached to particular social roles. For example, in discussing third-wave feminism, Rita Alfonso notes that way Riot Grrls (members of the underground feminist punk movement) dressed "in baby doll dresses, usually worn with combat boots, colorful but torn stockings, and any number of tiny plastic hair barrettes, but writing 'slut' on their bodies to preempt society's judgment of them."[28] Riot Grrls intentionally performed contradictory roles: young female in feminine baby doll dresses and tough adult in masculine combat boots, innocent girl wearing plastic barrettes and adult woman with torn stockings. Riot Grrls played with roles because they wanted to challenge the officially accredited social values.

Mystification. Sometimes rhetors perform roles that possess an element of mystery, giving them social distance from, rather than a connection to, the audience. **Mystification** is *the process of distancing the rhetor from the audience so the audience grants the rhetor authority.* Goffman describes mystification as "a widely held notion that restrictions placed upon contact, the maintenance of social distance, provide a way in which awe can be generated and sustained in the audience."[29] Unlike identification, which creates closeness between the rhetor and the audience on the basis of similar interests, mystification requires social distance between the rhetor and the audience so that the audience perceives the rhetor as apart or different from the audience. The audience sits in awe of the rhetor and grants the rhetor power.

An attorney's office illustrates mystification in the way the attorney sets the stage for the role she plays. When you enter the office, you probably first enter a waiting room with a receptionist. Already, the attorney is physically separated from you. You must give your name and appointment information to the receptionist before you can see her. If you do not have an appointment, you probably will not be allowed to speak with the attorney, so a temporal separation exists; her office staff regulates the time of your interaction with her. As you enter the attorney's office, you notice diplomas and certificates on the wall that indicate expertise. The office is probably lined with books, all written in a jargon that a layperson does not comprehend. As you sit in a chair, you might face the attorney, who is sitting at a large, imposing desk—another separation to create authority. The physical space (diplomas, books, desk, and seating arrangements) possesses a mystical feel, as if you are seeking wisdom from on high. These trappings persuade you of the attorney's authority, because she has knowledge and ability you lack. As you discuss your issues with the attorney, she may answer you with jargon and descriptions of the legal process that you fail to fully understand, yet you grant her authority precisely because you fail to understand and because of the social distance she has created. Mystification creates authority through distance and difference. It is mysterious, yet impressive.

Mystification is part of a rhetor's social performance. The rhetor performs the duties of a mystic, a person who inspires a sense of mystery and wonder, and is granted authority because of the audience's belief in the ritual performance. Because US society privileges the scientific and rational, it might seem strange to be talking about mysticism and ritual, but that is precisely what is happening in such a display of power. People do not tend to think of lawyers' offices as fraught with mystery, and instead just speak of them as impressive places. The ritualistic and repeated invocation of symbols guide their reactions.

Mystification is also a central part of presidential inauguration processes. When a new president is inaugurated, a transfer of power occurs. The audience cannot physically see this transfer; it is mysterious. Instead, the transfer suggests itself through the symbolism of the inaugural ceremony, symbolism premised on creating a distance between the president and the citizens. The previous president congratulates the new president, to demonstrate that the transfer of power is peaceful. The new president takes an oath of office, which mystically finalizes the transfer of power from one person to another. The oath is an example of a ritual, a mystical act that changes those participating in it. In some societies, new presidents are given a sash or other symbol of authority to distinguish them from the rest of the populace. A peaceful transfer of power is accomplished through symbolic action because the audience believes in the social process and engages in a mystical leap of faith.

George Washington's first inaugural address, delivered on April 30, 1789, in New York, demonstrates the role of mystification in the inaugural process. Early in the speech, Washington pointed out the importance and uniqueness of the ceremony:

> I was summoned by my Country, whose voice I can never hear but with veneration and love, from a retreat which I had chosen with the fondest predilection . . . the magnitude and difficulty of the trust to which the voice of my Country called me . . . could not but overwhelm with dispondence, one, who, inheriting inferior endowments from nature and unpractised in the duties of civil administration, ought to be peculiarly conscious of his own deficiencies.[30]

He opened his speech by recognizing the magnitude of the office. He noted that he was "called" to take the office, creating the image that he was a reluctant leader, but willing to serve for the good of the country. This "call" also created the impression that he was special—the country summoned him, not someone else.

Washington then invoked an Almighty Being whose "benediction may consecrate to the liberties and happiness of the people." When he invoked the "invisible hand, which conducts the Affairs of men," he mystified the office of president as ordained by forces greater than human:

> No People can be bound to acknowledge and adore the invisible hand, which conducts the Affairs of men more than the People of the United

States. Every step, by which they have advanced to the character of an independent nation, seems to have been distinguished by some token of providential agency.

Through mystification, Washington endowed the new office of the president with power.

Identity

Identity refers to *the physical and/or behavioral attributes that make a person recognizable as a member of a group.* Identity ingredients that have attained social significance and functioned as the basis for group identification include, but are not limited to race, class, sex, sexual orientation, veteran status, religion, nationality, citizenship status, ability or disability, education, and profession. Your answer to the question "who/what are you?" provides a clue about how you understand identity.

Identity as Rhetorical. Assuming an identity when speaking is not a politically neutral act. When people say they are speaking as members of a race, class, sex, sexuality, nationality, or other group, they are assuming personae. For example, Joshua Packwood, the first white valedictorian at historically black, all male Morehouse College, said: "What Morehouse stands for at the end of the day, and what Dr. King epitomized, it's not about black or white, it's about the content of [a person's] character. It's about me, representing Morehouse in that light—not as a white man or a black man."[31] Packwood made clear he was not speaking as a white man, but as a Morehouse man. His persona was tied to belonging to a group defined by attendance at the school, not by a race. *his traits* *sexual orientation*

Rhetoric involves not only *what* people communicate (the words and images), but also *as whom* they communicate—the identities they foreground. You might begin a statement with the phrase: "Speaking as a student . . . ," thereby establishing an identity from which you are speaking. The phrase also constructs the message for the audience in a particular way. You are speaking as a student, not as a professor, parent, taxpayer, or administrator. You begin with this phrase not simply to make an objective observation about yourself, but to establish an identity from which you will speak, because you believe that "speaking as a student" gives you more rhetorical power than speaking as someone else.

The range of personae available to rhetors is constrained by the various identities in which the rhetors can participate. This does not mean that identities are fixed, immutable, or one-dimensional. In fact, scholars argue that identity should be understood as intersectional. Legal scholar Adrien Katherine Wing defines **intersectionality** as *the nature of identity as "multiplicative" rather than additive.*[32] Identity makes more sense if you think of its facets of identity as integral, interlocking parts of a single whole, rather than as the addition of each element on top of another. The way a person performs "man" is influenced by his race, gender, sexuality, religion, education level, and class. The way people perform "white" is influenced by the same characteristics.

The metaphor of "ingredients" helps explain intersectionality.[33] Just as a cake is composed of discrete parts (eggs, flour, milk, sugar, and so on), the parts become inextricably intertwined when they are melded together through the alchemic process of cooking. The eggs affect the flour, which affects the milk, and so on. The interaction among the initially discrete ingredients makes a cake a cake. Similarly, the interaction among identity ingredients as they meld together makes a person a person.

Intersectionality in identity emphasizes that your sex influences your performance of class, your class influences your performance of race, your race influences your performance of nationality, and your nationality influences your performance of sex. In other words, you cannot understand what it means to have a certain identity without examining how all your identity ingredients interact with and infuse each other. Thus, scholars have begun to explore how Protestant religion and masculinity intersect in their studies of "muscular Christianity,"[34] how race and sex intersect in their studies of black masculinity[35] and hegemonic white masculinity;[36] and how class, sex, and race intersect in their studies of motherhood.[37]

Studies of motherhood show how a woman's identity as mother intersects with her race and class. Many people (mostly upper-class white people) might think of "mother" as the gentle soul who provides unconditional love and protective nurturing. In contrast, sociologist Patricia Hill Collins describes a form of motherhood that developed among women who had to prepare children to face discrimination. She shows that many working-class people and African Americans think of "mother" not as the gentle nurturer who soothes all wounds, but as the person who gave them the strength and the ability to handle life's hard knocks. Communication scholar Mari Boor Tonn labels this identity as "militant motherhood."[38]

Militant motherhood appears not only in families, but also in public discourse. In her study of labor activist Mary Harris "Mother" Jones, Tonn describes how militant motherhood uses "assertive, even aggressive, modes of presentation. Militant mothers not only confront their children's enemy, but must also train their children to do likewise if the threat they face is ongoing and systematic."[39] Militant motherhood is not sweet and gentle, but uses "bawdy, rowdy, and irreverent personal expression . . . . Such mothers also may bait, tease, and otherwise provoke children in order to acclimate them to attack, to provide practice at fighting back, and to sharpen their emotional control."[40] The way a woman performs the identity of "mother" is influenced by her race and class. That identity is not static and fixed: multiple performances of "mother" exist.

Intersectionality theory highlights the unique combinations of characteristics that make up each individual and calls attention to the ways interlocking forms of privilege marginalize members of some groups. Legal scholar Kimberlé Crenshaw first used the word "intersectionality" to explain why existing civil rights law, which treats race and sex discrimination as two discrete forms of discrimination, did not work for black women. She explains, "Because the intersectional experience is greater than the sum of racism and sexism, any analysis that does not take intersectionality into account cannot sufficiently address the particular manner in which Black Women are subordinated."[41] As demonstrated in the cases Crenshaw studied, black women were not discriminated against because they were black, or because they were women, but because they were black women.

As feminist philosopher Sandra Harding points out, one should remember "that it is not just the marginalized who have a gender, race, and so on."[42] Intersectionality explains the complexity of all people's identities. "Man" is as much an identity as "woman"; "middle class" is as much an identity as "poor"; and "white" is as much an identity as "black" or "Hispanic" or "Asian," but people who belong to a dominant identity do not perceive it to be an identity. Because it is the norm, the dominant identity becomes invisible. In their article on white-ness as a strategic rhetoric, communication scholars Thomas K. Nakayama and Robert L. Krizek identify the ways whiteness is created and maintained rhetorically as (1) closely tied to power, (2) the norm, (3) natural, (4) indicative of nationality and citizenship, (5) beyond the necessity of racial identity labels, and (6) consciously tied to white people's European ancestry.[43] To illustrate the hidden nature of race, think about references you may have heard to "the Asian doctor," "the Hispanic lawyer," or the "black accountant." Some people may suggest that these are only objective descriptions, but consider "white" as a descriptor: "the white doctor," "the white lawyer," or the "white accountant." Do these phrases sound strange? The fact that they sound odd suggests that "white" is an identity that receives preference for positions of power and authority. A complex interaction between audience, the rhetor, and identity exists, a relation-ship that calls for an analysis of power.

People's identities are not fixed, but developed through the choices they make, even as those choices are delimited by cultural norms that have been reiterated across time. Political communication scholar Thomas A. Hollihan explains, "Although all human beings actively participate in the creation of their own images, these images are not painted on a blank canvas."[44] It may be difficult for a man to play the role of mother, because social norms have linked women with the mother role and men with the father role. An audience's past experience with a rhetor, as well as its perception of the rhetor's race, sex, class, sexual orientation, nationality, and religion, influence the rhetor's ability to create and perform a persona. When delivering the graduation address at Morehouse College, valedictorian Packwood could not speak "as a black man" because US society perceives race to be a binary; one is either black or white. Thus, Packwood created an identity shared with his fellow students based not on race, but on their common Morehouse experience. Likewise, it would be diffi-cult for Barack Obama to speak "as a white man" even though he is as white as he is black. US society sees him as a black man because the racial binary induces people to place others in the either/or identity category.

Scholars, such as feminist scholar Paula M. L. Moya, recognize that identi-ties are fluid even as the performance of those identities are constrained by the existing relationships between social groups and "the historically produced social facts which constitute social locations."[45] The social roles that people are allowed to play and the level of social authority that they are granted are constrained by their identities. For example, US society tends to listen to Microsoft founder Bill Gates because of his economic power; his role as a business magnate and the power that goes along with possessing vast amounts of money make him a compelling persona. In contrast, if you said exactly the same thing that Bill Gates said, people would not listen to you as attentively even if you attempted to perform the role of rich, white, male, computer genius.

Audiences read rhetors' personae through the identity they apply to the rhetors (hence, there is never a "blank canvas"), and often do not recognize that identities are intersectional. Thus, when some people look at United States Representative Keith Ellison, the first Muslim elected to the US Congress, they might only see Muslim or black, rather than US citizen, middle-class, college-educated, Muslim, African-American, man.[46] In the United States people who are categorized as black, Latino/Latina, or Asian are subjected to stereotypes on the basis of those categories.

People assume they know the rhetor's persona even before the rhetor performs it. These social assumptions are why identity matters: identities have real effects on how people live their lives. Moya argues that the external construction of peoples' identities influences their experiences, which then inform what they know and how they know it. She urges everyone to remember that although "people are not *uniformly* determined by any *one* social fact, . . . social facts (such as gender and race)" do influence who people are.[47] Even if identities are fictions, those fictions matter because they influence what and how people know.

Although social imposition of an identity may limit the range of persona options, identity is not fixed. It can be both an obstacle and an opportunity in constructing a persona. Communication scholar Karlyn Kohrs Campbell explains one may have the *opportunity* to choose to speak from an identity that has been accorded social power, or face the *obstacle* of speaking from an assigned identity that lacks social power. For Campbell, the concept of persona captures the "shifting but central character of the roles that we assume in the plays in which we participate."[48]

Barack Obama had both an obstacle and an opportunity arising from his status as the first US president of African descent. The obstacle arose from the 5 percent of the electorate who said they would never vote for a black candidate;[49] those people might never see Obama as the legitimate president even though he won the election. However, his race also provided an opportunity. He could use his race, his own self, as proof of the promise of the United States of America. In his inaugural address, he stated:

> This is the meaning of our liberty and our creed—why men and women and children of every race and every faith can join in celebration across this magnificent mall, and why a man whose father less than sixty years ago might not have been served at a local restaurant can now stand before you to take a most sacred oath.[50]

President Obama foregrounded his racial identity in order to make a point about the nation's progress toward equality. He spoke the oath for the highest office in the land in a city that, years earlier, had used Jim Crow segregation laws to deny equal treatment to people like him and his father.

Many rhetors will call forth particular ingredients in their identities, just as President Obama did with his race, to form their personae in particular speech acts. Rhetors may speak as and for women, men, women of color, African Americans, whites, immigrants, Muslims, US citizens, and so on. Even though each of those identity ingredients may be fluid and shifting, the rhetor chooses to fix one ingredient momentarily in order to speak from the social location attached to that identity. Claiming that identity becomes a strategic part of the communication act.

Strategic Essentialism. The differences among races or between women and men are not nearly as extensive as most popular culture literature would have you believe, but people often treat each other as more different than they really are. Thus, when others label you with an identity that is perceived as essential, meaning that it is fixed and immutable, how might you use that identity? If you have been assigned an identity by the larger society, thus limiting your range of personae, how might you use that assigned identity to enhance your communicative actions? A rhetor may have limited power because of sex, race, class, or nationality, yet still find creative and artistic ways to communicate.

Literary critic Gayatri Spivak describes **strategic essentialism** as *the process of making an identity ingredient the core part of one's persona that legitimizes the right to speak.*[51] It is strategic because it is an intentional construction of persona based on that single identity ingredient. A rhetor consciously picks an identity ingredient to foreground. That choice is essentialist because it positions one element of identity as fixed and determinative of the rhetor's identity and seeks to create group identification through the appeal to that one shared identity ingredient. Strategic essentialism chooses to ignore intersectionality, and instead focuses on a single identity ingredient. For example, in the 1960s and 1970s, African Americans appealed to the single identity ingredient of race with their slogan "Black Power";[52] women appealed to the single identity ingredient of sex with their proclamation that "Sisterhood is Powerful";[53] and Native Americans appealed to their nationality/race with "Red Power."[54] Marginalized groups tend to be the ones to employ strategic essentialism because they are the people who are fighting misrepresentations of their group identity.

Strategic essentialism as a rhetorical technique has two important characteristics. First, the so-called essential attributes of the group are defined by the group members themselves. The members of a marginalized group accept their identity as a group, but seek to control how they are defined. Instead of passively being labeled by the dominant group, they actively take possession of an identity and define it in their own terms. "Black" does not mean powerless and enslaved, but powerful. "Sisterhood" means women are not divided cat-fighting individuals, but unified and powerful. Native American identity is not extinct, but vibrant and alive. Second, even as the group members engage in essentialism, they recognize that identity is always artificially constructed. Spivak recognizes that strategically appealing to an essential understanding of identity can sometimes be politically productive, but it must be done "in a scrupulously visible political interest."[55] Thus, people must *consciously* appeal to an essential identity in order to achieve a particular goal; once that goal has been achieved, they should consciously question that essentialism. If they are to have agency or some degree of control over persona production, then they must consciously perform and question that persona.

thorough

Throughout this discussion, we have tried to make clear that even as identities are used to form a persona, they should also be critically examined. Sometimes, people strongly embrace the identities in order to create a sense of belonging. Other times, identity ingredients are de-emphasized so alliances can be built on the basis of other ingredients. Identities can be defined in order to create unification, but the process creates divisions. If a group unifies on the basis of a common ethnic background, it excludes those who do not share that background. Thus, the deployment of identity must be carefully considered in order to avoid creating a permanent division. Chicana author, scholar, and activist Gloria Anzaldúa offers an elegant metaphor for this multilayered process in her essay, "Bridge, Drawbridge, Sandbar or Island: Lesbians-of-Color *Hacienda Alianzas*."[56] Groups who build bridges to other groups find, at times, that moments of separation are needed, and raise the drawbridge. Sometimes no bridge is built, because the group needs the isolation of an island. Sometimes permanent bridges are built so the connections to others can always be maintained.

Identity is performed. Thus, when people are seeking to present a particular persona by strategically foregrounding an identity ingredient, they should remember that a persona is a mask, which can become suffocating if it is fixed and permanent.

Authority

Authority is *a rhetor's possession of socially recognized power.* Sometimes rhetors are able to persuade audiences because of their authority. If a classmate stands up before the professor arrives and instructs everyone to take out a pen and paper for a quiz, the other students probably would ignore these instructions because they do not recognize the student's authority to give those instructions. If the professor arrives and instructs the students to get ready to take a quiz, however, they would likely follow the professor's instructions because they recognize the professor's authority. To show how authority is a facet of persona, we first outline the way authority operates as social power. Second, we apply the concept of authority to the performance of identity to show how authority both enables and constrains.

Social Power. **Social power** is *the influence that people possess within a particular social structure, and that enables them to induce others to act.* For example, students in a course will probably follow the directives of their instructor not because of the instructor's ethos (although it helps induce cooperation), but because of the instructor's position in the social structure of the university. Instructors have ethos because students assume they possess the qualifications to teach the class. They also work to develop ethos during their classes so the coercive power of the grade book is not their only source of influence. Upon entering a classroom for the first time, however, students usually defer to instructors not because they necessarily perceive the instructors' credibility, but because social power is attached to the role of instructor.

The social power a rhetor brings to a situation is relevant only insofar as the audience perceives it. People do not have or lack power in an absolute sense, rather, they have more or less power in relation to others. Rhetors can possess various types and degrees of social power, including reward power (the perceived authority of the rhetor to reward or benefit the audience), coercive power (the perceived authority of the rhetor to punish the audience), expert power (the perceived authority of the rhetor stemming from knowledge, talent, or skill), referent power (the perceived authority of the rhetor due to the audience's identification with the rhetor), and legitimate power (based on the audience's perception of the rhetor's assigned position in a social structure).[57] For example, you might be responsive to your professors' messages because you believe they have expert power when discussing their particular subjects. You also might perceive their reward and coercive power, related to giving grades and course credit. Professors also have some degree of legitimate power because they have particular positions in a university that grants authority within that social structure. Additionally, they might be perceived as having legitimate power or authority beyond the university, in the larger society, if the society places social importance on the teaching profession. Finally, you might admire professors' knowledge and want to identify with them, thus granting them referent power.

A professor's race, sex, citizenship status, and sexuality interact with the ability to exercise the various forms of power. Research indicates that Euro-American white professors are more likely than minority professors to possess referent power with white students,[58] male professors more easily exercise expert power than female professors,[59] and professors perceived to be heterosexual are more likely to be granted legitimate power than professors perceived to be homosexual.[60]

Identity and social power intersect. People's positions in a social structure are influenced by all ingredients of their identities. Even though a police officer may have legitimate power, an audience may place limits on that power because of the officer's sex. In an ethnographic study of the traditionally masculine profession of police officer, women officers on the Pittsburgh police force talked about learning "not to smile" to reduce the risk that others would see them as incompetent or unprofessional.[61] In other words, they managed their smiling behavior to comply with public expectations for officers. Recognizing that their sex negatively impacted their legitimate power, they sought ways to perform the persona of police officer in a way that would maximize its legitimate power.

Authority to Perform. Audience bias about identity limits a person's ability to access authority. Harvard professor Cornell West tells of a time he was stopped by police:

> Years ago, while driving from New York to teach at Williams College, I was stopped on fake charges of trafficking cocaine. When I told the police officer I was a professor of religion, he replied "Yeh, and I'm the flying Nun. Let's go, nigger!" I was stopped three times in my first ten days in Princeton for driving too slowly on a residential street with a speed limit of twenty-five miles per hour.[62]

Professor West had attained a level of social power because of his educational and professional status, but the police denied him access to it because of race bias. The police officer who stopped West did not believe West's performance of his power because he did not believe a black man had the authority to perform the role of professor. *In JAW, need for change & loss of influence b/c managerian*

Social power is a resource, but it is constrained when people are not given the authority to perform particular roles. When women activists struggled for their rights during the 1960s and 1970s, they sought to perform a new form of womanhood, but they were not totally free to perform "womanhood" in any way they wanted, free from social sanction. Communication scholar Karlyn Kohrs Campbell notes how the social status of women placed them at odds with the persona of "rhetor," which called for "self-reliance, self-confidence, and independence."[63] If a woman performed the persona of "woman," then she did not enact the persona of "rhetor;" if she performed the persona of "rhetor," then she might not be perceived as enacting "woman." Campbell argues that feminist rhetoric during this era, "no matter how traditional its argumentation, how justificatory its form, how discursive its method, or how scholarly its style, . . . attacks the entire psychosocial reality, the most fundamental values, of the cultural context in which it occurs."[64] *wires as lowans*

When a persona pushes at the social expectations attached to the body performing it, the audience may reject the performance as unauthorized. Because not all rhetors have equal authority to perform a role, analysis of performances should focus on the power to perform, rather than on the truth of a performance. As Goffman states: "Sometimes when we ask whether a fostered impression is true or false we really mean to ask whether or not the performer is authorized to give the performance in question, and are not primarily concerned with the actual performance itself."[65] Even though personae are performances, people are not free to play any role they wish.

For example, a person's gender identity (tending toward feminine, tending toward masculine, or a creative mix of both) is a performance. Gender (as opposed to biological *sex*) is something people do, not something they are—a performance, a series of repeated actions, postures, and statements. Rhetoric professor Judith Butler aptly describes the relationship between gender and identity: "Gender is the repeated stylization of the body, a set of repeated acts within a rigid regulatory frame that congeal over time to produce the appearance of substance, of a natural kind of being."[66] Consider the ways you do gender through your dress, hairstyle, body posture, language choice, hand gestures, areas of interest, and so on. When humans (consciously or unconsciously) behave in gendered ways, they construct, maintain, and transform their own and others' notions of gender identity. These performances are repeated so frequently they become unconscious, if not involuntary, and might even appear natural and determined rather than performed. Yet, they are still actions, not some inherent identity a person possesses.

Butler explains that even though "gender is a kind of doing, an incessant activity performed, in part, without one's knowing and without one's willing," it is not "automatic or mechanical."[67] She asks people to think about gender as "a practice of improvisation within a scene of constraint."[68] It is a performance, but one where the actors maintain only some level of control over the content of the scene. When you wake up every day, you make choices about how to do gender; about how to dress, move, sit, and talk. You could choose to "do gender" differently, but first you would have to see those choices as options. If a man wanted to do his gender differently, he would need to see wearing a dress and heels as a viable option; most men do not. Although women can now wear pants and still be perceived as feminine (which was not true until the latter half of the twentieth century), a man who decided to wear a skirt would face serious social censure. Thus, the performance of gender is constrained; the script has already been written with only limited space for improvisation.

Race is another identify ingredient that affects a rhetor's authority to perform particular personae. Whiteness in US society operates as a form of privilege that nonwhites cannot access. White rhetors of European ancestry have an advantage for many US audiences, without explicitly stating the fact that they are white, because white is defined as the norm. The Birther Movement's challenges to President Obama's citizenship highlight the way in which people consider whiteness to be interlinked with US nationality and citizenship. Despite an officially recognized Hawaiian birth certificate and Honolulu newspaper birth announcements, the Birther Movement refuses to accept that Obama was born in the United States as the Constitution requires the president to be.[69] Birthers' implication is that Obama does not have the authority to perform the role of president. Some people argue that part of their questioning of his authority is related to his race, and that challenges to President Obama's citizenship would not have gained as much traction if he were perceived as white.

Image

When news broke that Tiger Woods had crashed his car on Thanksgiving night, reportedly after a fight with his wife over allegations of marital infidelity, one primary talking point for commentators was the effect the accident would have on his image. A *Sports Illustrated* writer commented, "The shattering of a public image has become an event, a topic of speculation much like the Super Bowl."[70] From late November 2009 to mid-January 2010, almost 1000 newspaper articles and 750 radio and television stories discussed the effect of the accident on Woods's image, because his image had made him the first athlete to pass the $1 billion earnings mark. A *Sports Illustrated* story explained: "The public, of course, knows when it is being sold an image, and we truly aren't averse to that. The problem for Woods is that his carefully cultivated aura—committed family man, ruthlessly disciplined, always in total control—has been exposed as clearly false."[71] An image's changeability makes clear that it is created, a rhetorical construction.

An **image** is *a verbal and visual representation, emphasizing particular qualities and characteristics, that creates a perception of the rhetor in the audience's minds.* Image is an aspect of persona, but also an effect of it. Across time, an image is created by the performance of persona. An image is most persuasive, according to historian Daniel Boorstin, when it builds a reputation and does not outrage common sense.[72] Prior to Thanksgiving 2009, Tiger Woods's image had been of a hardworking, controlled, and precise golfer, the best in history, with an ideal family life. Manufacturers (including Nike, Gatorade, Swiss luxury watchmaker Tag Heuer, and Gillette) used that image to sell products by associating them with the qualities of hard work, control, and precision.

In his book critiquing the rise of hollow images and pseudo-events, Boorstin identifies a number of characteristics of an image. His purpose in analyzing images is to condemn them, but these characteristics can be useful in our study of how image works more generally. For Boorstin, an image is (1) synthetic, (2) believable, (3) passive, (4) vivid and concrete, (5) simplified, and (6) ambiguous.[73]

By *synthetic*, Boorstin means that an image is "planned: created especially to serve a purpose, to make a certain kind of impression."[74]

Yet an image must be perceived as authentic to be effective: It must be *believable*. As Boorstin explains, an image "serves no purpose if people do not believe it."[75] The believability of the image is not determined simply by the rhetor's ability to project an image, but also by the audience's willingness to accept it. Thus, commentators noted that Woods and the companies he endorsed created a "carefully constructed public image,"[76] showing him making impossible putts and concentrating as he bounced a golf ball on his club before hitting it an amazing distance. Despite his periodic cursing and club tossing on the course, most people continued to accept Woods's image as a controlled golfer because of his incredible success. Once the allegations of marital infidelity and the pictures of his wrecked (out of control) car hit the airwaves in November of 2009, however, the image of Woods as controlled was no longer believable.

Although images are actively constructed, they are most believable when they appear *passive*, not something the rhetor strives for, but that occurs naturally. Conformity and image go hand in hand, because conforming to norms always appears easier than challenging them. When Woods's control on the golf course appeared to match control in his personal life, people were willing to accept his image. When it began to appear that his domestic life was out of control, however, it was more difficult for Woods to fit the image of a controlled golfer. It did not appear natural.

In order for constructed images to influence an audience, they must be *vivid* and *concrete*, yet *simplified*. Because they are meant to invite identification, they must be *ambiguous* enough for multiple audiences to feel similarity, yet vivid enough to give them a sense of who the rhetor is. Woods's image as hardworking is vivid and simple; in US society, hard work is valued and understood. "Hardworking" also is vague enough that many people could identify with it. Even a person who worked really hard would probably not become as good a golfer as Woods, but could still be a hard worker like Woods.

Images are not always positive creations meant to enhance a rhetor's appeal. Sometimes, negative images are imposed on a rhetor. Gerald Ford, who served as president from 1974 to 1977, was arguably one of the most athletic presidents in the nation's history. He had been a star athlete on the University of Michigan football team and turned down contract offers from the Detroit Lions and Green Bay Packers. Nevertheless, he was painted as a well-meaning nice guy whose incompetence was reflected in his physical bumblings. After news footage showed him slipping on the steps as he exited Air Force One and hitting golf spectators with the ball, comedian Chevy Chase began lampooning Ford on *Saturday Night Live*. Chase did not wear makeup or hairpieces to make him look like Ford. Chase just fell down, often, and thus cemented the public's image of Ford,[77] and of his effectiveness as president.

Although Boorstin is extremely critical of images (especially as deployed by those with power), referring to them as "pseudo-events," contemporary scholars find that image events have a productive role in contemporary protest. Movements, groups, and organizations outside the mainstream political order also can construct images. Images not only conform, keep things the way they are, and squelch dissent, but also shake things up. Particularly in an increasingly multimediated world, rhetors recognize the need to have their images appear on the public screen.

RHETOR ANALYZED

Sojourner Truth is one of the most widely known antislavery and women's rights agitators of the 1800s. A black woman born into slavery, she originally spoke Dutch; she did not learn English until she was around nine years old. As a slave, she had been denied access to education. She never learned to read or write, even after she was freed, so what survives of her speaking is what was transcribed by audience members. Her speeches survived because, as communication scholar Suzanne Pullon Fitch explains, she "was an orator of great personal power whose words [according to abolitionist Lucy Stone] 'came with direct and terrible force, moving friend and foe alike.'"[78] Her status as a freed black woman provided her with a resource to speak to the causes of abolition and woman's suffrage, but she also faced the challenge that she was speaking as a black woman. African Americans and women were two groups who did not possess much social power at the time.

At the May 1851 Women's Rights Convention, Truth challenged the white women present to recognize that black women were women too—arguing that white women working for woman's suffrage should also work for black women's right to vote. Truth artistically created ethos for herself by performing a persona that incorporated her identity as a woman and as a former slave.

Sojourner Truth
"On Women's Rights"
Ohio Women's Rights Convention, Akron, Ohio
May 1851

1. Well, children, where there is so much racket there must be something out of kilter. I think that 'twixt the Negroes of the South and the women at the North, all talking about rights, the white men will be in a fix pretty soon.

2. But what's all this here talking about? That man over there says that women need to be helped into carriages, and lifted over ditches, and to have the best place everywhere. Nobody ever helps me into carriages, or over mud-puddles, or gives me any best place. [*And raising herself to her full height and her voice to a pitch like rolling thunder, she asked*] And aren't I a woman? Look at me! Look at my arm. [*And she bared her right arm to the shoulder, showing her tremendous muscular power.*] I have plowed and planted and gathered into barns, and no man could head me. And aren't I a woman? I could work as much and eat as much as a man—when I could get it—and bear the lash as well. And aren't I a woman? I have borne thirteen children, and seen them most all sold off into slavery, and when I cried out with a mother's grief, none but Jesus heard me! And aren't I a woman?

3. Then they talk about this thing in the head; what's this they call it? ("Intellect," whispered someone near.) That's it, honey. What's that got to do with women's rights or Negroes' rights? If my cup won't hold but a pint and yours holds a quart, wouldn't you be mean not to let me have my little half-measure full? [*And she pointed her significant finger and sent a keen glance at the minister who had made the argument. The cheering was long and loud.*]

4. Then that little man in black there, he says women can't have as much rights as men, 'cause Christ wasn't a woman. Where did your Christ come from? Where did your Christ come from? Where did your Christ come from? From God and a woman! Man had nothing to do with Him.

5. If the first woman God ever made was strong enough to turn the world upside down all alone, these together ought to be able to turn it back and get it right side up again. And now they is asking to do it, the men better let them.

6. Obliged to you for hearing on me, and now old Sojourner hasn't got nothing more to say.[79]

Given the social norms of the time, Truth was not authorized to perform any persona she wanted; she could not claim the expert power of a white male lawmaker or the social power of an upper-class woman. However, she did not choose to ignore her identity. Instead, as rhetoric scholar Karlyn Kohrs Campbell argues, Truth artistically used her black, female, former slave identity to construct her persona as a person of strong character, whose knowledge of slavery and of her own abilities as a woman gave her the authority to speak on the topics of slavery and woman suffrage.[80] Her labor in the fields meant she did not meet the social norms for womanhood, yet she *was* a woman. When she explained to the audience that she had watched her own children sold into slavery, she reminded them of her sex and of the horrors of slavery. Her personal experiences gave her the authority to speak. Her skillful arguments and use of humor gave insight to her character.

Campbell argues that the way Truth's speech was perceived and recorded also provides insight into how social power and privileges can affect the perception of a rhetor's persona. Truth spoke English as a second language, having been owned by a Dutch master, and prided herself on correct English usage; thus, according to Campbell, she most likely used the phrase "Aren't I a Woman?" The initial transcription of her speech by Frances Dana Gage, a white woman-suffrage and abolition advocate, powerfully defined how the speech was remembered, however. The phrase "Ain't I a Woman?" was not likely to be used by a person who learned English as a second language. It is more akin to speech styles found in racist caricatures and blackface minstrel shows.[81] Truth's persona, as preserved in Gage's version of the speech, imposed on Truth the social perceptions of slaves as ignorant. Although illiterate, Truth was not ignorant.

Truth's performance of persona in her speech makes clear the ways in which ethos and identity can be used as resources, even by rhetors who belong to groups denied social authority. The transcription of Truth's speech also points to the constraints on performances of persona. Truth probably tried to speak with correct grammar, yet even someone who was sympathetic to her point heard her through the filter of racism.

CONCLUSION

Understanding the rhetor is central to understanding rhetoric. Conceiving of the rhetor through the concept of persona enables us to recognize that the rhetor simultaneously produces and is produced through rhetorical action.

As a civic actor, you play various roles even as others' rhetoric constructs your role as a civic actor. Thus, when you contemplate producing a rhetorical action, pay attention to the way you produce yourself as rhetor in that action. Because seeking agreement with a claim invites assent not only to what was said, but who says it, attention to persona is central to understanding how rhetoric operates.

Persona is a holistic term referring to the character, role, identity, authority, and image a rhetor portrays during a rhetorical act. When you communicate, you may do so from a range of personae. You can develop ethos or trustworthy character, play a role, embrace an identity, claim authority, or project an image.

Regardless of where you find the resources for your performance, a persona is something you do, something you perform, not merely something you are. You possess agency not only in relation to what you say, but as whom you say it. Despite this agency, rhetors are not free to construct just any persona, because audiences and societies place meaning and value on characteristics such as gender, race, socioeconomic status, and ethnicity.

DISCUSSION QUESTIONS

1. What identity ingredients are available to you as you perform a persona? In what ways do you have the privilege (or opportunity) to choose between multiple personae? In what ways do the identities that others assign to you present an obstacle to your communication acts?
2. Is the Sojourner Truth speech an example of strategic essentialism? If so, in what ways does Truth embrace a particular identity? In what ways does she critically reflect on what that identity means?
3. Find an example of a speaker using visuals to present authority. What visual elements produce the image of authority? How does the audience interact with the images? How do the images of authority produce mystification?
4. Give an example of a person's character getting in the way of a persuasive message. How did the person's persona create obstacles for persuasion? What could the person have done to correct these obstacles?
5. Throughout this text, we qualify the people we cite by listing their academic credentials. What form of social power does this practice access? Does it impose a particular identity upon these people? Would their identities be different if we also listed the schools at which they teach or their marital statuses, sexes, races, and classes?

RECOMMENDED READINGS

Campbell, Karlyn Kohrs. "Agency: Promiscuous and Protean." *Communication and Critical/Cultural Studies* 2, no. 1 (March 2005): 1–19.

Goffman, Erving. *The Presentation of Self in Everyday Life*. New York: Anchor, 1959.

Nakayama, Thomas K., and Robert L. Krizek. "Whiteness: A Strategic Rhetoric." *Quarterly Journal of Speech* 81 (August 1995): 291–309.

ENDNOTES

[1] Michael Weiler and W. Barnett Pearce, eds., *Reagan and Public Discourse in America* (Tuscaloosa: University of Alabama Press, 1992), 4.
[2] Frank Newport, Jeffrey M. Jones, and Lydia Saad, "Ronald Reagan from the People's Perspective: A Gallup Poll Review," *Gallup*, June 7, 2004, http://www.gallup.com/poll/11887/ronald-reagan-from-peoples-perspective-gallup-poll-review.aspx (accessed January 15, 2010).
[3] Weiler and Pearce, *Reagan*, 4.

4 J. Jeffery Auer, "Acting Like a President; Or What Has Ronald Reagan Done to Political Speaking?" in *Reagan and Public Discourse in America*, ed. Michael Weiler and W. Barnett Pearce, 93–120 (Tuscaloosa: University of Alabama Press, 1992), 101.

5 James Nuechterlein, in Stephen E. Ambrose, M. E. Bradford, Alonzo L. Hamby, Forrest McDonald, George H. Nash, James Nuechterlein, and Karl O'Lessker, "How Great Was Ronald Reagan?" *Policy Review* (Spring 1989), http://www.hoover.org/publications/policyreview/7908317.html (accessed January 15, 2010).

6 M. E. Bradford, in Ambrose, et al., "How Great."

7 Karlyn Kohrs Campbell and Kathleen Hall Jamieson, *Deeds Done in Words: Presidential Rhetoric and the Genres of Governance* (Chicago: University of Chicago Press, 1990).

8 Auer, "Acting," 101.

9 Wayne Booth, *The Rhetoric of Fiction* (Chicago: University of Chicago Press, 1961), 74–75.

10 Erving Goffman, *The Presentation of Self in Everyday Life* (New York: Anchor, 1959), 15, italics added.

11 Randall Lake, "The Implied Arguer," in *Argumentation Theory and the Rhetoric of Assent*, ed. David C. Williams and Michael D. Hazen, 69–90 (Tuscaloosa: University of Alabama Press, 1990), 83.

12 B. L. Ware and Wil A. Linkugel, "The Rhetorical *Persona*: Marcus Garvey as Black Moses," *Communication Monographs* 49 (1982): 50–64, 50.

13 Ware and Linkugel, "Rhetorical," 50.

14 George A. Kennedy, *A New History of Classical Rhetoric* (Princeton, NJ: Princeton University Press, 1994), 57–60.

15 James M. May, *Trials of Character: The Eloquence of Ciceronian Ethos* (Chapel Hill: University of North Carolina Press, 1988).

16 Cicero, *On the Ideal Orator (De Oratore)*, trans. James M. May and Jakob Wisse (New York: Oxford University Press, 2001), 2.182.

17 Aristotle, *On Rhetoric*, trans. George A. Kennedy (New York: Oxford University Press, 1991) 2.1 [1378a].

18 Aristotle, *On Rhetoric*, 2.1 [1378a].

19 Aristotle, *On Rhetoric*, 1.9.

20 Quoted in Phillip Rawls, "Giuliani Seeks Votes in Alabama," *Tuscaloosa News*, April 11, 2007, http://www.tuscaloosanews.com/article/20070411/NEWS/704110343/1010/NEWS05 (accessed April 15, 2007).

21 Rudy Giuliani presidential campaign website, http://www.joinrudy2008.com/index.php?section=1 (accessed April 15, 2007).

22 Aristotle, *On Rhetoric*, 1.9 [1367a].

23 Aristotle, *On Rhetoric*, 2.1 [1378a].

24 Barack Obama, "Announcement for President," February 10, 2007, http://www.barackobama.com/2007/02/10/remarks_of_senator_barack_obam_11.php (accessed April 15, 2007).

25 Edwin Black, "The Second Persona," *Quarterly Journal of Speech* 56, no. 2 (April 1970): 109–119, 111.

26 Goffman, *Presentation*, 6.

27 Goffman, *Presentation*, 35.

28 Rita Alfonso and Jo Trigilio, "Surfing the Third Wave: A Dialogue between Two Third Wave Feminists," *Hypatia* 12, no. 3 (Summer 1997), 13, 7–16.

[29] Goffman, *Presentation*, 67. See also Kenneth Burke, *A Rhetoric of Motives* (Berkeley: University of California Press, 1969), 101–123.

[30] George Washington, "Washington's Inaugural Address of 1789," National Archives and Records Administration, http://www.archives.gov/exhibits/american_originals/inaugtxt.html (accessed April 22, 2009).

[31] Quoted in Dana Rosenblatt and Don Lemon, "White Valedictorian: A First for Historically Black Morehouse," "Black in America 2," CNN.com/US, http://www.cnn.com/2008/US/05/16/white.valedictorian/index.html (accessed January 16, 2010).

[32] Adrien Katherine Wing, "Brief Reflections toward a Multiplicative Theory of Praxis and Being," in *Critical Race Feminism: A Reader*, ed. Adrien Katherine Wing, 27–34 (New York: New York University Press, 1997).

[33] The inspiration for the metaphor of ingredients comes from Audre Lorde, *Sister Outsider* (Trumansberg, NY: Crossing, 1984), 120.

[34] Donald E. Hall (ed.), *Muscular Christianity: Embodying the Victorian Age* (Cambridge, UK: Cambridge University Press, 1994).

[35] Herman Gray, "Black Masculinity and Visual Culture," *Callaloo* 18, no. 2 (1995): 401–405.

[36] Nick Trujillo, "Hegemonic Masculinity on the Mound: Media Representations of Nolan Ryan and American Sports Culture," *Critical Studies in Mass Communication* 8 (1991): 290–308.

[37] Patricia Hill Collins, "Shifting the Center: Race, Class, and Feminist Theorizing about Motherhood," in *Representations of Motherhood*, ed. Donna Bassin, Margaret Honey, and Maryle Mahrer Kaplan, 56–74 (New Haven: Yale University Press, 1994).

[38] Mari Boor Tonn, "Militant Motherhood: Labor's Mary Harris 'Mother' Jones," *Quarterly Journal of Speech* 82 (February 1996): 1–21, 1.

[39] Tonn, "Militant," 5.

[40] Tonn, "Militant," 6.

[41] Kimberlé Crenshaw, "Demarginalizing the Intersection of Race and Sex: A Black Feminist Critique of Antidiscrimination Doctrine, Feminist Theory and Antiracist Politics," *University of Chicago Legal Forum* (1989): 139–167, 59.

[42] Sandra Harding, "Subjectivity, Experience, and Knowledge: An Epistemology from/for Rainbow Coalition Politics," in *Who Can Speak? Authority and Critical Identity*, ed. Judith Roof and Robyn Weigman, 120–136 (Urbana: University of Illinois Press, 1995), 121.

[43] Thomas K. Nakayama and Robert L. Krizek, "Whiteness: A Strategic Rhetoric," *Quarterly Journal of Speech* 81 (August 1995): 291–309.

[44] Thomas A. Hollihan, *Uncivil Wars: Political Campaigns in a Media Age* (Boston: Bedford/St. Martin's, 2001), 56.

[45] Paula M. L. Moya, "Postmodernism, 'Realism,' and the Politics of Identity: Cherríe Moraga and Chicana Feminism," in *Feminist Genealogies, Colonial Legacies, Democratic Futures*, ed. M. Jacqui Alexander and Chandra Talpade Mohanty, 125–150 (New York: Routledge, 1997), 127.

[46] "First Muslim Elected to Congress," MSNBC, November 7, 2006, http://www.msnbc.msn.com/id/15613050 (accessed April 29, 2009).

[47] Moya, "Postmodernism," 132.

[48] Karlyn Kohrs Campbell, "Agency: Promiscuous and Protean," *Communication and Critical/Cultural Studies* 2, no. 1 (March 2005): 5.

[49] New York Times/CBS News Poll, "Whites, Race and the Election," August 9, 2008, http://www.nytimes.com/imagepages/2008/08/09/opinion/09blow_art.ready.html ?scp=3&sq=whites%20race%20election&st=cse (accessed April 29, 2009).

[50] Barack Obama, Presidential Inaugural Address, "What is Required: The Price and the Promise of Citizenship," January 20, 2009, http://www.americanrhetoric.com /speeches/barackobamabarackobamainauguraladdress.htm (accessed April 27, 2009).

[51] Gayatri Chakravorty Spivak, *The Spivak Reader*, ed. Donna Landry and Gerald MacLean (New York: Routledge, 1996), 159, 214.

[52] Stokely Carmichael, "Black Power," October 1966, http://www.americanrhetoric.com/speeches/stokelycarmichaelblackpower.html (accessed April 29, 2009).

[53] Robin Morgan, ed., *Sisterhood is Powerful* (New York: Random House, 1970).

[54] Vine Deloria, Jr., and Daniel R. Wildcat, *Power and Place: Indian Education in America* (Golden, CO: Fulcrum, 2001).

[55] Spivak, *Reader*, 214.

[56] Gloria Anzaldúa, "Bridge, Drawbridge, Sandbar or Island: Lesbians-of-Color *Hacienda Alianzas*," in *Bridges of Power: Women's Multicultural Alliances*, ed. Lisa Albrecht and Rose M. Brewer, 216–231 (Philadelphia: New Society, 1990).

[57] John R. P. French and Bertram Raven, "The Bases of Social Power," in *Studies in Social Power*, ed. Dorwin Cartwright, 150–167 (Ann Arbor: University of Michigan Press, 1959).

[58] Mia Alexander-Snow, "Dynamics of Gender, Ethnicity, and Race in Understanding Classroom Incivility," *New Directions for Teaching & Learning* 99 (Fall 2004): 21–31.

[59] Bernice Resnick Sandler, "Women Faculty at Work in the Classroom, or, Why It Still Hurts To Be a Woman in Labor," *Communication Education* 40, no. 1 (January 1991), 6–15.

[60] Travis L. Russ, Cheri J. Simonds, and Stephen K. Hunt. "Coming Out in the Classroom . . . An Occupational Hazard?: The Influence of Sexual Orientation on Teacher Credibility and Perceived Student Learning," *Communication Education* 51, no. 3 (2002): 311–324.

[61] Bonnie S. McElhinny, "'I Don't Smile Much Anymore': Affect, Gender and the Discourse of Pittsburgh Police Officers," in *Locating Power: Proceedings of the 1992 Berkeley Conference on Women and Language*, ed. Kira Hall and Birch Moonwomon, 386–403 (Berkeley, CA: Berkeley Women and Language Group, 1992).

[62] Cornell West, *Race Matters* (Boston: Beacon, 1993): x–xi.

[63] Karlyn Kohrs Campbell, "The Rhetoric of Women's Liberation: An Oxymoron," *Quarterly Journal of Speech* 59 (February 1973): 75.

[64] Campbell, "Rhetoric," 75.

[65] Goffman, *Presentation*, 59.

[66] Judith Butler, *Gender Trouble* (New York: Routledge, 1990), 33.

[67] Judith Butler, *Undoing Gender* (New York: Routledge, 2004), 1.

[68] Butler, *Undoing Gender*, 1.

[69] Jeff Zeleny, "Persistent 'Birthers' Fringe Disorients Strategists," *New York Times on the Web* (August 5, 2009), http://0-www.lexisnexis.com.unistar.uni.edu/us/lnacademic /results/docview/docview.do?docLinkInd=true&risb=21_T7120640045&format= GNBFI&sort=RELEVANCE&startDocNo=1&resultsUrlKey=29_T7120640054& cisb=22_T7120640052&treeMax=true&treeWidth=0&csi=6742&docNo=12 (accessed August 10, 2009).

[70] Phil Taylor, "The Sadness," *Sports Illustrated* (December 14, 2009), 48–51, 50. The February issue of *Golf Magazine* contained a two-page spread reproducing twenty front-page stories from gossip magazines and tabloids. An article on Golf.com declared that 2009 "will be remembered as the year that Tiger's impeccable image took a serious hit." Gary Van Sickle, "Tiger Woods's Image Will Be Tarnished after Recent Drama," Golf.com, December 2, 2009, http://www.golf.com/golf/tours_news/article/0,28136,1945114,00.html (accessed January 17, 2010).

[71] Taylor, "The Sadness," 50.

[72] Daniel J. Boorstin, *The Image: A Guide to Pseudo-Events in America*, 25th anniversary ed. (New York: Athenaeum, 1987), 188–189.

[73] Boorstin, *Image*, 185–193.

[74] Boorstin, *Image*, 185.

[75] Boorstin, *Image*, 188.

[76] Phil Taylor, "Shattering of Tiger Woods's Carefully Constructed Public Image is Grist for Gossip, but It's Just a Sad Story," Golf.com, December 9, 2009, http://www.golf.com/golf/tours_news/article/0,28136,1946679,00.html (accessed January 17, 2010).

[77] Mark Caro, "Ford Still Defined by Chevy: Fair or Not, Ford's Enduring Image as a Bumbler Was Sealed by a National Lampoon," *Chicago Tribune*, December 28, 2006, http://archives.chicagotribune.com/2006/dec/28/image/chi-0612280251dec28 (accessed May 6, 2009).

[78] Suzanne Pullon Fitch, "Sojourner Truth," in *Women Public Speakers in the United State, 1800–1925*, ed. Karlyn Kohrs Campbell, 421–433 (Westport, CT: Greenwood Press, 1993), 421.

[79] Sojourner Truth, "On Women's Rights," Ohio Women's Rights Convention, Akron, OH, 1851. Speech text accessed April 12, 2007, from http://people.sunyulster.edu/voughth/sojourner_truth.htm. Descriptive comments in the speech drawn from Karlyn Kohrs Campbell, *Man Cannot Speak For Her*, vol. 2 (New York: Praeger, 1989), 100.

[80] Campbell, "Agency."

[81] Campbell, "Agency."

Chapter 7

Audiences

Key Concepts

attitudes

audience

beliefs

consubstantiality

eavesdropping audience

first persona

fourth persona

identification

rhetorical agency

rhetorical audience

second persona

third persona

values

On May 17, 1954, the United States Supreme Court issued the *Brown v. Board of Education* decision, authored by Chief Justice Earl Warren, ordering the desegregation of public schools. Typically, judges write decisions in a style appropriate for members of the legal profession, focusing their attention on either of two questions: questions of fact or questions of law. Trial courts focus on questions of fact to determine what happened, who was involved and to what degree, and whether there were extenuating circumstances. Appellate courts, including the US Supreme Court, address questions of law to determine whether the court has jurisdiction, whether the legal process was followed, which precedents and legal principles apply, whether the law is constitutional, and how the law should be interpreted.[1] Given the specialized audience and evidentiary requirements, legal decisions tend to participate in technical (rather than public) argument.

In *Brown v. Board of Education*, the Court clearly articulated the technical question of law at hand: "Does segregation of children in public schools solely on the basis of race, even though the physical facilities and other 'tangible' factors may be equal, deprive the children of the minority group of equal educational opportunities?"[2] The *Brown* decision was unique. The decision, examining whether the "separate but equal" doctrine established by *Plessy v. Ferguson*[3] in 1896 violated the equal protection clause of the Fourteenth Amendment, was not written in the typical legal style. Read aloud in its entirety from the bench, it overtly declared that precedent alone did not govern the Court's interpretation of the Constitution. It was short, deliberately written in a length that could be reproduced on a single page of newsprint and understood by the general public. (The *Brown* decision was approximately 1,775 words. By comparison, the 1973 *Roe v. Wade* decision was approximately 11,667 words long.)

The *Brown* decision engaged in public argument, rather than technical legal argument. The Court explained its reliance on social factors rather than on legal precedent:

Segregation of white and colored children in public schools has a detrimental effect upon the colored children. The impact is greater when it has the sanction of the law, for the policy of separating the races is usually interpreted as denoting the inferiority of the negro group. A sense of inferiority affects the motivation of a child to learn. Segregation with the sanction of law, therefore, has a tendency to [retard] the educational and mental development of negro children and to deprive them of some of the benefits they would receive in a racial[ly] integrated school system.

Whatever may have been the extent of psychological knowledge at the time of *Plessy v. Ferguson,* this finding is amply supported by modern authority. Any language in *Plessy v. Ferguson* contrary to this finding is rejected.[4]

Compared to most court decisions, this one is easily understood by a general audience. It avoids the use of legal jargon, focuses on the question of right and wrong, and refuses to be governed by *stare decisis* (the legal principle that says that, in deciding a case, a court should be governed by the precedents set in earlier decisions). The decision refers to the psychological effects of the *Plessy* decision on schoolchildren, a type of evidence unexpected in an appellate court ruling that typically would look to legal precedents (not their effects) to guide the present case.

What induced the Court to write such an atypical decision? Chief Justice Warren, in his memoirs written two decades after the ruling, explains: "It was not a long opinion, for I had written it so it could be published in the daily press throughout the nation without taking too much space. This enabled the public to have our entire reasoning instead of a few excerpts from a lengthier document."[5] By addressing the decision to the US public, and not just the technical sphere of the law, the Court participated in the public discussion about race and segregation.

Much debate ensued. Appellate judge and judicial philosopher Learned Hand derided the decision because it failed to follow precedent and did not exhibit judicial restraint.[6] Judge Hand's reaction can be explained in part because the decision was not written to persuade him as a fellow legal expert and, thus, violated the technical rules of legal argument.

Not everyone in the public was persuaded, however. In 1956, 101 southern senators and congressional representatives wrote a Southern Manifesto that "pledged the signers to exert 'all lawful means' toward reversing the Supreme Court's desegregation decision."[7] In response, Warren pointed out that the decision did not seek to end desegregation by court decree but to give Congress and the public the ability to act politically to end segregation.[8] By targeting its discourse to a wider audience, the Court also helped persuade the general public of the social and political importance of desegregation. Separate could not be equal.

This example illustrates the important role of the audience in rhetoric. The Supreme Court was a rhetor possessing both referent and legitimate power, but it did not rely solely on that social power to persuade the country. "Because we say so" was not enough to persuade the public. The Court realized its decision, alone, could not create the necessary social change if only other lawyers and judges understood the decision: the society as a whole had to change.

In this chapter we examine the complex relationship among audiences, rhetors, and symbolic actions. First, we discuss how rhetoric is adapted to audiences. Because rhetoric is addressed to other people, understanding audience is central to rhetoric. Second, we analyze audience agency, recognizing that not all audiences possess the same degree of power to effect change in the world. Third, we discuss how audiences can be adapted to rhetoric; or how rhetoric can constitute, or bring into being, a particular audience.

ADAPTING RHETORIC TO AUDIENCES

Audience is the element that distinguishes rhetoric from purely expressive forms of communication (such as shouting "ouch" when you stub your toe, or drawing for the pure pleasure of artistic creation). Rhetorical scholar Kenneth Burke identifies the central element of rhetoric as "its nature as *addressed*, since persuasion implies an audience."[9] He describes rhetoric as "the use of words by human agents to form attitudes or to induce actions in other human agents."[10] We would expand Burke's definition to include the use of any symbolic action, but we embrace his emphasis on rhetoric as addressed to other people—an audience. In the next section, we explain what we mean by "rhetoric as addressed." We then outline a few means of adaptation: identification, pathos, and values.

Rhetoric as Addressed

Recognizing that rhetoric is addressed to an audience is not as simple as it might first appear. **Audience** can mean *any person who hears, reads, or sees a symbolic action; the group targeted by a message, even if it is not present; or the group capable of acting in response to the message.* Multiple audiences may exist for any given symbolic action.

In interpersonal interactions, the audience is usually easy to identify: it is the person to whom you are speaking (unless—in a particularly middle-school moment—you are hoping that person will pass along what you said to your intended audience). Identifying the audience is more complicated in public address. The group of people who might hear a public address is large and diverse. Its members may carry conflicting expectations. Sometimes, everyone present is the intended recipient of the symbolic action; other times, only some of those present are the audience for the message.

When you speak to a large group, not every member may be part of the **rhetorical audience,** or *the audience that "consists only of those persons who are capable of being influenced by discourse and of being mediators of change."* In this definition, rhetoric scholar Lloyd Bitzer distinguishes a rhetorical audience from all those who might hear a speech.[11] For Bitzer, a rhetorical audience preexists the rhetorical action; it is empirically real and already possesses the ability to implement the change that the rhetor calls for. In Bitzer's approach, rhetors and critics need to analyze the audience members who are agents capable of bringing about the action, not just anyone who might receive the message.

Bitzer's understanding of the rhetorical audience finds its roots in the classical tradition, which defined the audience as that group who was capable of acting in response to a message. Aristotle points out, "A speech consists of three things: a speaker and a subject on which he [or she] speaks and someone addressed, and the objective of the speech relates to the last."[12] Aristotle argues that rhetoric is persuasive to a *particular* audience, which he defines as those who make judgments concerning the issue or issues at hand. The objective of the speech is, in turn, determined by the audience, as the audience holds the power to act on the message.[13]

Philosophers Chaïm Perelman and Lucie Olbrechts-Tyteca[14] note the classical rhetorical tradition's emphasis on "the discursive ways of acting upon an audience, with a view to winning or increasing its adherence to the theses that were presented to it for its endorsement."[15] They agree with Aristotle, explaining: "It is indeed the audience which has the major role in determining the quality of argument and the behavior of orators."[16] Whenever you consider the function of symbolic action, it is essential to assess the audience to whom the rhetor addresses the message. For example, when students go through a graduation ceremony, they may appreciate a commencement address their parents condemn.

You can probably recall times when you made rhetorical choices according to the audience to whom you spoke; that is, you adapted to the rhetorical audience. For example, when requesting an extension on a paper due for a class, you probably tailor your request to the professor from whom you are requesting the extension. Some professors might be more persuaded by a pity appeal, while others would only be persuaded if you proved you had not procrastinated. You might not even make such a request to some professors because you believe they are not likely to grant the request. In all these instances, you frame your message to speak to the particular audience. You adapt because your audience determines and delimits the objective of your symbolic action.

When identifying the audience(s) for a rhetorical act, remember that multiple audiences may be targeted. When President Barack Obama spoke at Cairo University on June 4, 2009, commentators noted that he addressed multiple audiences in his attempt to respond to the problems that arose in US-Muslim relations in the wake of 9/11. NBC's chief White House correspondent, Chuck Todd, explained during the NBC *Nightly News* that President Obama sought "to talk to three or four different audiences, including explaining Islam to Americans, explaining America to Muslims [in the Arab world], and trying to jumpstart a conversation between Israelis and the Arab world."[17] The speech was not simply a single message to a homogenous audience, but a complex set of messages directed to heterogeneous audiences that operate from diverse cultural orientations, participate in distinct ideologies, and possess a range of different values, beliefs, and attitudes. Although he spoke to multiple audiences, he attempted to create identification with all of them. To speak effectively to all these audiences, President Obama reportedly began working on the speech even before he was elected to office.[18]

Appealing to an Audience

How might you go about adapting to an audience? A range of overlapping rhetorical techniques exists. First, you can seek to create identification, or a sense of commonality between you and the audience. Second, you can employ pathos appeals, trying to put the audience members in a state of mind where they are most open to the arguments offered. Third, you can work with factors that influence audience perceptions, which include attitudes, values, and beliefs. These factors guide audiences' assessments of symbolic action, sometimes justifiably and sometimes in the form of unwarranted bias.

Identification. The concept of identification plays a central role in describing the relationship between rhetors and audiences. **Identification** is *a communicative process through which people are unified on the basis of common interests or characteristics*.[19] Through identification, you make a connection with the audience on a psychological level, not simply on a demographic level. On the surface you might identify with another student simply because of the shared demographic characteristic—the other person is also a student. However, identification can be deeper if you do not take it for granted, but actively produce it through rhetoric. If you wanted to create identification on the basis of shared student status, you would not simply take for granted that other students would agree with you. Instead, you would use evidence based on experiences students share, speak from the persona of a student, and emphasize values and concerns that are prominent in students' lives.

Rhetors and audience members are both similar and different. Identification can be achieved by emphasizing similarities. Burke explains that "two persons may be identified in terms of some principle they share in common, an 'identification' that does not deny their distinctness."[20] Notice that Burke does not reduce identification to shared demographic characteristics, but argues that a shared principle must be identified. Identification does not require that a rhetor and audience member be identical, only that points of agreement and consubstantiality be identified. These moments of **consubstantiality,** in which *two unlike things momentarily become one*, are at the heart of persuasion and rhetoric. Burke posits, "Here is perhaps the simplest case of persuasion. You persuade a man [or woman] only insofar as you can talk his [or her] language by speech, gesture, tonality, order, image, attitude, idea, *identifying* your ways with his [or hers]."[21] If you are connected to a person in some way, you probably have a better chance of persuading that person than if you were a stranger or completely alien to her or him.

Understanding the process of identification is central to understanding rhetoric as addressed. Thus, critics need to explore how rhetors seek to create identification with their audiences. In President Obama's 2009 speech at Cairo University,[22] he sought to create identification with each audience to whom he spoke. He opened by identifying with Muslims, using the customary Muslim greeting "Assalaamu alaykum."[23] He reaffirmed that identification by outlining his other personal connections to Islam: "[M]y father came from a Kenyan family that includes generations of Muslims. As a boy, I spent several years in Indonesia and heard the call of the azaan at the break of dawn and at the fall of dusk. As a young man, I worked in Chicago communities where many found dignity and peace in their Muslim faith."[24] He identified with Christians by testifying to his own Christianity, saying "I'm a Christian."[25] He highlighted the identification of political interests between the United States and Israel: "America's strong bonds with Israel are well known. This bond is unbreakable. It is based upon cultural and historical ties, and the recognition that the aspiration for a Jewish homeland is rooted in a tragic history that cannot be denied."[26] Finally, he created identification between the United States and Arab countries by recognizing the common interests they have in stopping the suffering of Palestinians:

> On the other hand, it is also undeniable that the Palestinian people—Muslims and Christians—have suffered in pursuit of a homeland. For more than 60 years they've endured the pain of dislocation. Many wait in refugee camps in the West Bank, Gaza, and neighboring lands for a life of peace and security that they have never been able to lead. They endure the daily humiliations—large and small—that come with occupation. So let there be no doubt: The situation for the Palestinian people is intolerable. And America will not turn our backs on the legitimate Palestinian aspiration for dignity, opportunity, and a state of their own.[27]

Even though President Obama spoke to audiences with different, if not conflicting, interests and identities, he was able to create the impression that he as a person, and the United States as a nation, were consubstantial with Muslims and Christians, Arabs and Israelis. His need to create identification with multiple audiences can be explained by the various audiences' abilities to effect the change for which he called.

Pathos. Aristotle, focusing on the importance of pathos, explained that rhetors must consider the emotional state of the audience.[28] He noted that people make judgments differently depending upon their state of mind.[29] An angry person makes judgments differently from the way a happy person does. Aristotle's treatment of human emotions was perhaps the earliest systematic treatment of psychology.[30] He placed emotions in contrasting pairs: anger/calmness; friendliness/enmity; fear/confidence; shame/shamelessness; kindness/unkindness; pity/indignation; envy/emulation. To relieve fear, a rhetor must shift the emotional state of the audience to confidence. Pathos appeals lead audience members to particular emotional states of mind.

You have thought about the emotional state of your audience when you have considered someone's mood before initiating a difficult conversation. Suppose you want to talk to a housemate about redistributing chores. If you ask a mutual friend what kind of mood your housemate is in before you talk, you are considering the emotional state of the audience in constructing your request. You might even choose not to make the request that day if you conclude that your housemate is not in the appropriate state of mind to consider your request, or you might think about how to alter your housemate's state of mind to be more open to a conversation about shared housework. Pathos appeals recognize the effect of emotion on an audience's receptiveness, so they are chosen to induce a particular emotion in order to enhance a persuasive appeal.

For example, fear is a strong emotion that can lead people to make particular choices they might not make otherwise. For Aristotle, fear is "pain or agitation derived from the imagination of a future destructive or painful evil."[31] Quit Smoking campaigns often rely on pathos appeals, speaking to human beings' fear of death. Just Eliminate Lies (or JEL), an Iowa-based youth-targeted campaign created in 2000, has focused on smokers as well as on the tobacco industry. In one print advertisement, it uses the pathos appeal of imminent death, showing a draped body on a gurney with the caption "Smoking, table for one."[32] If the advertisement works, it will persuade you not to smoke cigarettes because of the fear of dying a painful and premature death from lung cancer. In choosing not to smoke, you are psychologically comforted that the danger of dying from lung cancer is significantly reduced. We all know people who continue to smoke despite constant fear appeals to quit smoking, though, so clearly rhetoric never involves a simple cause-and-effect relationship.

Perelman and Olbrechts-Tyteca observe that images that the rhetor provides will create emotions in audiences.[33] Emotions cannot be triggered merely by saying "Be afraid, be very afraid!" Instead, they are created through complex rhetorical forms, such as myths and narratives. A rhetor who is able to construct images to which an audience attaches emotions can move the audience to a particular emotional state in which it is more open to persuasion.

To illustrate the complexities involved in a pathos appeal, consider the 2009 outbreak of the H1N1 (also known as swine flu). The World Health Organization declared the flu outbreak a pandemic, outlining health concerns and warnings because the strain had never been seen before and was affecting people on several continents.[34] Although "pandemic" refers to how widespread a disease is, and not necessarily its mortality rate, the label likely induced fear because of movies such as *Pandemic* (2007), *Outbreak* (1995), *28 Days Later* (2003), and *Contagion* (2011), all of which threatened death to everyone. Media coverage of H1N1 intensified fear, by including images of people wearing protective masks, Vice President Joseph Biden remarking that he would advise his own family members to avoid public transportation and confined places,[35] and local news reports of confirmed cases and deaths. The anticipation of a flu outbreak and the rhetorical depictions of the flu cases created a situation in which public fear could take control of people's decision making.

To counter this fear, President Obama issued a statement noting that the government was monitoring the situation and outlining specific steps the government was taking. He concluded with practical advice: "I've asked every American to take the same steps you would take to prevent any other flu: Keep

of health and welfare studies at the Cato Institute (a nonprofit public policy research foundation based on the principles of limited government, free markets, individual liberty, and peace), argues:

> The broad and growing trend is to move away from centralized government control and to introduce more market-oriented features. The answer then to America's health care problems lies not in heading down the road to national health care but in learning from the experiences of other countries, which demonstrate the failure of centralized command and control and the benefits of increasing consumer incentives and choice. . . . [A] closer look at countries with national health care systems shows that those countries have serious problems of their own, including rising costs, rationing of care, lack of access to modern medical technology, and poor health outcomes. Countries whose national health systems avoid the worst of these problems are successful precisely because they incorporate market mechanisms and reject centralized government control. In other words, socialized medicine works—as long as it isn't socialized medicine.[44]

His opposition to a national or single-payer health care program is based on particular values, beliefs, and attitudes informed by a free market economic system. From that perspective, anything that does not embrace the value of freedom of choice might be labeled as socialism, which is perceived to be capitalism's opposite. If you value choice as the central principal of freedom in a capitalist economy, then you might have a negative attitude toward any program that you perceive limits your choice. We could describe Tanner's values, beliefs, and attitudes as follows:

> *Value:* Free market (capitalism) is good; centralized government control (socialism) is bad.
>
> *Belief:* Market-oriented features, such as consumer incentives and choice, work.
>
> *Attitude:* Any government program that centralizes control or limits individual health care choice is suspect.

In this example, the negative attitude toward a government program is guided by the belief in individual choice and the values of a free market economy.

To respond to Tanner, a person advocating a single-payer system could focus on beliefs, attitudes, or values. For example, you could challenge his belief that the market always works, that choice actually exists now, or that free enterprise profit motives work in health care; or the attitude that government is inept. Altering someone's values is more difficult because it requires altering core organizing principles. It would require you to challenge ideographs, perhaps by offering a competing ideograph: you could argue that access to health care is a right, not a privilege for those who can afford to pay; or that the value of individual choice does not apply to this case.

For an example of a person operating with a different set of values, beliefs, and attitudes, we turn to a radio interview with bioethicist Arthur Caplan,[45] director of the Center for Bioethics and chair of the Department of Medical Ethics at the University of Pennsylvania, and one of *Discover* magazine's ten most influential people in science. Like Tanner, Caplan points to other countries' approaches to health care, not to argue that the market is the best way to solve the health care crisis, but to make explicit the way in which particular values influence US beliefs about health care and attitudes toward its provision. Caplan explains that Germany, Taiwan, and England do not say you must work in order to have health insurance. It is not a perk of work or something you earn. Caplan argues this value orientation from a moral perspective, stating: "Morally, it doesn't make sense to say you have to earn your health insurance." He argues that if people are sick and without health insurance, the choice is to leave them on the street or care for them. To argue that people earn or deserve health insurance because they have jobs seems morally wrong to him. Thus, Caplan argues for universal coverage not because it is efficient or an investment, but on the grounds that it is a basic human right—and "more than anything else about the right." He seeks to make access to health insurance a prerequisite to the free market, rather than as a good provided by it.

Caplan's interview illustrates the central role values play. He is adamant that a solution to the problem of health care costs and access cannot be achieved until US citizens hold a set of common values. Unless people in the United States see health care as an ethical issue, rather than as an economic one, no solution is possible. People, he says, will apologize for the millions of people lacking health insurance but argue that "they don't have a right to it." For Caplan, aligning values is a prerequisite for changing beliefs, attitudes, and policy.

The point is that audiences are not passive recipients of a message, but active participants in the process of rhetoric. Audiences matter. In addition, if a rhetor is seeking to induce some sort of action in an audience, the rhetor must consider the limits of audience agency, of the audience's ability to take the action. You can try to adapt rhetoric to an audience in order to create a desired change, or you can try to adapt the audience to your rhetoric. In order to show why rhetors must sometimes adapt audiences to rhetoric, we need to explain the concept of audience agency.

AUDIENCE AGENCY

Recall, from Chapter 1, that Karlyn Kohrs Campbell defines **rhetorical agency** as *"the capacity to act, that is, to have the competence to speak or write in a way that will be recognized or heeded by others in one's community."*[46] We amended her definition to include competence not just in the verbal forms of speaking and writing, but also in visual rhetoric.

Both rhetors and audiences possess agency. Just as rhetors may possess various degrees of agency because they have various positions in the socio-economic order, cultural norms, or ideologies, so, too may audiences possess various degrees of agency, or various capacities to act on or respond to rhetors' symbolic actions. Campbell argues that traditional understandings of the audience as the group to whom a symbolic action is addressed and that is capable of enacting the called-for change are overly limiting. Not all audiences who are addressed already possess agency; they are not already rhetorical audiences, but must be constituted as such. In some cases, rhetors may need to construct audiences as agents of action.

For example, in the rhetoric of women's liberation that emerged in the 1960s and 1970s, a central goal of the rhetoric was empowerment: convincing women that they could, indeed, be agents of change. Campbell argues, "The [traditional] concept of the audience does not account for a situation in which the audience must be *created under the special conditions* surrounding women's liberation."[47] Women activists faced the challenge of figuring out how to perform the public role of rhetor when social demands on how to perform the role of woman pushed them to stay out of public affairs. In addition, even though women really were not equal under the law, not all women perceived inequality to be a problem. Those who did were uncertain they had the ability to effect change in the law or culture. As women appealed to other women to act, they had to make clear that the audience members possessed the agency with which to act; they had to construct audiences as having agency as one of their characteristics.

Given all the complexities associated with the audience, when you consider the interplay of rhetoric and audience, you need to decide whether the audience is (1) the group of people who happened to receive the symbolic action, (2) the group or groups targeted by the rhetor, (3) the group with whom the rhetor sought to create identification, or (4) the audience called into being by the rhetoric. We now turn to a more in-depth analysis of this last form of audience.

ADAPTING AUDIENCES TO RHETORIC

Audiences, even those already capable of acting, are molded by the rhetoric addressed to them. Rhetoric scholar Barbara Biesecker suggests that identities of audiences and of rhetors are not fixed; that rhetorical action is "an event that makes possible the production of identities and social relations."[48] Rhetors can call audiences into being. An audience can be understood not only as Bitzer's objectively identifiable empirical audience that is capable of acting, but also as a rhetorical creation.

A rhetor addresses an audience in the hope of affecting that audience in some way. However, people often take for granted what constitutes the audience—that the audience is the people who receive the message. Think about your preparations for a speech in class. How much time do you spend thinking about who your audience is? Do you just assume it is your classmates? Or your instructor? In other words, do you assume that an audience preexists the message? Or, do you think about how you could actually change the character of the class with your message, how you could target your message to only some people in your class, or even how you might address an audience who is totally absent? Your audience might come into being because of your message.

One of the most analyzed examples of bringing an audience into existence is found in scholarly examinations of "the people." Political discourse often takes for granted that a group known as "the people" exists, and is the group to whom political discourse is directed. For example, Speaker of the House John Boehner released a column two days after the 112th Congress was sworn in, in which he declared, "The new Majority is wasting no time answering the call of the American people to cut spending immediately, repeal ObamaCare and change the way Congress works."[49] "The people" does not really exist as a discreet entity, however. Given that Gallup polls taken at the time concerning the health care law indicated that "Americans are broadly divided on the issue, with slightly more favoring repeal (46%) than opposing it (40%)" and 14% having no opinion,[50] it is clear that not *all* the American people favored repealing the law. Who, then, are "the people?"

Communication scholar Michael C. McGee points out that the concept of "the people" is a rhetorical construction. He explains that "'the people,' even though made 'real' by their own belief and behavior, are still essentially a mass illusion. In purely objective terms, the only human reality is that of the individual; groups, whether as small as a Sunday school class or as big as a whole society, are infused with an artificial identity."[51] The individuals who compose an audience are real, but the belief that the collection of individuals represents a unit is a social construction. To say an audience is a social construction does not mean, however, that it is illusory or meaningless. How an audience is constructed matters to how it acts. Rhetoric matters.

Just as McGee analyzes "the people," scholars have explored the rhetorical creation of other groups. Such a creation is not the result of a single rhetorical act, but the repeated invocation of that group across multiple messages. When a rhetor constructs an audience as a group of people who identify with one another, a second persona has been created. Yet, whenever identification is created within a group, division is also created. Thus, an assessment of the third persona, the excluded or denied audience, is necessary. The rhetor may also create an audience that is a fourth persona, an audience that is indirectly or surreptitiously addressed.

Second Persona

The **first persona** is *the author implied by the discourse*. Rhetorical theorist Edwin Black posits that just as the rhetor may construct a persona for the "I" who is speaking, so too may a rhetor create a **second persona** for the "you" to whom the rhetor speaks, *the implied audience for whom a rhetor constructs symbolic actions*.[52] He challenges critics to look beyond the immediate audience and to recognize the larger social context in which symbolic action worked.

At the beginning of this chapter we discussed the example of the Supreme Court decision in *Brown v. Board of Education,* which was written for the general public. The use of public reasoning rather than legal precedent pointed to the wider public as the implied audience, the second persona, rather than the narrower legal community. In addition, the public is but a particular type of public—one who is called to accept the equal humanity of all people. When analyzing the audience from this perspective, a critic does not ask: To what group of bodies does a rhetor speak? Instead, the more pertinent question is: What auditor is implied within the rhetorical discourse? Identifying the implied auditor is important, Black says, because "the critic can see in the auditor implied by a discourse a model of what the rhetor would have his [or her] real auditor become."[53]

Examples of second persona abound in public discourse. From Franklin Delano Roosevelt's "the only thing we have to fear is fear itself,"[54] to George H. W. Bush's "thousand points of light,"[55] to William J. Clinton's "spring reborn in the world's oldest democracy, that brings forth the vision and courage to reinvent America,"[56] we can see appeals to an audience to be something it is not yet. Such rhetoric holds out ideals to which an audience can aspire, yet presents those ideals as already in existence, thus constituting the US citizenry as beings of a particular type (fearless, philanthropic, reborn). Each of these presidents spoke to a particular "you," constructing the audience so that it was adapted to fit the rhetorical message, rather than adapting the message to fit some objectively existing audience.

Politicians often talk about how "we" need to do something, or that "we" as a nation believe in particular values, when in reality they are referencing a particular segment of the population who, they hope, will vote for them. Granted, it is extremely easy to fall into using "we," especially when a person wants to create a sense of identification and community. As Burke points out, however, whenever identification is used, one must "confront the implications of *division*. . . . Identification is compensatory to division."[57] When a group says "we are alike," it implies that others are *not* like them.

In one example, Manuel Miranda (a former aide to Senator Bill Frist), in a Heritage Foundation luncheon explaining how conservatives could woo the Latino/a vote, said: "Hispanic polls, Hispanic surveys, indicate that Hispanics think just like everyone else. We're not like African-Americans. We think just like everybody else."[58] By identifying Hispanics with "everybody else," then dissociating African Americans from that group, Miranda suggests that "everyone else" as a group does not include, literally, everyone else. Instead, Miranda's rhetoric says "everyone else" means whites, of which African Americans are not a part. Whenever a rhetor seeks to create identification among group members, disidentification is a necessary counterpart. If you create an "us," you also create a "them." From this dialectic relationship comes the reality of a third persona, an "it" who not only is excluded from address, but whose humanity is questioned.

Third Persona

If rhetors can call an audience into being, they can construct other people as lacking being. Rhetorical scholar Philip Wander labels these people the

third persona: *"audiences not present, audiences rejected or negated through the speech and/or the speaking situation."*[59]

Recognition of such an audience is essential in tracking the ways in which rhetoric enacts ideology. Just as rhetoric can affirm a set of values, beliefs, and attitudes, so too can it erase or deny values. Thus, whenever one studies the audience that is present in the rhetorical action, one should also ask about the audience members who have been excluded. Wander explains, "What is negated through the Second Persona forms the silhouette of a Third Persona—the 'it' that is not present, that is objectified in a way that 'you' and 'I' are not. . . . The potentiality of language to commend being carries with it the potential to spell out being unacceptable, undesirable, insignificant."[60] The third persona is the group treated as an object and dehumanized, while the second persona is the audience treated as a subject and recognized or commended. If the first persona is an "I," and the second persona a "you," then the third persona is an "it."

The construction of a third persona involves more than speaking to one group of people rather than another. Rhetors cannot speak to all people all the time. In some instances, messages really are meant for a particular audience. In many cases, however, constituting one audience by including some people necessarily excludes other people. For Wander's purposes, the third persona

> refers not merely to groups of people with whom "you" and "I" are not to identify, who are to remain silent in public, who are not to become part of "our" audience or even be allowed to respond to what "we" say. Beyond its verbal formulation, the Third Persona draws in historical reality, so stark in the twentieth century, of peoples categorized according to race, religion, age, gender, sexual preference, and nationality, and acted upon in ways consistent with their status as non-subjects. The Third Persona directs our attention to beings beyond the claims of morality and the bonds of compassion.[61]

In calling some groups into being, rhetoric also can deny the existence of others, or erase them. Wander's exploration of the third persona emphasizes the power of language to name, interpret, and construct human understandings of reality.

The clearest contemporary example of the construction of a third persona can be found in the recent debates over immigration. Instead of addressing the people who immigrate illegally (attempting to persuade them not to cross the border illegally), critics of illegal immigration turn them into a third persona. Media figures dehumanize illegal immigrants by describing them as a "flood," "tide," "pollutant," "infestation," "infection," and "disease."[62] Once denied humanity, immigrants also are denied compassion. They become an infestation to be fought, a tide to be held back, a pollutant in need of cleansing.

A third persona can be created even when speakers appear to use inclusive language. Political scientist Jane Mansbridge analyzes how the use of the collective "we" in political discourse can be used to represent a particular few by making invisible a distinct other. She explains, "'We' can easily represent a false universality, as 'mankind' used to."[63] Thus, "the very capacity to identify with others can easily be manipulated to the disadvantage of" a subordinated group because "[t]he transformation of 'I' into 'we' brought about through political deliberation can easily mask subtle forms of control."[64] The earlier example from Manuel Miranda is one illustration.

The perniciousness of a falsely universal "we" is evident even in a speech that was meant to celebrate inclusion. In 1998, President William J. Clinton delivered a speech announcing his Race Initiative, a series of national conversations and policy initiatives meant to counter racism in the United States. His speech provides a review of history, which uses the inclusive language of "we," but actually excludes some groups because of their absence from the historical occurrences he outlines. As you read this passage, ask yourself: who is "we"?

> *We* were born with a Declaration of Independence which asserted that *we* were all created equal and a Constitution that enshrined slavery. *We* fought a bloody Civil War to abolish slavery and preserve the Union, but *we* remained a house divided and unequal by law for another century. *We* advanced across the continent in the name of freedom, yet in so doing *we* pushed Native Americans off their land, often crushing their culture and their livelihood. *Our* Statue of Liberty welcomes poor, tired, huddled masses of immigrants to our borders, but each new wave has felt the sting of discrimination. In World War II, Japanese-Americans fought valiantly for freedom in Europe, taking great casualties, while at home their families were herded into internment camps. The famed Tuskegee Airmen lost none of the bombers they guarded during the war, but their African-American heritage cost them a lot of rights when they came back home in peace. [emphasis added][65]

The first "we" most likely does not refer to everyone, even though Clinton had earlier noted that the audience was composed of people of "many backgrounds." It refers only to white US citizens of European descent, the group granted rights by a "Constitution that enshrined slavery." Clearly, not everyone was born equal under the nation's founding documents. The "we" who fought the Civil War could include white and black people, yet black people were probably not a "house divided" after the war. Instead, the divided "we" seems to refer to white southerners and northerners. Although Clinton does recognize that "we" drove Native Americans off their lands, such a use of "we" is interesting because US citizens of European descent were primarily responsible for the genocide against Native Americans. This statement also implies they (Native Americans) are not part of us (Americans).

The use of "we" is complicated further by the use of truncated passives. In the first few sentences, a "we" is present. Yet, when Clinton begins to describe specific examples of discrimination, the agent of those acts becomes invisible. He explains that each new wave of immigrants "felt the sting" of discrimination, but does not identify who discriminated against them. Japanese families were "herded into internment camps," but Clinton does not identify who herded them. Finally, their "African-American heritage cost" the Tuskegee Airmen their rights; the bigotry of white people ("we") did not deny them their "inherent dignity." Thus, responsibility either lies with no one, or with the heritage of those who faced racism. Although Clinton's historical narrative might attempt to expose the hypocrisy of the dominant myths of democracy, exploration, and equality, it fails to unmask the agency of white Americans.

Indirectly Addressed Audiences

Thus far, we have explored the first persona (the implied author), the second persona (the implied audience), and the third persona (the excluded and denied audience). However, an audience type is missing from this list: the covertly or indirectly addressed audience. Scholars have written about two types of covert audiences: the fourth persona and the eavesdropper.

The **fourth persona** is *an audience who recognizes that the rhetor's first persona may not reveal all that is relevant about the speaker's identity, but maintains silence in order to enable the rhetor to perform that persona.* A rhetor's persona may require an act of passing, or convincing an audience that the rhetor's persona participates in an acceptable identity category. Gay people sometimes attempt to pass as heterosexual. Historically, some light-skinned black people passed as white. During the Holocaust, some Jewish children passed as Christian.

Rhetors often engage in rhetorical passing, while some members of the audience are aware of the attempt to pass. Rhetoric scholar Charles Morris posits that rhetors enact passing "by means of the *fourth persona:* a collusive audience constituted by the textual wink. Similar to its counterpart, the second persona, the fourth persona is an implied auditor of a particular ideological bent . . . ."[66] Passing only works if those who know otherwise enable the rhetor to perform the passing persona.

Any time you perform a persona that may not comport with the persona with which you most often operate, you rely on those people who know you differently to not interfere with your performance. You call an audience to silence, but unlike the third persona's forced silence, in this case "silence functions constructively as the medium of collusive exchange. What is not said is nonetheless performative, a speech act that can be read by certain audiences, and calls those audience members into being as abettors."[67]

An **eavesdropping audience** is *an audience whom the rhetor desires to hear the message despite explicitly targeting the message at a different audience.*[68] The targeting can be for two reasons: (1) to limit room for response by, or the agency of, the eavesdropping audience or (2) to allow the eavesdropping audience to feel empowered because they are not being criticized even as they hear criticisms made against others.

In the first instance, by constructing the audience as an eavesdropper, the rhetor limits the options available to the audience; they were not being addressed, so how can they answer or participate in the discussion? Such a technique is used when a rhetor wants to center attention on one audience in order to maximize its agency while limiting the agency of the eavesdropping audience. One powerful example is Gloria Anzaldúa's "Speaking in Tongues: A Letter to Third World Women Writers," originally written for *Words in Our Pockets,* the

Feminist Writers' Guild handbook, and later appearing in two other books, *This Bridge Called My Back* and *Speaking For Ourselves: Women of the South*. All three books bring the letter to an audience broader than the one addressed in its title.[69]

Although the letter is addressed to third world women writers, first world women are an audience. In the introduction to their coedited volume, *This Bridge Called My Back*, Cherríe Moraga and Anzaldúa note that the book was created "to express to all women—especially to white middle-class women—the experiences which divide us as feminists."[70] They exhort teachers to use the book in the classroom, again recognizing that white women and men are an audience. In her foreword to the second edition of the book, Anzaldúa further clarifies the existence of a complex audience: "We have come to realize that we are not alone in our struggles nor separate nor autonomous but that we—white black straight queer female male—are connected and interdependent. We are each accountable for what is happening down the street, south of the border or across the sea."[71] Anzaldúa knows first world women and men will read the letter, and she wants them to.

Despite (or because of) the broader audience, Anzaldúa addresses her letter to a specific group of women, "third world women," not to all women (and not to any men). She linguistically and symbolically reinforces this address in the first and last sections by opening with "mujeres de color,"[72] thus placing first world women (and men) in the position of reading mail unintended for them. The letter moves first world women (and all men) to a borderland when it does not address the letter to them, while it empowers third world women by literally addressing them as the primary subjects. First world women are written about. Men are just absent; they are not written to, nor do they write. Men and first world women are uninvited eavesdroppers and, hence, suspended from a critical position. They are reminded of their difference. They are reminded that they constantly tokenize third world women and deny differences among women. The letter reverses power relationships so that first world women are allowed access without input, a condition third world women often experience.

The letter's exclusive address operates heuristically; it creates, for anyone not a third world women, an experience of exclusion from which they can learn. Men and white women are made to feel like outsiders, much like women of color are made to feel in US culture. They learn, through experience, what it means to be marginalized, and why marginalization might make people angry. When the letter addresses third world women, it knocks first world readers out of the position that assumes white, Western, and male is the norm.

At the same time that the letter marginalizes men and first world women, it creates a community in which third world women are foregrounded. It quotes numerous third world women and, through this referencing, physically and mentally centers them. They are written to and they write. They are visualized early in the letter: "Black woman huddles over a desk. . . . [A] Chicana fanning away mosquitos. . . . Indian woman walking to school or work. . . . Asian American, lesbian, single mother, tugged in all directions by children, lover or ex-husband, and the writing."[73] The letter reminds women of color of their worth and ability, of their identification with Anzaldúa, when she refers to her "brown hand clutching the pen."[74] Third world women are present throughout the letter in all the examples, thus proving that third world women *do* write. In addition, the letter form operates as empowerment by eliciting a response, encouraging women of color to write back—to answer the letter.[75]

The empowerment function points to the second way that eavesdropping can be used. Criticisms can be targeted at one audience, in the hope that another audience overhears them and feels empowered. Communication scholars Michael Leff and Ebony A. Utley argue that Martin Luther King, Jr., did just this in his "Letter From Birmingham Jail."[76] Even though the letter is addressed to "My Dear Fellow Clergymen"—meaning white moderates, it also indirectly speaks to all black people in the United States as King attempts to persuade them to risk their bodies in nonviolent civil disobedience in civil rights protests. White moderates appear unwilling to act, so it is other African Americans who must be persuaded to push for social change. Leff and Utley argue King's persona in his letter is one

> that black readers can use as a model for becoming effective actors on the American scene. Like King, they can view themselves as agents who need not and will not suffer the indifference of white moderates, who can break free of external restraints without losing self-restraint, and who can work from within American society to make fundamental changes in the way they conceive themselves and are conceived by others.[77]

Eavesdroppers' agency was not limited, but enhanced, as King modeled for them how to be an agent of action.

These examples demonstrate that the overtly addressed audience is not necessarily the only, or even the most important, audience. A careful analysis of symbolic acts is required to understand the range of audiences to whom a rhetor speaks and the way in which the rhetoric positions that audience.

CONCLUSION

Rhetoric is always addressed to another. Thus, a rhetor must consider ways to create identification with the audience or to construct the audience in such a way that it is capable of being an agent of action. Audience members should consider whether they are, indeed, the audience spoken to (the second persona), simply a body that is present, or a person who is excluded from address. The concept of audience is much more complex than just the random group of people who may be gathered to hear a message. Audiences are actively created by rhetors. They are active recipients of messages, able to accept, question, and reject them.

Civic engagement means engaging with another, an audience, but rhetoric may also exclude people. If the ideal civil society is, in principle, open to the participation of all people, then rhetoric that excludes people works against civic ideals.

DISCUSSION QUESTIONS

1. Advertisers market their products to particular audiences. Find an advertisement and figure out who its audience is. Does the advertisement construct an audience? How? What beliefs, attitudes, or values does the advertisement use? Does it create audience agency? Does it use identification or pathos?
2. When you attempt to persuade someone, how does your audience frame and alter your message? What is an example of a particular audience that was difficult for you to persuade?
3. How should a rhetor attempt to persuade a hostile audience? Is it possible to persuade an audience that does not share your values?
4. Find a symbolic action and identify the audiences. Who is the second persona? Who is the third persona? What is the audience agency?
5. Politicians frequently refer to "the people." Find examples of these references and explain how the rhetor is defining and conceptualizing "the people." Who is the second persona in the reference to "the people?" Who is the third persona? What does the politician's use of "the people" tell you about the rhetor and the issue?
6. In writing this book, we made choices about how to write because we have chosen to target an audience of students. What are some of the clues that we targeted our writing to students, rather than to other professors?

RECOMMENDED READINGS

Balthrop, V. William. "Culture, Myth, and Ideology as Public Argument: An Interpretation of the Ascent and Demise of 'Southern Culture.'" *Communication Monographs* 51 (December 1984): 340–352.

Black, Edwin. "The Second Persona." *The Quarterly Journal of Speech* 56 (April 1970): 109–119.

McGee, Michael Calvin. "In Search of 'The People': A Rhetorical Alternative." *The Quarterly Journal of Speech* 61 (1975): 235–249.

Wander, Philip. "The Third Persona: An Ideological Turn in Rhetorical Theory." *Central States Speech Journal* 35 (Winter 1984): 197–216.

ENDNOTES

[1] Stephen Toulmin, Richard Rieke, and Allan Janik, *An Introduction to Reasoning,* 2nd ed. (New York: Macmillan, 1984), 306–307.

[2] *Brown v. Board of Education,* 347 U.S. 483 (1954). National Park Service, Department of the Interior, National Historic Site, http://www.nps.gov/brvb (accessed May 20, 2009).

[3] *Plessy v. Ferguson,* 163 U.S. 537 (1896).

[4] *Brown v. Board of Education.*

[5] Earl Warren, *The Memoirs of Earl Warren* (New York: Doubleday, 1977), 3.

[6] Ed Cray, *Chief Justice: A Biography of Earl Warren* (New York: Simon and Schuster, 1997), 351; Learned Hand, *The Bill of Rights* (Cambridge: Harvard University Press, 1958).

7 "The Southern Manifesto," *Time*, March 26, 1956, http://www.time.com/time/magazine/article/0,9171,824106,00.html (accessed May 20, 2009); Jim Newton, *Justice for All: Earl Warren and the Nation He Made* (New York: Riverhead, 2006), 339–40; Ed Cray, *Chief Justice*, 320, 342–47.

8 Warren, *Memoirs*, 297.

9 Kenneth Burke, *A Rhetoric of Motives* (University of California Press, 1969), 38.

10 Burke, *Rhetoric*, 41.

11 Lloyd F. Bitzer, "The Rhetorical Situation," *Philosophy and Rhetoric* 1 (1968), 7, italics added.

12 Aristotle, *On Rhetoric*, trans. George A. Kennedy (New York: Oxford University Press, 1991), 47 [1.3.1; 1358b].

13 Aristotle, *On Rhetoric*, 1.2.11 [1356b], 47 [1.3.1; 1358b].

14 Lucie Olbrechts-Tyteca's contributions to this work often are undervalued. For a discussion of her scholarship, see Barbara Warnick, "Lucie Olbrechts-Tyteca's Contribution to *The New Rhetoric*," in *Listening to Their Voices: The Rhetorical Activities of Historical Women*, ed. Molly Meijer Wertheimer (Columbia: University of South Carolina Press, 1987), 69–85.

15 Chaïm Perelman, "Rhetoric and Philosophy," *Philosophy and Rhetoric* 1 (1968), 15.

16 Chaïm Perelman and Lucie Olbrechts-Tyteca, *The New Rhetoric*, trans. John Wilkinson and Purcell Weaver (Notre Dame, IN: University of Notre Dame Press, 1969), 24.

17 "Highlights of Obama's Speech to Muslim World," NBC *Nightly News* 6:30 PM EST, NBC News Transcripts, June 4, 2009, LexisNexis (accessed June 5, 2009).

18 "Highlights."

19 Burke, *Rhetoric*, 20.

20 Burke, *Rhetoric*, 21.

21 Burke, *Rhetoric*, 55.

22 Barack Obama, "A New Beginning: Speech at Cairo University," June 4, 2009, http://www.americanrhetoric.com/speeches/barackobama /barackobamacairouniversity.htm (accessed June 9, 2009).

23 Stephen Prothero, "In Egypt, a Theologian in Chief," *USA Today*, June 8, 2009, 11A.

24 Obama, "New Beginning," para. 7.

25 Obama, "New Beginning," para. 7.

26 Obama, "New Beginning," para. 29.

27 Obama, "New Beginning," para. 31.

28 Aristotle, *On Rhetoric*, 2.1.2 [1378a]

29 Aristotle, *On Rhetoric*, 1.2.5 [1356a].

30 George A. Kennedy, *Classical Rhetoric and Its Christian and Secular Tradition*, 2nd ed. (Chapel Hill: University of North Carolina Press, 1999), 89.

31 Aristotle, *On Rhetoric*, 2.5.1.

32 Iowa Department of Public Health, Just Eliminate Lies (advertisement), http://www.idph.state.ia.us/Tobacco/jel.asp (accessed August 6, 2009).

33 Perelman and Olbrechts-Tyteca, *New Rhetoric*, 147.

34 World Health Organization, "Influenza A(H1N1)," http://www.who.int/csr/disease/swineflu/en/index.html (accessed June 19, 2009).

35 "Foot-in-Mouth Disease: The Vice President Isn't Helping to Calm an Anxious Public," *Washington Post*, http://www.washingtonpost.com/wp-dyn/content/ article/2009/04/30/AR2009043002660.html, May 1, 2009 (accessed June 19, 2009).

36 Barack Obama, Press Conference, April 30, 2009, http://www.whitehouse.gov/blog/09/04/30/The-Presidents-Remarks-on-H1N1 (accessed June 19, 2009).

37 Coco Ballantyne, "Will Egypt's Plans to Kill Pigs Protect It from Swine—Sorry, H1N1 Flu?" *Scientific American*, May 1, 2009, http://www.scientificamerican.com/blog/60-second-science/post.cfm?id=will-egypts-plans-to-kill-pigs-prot-2009-05-01 (accessed August 6, 2009).

38 Philip Alcabes, *Dread: How Fear and Fantasy Have Fueled Epidemics from the Black Death to the Avian Flu* (Philadelphia: PublicAffairs, 2009), 4.

39 Alcabes, *Dread*, 4.

40 Erving Goffman, *The Presentation of Self in Everyday Life* (New York: Anchor, 1959), 34–35.

41 Goffman, *Presentation*, 9.

42 R. Jay Wallace, *Responsibility and the Moral Sentiments* (Cambridge, MA: Harvard University Press, 1994), 53.

43 Quoted in Brian Mann, "N.Y. Gov. Threatens to Mothball More Prisons," NPR: *All Things Considered* (January 27, 2011), http://www.npr.org/2011/01/27/133276372/new-york-gov-threatens-to-mothball-more-prisons (accessed February 21, 2011).

44 Michael Tanner, *The Grass Is Not Always Greener: A Look at National Health Care Systems around the World*, Policy Analysis No. 613, March 18, 2008, pp. 1–3, http://www.cato.org/pubs/pas/pa-613.pdf (accessed June 1, 2009).

45 Arthur Caplan, "Bioethics and the Obama Administration," interview with Terry Gross, *Fresh Air*, December 17, 2008, http://www.lexisnexis.com/us/lnacademic/search/homesubmitForm.do (accessed May 22, 2009). Audio recording available at http://www.npr.org/templates/story/story.php?storyId=98387481.

46 Karlyn Kohrs Campbell, "Agency: Promiscuous and Protean," *Communication and Critical/Cultural Studies* 2 (2005), 3, italics added.

47 Karlyn Kohrs Campbell, "The Rhetoric of Women's Liberation: An Oxymoron," *The Quarterly Journal of Speech* 59 (February 1973): 74–86, 85.

48 Barbara Biesecker, "Rethinking the Rhetorical Situation from within the Thematic of *Différance*," *Philosophy and Rhetoric* 22 (1989), 126.

49 John Boehner, "Focused on Cutting Spending and Growing the Economy, New Majority Moves Forward with Repealing ObamaCare," January 7, 2011, http://johnboehner.house.gov/News/DocumentSingle.aspx?DocumentID=219296 (accessed January 9, 2011).

50 Jeffrey M. Jones, "In U.S., 46% Favor, 40% Oppose Repealing Healthcare Law," January 7, 2011, http://www.gallup.com/poll/145496/Favor-Oppose-Repealing-Healthcare-Law.aspx (accessed January 9, 2011).

51 Michael Calvin McGee, "In Search of 'The People': A Rhetorical Alternative," *Quarterly Journal of Speech* 61 (1975), 242.

52 Edwin Black, "The Second Persona," *Quarterly Journal of Speech* 56 (April 1970): 109–119.

53 Black, "Second Persona," 113.

54 Franklin Delano Roosevelt, "First Inaugural Address," March 4, 1933, http://www.americanrhetoric.com/speeches/fdrfirstinaugural.html (accessed July 24, 2009).

55 George H. W. Bush, Inaugural Address, January 20, 1989.

56 William Jefferson Clinton, Inaugural Address, January 21, 1993.

57 Burke, *Rhetoric*, 22.

58 "Manuel Miranda: Hispanics 'Not Like African-Americans, and We Think Just Like Everybody Else,'" http://www.youtube.com/watch?v=NbDPuVSb12Y (accessed June 5, 2009).

59 Philip Wander, "The Third Persona: An Ideological Turn in Rhetorical Theory," *Central States Speech Journal* 35 (Winter 1984): 197–216, 209, italics added.

60 Wander, "Third Persona," 209.

61 Wander, "Third Persona," 216.

62 J. David Cisneros, "Contaminated Communities: The Metaphor of 'Immigrant as Pollutant' in Media Representations of Immigration," *Rhetoric and Public Affairs* 11, no. 4 (Winter 2008): 569–602; Anne Demo, "Sovereignty Discourse and Contemporary Immigration Politics," *Quarterly Journal of Speech* 91 (2005): 291–311; Hugh Mehan, "The Discourse of the Illegal Immigration Debate: A Case Study in the Politics of Representation," *Discourse and Society* 8 (1997): 249–70; Kent A. Ono and John M. Sloop, *Shifting Borders: Rhetoric, Immigration, and California's Proposition 187* (Philadelphia: Temple University Press, 2002); and Otto Santa Ana, *Brown Tide Rising: Metaphors of Latinos in Contemporary American Public Discourse* (Austin: University of Texas Press, 2002).

63 Jane Mansbridge, "Feminism and Democracy," in *Feminism and Politics*, ed. Anne Phillips, 142–158 (New York: Oxford University Press, 1998), 152.

64 Mansbridge, "Feminism," 143.

65 William Jefferson Clinton, "Remarks at the University of California San Diego Commencement Ceremony in La Jolla, California," *Public Papers of the Presidents of the United States: William J. Clinton* (Washington: GPO, 1998), 877, italics added.

66 Charles E. Morris III, "Pink Herring and the Fourth Persona: J. Edgar Hoover's Sex Crime Panic," *Quarterly Journal of Speech* 88, no. 2 (May 2002): 228–244, 230.

67 Morris, "Pink Herring," 230.

68 This concept of audience is discussed extensively in James L. Golden and Richard D. Rieke, *The Rhetoric of Black Americans* (Columbus, OH: Charles E. Merrill, 1971).

69 Gloria Anzaldúa, "Speaking in Tongues: A Letter to Third World Women Writers," in *This Bridge Called My Back,* 2nd ed., ed. Cherríe Moraga and Gloria Anzaldúa (New York: Kitchen Table, 1981), 165–173.

70 Cherríe Moraga and Gloria Anzaldúa, "Introduction," *This Bridge*, xxiii.

71 Anzaldúa, *This Bridge*, iv.

72 Anzaldúa, "Speaking," 165, 171.

73 Anzaldúa, "Speaking," 165.

74 Anzaldúa, "Speaking," 169.

75 This analysis is adapted from Catherine Helen Palczewski, "Bodies, Borders and Letters: Gloria Anzaldúa's 'Speaking in Tongues: A Letter to 3rd World Women Writers,'" *Southern Communication Journal* 62, no. 1 (Fall 1996), 1–16.

76 Martin Luther King, Jr., "Letter from Birmingham Jail," April 16, 1963, http://www.africa.upenn.edu/Articles_Gen/Letter_Birmingham.html (accessed August 5, 2009).

77 Michael Leff and Ebony A. Utley, "Instrumental and Constitutive Rhetoric in Martin Luther King Jr.'s 'Letter from Birmingham Jail,'" *Rhetoric and Public Affairs* 7, no. 1 (2004): 37–51.

Chapter 8
Rhetorical Situations

Key Concepts

antecedent genre	exigence
conformity	fitting response
constraints	forensic discourse
contextual reconstruction	genre
deliberative discourse	nonparticipation
desecration	rhetorical audience
epideictic discourse	rhetorical situation

Different rhetors, messages, and audiences require different means of persuasion. For example, when you request an extension on an assignment, you consider many situational elements in constructing the request to your professor. You think about whether it is generally acceptable to ask for an extension for an assignment, your professor has particular rules about late assignments, the professor has given clear instructions for the assignment, and the deadlines are more or less firm. You consider your particular relationship with the professor, your performance in the class, and whether you have asked for an extension in the past. You also consider how and where you will make the request: by e-mail, face-to-face, during the professor's office hours, after class in the hallway, before class in the classroom, in a phone message, and so on.

When Aristotle defined rhetoric as "an ability in each [particular] case, to see the available means of persuasion,"[1] he made clear that the options open to rhetors and the demands placed on them differ from situation to situation.[2] The challenge to a rhetor is to determine what options exist to communicate a message in the particular situation. Communication does not occur in a vacuum, but in a particular place, at a particular time, as part of a particular socioeconomic and cultural context, about a particular topic, and to a particular audience. Some situations recur, however, and rhetors learn from their recurrence.

Aristotle offered an early description of the interplay of audience, topic, and rhetor in a situation. For Aristotle, the composition of the audience determines the rhetorical situation because the audience determines the expectations the rhetor will need to fulfill. He divided rhetoric into three situational classifications on the basis of three distinct audiences to which those speeches are delivered: deliberative, forensic, and epideictic.[3] Each of these three classifications had a particular form, style, and range of arguments, and called for different temporal orientations. Aristotle explains: "Each of these has it own 'time': for the deliberative speaker, the future . . . ; for the speaker in court, the past . . . ; in epideictic, the present is the most important; for all speakers praise or blame in regard to existing qualities, but they often also make use of other things, both reminding [the audience] of the past and projecting the course of the future."[4]

Deliberative discourse is *rhetoric that addresses broad public audiences and concerns the merits of proposals for future courses of action.* It responds to policy issues, such as ways and means, war and peace, and legislation.

For Aristotle, **forensic discourse** is *rhetoric that occurs when a designated audience (such as a jury) judges the arguments about events in the past and accusations of wrongdoing.* The language of forensic discourse tends to be "accusation" or "defense" (apologia)."[5]

Epideictic discourse consists of *speeches of praise or blame, usually delivered to audiences assembled during ceremonial occasions, and oriented to the present moment, while calling on the past to inform the future.* Its focus on praise or blame means the audience is called to determine the fittingness of the values that the rhetor uses, and to judge the virtues and vices of the rhetor's subject.

For most of the history of rhetorical studies, Aristotle's model was the dominant perspective on rhetorical situations, but more complex theories have evolved since then. We begin this chapter by reviewing a theory that claims "rhetoric is situational," that rhetorical action is a response to a rhetorical situation. Next, we review a response to this theory that argues "situations are rhetorical," that we cannot understand a situation except through rhetoric. Each of these approaches, taken alone, has limits, so we combine the most insightful parts of the two approaches to explore how situations and rhetoric constantly interact with and affect each other. That is, situations can delimit a rhetor's rhetorical choices and the rhetorical choices of a rhetor can define the situation. We conclude the chapter by reconsidering which rhetorical actions constitute a fitting response to the situation, and why we sometimes may not want to provide a fitting response at all.

RHETORIC AS SITUATIONAL

Communication scholar Lloyd Bitzer argues that "rhetoric is situational."[6] He proposes that rhetoric is produced at a specific time, for a particular audience, and in response to a particular issue. He distinguishes the "meaning-context" formed by previous communication from the "rhetorical situation" formed by a particular event in the world. Context and situation are not synonymous for Bitzer.[7]

For instance, when voting rights activist Fannie Lou Hamer delivered her testimony to the 110 members of the 1964 Democratic National Convention Credentials Committee, she was asking the Democratic Party Convention to recognize and seat the Mississippi Freedom Democratic Party as the official delegation from Mississippi instead of the already recognized, all-white, anti–civil rights, regular Democratic Party delegation. As she detailed the repeated abuse she had faced at the hands of police because of her attempts to vote and register others to vote, she had to consider much more than the setting and immediate audience. The rhetorical situation included expectations attached to convention speeches; Hamer's relationship to the Civil Rights movement, the Mississippi Freedom Democratic Party, and the Democratic Party; the audiences she hoped to influence, ranging from the Credentials Committee, other African Americans, and the nation as a whole; the social and cultural history of voting rights for African Americans; and her reputation as an activist and vice-chair of the Mississippi Freedom Democratic Party.[8] As this example shows, and Bitzer points out, all messages occur in a context, but only a rhetorical situation demands a rhetorical response, insofar as "rhetorical discourse . . . obtain[s] its character-as-rhetorical from the situation which generates it."[9] In other words, Bitzer believes that the things he labels *rhetorical situations* are distinct from context because rhetorical situations should elicit particular responses from rhetors.

For Bitzer, rhetoric is a special kind of communication, one that intends to produce some change in the world. Rhetoric is instrumental, or pragmatic, and "is always persuasive."[10] People engage in rhetorical action to respond to some external and preexisting problem. Given this understanding of rhetoric, Bitzer defines the **rhetorical situation** this way:

> *a complex of persons, events, objects, and relations presenting an actual or potential exigence which can be completely or partially removed if discourse, introduced into the situation, can so constrain human decision or action as to bring about the significant modification of the exigence.*[11]

He defines **exigence** as "*an imperfection marked by urgency; it is a defect, an obstacle, something waiting to be done, a thing which is other than it should be.*"[12] The exigence calls for, or demands, a rhetorical response. If rhetoric cannot create a change in the exigence, then it is not a rhetorical situation. Although a hurricane is a problem, it is not a rhetorical exigence because rhetoric cannot stop the onslaught of wind and water. People's reactions to a hurricane (usually panic) do present an exigence. Rhetorical appeals not to panic, to prepare, and to evacuate in an orderly manner can alter the exigence. When Hurricane Ike threatened the Gulf Coast during the Atlantic storm season of 2008, Texas officials asked Houston residents not to evacuate and instead to remain in Houston and seek shelter in place, even though hundreds of thousands of other Texans living in low-lying areas were told to evacuate or face certain death. All Texans faced the same storm, but different exigences presented themselves to disaster officials. Evacuation from less populated areas could occur in an orderly manner, but in more densely populated areas, as the experience with Hurricane Rita in 2005 had made clear, more people might die from the evacuation than from the storm itself.[13] The exigence was people's panic, not the storm.

In the example of a student persuading a professor to grant an extension, the exigence is the looming deadline for an assignment the student cannot complete in time. Bitzer believes that rhetoric "comes into existence as a response to a situation, in the same sense that an answer comes into existence in response to a question, or a solution in response to a problem."[14] The student responds to the situation of the assignment deadline by requesting an extension. The student's request creates a situation calling for a response from the professor, which, in turn, comes into existence because of the student's request. The situation invites and guides both rhetors' responses.[15]

Another example of how situations invite a response arises when a person dies. In many cultures discourse is expected in response to the death, such as eulogies, sympathy cards, expressions of condolences to family and friends, and obituaries. The situation gives the rhetorical acts their significance. When a situation has importance, the persuasive responses to that situation are given importance.

Bitzer urges rhetorical critics to consider whether a rhetorical situation induced a rhetorical action so they can fully understand what the rhetor was hoping to achieve, what was possible to achieve, and what was actually achieved. Placing a rhetorical act within its rhetorical situation is more complex than identifying the historical moment at which it occurred. Knowing the historical context of a speech gives you an understanding of its contextual meaning. Knowing the rhetorical situation helps you understand the rhetorical choices that the rhetor made in response to it.

Bitzer identifies three elements of any rhetorical situation: *exigence, audience,* and *constraints.* These elements are present prior to any rhetorical act and compose the "situation which calls the discourse into existence."[16] According to Bitzer, a rhetor should consider these elements when constructing a rhetorical act. When critically analyzing a rhetorical act, critics should begin by identifying the components of the rhetorical situation in which the rhetorical act occurs.

Exigence

On September 11, 2001, when planes crashed into the Twin Towers of the World Trade Center, the Pentagon, and a field in Pennsylvania, events demanded a response. The public reaction to the events created an evolving exigence. President George W. Bush delivered three statements throughout the day. His first statement (lasting 68 seconds) was from Emma E. Booker Elementary School in Sarasota, Florida, immediately after the Twin Towers had been hit. The second statement (lasting 130 seconds) was from Barksdale Air Force Base in Louisiana, after the Pentagon had also been hit.[17] Finally, on the evening of September 11, when it appeared the attacks were over, President Bush delivered a seven-minute address to the country from the Oval Office to make sense of the day's events. The magnitude of the developing events motivated him to respond rhetorically to the situation three times in one day. In each speech, he was responding to the urgency of the situation at that moment, the exigence.

President Bush had choices regarding how to respond. One choice could have been to ignore the events and not deliver any public statements. He probably felt compelled to speak directly about the events, because to ignore them could have created additional problems that would have been more damaging than the risks he faced in responding. If he had not responded, people would have believed he failed to see the magnitude of the events;[18] they would have seen the president as out of touch, incompetent, or afraid.

Rhetorical theorist Bruce Gronbeck explains the very unexpectedness of events "calls for particular messages at particular times . . . . the unexpectedness of impending harm produces public uncertainty, especially if the event is unique rather than cyclical; public uncertainty produces public fear, which consequently calls for explanation, [and] reassurance."[19] President Bush sought to calm the initial fears and uncertainties through his rhetorical acts.

Most rhetors have an inherent sense of exigence, recognizing a need to say something in response to unexpected events; they feel they are "invited" or "called" to respond to the situation. The feeling that you have to say something is an indication that an out-of-the-ordinary event has occurred that demands an immediate (urgent) response. Of course, urgency must be defined relative to the situation. Explaining why you might be late to a party is less urgent than explaining to your boss that you will be late for work. If you are going to be late to a party, you might not feel that you must contact the hosts immediately, even though you might call as a courtesy. If you are late for work, however, you probably feel a greater sense of urgency. Being late for work is more important than being late to a party.

Audience

The second component of the rhetorical situation is the **rhetorical audience** (discussed in Chapter 7), which Bitzer believes is *an audience that "consists only of those persons who are capable of being influenced by discourse and of being mediators of change."*[20] Bitzer distinguishes the entire group of people who might hear a speech or read an essay from the rhetorical audience, the group to whom a rhetor targets a message because that group is composed of agents of change who can respond. Just because you are reading or watching a speech does not mean that you are the rhetorical audience for the speech. You would have to have the ability to remedy the exigence in order to be part of the rhetorical audience.

Mediators of change are those people who are capable of taking the actions that the rhetor suggests, but it can be difficult to determine who that audience is. The perceived mediators of change are not a constant, as presidential campaign strategy demonstrates. From the 1980 presidential campaign (which saw the emergence of the Reagan Democrats) until 2004, presidential campaigns tended to focus on wooing swing voters. Campaigns identified voters without a strong party identification as their rhetorical audiences because they were the people who could swing a presidential election in favor of one side or another. When Republican campaign strategist Matthew Dowd analyzed the electorate after the 2000 election, however, he discovered that "independents or persuadable voters in the last 20 years had gone from 22 percent of the electorate to

7 percent of the electorate in 2000." Using this information, campaign strategists for the 2004 Republican election campaign developed what came to be known as "the base strategy" which attempted "to focus on delivering votes from reliable Republicans."[21] These strategists saw the Republican Party's base as the key mediators of change. As a result, the Republican presidential campaign limited rallies to invitation-only events; tickets were given only to people willing to state their allegiance to George W. Bush.[22] The campaign redefined the rhetorical audience by suggesting that the key to winning elections (the exigence) was not about persuading undecided or centrist voters, but about mobilizing dedicated party supporters to go to the polls.

In 2008, however, the Republican campaign saw the rhetorical audience as broader than the base, so it used a mix of appeals to the base (including the selection of Sarah Palin as the vice-presidential candidate) and to independents (including the emphasis on John McCain as a maverick). The 2008 Democratic campaign also redefined the rhetorical audience. Instead of simply looking at voters as the audience, the Obama campaign looked at all those who were eligible to vote. On April 25, 2008, the Democrats launched a fifty-state voter registration drive to attract first-time voters, targeting youth and minority voters who might have felt disenfranchised by politics in the past.

Rhetors need to determine which audiences can be influenced to effect change, then tailor their messages to those audiences. For example, to persuade Congress to pass a particular piece of legislation, the president could choose to focus on members of Congress, who are mediators of change because they actually enact the legislation. Alternatively, the president might go directly to the voters, to get them to pressure members of Congress to pass the legislation. In the latter case, the voters are the rhetorical audience that the president defines.

Sometimes rhetors cannot choose audiences; the audiences are chosen for them, and they must adjust their messages to these audiences. For instance, the plaintiff in a legal proceeding cannot choose which judge to persuade. The judge (audience) is selected for the case and the attorney (rhetor) must adapt accordingly.

Not only does the rhetor respond to the audience, the audience responds to the exigence. Bitzer believes that the audience is guided by the situation, as is the rhetor.[23] The rhetor is seeking to influence change; the audience brings about that change. The choices a rhetor faces are not only about how to respond to the audience, but also about which audiences to respond to. Because the audience is the mediator of change, the change the rhetor seeks might guide which audience the rhetor chooses to address.

Constraints

The third component of a rhetorical situation, according to Bitzer, is **constraints**, *"persons, events, objects, and relations which are parts of the situation because they have the power to constrain decision and action needed to modify the exigence."*[24] Constraints restrain and enable choices that a rhetor might make in response to the exigence, audience, and the rhetor's own history. They do not determine or dictate a specific response to a situation; rather, they limit and provide opportunities for the rhetor's persuasive choices.[25]

People who come from marginalized groups in a society as a result of sex, race, or class often face greater constraints and have fewer opportunities than people from privileged groups. In the 1960s, for example, when engaging in lunch counter sit-ins to protest Jim Crow segregation laws, young African-American women and men would dress very conservatively and properly. They would politely ask to be served. The simple reality of African Americans and whites eating together was so radical and confrontational, they had to moderate all their other actions. They also had to counteract white people's irrational perceptions that African Americans were violent and unruly. The protesters very intentionally sought to counter these constraints. John Lewis, one of the participants in the Nashville sit-ins, explains, "It was like going to Church, I guess. You would put on your church-going clothes, Sunday clothes, and we took books and papers and did our homework at the lunch counter, just quiet and trying to be as dignified as possible."[26]

As a counterexample, consider performance artist Bill Talen's character of Reverend Billy. Located in New York, Talen uses street theatre to protest the rise in consumerism and the invasion of Times Square by transnational corporations such as Disney and Starbucks.[27] Reverend Billy begins his sermon in a local theatre, but takes it directly into a store to challenge shoppers. He preaches at them about the evils of consumption, or whispers in their ears that the cute stuffed Dumbo was made by sweatshop labor. His race, sex, and class provide him an opportunity, rather than a constraint. He recognizes that as a white man, he is able to get away with more. As he explains: "I don't suffer from racial profiling. If a cop stops me, he knows immediately that I have a college education and dental work."[28] He is able to gain access to spaces and command attention from those who might otherwise dismiss the message.

All rhetors are confronted with constraints. Communication scholars Karlyn Kohrs Campbell and Susan Schultz Huxman provide a more expansive assessment of constraints in their examination of "the rhetorical problem."[29] Adapting their work and applying it to the framework of the rhetorical situation, we can see constraints stemming from the exigence, audience, and rhetor.

Constraints arising from the exigence include the complexity of the exigence and its cultural history.[30] The exigence can be more or less complex; the level of expertise needed to understand it varies from subject to subject. In the case of the student request for an extension, the exigence is fairly straightforward and clear. The student's reasons for the extension might make the exigence more complex, but the obstacles that the student must overcome include the professor's stated (or unstated) deadline policies and the academic culture of the institution or department.

In contrast, some exigences are extremely complex. When the United States was in the throes of the Great Depression, following the 1929 stock market collapse, President Franklin Delano Roosevelt faced the daunting task of explaining to the public what was happening, why, and how the government would respond. When he was inaugurated on March 4, 1933, five thousand banks had already folded; ten million people in the United States had lost their savings; 25 percent were unemployed; hundreds of thousands of families had lost their homes; and farmers were leaving crops to rot in the fields because commodity prices had fallen so far they could not afford to harvest their crops.[31] On March 12, 1933, Roosevelt delivered, via the relatively new medium of radio, his first presidential fireside chat, the subject of which was banking.[32] He sought to explain the federal "banking holiday" he had declared, in terms that would be understood by "the average citizen."[33] He faced the exigence of an extremely complex and volatile situation, which called forth rhetoric that would explain and calm. In an interesting parallel, as the economic crisis that had begun in the October 2008 intensified during early 2009, many commentators encouraged President Barack Obama to respond to his complex exigence in the same way Roosevelt had. Mary Kate Cary of *U.S. News and World Report* argued that "a series of one-on-one talks with the American people explaining the crisis and the government's response—as well as a go-get-'em confidence builder at the end—might work wonders."[34]

Constraints arising from the audience capable of acting include whether it can be reached by the rhetor, is likely to misinterpret or misperceive the message, can be motivated to act despite potential costs, perceives itself as an agent of change, and has control over the action asked of it.[35] If the rhetor is unable to deliver a persuasive message to the audience, then the audience is unreachable. Even if the rhetor delivers the message to the audience, the audience must perceive and interpret the situation as described in the message in a way that is consistent with how the rhetor interprets and perceives it. Further, audience members must be motivated and believe they can make a change, that they have agency to act on the exigence. In some cases, responding to an exigence will present costs to the audience, which could include money, time, or the risk of social disapproval.

When a student asks for an extension, the professor clearly is an audience with agency; control is not the most significant constraint arising from this audience. Instead, it is the cost, which, from the professor's perspective might be the perception of unfairness to other students or the time the professor needs to grade the assignment. (If the extension is granted, the professor has less time to evaluate it.)

Constraints can also arise from audience agency. If you are trying to encourage other students to join a protest against building a road through a campus green space, you might encounter apathy. You might need to persuade them that they can make a difference. You might need to motivate them to become involved, even if they agree that the road should not be built.

Finally, constraints arising from the rhetor include the rhetor's reputation, ability to create identification with the audience, and social power.[36] These same areas can present opportunities for the rhetorician, however. A rhetor who has credibility with an audience can use that credibility to persuade the audience. For example, as Roosevelt's term in office progressed, he developed credibility with the public. His fireside chats and constant communication instilled confidence to such an extent that in their letters to him, people described him as "a gift from God, and a 'friend-next-door,' a supreme being and a real fellow who did not talk down to the public."[37] Because of his reputation, Roosevelt was able to persuade audiences by relying on his relationship with them. Conversely, rhetors who have negative images or tarnished reputations would have to overcome them in order to persuade their audiences.

Fitting Response

Bitzer concludes that although a rhetorical situation invites a response, not all responses are fitting. A **fitting response** is *a response that meets the expectations of the rhetorical situation.* Bitzer points out that "every situation prescribes its fitting response; the rhetor may or may not read the prescription accurately."[38] A successful persuasive message is one that is appropriate for the exigence, audience, and constraints of the rhetorical situation.

To be fitting, a response must also meet the expectations established by responses to preceding situations that the audience perceives to be analogous. When a rhetorical situation (or a particular interaction of audience, exigence, and constraints) repeatedly recurs, stylistic and substantive expectations become attached to that situation.[39] Stylistic expectations can involve the formality of language, attitudes toward the subject and audience, and the structure of the speech. Substantive expectations include the types of subjects and evidence. When requesting an extension on an assignment, even a student who has never made such a request before probably knows the expectations attached and would probably frame the request as a polite appeal to the professor, offering reasons for the request. If the student stood on a desk during a class session and shouted in an angry tone to demand an extension, the professor and other students would see that response as inappropriate because it failed to meet stylistic and substantive expectations.

Similarly, even if you have never given or heard a eulogy, you probably have a general sense of what it should include. As Campbell and Jamieson note, Western audiences expect that a eulogy "acknowledges the death, transforms the relationship between the living and the dead from present to past tense, eases the mourners' terror at confronting their own mortality, consoles them by arguing that the deceased lives on, and reknits the fabric of the community."[40]

What you expect to hear in a eulogy is determined not just by the particular death, but by all the eulogies that have gone before. If someone were to give a speech that did not even mention the person who had died, people would probably not see that speech as fitting and say, "It wasn't really a eulogy."

Situations familiar to an audience call for responses that fit audience expectations of that type of situation. As Bitzer points out, "some situations recur . . . and, because we experience situations and the rhetorical responses to them, a form of discourse is not only established but comes to have a power of its own—the tradition itself tends to function as a constraint upon any new response in the form."[41] To determine whether a response is fitting, a rhetor must accurately assess the situation, the demands of the subject, her or his own credibility, and the audience's needs. If a situation is recurrent and, thus, has generated audience expectations across time, an advocate also must consider whether the rhetorical action addresses the stylistic and substantive expectations attached to that situation.[42] For this reason, a rhetor's decisions about how to respond to a situation must account not only for the specific situation, but also for the way others have responded to it in the past.

Rhetors respond to common elements in exigencies, contexts, responses, or audiences. These responses often lead to the formulation of genres. A **genre** is *a rhetorical form created by the recurrent elements of the rhetorical situation, which create clusters of discourse that share style, substance, and purpose.* Genres create constraints and opportunities for rhetors as they respond to situations. One special type of genre is the **antecedent genre,** or *a genre that arises because of audience expectations based on the ways others have responded to similar situations.* An antecedent genre affects the range of options a rhetor has available. Thus, it is not solely the present situation that generates constraints on and resources for a rhetor, but also the previous situations that have created an antecedent genre—"the chromosomal imprint of ancestral genres."[43]

Analysis: The *Challenger* Explosion

President Ronald Reagan's speech after the explosion of the *Challenger* space shuttle illustrates how a rhetor responds to a rhetorical situation and how critics can use the concept of the rhetorical situation to analyze a rhetorical act.

On January 28, 1986, NASA launched the *Challenger* in what it believed to be a routine mission even though there had been five liftoff delays. On board were seven astronauts: Gregory Jarvis, Christa McAuliffe, Ronald McNair, Ellison Onizuka, Judith Resnik, Dick Scobee, and Michael J. Smith. NASA had been plagued by declining public interest in its space missions, but many people in the United States, particularly schoolchildren, watched the launch live because of schoolteacher Christa McAuliffe, the first member of the Teacher in Space Project. A little over a minute after the launch, the shuttle exploded in flight, killing all seven astronauts. Although the only live coverage of the launch was on newly formed CNN and via a satellite feed of NASA TV targeted at schools, one study reported that 85 percent of those surveyed had heard the news within an hour of the accident as a result of the extensive media coverage.[44]

The vivid imagery of the explosion shocked the nation.[45] Within minutes, the networks replaced regular programming with coverage of the explosion. The nation watched in horror as their televisions repeatedly showed the shuttle exploding and debris raining down. Despite all the coverage, in the hours after the explosion, the public was left with a void of meaning. People did not know what had happened or why. They could have interpreted the explosion as proof that NASA was inept and the benefits of space exploration were not worth the costs, or as an inexplicable and irredeemable loss of human life. Knowing that the situation demanded a response, President Reagan cancelled his scheduled State of the Union address to speak to the country about the *Challenger* disaster.

President Ronald W. Reagan
"The Space Shuttle *Challenger* Tragedy Address"
Oval Office
January 28, 1986

1. Ladies and Gentlemen, I'd planned to speak to you tonight to report on the state of the union, but the events of earlier today have led me to change those plans. Today is a day for mourning and remembering. Nancy and I are pained to the core by the tragedy of the shuttle *Challenger*. We know we share this pain with all of the people of our country. This is truly a national loss.

2. Nineteen years ago, almost to the day, we lost three astronauts in a terrible accident on the ground. But we've never lost an astronaut in flight. We've never had a tragedy like this. And perhaps we've forgotten the courage it took for the crew of the shuttle. But they, the *Challenger* Seven, were aware of the dangers, but overcame them and did their jobs brilliantly. We mourn seven heroes: Michael Smith, Dick Scobee, Judith Resnik, Ronald McNair, Ellison Onizuka, Gregory Jarvis, and Christa McAuliffe. We mourn their loss as a nation together.

3. For the families of the seven, we cannot bear, as you do, the full impact of this tragedy. But we feel the loss, and we're thinking about you so very much. Your loved ones were daring and brave, and they had that special grace, that special spirit that says, "Give me a challenge, and I'll meet it with joy." They had a hunger to explore the universe and discover its truths. They wished to serve, and they did. They served all of us.

4. We've grown used to wonders in this century. It's hard to dazzle us. But for twenty-five years the United States space program has been doing just that. We've grown used to the idea of space, and perhaps we forget that we've only just begun. We're still pioneers. They, the members of the *Challenger* crew, were pioneers.

5. And I want to say something to the schoolchildren of America who were watching the live coverage of the shuttle's take-off. I know it's hard to understand, but sometimes painful things like this happen. It's all part of the process of exploration and discovery. It's all part of taking a chance and expanding man's horizons. The future doesn't belong to the fainthearted; it belongs to the brave. The *Challenger* crew was pulling us into the future, and we'll continue to follow them.

6. I've always had great faith in and respect for our space program. And what happened today does nothing to diminish it. We don't hide our space program. We don't keep secrets and cover things up. We do it all up front and in public. That's the way freedom is, and we wouldn't change it for a minute.

7. We'll continue our quest in space. There will be more shuttle flights and more shuttle crews and, yes, more volunteers, more civilians, more

its character-as-rhetorical from the situation which generates it," but situations obtain their character from the rhetoric which surrounds them or creates them.[50]

Vatz argues that rhetoric constructs the situation. He rejects the idea that one can find meaning in a situation, then respond to that preset meaning. Instead, he says, "meaning is not discovered in situations, but *created* by rhetors."[51] The meaning, or the definition of a situation, is not always clear. Consequently, the demand for a response is not necessarily self-evident to the audience or the rhetor. Instead, people's responses to situations make those events meaningful. Thus, "the rhetor is responsible for what he [or she] chooses to make salient."[52]

In Bitzer's formulation, the meaning intrinsic to the situation causes rhetoric. He argues that "the situation is objective, publicly observable, and historic [which means] that it is real or genuine . . . ."[53] A fitting response, according to Bitzer, would not attempt to alter or (re)define the situation; he rejects the attempt to create or alter a situation as illegitimate. In Vatz's formulation, however, rhetoric creates the meaning of the situation. Attempts to define the situation, or challenge another's interpretation of it, are perfectly reasonable.

Vatz recognizes the power of rhetoric to create a situation. Of the three elements of the rhetorical situation (exigence, audience, and constraints), Vatz most objects to Bitzer's notion of exigence.[54] Vatz argues that exigence is not intrinsic to the situation, but interpreted. Thus, critics and audiences must examine how rhetors define the exigence, and not simply accept the rhetor's description of it.

The exigence of a situation is not always clear or even known. In fact, the audience members may not perceive the urgency until the rhetor introduces the problem to them. For example, in 1962 Rachel Carson, a scientist who worked for the US Fish and Wildlife Service, wrote *Silent Spring* in order to galvanize action to ban the pesticide DDT.[55] Having researched and written several articles on ecologies, she had become concerned at the rapidly increasing use of chemical pesticides. She wrote *Silent Spring* to challenge their use and warn the public of their dangers.[56]

Prior to the publication of her book, people had not known about the dangers of chemical pesticides or recognized the urgency of the problem. They did not perceive an exigence. Technological progress was accepted as an unassailable good. Few people believed that nature was vulnerable to human intervention. Carson's book created a firestorm of controversy over pesticide use, an exigence to which chemical industries and the government had to respond, ultimately by banning DDT. Carson's rhetorical actions helped create the meaning and importance of the exigence to which the audience needed to respond.

Another example of defining an exigence can be seen in President Reagan's *Challenger* speech. He began by calling the event a "national tragedy." He clarified the exigence by stating "We're still pioneers. They, the members of the *Challenger* crew, were pioneers." In this way, he gave meaning to the disaster. In his view, the accident was part of US pioneer spirit, not an indication of the failure of NASA or the end of space travel.

The disagreement between Bitzer and Vatz appears to be irresolvable because Vatz frames his response as a direct refutation of Bitzer's position. For Bitzer, the situation produces rhetoric. For Vatz, rhetoric produces the situation. Does the situation control rhetoric or does rhetoric construct the situation?

A SYNERGISTIC UNDERSTANDING OF RHETORIC AND SITUATIONS

The rhetorical situation is complex. Symbolic action constructs human beings' understanding of reality and, hence, their understanding of situations. This statement does not mean that nothing exists outside of symbolic action, but that the meaning of the material world is always mediated through symbols and language. A synergistic relationship emerges between rhetoric and situation, one in which situations guide rhetorical responses *and* rhetoric constructs situations. The interaction results in something larger and distinct from the sum of the individual effects. Events happen, but their relative importance is given to them through interpretations, which are rhetorically constructed.

Although we recognize the importance of Bitzer's work, we question his assumption of an objectively knowable situation. Although we are sympathetic to Vatz's position, we recognize that rhetoric does not occur in a vacuum. A rhetor does not, all alone, define a situation. Human beings do not come to understand situations unmediated by discourse, but no rhetor comes to a situation with only her or his own discourse as the means of mediation. Other rhetors have already responded; a subject's cultural history has developed across time; and individuals may have watched an event on television or the Internet and are in search of meaning.

Rhetoric scholars Robert J. Branham and W. Barnett Pearce point out that rhetoric gets its meaning from the situation, but it also influences and helps create the situation.[57] For example, when you speak in class, you are aware that you are in a classroom with other students and a professor, so you probably speak differently from the way you do when you are at lunch with your friends. Once you speak in class, however, your communication shapes the class, helping to set a tone for the discussion. As people interact, the interaction begins to define the situation. Consequently, we believe a synergistic understanding of the rhetorical situation is needed, an approach that recognizes Bitzer's and Vatz's contributions.

Definition of the Situation

Argumentation theorist Robert Cox points out that a rhetor's definition of the situation determines which responses appear to be reasonable, rational, and coherent.[58] Cox argues that "actors' *definitions of the situation* emerge in their symbolic interactions with their environment"; they are not predetermined by the situation.[59] The way a rhetor defines a situation determines the exact nature of the exigence and, hence, what appear to be reasonable judgments about it and actions responding to it. Instead of the situation containing rules in the world. And no one will keep that light from shining. Today, our nation saw evil—the very worst of human nature—and we responded with the best of America. With the daring of our rescue workers, with the caring for strangers and neighbors who came to give blood and help in any way they could.

4. Immediately following the first attack, I implemented our government's emergency response plans. Our military is powerful, and it's prepared. Our emergency teams are working in New York City and Washington D.C. to help with local rescue efforts. Our first priority is to get help to those who have been injured, and to take every precaution to protect our citizens at home and around the world from further attacks. The functions of our government continue without interruption. Federal agencies in Washington which had to be evacuated today are reopening for essential personnel tonight and will be open for business tomorrow. Our financial institutions remain strong, and the American economy will be open for business as well.

5. The search is underway for those who were behind these evil acts. I have directed the full resources of our intelligence and law enforcement communities to find those responsible and to bring them to justice. We will make no distinction between the terrorists who committed these acts and those who harbor them.

6. I appreciate so very much the members of Congress who have joined me in strongly condemning these attacks. And on behalf of the American people, I thank the many world leaders who have called to offer their condolences and assistance. America and our friends and allies join with all those who want peace and security in the world, and we stand together to win the war against terrorism.

7. Tonight, I ask for your prayers for all those who grieve, for the children whose worlds have been shattered, for all whose sense of safety and security has been threatened. And I pray they will be comforted by a Power greater than any of us, spoken through the ages in Psalm 23: "Even though I walk through the valley of the shadow of death, I fear no evil for you are with me."

8. This is a day when all Americans from every walk of life unite in our resolve for justice and peace. America has stood down enemies before, and we will do so this time. None of us will ever forget this day, yet we go forward to defend freedom and all that is good and just in our world.

9. Thank you. Good night. And God bless America.[64]

In the second paragraph of this speech, the attacks are described as "evil," "acts of terror" and "acts of mass murder," but not yet as "acts of war." Still, Bush established a rhetorical trajectory that made clear a military response was planned when he declared: "Our military is powerful, and it's prepared," then clarified that the US would "win the war against terrorism."

Not until September 12 did President Bush specifically refer to the attacks as "acts of war."[65] Naming them as "acts of war" and also declaring a "war against terrorism" defined the situation differently than if the acts had been described as criminal acts, a violation of international law, or crimes against humanity. Because President Bush was able to convince the public that the situation was an "act of war" in which terrorism was attacking freedom, a definition that media coverage echoed,[66] the course of action that appeared reasonable was a military response. By defining the situation as an act of war he stretched the definition of an act of war to encompass acts of terrorism that were believed to be sponsored by another country but perpetrated by nonstate actors. By declaring a war against terrorism, he expanded the idea of war to targets beyond aggressive nation states.

As the 9/11 example illustrates, President Bush's definition of the situation framed the types of evidence that were admissible (only US sources counted because the attackers were evil) and the information that was relevant (the "war" began on 9/11, and no earlier). By defining the terrorist attacks as "acts of war," he limited the appropriate response to the attacks. An act of war requires some sort of military response.

The rhetorical response, the rhetorical situation, the rhetor, and the audiences all influence each other, bringing into existence a situation at their nexus. Once a rhetor crafts a definition of the rhetorical situation and calls a particular audience into being, the rhetorical situation is defined for present, as well as future, rhetors. The events clearly happened on September 11, 2001, but what they meant was open to interpretation; depending on that interpretation, rhetors could defend particular reactions as the most reasonable. As events unfold, however, rhetorical action ensues and the rhetorical situation evolves, eliciting different interpretations. Definitions do not go unanswered or unchallenged. Competing definitions of the situation can sustain and generate arguments about what is an appropriate rhetorical response.

Analysis: 9/11 Redefined

At this point, given how deeply the US public has been immersed in rhetoric declaring 9/11 an "act of war," it seems unreasonable to think about whether a nonmilitary response would have been appropriate. At the time, over 80 percent of US citizens approved of the US-led invasion of Afghanistan as part of its war on terror.[67] The United States government declared the Afghanistan government harbored those who masterminded the 9/11 attacks. Afghanistan was controlled by the Taliban, who were supported by Osama bin Laden, who claimed credit for the 9/11 attacks.

The interpretation of 9/11 as an "act of war" is not the only way to understand it, however.[68] As Richard Vatz points out, "meaning is not discovered in situations, but *created* by rhetors."[69]

Pope John Paul II offered a different definition of the situation. In a papal audience one year later, he stated clearly that the attacks were unjustified, but that defining the attacks as an act of war was unacceptable.

so that the seeds are not sown for further events of this kind, find sites of intervention, help to plan strategies thoughtfully that will not beckon more violence in the future. One can even experience that abhorrence, mourning, anxiety, and fear, and have all of these emotional dispositions lead to a reflection on how others have suffered arbitrary violence at the hands of the US, but also endeavor to produce another public culture and another public policy in which suffering unexpected violence and loss and reactive aggression are not accepted as the norm of political life.[74]

Butler's call for a nonviolent ethics that understands the precariousness of life is at odds with the public discourse that has defined US reactions to 9/11. Her point is that invasion should not be perceived as the only option. Instead of constituting the audience as vengeful citizens of an attacked nation, she called on people to be empathic citizens of the world. If the audience members accepted Bush's definition of the situation as war, however, it would be difficult to persuade them to redefine the situation, as Butler attempted to do.

Ultimately, Butler argued that dissent is important, including dissent against definitions of situations that lead to labeling dissent as anti-American or, worse, treason. Recognition that situations are rhetorically defined is essential if we are to recognize the possibility of challenging the definition of a situation. Redefining a situation is not easy. Once an audience accepts a definition of a situation, it can be difficult to change that definition. When the US public accepted the definition of 9/11 as an act of war against the United States and identified another country as sharing responsibility, US support for military action was strong. Such strong support should not have meant that people who disagreed were anti-American or did not support the troops, but the definition of the situation became stable and, hence, presented a particular exigence to anyone who would question the US response.

FITTING RESPONSES RECONSIDERED

Identifying the components of a rhetorical situation and recognizing when symbolic actions have attempted to define the situation are useful steps in understanding how rhetoric functions. The relationships between the rhetor, argument, and components of the rhetorical situation (exigence, audience, and constraints) influence the range of communication possible. One way to assess the possibility of communication is to determine whether the response to the rhetorical situation is fitting. Like clothes, fit can be expansive or tight. If the situation is defined more expansively, then the issues to be considered become broader as well. As Butler asked about 9/11, do we mourn only the loss of US life, or all life? If the situation is defined expansively, it might call for a radically different response, such as the Pope's call to respect all human life and to reflect on the underlying conditions that might lead people to violence. If defined narrowly, the situation tends to demand a focused response. The focus on the loss of US lives constructs a definition of the situation that suggests armed conflict is necessary to protect US lives. In the next section, we identify possible influences on whether responses are fitting, including cultural variations in historical context and conscious decisions on the part of rhetors to challenge what is considered a fitting response.

Cultural Variations and Historical Context

Although the rhetorical situation is more than the historical context, placing a rhetorical act in its historical context assists our understanding of the choices available to a rhetor. Not all rhetors have equal access to the full range of persuasive possibilities. Furthermore, meaning is not only in texts, but in the audiences who interpret the texts. Various audiences' social norms influence what they consider appropriate even during a single historical moment.

Understanding the historical context is a necessary, but not sufficient, condition for understanding how a response fits a rhetorical situation. Communication scholars Robert J. Branham and W. Barnett Pearce point out that an audience interprets a rhetorical text within the rhetorical situation.[75] If you read the Gettysburg Address without knowing the rhetorical situation of the speech, you might read it as a piece of literature and miss how it responds to a very particular situation. Knowing that it was given on the battleground of the bloodiest battle in the US Civil War gives meaning to the speech and the persuasive choices President Lincoln made.

The context is not simply the historical facts and events surrounding a persuasive response. It also includes the participants' cultural orientations and how they influence interpretations of those events and facts. What today might be viewed as unfitting or as inappropriate language choice, form, topic, style, or approach might have been viewed as an acceptable or fitting response when a speech was first delivered. For example, expectations concerning the appropriate length of speeches have changed dramatically. In 1841, William Henry Harrison delivered a 105-minute inaugural speech. After the advent of radio in the 1920s, most speeches lasted no more than an hour. By the 1940s, the 30-minute speech was the norm; almost all major political speeches were reprinted in their entirety in newspapers. Now, most political speeches average about 20 minutes in length. Speakers hope to receive evening news coverage with 5-, 10-, or 15-second sound-bites.[76] Barack Obama's 2009 inaugural was barely 22 minutes long.

An even more extreme time shrinkage can be seen in political debates. When senatorial candidates Abraham Lincoln and Stephen A. Douglas debated seven times in 1858 on the single issue of slavery (particularly the expansion of slavery into the territories), each debate lasted three hours. The first person spoke for 60 minutes, the second for 90 minutes; then the first person had a rejoinder speech of 30 minutes. By comparison, in the September 5, 2007, Republican presidential primary debate in Durham, NH, in which seven candidates participated, each person was given 60 *seconds* to answer, and a 30-*second* rebuttal.

The length of speeches is not the only thing that has changed. What you might take for granted as appropriate now could have been extremely shocking in a different era. For example, political communication scholar Kathleen Hall Jamieson traces how a style that was once condemned as effeminate (soothing, ornamental, personal, self-disclosing, and using dramatic narratives), became the norm for contemporary politicians speaking in an electronic age.[77] Television is a visual medium, in which the visual elements combine intimately with the verbal elements.[78] Television has given the public a closer view of their leaders speaking than was possible before television; and people expect the words from speakers who are close-up to be intimate and personal.[79] Additionally, television gives the illusion that the rhetor is speaking to them individually, rather than to a large audience. Hence, it invites a more personal style than did the oratory of a pretelevision age.[80]

In fact, some rhetorical acts are intended to contribute to changes in social norms. For example, for a woman to speak (or even vote) on public policy was considered absolutely inappropriate and "unfitting" in the United States until the early 1900s. Daniel Webster (lawyer, congressperson, and statesperson) declared that "The rough contests of the political world are not suited to the dignity and the delicacy of your sex." Cardinal Gibbons (Catholic archbishop and the youngest prelate at the First Vatican Council) worried that "If woman enters politics, she will be sure to carry away on her some of the mud and dirt of political contact." Dr. S. Weir Mitchell (celebrated clinician and neurologist) exhorted women to "accep[t] the irrevocable decree which made her woman and not man. Something in between she cannot be."[81] Those societal norms have significantly shifted to the point that it would now be considered inappropriate to suggest explicitly that women have no place in public policy argument.

Responses to Rhetorical Situations

How does one explain persuasive responses that, at first glance, do not appear to fit the rhetorical situation, but still persuade an audience? Sometimes a rhetor might respond in an "unfitting" way in order to draw attention to an issue or shock an audience into awareness. Civil rights activists' lunch counter sit-ins of the 1960s and AIDS activists' die-ins of the 1980s did not persuade in a conventional way.[82]

Rhetors may choose to respond in an untraditional way if they do not interpret the situation in a conventional way. As Branham and Pearce explain, "not all texts are conventional, not all contexts are stable, and not all situations imply recognizable techniques or consensual standards of interpretation."[83] They offer four ways in which a rhetor can respond to a rhetorical situation: conformity, nonparticipation, desecration, and contextual reconstruction. We begin with their description of conformity, which echoes Bitzer's idea of the fitting response to the rhetorical situation.

Conformity. Rhetors use **conformity** when they employ *a conventional response to a situation*.[84] A person who is upset by a particular law might write a letter to a legislator that outlines the ways in which the law is flawed. This is a conventional way of expressing opinions about a legislative issue; it conforms to the traditional method of persuasion. Conformity adapts the persuasive message to the norms and expectations of the audience it addresses.

Societal norms affect what is considered a conforming response. Audiences have expectations that rhetors may decide to follow in order to have their messages heard and accepted. Much of our everyday communication conforms. For example, when you attempt to persuade your professor to alter an assignment that you think is too difficult or time consuming, you probably make an argument in a polite way, offering support for your position. You probably suggest alternatives to the assignment or ways to make the assignment more workable for you and your classmates. You are attempting to persuade your professor conventionally, using a style and arguments that are expected in this situation.

Nonparticipation. Some rhetors may choose not to respond to a situation within the established context because they do not believe the context is legitimate. **Nonparticipation** is *a response that denies the legitimacy of the rhetorical situation.*[85] Some people might perceive nonparticipation as an unfitting response.

In the 2008 Zimbabwe presidential elections, opposition leader Morgan Tsvangirai refused to participate in the run-off election with incumbent President Robert Mugabe, even though Tsvangirai claimed to have won more than 50 percent of the vote in the first round—which would have meant that a second round of voting was not needed. Despite charges of election fraud, however, the Mugabe administration claimed that Tsvangirai had not actually won the first round of voting outright; that Tsvangirai had received 48 percent of the vote while Mugabe got 43 percent, necessitating a run-off election.[86] During the campaign for the run-off, Tsvangirai was arrested and detained. Many of his supporters were harassed and beaten; some were killed. Fearing for his supporters and believing the election would not be fair, Tsvangirai dropped out of the run-off election. He refused to participate because he believed the situation was not a legitimate election. Although he believed in democratic processes, he also believed that the current system was unfair. By refusing to participate, he sent that message to his country and to the world. His nonparticipation further eroded the legitimacy of the election and Mugabe's rule.

Nonparticipation as a strategy is not odd. In his study of how people react to the failure of an organization to provide a high quality service or product, noted economist and political theorist Albert O. Hirschman argues that consumers and citizens have two choices: exit or voice, exit representing nonparticipation and voice representing participation.[87] He argues that exit occupies a privileged position in US ideology, tradition, and practice, because the nation was founded by an act of exit/nonparticipation: in the Declaration of Independence, the colonies exited the British empire and declared they would no longer participate in it. Hirschman believes the countercultural movements of the 1960s and '70s followed this tradition with their calls to "turn on, tune in, drop out."[88] He explains, "Once again dissatisfaction with the surrounding social order leads to flight rather than fight, to withdrawal of the dissatisfied group and to its setting up a separate 'scene.'"[89]

Desecration. While nonparticipation refuses to grant legitimacy to a situation through participation in it, **desecration** is *a response that violates what would be considered an appropriate response; it participates, but in a way that overtly challenges expectations.* The rhetor ridicules the situation and/or those who take part in it. This response violates norms and conventions in order to question the legitimacy of the situation.[90] When protesting the Vietnam War, for example, some activists chose to desecrate the situation by burning their draft cards. In this way, they questioned the legitimacy of the government's use of selective service and the legitimacy of the war. Protestors of the 1960s engaged in rhetorical actions that intentionally violated expectations of decorum. In some cases, they considered the acts of confrontational protest to be ends in themselves because they declared a sense of self-worth and demanded to supplant the existing order.[91]

Desecration can be funny, as the rhetor creates what Burke refers to as "perspective by incongruity" for the audience.[92] Basically, the rhetor creates a response that is funny in its absurdity, even though there are some elements of truth in that response. For example, *The Daily Show* mimics the form of a conventional news program, but at key moments departs from the form in order to expose how media outlets have failed to live up to their journalistic duty in a democratic society. Even as it appears to conform, its departure from form make clear the show is not a news show, but a "fake news program." For example, on March 4, 2009, the show criticized CNBC (the Consumer News and Business Channel) for its failure to report the financial crisis accurately. *Mad Money* host Jim Cramer, one of the more prominent faces of CNBC, took this criticism personally and started a round of appearances on other NBC-owned shows. In response, *Daily Show* host Jon Stewart focused a segment on Cramer (whose show CNBC promoted with the motto "In Cramer We Trust") and his fabulously bad advice to hold Bear Stearns stock in the days before the financial firm collapsed. Cramer indicated that Stewart had taken his advice out of context and dismissed Stewart as a "comedian" on a "variety show."[93] On his March 9 show, Stewart compiled a series of clips showing Cramer specifically telling people to buy the stock in the weeks before the collapse. At the end of this series, Stewart broke from the form of reporting (where reporters are supposed to be objective and not personally invested in a story), and yelled a phrase that rhymes with "MUCK YOU!"[94] Stewart literally desecrated the form of news reporting by yelling an obscenity. He also desecrated it stylistically by intentionally rejecting the decorous persona that news anchors often assume.[95]

What is most interesting, however, is that this fake program often does the job of critically reporting world events better than its supposedly real counterparts do. As host Jon Stewart explains in an exchange on *Crossfire* (an ostensibly real news show): "the absurdity of the system provides us the most material."[96] The reporters on *The Daily Show* desecrate the news to create messages about the way media report stories as well as to desecrate the subjects of the stories themselves.

Contextual Reconstruction. **Contextual reconstruction** is *a response in which a rhetor attempts to redefine the situation.* These responses might appear to conform to the situation, but actually challenge the expectations of what they are meant to achieve, sometimes quite overtly, as part of the rhetorical act. In these instances, Branham and Pearce say, "Speaking itself is both the subject and object of such discourse."[97] Instead of "accepting the rhetorical situation as presented," a rhetor "dismantles and then reconstructs it."[98] In contextual reconstruction, the rhetor recognizes the traditional meaning of the rhetorical situation, but seeks to redefine it.

Branham and Pearce offer Abraham Lincoln's Gettysburg Address as an example of contextual reconstruction.[99] President Lincoln had been invited to make "a few appropriate remarks"[100] to dedicate a cemetery for the soldiers who had died fighting a horrific Civil War battle that saw fifty-one thousand casualties during a three-day period in July 1863.[101] Such a situation asked President Lincoln to look backward, which he appeared to acknowledge when he stated: "We are met on a great battle-field of that war. We have come to dedicate a portion of that field, as a final resting place for those who here gave their lives that that nation might live. It is altogether fitting and proper that we should do this."[102] He directly reinterpreted the exigence, however, by stating that the assumed exigence was not accurate: "But, in a larger sense, we can not dedicate—we can not consecrate—we can not hallow—this ground." Instead of looking backward in consecration, he shifted the orientation to the future. He reinterpreted the situation by creating a new exigence of renewal.[103]

Harkening back to Pericles's funeral oration delivered 2,394 years earlier,[104] President Lincoln questioned whether a verbal response was even fitting: "The brave men, living and dead, who struggled here, have consecrated it, far above our poor power to add or detract. The world will little note, nor long remember what we say here, but it can never forget what they did here." Finally, he solidified his reconstruction of the situation to a future orientation, calling for a renewed commitment to the war effort:

> It is for us, the living, rather, to be dedicated here to the unfinished work which they who fought here have thus far so nobly advanced. It is rather for us to be here dedicated to the great task remaining before us . . . that from these honored dead we take increased devotion to that cause for which they gave the last full measure of devotion; that we here highly resolve that these dead shall not have died in vain; that this nation, under God, shall have a new birth of freedom; and that government of the people, by the people, for the people, shall not perish from the earth.

On one level, the Gettysburg Address, considered by many to be one of the greatest speeches in US history, was not a fitting response because the purpose of the gathering was to consecrate part of the battlefield as a cemetery. Yet, as Branham and Pearce point out, President Lincoln reconstructed the situation and offered a new interpretation to the audience[105] that focused on renewal, not consecration. Lincoln knew he was faced with eulogizing the largest number of US soldiers ever killed in battle, and that the reality of the tragedy could have a demoralizing effect on Union supporters. Not all of the North was committed to the war effort. His interpretation of the meaning of the situation transformed the understanding of the battle and the memorial.[106]

[14] Bitzer, "Rhetorical Situation," 5.

[15] Bitzer, "Rhetorical Situation," 5–6.

[16] Bitzer, "Rhetorical Situation," 2.

[17] David Kohn, "The President's Story: The President Talks in Detail about His Sept. 11 Experience," *60 Minutes*, September 10, 2003, http://www.cbsnews.com/stories/2002/09/11/ 60II/main521718.shtml (accessed February 14, 2009).

[18] Some people perceived failure to respond. After President Bush was informed that the second tower had been hit, he continued to listen to sixteen second-graders take turns reading *The Pet Goat*. The perception of a failure to respond is most detailed in Michael Moore's controversial documentary, *Fahrenheit 9/11* (2004).

[19] Bruce E. Gronbeck, "Rhetorical Timing in Public Communication," *Central States Speech Journal* 25 (1974): 91.

[20] Bitzer, "Rhetorical Situation," 7, italics added.

[21] Matthew Dowd, "Interview from 'Karl Rove—The Architect,'" *Frontline*, January 4, 2005, posted April 12, 2005, http://www.pbs.org/wgbh/pages/frontline/shows/architect/interviews/dowd.html (accessed June 17, 2008).

[22] Tim Harper, "It's Very Difficult to Ambush Bush: 'Bush Bubble' Keeps Fans in Line for Hours, Campaign Events Strictly Limited to Loyal Republicans," *NewsCenter*, September 24, 2005, http://www.commondreams.org/headlines04/0925-24.htm (accessed June 17, 2008). In response to the strict control of access to campaign events, professors at Allegheny College in Meadville, Pennsylvania, created the Soapbox Alliance (http://cpp.allegheny.edu/soapboxalliance/ index.php). See Oren Dorell, "College Criticizes Invitation-Only Political Rallies," *USA Today*, updated November 19, 2007, http://www.usatoday.com/news/politics/election2008/2007-11-19-soapbox_N.htm (accessed June 17, 2008). The invitation-only strategy continued during Bush's presidency. See Michael A. Genovese and Lori Cox Han, "The 'Invitation Only' Presidency of George W. Bush," *HistoryNewsNetwork*, December 5, 2005, http://hnn.us/articles/18302.html (accessed June 17, 2005).

[23] Bitzer, "Rhetorical Situation," 6.

[24] Bitzer, "Rhetorical Situation," 8, italics added.

[25] Martha Cooper, *Analyzing Public Discourse* (Prospect Heights, IL: Waveland, 1989), 22.

[26] John Lewis, "John Lewis," in *My Soul is Rested: The Story of the Civil Rights Movement in the Deep South*, ed. Howell Raines (New York: Penguin, 1977), 99.

[27] For examples, see his website: http://www.revbilly.com (accessed October 12, 2011).

[28] Quoted in Jill Lane, "Reverend Billy: Preaching, Protest and Postindustrial Flânerie," *The Drama Review* 46, no. 1 (Spring 2002): 60–84, 71.

[29] Karlyn Kohrs Campbell and Susan Schultz Huxman, *The Rhetorical Act*, 3rd ed. (Belmont, CA: Thomson/Wadsworth, 2003), 184–198, 206–214, 224–236.

[30] Campbell and Huxman, *Rhetorical Act*, 207–212.

[31] H. W. Brands, "15 Minutes That Saved America," *American History* 43, no. 4 (October 2008): 34–41.

[32] David Michael Ryfe, "Franklin Roosevelt and the Fireside Chats," *Journal of Communication* 49, no. 4 (Autumn 1999), 80–103.

[33] Franklin D. Roosevelt, First Fireside Chat, "The Banking Crisis," March 12, 1933, http://www.americanrhetoric.com/speeches/fdrfirstfiresidechat.html (accessed March 17, 2009). For a detailed analysis of this speech, see Amos Kiewe, *FDR's*

First Fireside Chat: Public Confidence and the Banking Crisis (College Station: Texas A&M Press, 2007).

[34] Mary Kate Cary, "Obama Should Make Roosevelt-Style Fireside Chats on the Banking Crisis," Opinion, *U.S. News and World Report* online, March 12, 2009, http://www.usnews.com/blogs/mary-kate-cary/2009/3/12 /obama-should-make-roosevelt-style-fireside-chats-on-the-banking-crisis.html (accessed March 17, 2009).

[35] Campbell and Huxman, *Rhetorical Act*, 184–198, 212–214.

[36] Campbell and Huxman, *Rhetorical Act*, 224–236.

[37] Ryfe, "Franklin Roosevelt," 99.

[38] Bitzer, "Rhetorical Situation," 10.

[39] Karlyn Kohrs Campbell and Kathleen Hall Jamieson, "Form and Genre in Rhetorical Criticism: An Introduction," in *Form and Genre: Shaping Rhetorical Action*, ed. Karlyn Kohrs Campbell and Kathleen Hall Jamieson (Falls Church, VA: Speech Communication Association, 1978), 19.

[40] Karlyn Kohrs Campbell and Kathleen Hall Jamieson, *Deeds Done in Words* (Chicago: University of Chicago Press, 1990), 37.

[41] Bitzer, "Rhetorical Situation," 13.

[42] Campbell and Jamieson, "Introduction," 19.

[43] Kathleen M. Jamieson, "Antecedent Genre as Rhetorical Constraint," *Quarterly Journal of Speech* 61 (1975): 406.

[44] Daniel Riffe and James Glen Stovall, "Diffusion of News of Shuttle Disaster: What Role for Emotional Response," *Journalism Quarterly* 66 (Autumn 1989): 551–556.

[45] You can watch footage of the explosion on YouTube: "*Challenger* Disaster Live on CNN" at http://www.youtube.com/watch?v=j4JOjcDFtBE (accessed October 12, 2011).

[46] Ronald W. Reagan, "The Space Shuttle 'Challenger' Tragedy Address," January 28, 1986, http://www.americanrhetoric.com/speeches/ronaldreaganchallenger.htm (accessed June 18, 2008). A video of the speech is available on this site.

[47] One also should note that the Soviet Union was likely an audience, especially with Reagan's thinly veiled reference to the Soviet penchant for secrecy in paragraph 6.

[48] For additional analysis, see "Special Issue: The Space Shuttle *Challenger*," *Central States Speech Journal* 37 (Fall 1986). For analysis of the interactions between the visuals of the explosion and Reagan's rhetoric, see Kathleen Hall Jamieson, *Eloquence in an Electronic Age: The Transformation of Political Speechmaking* (New York: Oxford University Press, 1988), esp. pp. 126–133.

[49] Richard E. Vatz, "The Myth of the Rhetorical Situation," *Philosophy and Rhetoric* 6 (1973): 159.

[50] Vatz, "Myth," 159.

[51] Vatz, "Myth," 157.

[52] Vatz, "Myth," 159.

[53] Bitzer, "Rhetorical Situation," 11.

[54] Vatz, "Myth," 155–156.

[55] Rachel Carson, *Silent Spring*, 40th anniversary ed. (New York: Mariner, 1962/2002).

[56] Linda Lear, "The Life and Legacy of Rachel Carson," 1998, http://www.rachelcarson.org/Biography.aspx (accessed January 30, 2009).

[57] Robert J. Branham and W. Barnett Pearce, "Between Text and Context: Toward a Rhetorical Contextual Reconstruction," *Quarterly Journal of Speech* 71 (1985): 19–36, 19.

[58] J. Robert Cox, "Argument and the 'Definition of the Situation,'" *Central States Speech Journal* 32 (1981): 197–205, esp. 200.

Chapter 9

Publics and Counterpublics

Key Terms

counterpublics	public
cyberpublics	public screen
enclaved publics	public sphere
hybrid publics	strong publics
oscillating publics	weak publics

Immigration has long been a topic that sparks intense debate in the United States. Legislative attempts to limit immigration have occurred throughout US history, even though the United States of America was founded as a nation of immigrants and the Statue of Liberty declares:

> Give me your tired, your poor,
> Your huddled masses yearning to breathe free,
> The wretched refuse of your teeming shore.
> Send these, the homeless, tempest-tost to me,
> I lift my lamp beside the golden door!

Despite this welcome, immigration restrictions have, over time, targeted Asians, Eastern and Southern Europeans, and Latinos. In 1882, Congress passed the Chinese Exclusion Act, which prohibited for ten years the immigration of people from China to the United States. The Immigration Act of 1917 restricted the amount of immigration from Asia generally. During the first two decades of the 1900s, more than 14 million people emigrated to the United States, mostly from Southern Europe, Eastern Europe, and Asia. In response, the Immigration Act of 1924 sought to lock in the then-current ethnic distribution for immigration. In 1954, the United States Immigration and Naturalization Service launched "Operation Wetback," which sought the forcible deportation of 1.2 million migrant workers, mostly from Mexico. In 1994, California passed Proposition 187, which eliminated public health, education, and welfare provisions for undocumented workers. The spring of 2006 saw public demonstrations in response to US Congressional debates over immigration policy.[1]

In the 2006 debates, people, not just politicians, made clear the stakes they held in the public discussion. The debate was not reserved to the halls of Congress. Rallies across the country that demonstrated the broad public concern included gatherings of 500,000 in Los Angeles, 350,000–500,000 in Dallas, and 400,000 in Chicago. Pro-immigration rallies occurred in 140 cities across the country from March to May 2006. In addition, the anti–illegal immigration

Minuteman Project held a 13-city campaign tour, culminating in a rally outside the US Capitol building.

The debates over immigration illustrate a number of things about publics and public deliberation. First, they illustrate how, as people present their concerns for public consideration, they constitute a public—that is, they navigate who is entitled to participate in forming public culture and public policy. For our purposes, a **public** is formed by *people coming together to discuss common concerns, including concerns about who they are and what they should do, and as a result constructing social reality together.* The goal of public deliberation is not always consensus; sometimes it is to unsettle existing agreement. Regardless of the goal, publics use rhetoric to discuss matters of common concern (and determine what they are), constitute identity, and construct their shared reality.

Second, discussions about immigration illustrate how public discourse includes both deliberative debates about policy and cultural debates about civic identity—who can and should participate in public deliberations about national policy and national identity. Communication scholar Anne Demo notes that anxiety has grown "over the nation's changing ethnic demographics, characterized in the popular press as 'the browning of America.'"[2] As a result, these debates are not just about whom to let into the country, but also about what it means to be a US citizen, how to define the country's identity, and what power and privilege comes with citizenship.[3]

Third, these discussions show that "public" is a complex concept. The term carries diverse meanings. News coverage noted various ways in which these rallies and debates had a public character. Reports described the gatherings as "massive public rallies organized by immigrants' rights groups"[4] and as a "wave of public protests."[5] Representative Tom Tancredo talked about the public as audience: "Millions of people are flaunting the fact that they are here illegally and are demanding special treatment. I don't think that flies with John Q. Public."[6] In response, rally organizers encouraged protestors to carry more US flags because they "did not want to alienate the broader public."[7] Public opinion became a thing to be moved: reports noted that the "immigrant groups face several hurdles in their attempt to sway politicians and public opinion."[8] The audience was also described as complex, as containing both politicians and the public. One story noted, "it is encouraging that politicians and the public at least are thinking about" immigration issues.[9] Other stories examined whether the rallies were a possible influence on "the public debate on immigration"[10] and referenced scholarly reports that "demonstrations represent the largest effort by immigrants to influence public policy in recent memory."[11] Opponents to illegal immigration argued that immigrants were "invading" the United States, creating economic problems such as job loss, and that "illegal aliens bring diseases and drain public services."[12] Ultimately, media reports said a congressional bill was unlikely to pass because of "deep public divisions."[13] In these descriptions, at various times, the term "public" describes the rallies, a place, a people, policy, opinion, services, and nonpoliticians.

Fourth, the debates show that an understanding of the meaning of publicity and publics is central to understanding the role of rhetoric in civic life. Which issues are considered worthy of public consideration? What discussions are part of public discourse? Which people are given access to the public sphere? Who is included in the public? To understand rhetoric in civic life, you need to understand the concept of public.

Fifth, these debates show that a multitude of voices are present in the public sphere. Various perspectives and actions emerged on the issue, including former CNN news anchor Lou Dobbs's discussions of the economic impact of the "invasion of illegal aliens";[14] the Minuteman Project's frustrations with the lack of federal enforcement of immigration law; the work of La Raza, a Hispanic civil rights organization, on immigrants' rights; various governors' concerns about the fiscal impact of illegal immigration on states' budgets; President George W. Bush's attempts to link improved border security and workplace enforcement to the legalization of twelve million illegal immigrants; and the creation of a temporary worker program. Rhetoric scholar Gerard A. Hauser notes that this diversity of activity is central to the public sphere, for "it is only when a multitude of voices is heard that social actors begin to realize that they can do more than respond; they can choose."[15]

This chapter introduces you to an understanding of publics and the role rhetoric plays in them, but we do not end the discussion there. As with all communication, power plays a role. Not all people have equal rhetorical power. Thus, the question arises: if a group is not represented in the dominant public, how can its members develop a vocabulary that articulates their identity, interests, and needs? To answer this question, we explore the concept of *counter*public spheres—arenas of public deliberation that arise in response to exclusions from the dominant public. We also explore the increasing role of the Internet and the challenges it poses to the very idea of what is public. Finally, we discuss the expanding roles of visual rhetoric and media proliferation, and why these call for a reconsideration of the public sphere as a public screen.

THE PUBLIC SPHERE

Most contemporary understandings of the public sphere rely on German sociologist Jürgen Habermas's groundbreaking work.[16] Habermas studied nations that shifted from monarchical and feudalistic forms to democratic societies, such as Britain, France, and Germany during the eighteenth and early nineteenth centuries. These societies had in common the emergence of a bourgeois public sphere composed of people who influenced culture and possessed control over the means of production (artisans and tradespeople who formed guilds and companies), and who engaged in practices that enabled them to serve as an intermediary between the state (the executive power of official government) and society (associational activity among private individuals). Habermas believed the needs and interests of individuals can come together as a public to check the exercise of state power and to make sure that power always acts in the interest of those it governs. Habermas's study of these social changes led to his definition of the public sphere.

Habermas defines the **public sphere** as *"a domain of our social life in which such a thing as public opinion can be formed"* and that *"is constituted* *in every conversation in which private persons come together to form a public."*[17] By "public opinion," Habermas does not mean the survey responses that Roper tracks or the call-in polls your local evening news conducts. Instead, he says, public opinion is formed only when "a public that engages in rational discussion exists" to create informed opinion, which he contrasts to "mere opinions."[18] As an illustration, Habermas describes how, between 1680 and 1730, coffee houses opened in Britain and Germany and served as places where a variety of people (mostly men) could meet and talk about contemporary moral, literary, and political issues.[19] London, alone, had three thousand coffee houses, each with its own regulars. For Habermas, the conversations in these coffee houses were central to the formation of a public sphere.

Notice that Habermas defines the public sphere in terms of *communication*. A public sphere is not brought into being by a particular group of people, a location, or a set of topics. Instead, it is constituted by the *conversations* (rhetorical acts) of people as they discuss topics of general interest.[20] Political and social theorist Nancy Fraser describes Habermas's public sphere as an arena of discourse "in which political participation is enacted through the medium of talk" as people come together to "deliberate about common affairs."[21]

Habermas's definition is both descriptive and prescriptive. It describes the way public discourse is enabled and constrained within a given society by its institutions, legal rights, and norms. It also prescribes an ideal to work toward. An ideal public sphere has certain characteristics. It must (1) be "open in principle to all citizens," (2) address "matters of general interest," and (3) be free from coercion.[22] This ideal of the public sphere is central to democracy. Free and open communication, in which anyone can participate, about issues that transcend personal interest is essential to a fully functioning democracy and open society.

It is challenging to point to an example of a public sphere because it is difficult to identify a specific place or arena of discourse. Instead, one knows a public sphere has come into being because one can identify trace elements of it in rhetoric. The immigration rhetoric described in the introduction to this chapter is an example of public sphere discourse. People enacted political participation through their rhetorical acts (conversations, speeches, parades, signs, letters to the editor, and protest meetings) about an issue of common concern. Although the hope was that public opinion, and not mere opinion, was formed, it would be difficult to prove that all the rhetorical acts in these debates were "rational discussion." Still, the debates suggest the rise of a public sphere.

Another example is the February 2011 debate over the collective bargaining rights of unions of public employees in Wisconsin. In response to record state budget deficits, Governor Scott Walker proposed a "budget repair bill"[23] to balance the budget. The bill not only proposed cuts to public workers' compensation, it also eliminated almost all collective bargaining rights for most public employees (except police, firefighters, and the state patrol). The rhetoric about the bill provides ample trace evidence of a public sphere, as citizens talked about issues of common concern: the budget deficit, the vitality of public unions, and the legislative impasse caused when fourteen Democratic state senators fled the state in order to deny a quorum to Republican senators seeking to pass the bill. A public sphere was constituted in protests as tens of thousands of citizens filled the Wisconsin state capitol square and rotunda; as union members, citizens, and students took part in public hearings; as state representatives and senators, as well as the governor, talked in various media outlets and during legislative debates; and as citizens around the state talked to each other about the bill. The constitution of the public sphere was not confined to the events at the capitol building or the statements of lawmakers; it also occurred in coffee shops such as the Coffee Vault in Dousman[24] and EVP Coffee in Madison. In the tradition of Habermas's European coffee houses, many regulars at EVP Coffee (including public sphere scholar Robert Asen) engaged in conversations about public affairs, including the governor's bill. The protests, testimony, media interviews, and coffee shop conversations across the state enacted political participation through talk.

In an example on a smaller scale, at the university at which two of us teach, a vibrant discussion occurred about how to reform the Liberal Arts Core (LAC) requirements for students. The university is a sort of microcosm or parallel of a nation (with an administration, budget, and citizens). In the process of discussion, a public sphere was formed. Even people who were not personally involved in teaching LAC courses participated; the discussion was of general interest. People talked about the public purpose of a university education, the skills and knowledge people needed to succeed as citizens and in the economy, and whether LAC courses should be perceived to be relevant to students or change what students perceived to be relevant. Feedback from students on their perceptions of the LAC was sought and considered. Not everyone agreed, but a general public opinion began to emerge about what the LAC should do and how it had to be changed to be able to do that.

When the members of the university came together, they formed a public—a group unified by its identification with the larger institution of the university—and formed an opinion about what those who govern the university (the administration and faculty senate) should do as a result of public sphere discussions. The debate would not have brought a public sphere into being if only tenured professors were represented, or if the university president had said "if you speak negatively about the present LAC you will be fired." The discussion was a matter of general interest because all students are required to take the LAC. Even professors who do not teach LAC courses had an interest, because these courses are meant to prepare students to succeed in their non-LAC and major courses. Yet, this was not a complete public sphere: Faculty opinions were privileged. People who were not members of the university (the equivalent of noncitizens) were not invited. Some voices (such as that of the dean of students) were given more power than others, in that time was set aside for them to speak.

Habermas's ideal of open, public, and coercion-free communication may never have existed in reality,[25] but scholars herald it as an ideal toward which democratic societies should strive.[26] Civic engagement requires open and reasoned communication between informed citizens. Imagine if public debate about an issue such as health care was open only to those who were already covered by health insurance. A part of the citizenry would be voiceless about an issue that deeply affects them. Or imagine that during debates, people who disagreed with the government were jailed or threatened, as happened in Iran during the 2009 elections. When Iranian citizens protested the results of the re-election of Mahmoud Ahmadinejad, arguing that electoral fraud led to the defeat of Mir-Hossein Mousavi, they were met with force from police and para-military groups.

As we end our discussion of the definition of the public sphere, we want to warn you against conflating and confusing the complex meanings of "public" identified in the chapter's introduction.[27]

When you think of "public," you might think of anything outside the domestic sphere or family. In this formulation, that which is public is not private and that which is private is not public. This formulation shapes common understanding in phrases such as "public officials" (people who work for the state), "public opinion" (as polled by Roper), and "public figures" (people who can be identified by a substantial portion of the population, even if they have nothing to do with the discussion of issues of common interest). Fraser argues that this common understanding of "public" collapses four analytically distinct ideas: (1) the state, (2) the economy, (3) arenas of public discourse, and (4) people to whom the state should be accountable. When discussing public spheres in this chapter, we use Habermas's ideal as referenced in Fraser's third sense—arenas of public discourse. The public sphere is distinct from the state; ideally, discourse in the public sphere can critique and challenge state actions. The public sphere is also distinct from the economy; it is not a location in which to buy and sell, but to deliberate about policy and form collective identities. Finally, although people's discourse forms the public sphere, the people are not identical to it. Just because many people may be present does not mean that a public sphere has formed.

The boundaries of the public sphere are not static. As communication scholars Robert Asen and Daniel Brouwer explain, "'Public' and 'private' are not fixed, content-specific categories that structure the public sphere prior to discourse."[28] What counts as an issue of general interest can change over time. The question of what counts as a public issue is, itself, a topic to be discussed and debated in the public sphere. Communication scholars Valeria Fabj and Matthew J. Sobnosky note that, for example, for many years, HIV/AIDS was perceived to be a personal issue, a "gay disease." As a result of public activism, it was recognized as a public health issue about which everyone should be concerned and to which the state should respond.[29]

Habermas's description of the role of public sphere rhetoric in civil society is the foundation of more nuanced descriptions of civic participation. Because power plays a role in rhetoric, we now explore how power affects publics.

Strong and Weak Publics

Although Habermas held out the ideal of an overarching public sphere that could represent universal human interests in an arena distinct from the state, other scholars have noted that it makes more sense to speak of multiple publics, the way representative assemblies of the state can function as publics, and the interactions among publics.[30] In contrast to Habermas's description of the state as distinct from the public sphere, some scholars note, democratic parliaments and legislative assemblies can participate in public sphere discourse. Fraser distinguishes between weak publics and strong publics. She defines **weak publics** as *"publics whose deliberative practice consists exclusively in opinion formation and does not also encompass decision making."*[31] She defines **strong publics** as *"publics whose discourse encompasses both opinion formation and decision making."*[32] "Strong" and "weak" here refer to the power to make decisions or legislate, not to the general ability to dominate public opinion.

In the example of the immigration rallies and debates, both the Minuteman Project and immigrant groups represent weak publics; they cannot pass laws, but they seek to affect the opinions of politicians, who are members of strong publics. A weak public also participates in the formation of identity for those who are part of it. Communication scholars Kent A. Ono and John Sloop document how the discourse of the strong public (politicians) and dominant media, both for and against California's Proposition 187, constructed an identity of illegal immigrants (and Latinos) as prone to criminality, diseased, and of value only as an economic commodity (as workers).[33] In response, the weak public of immigrant groups sought to redefine their identity by celebrating immigrants' contributions to the United States, creating unity around a conception of La Raza, and developing counterhistories of immigration law.[34] For example, immigrant groups repeatedly used the slogan, "we didn't cross the border, the border crossed us," to highlight that much of what is the western United States once belonged to Mexico.[35]

Strong publics engage in instrumental acts of governance. Governing bodies made up of representatives of the people (such as the US Congress or sovereign parliaments) are examples of strong publics. Where a democratically elected body exists through which the people's will can be voiced, Fraser says, it can function not as an arm of the state, but as "the site for the discursive authorization of the use of state power."[36] Thus, democratically elected representative bodies begin to blur the distinction that Habermas draws so clearly between the state and civil society. Strong publics are important because "the force of public opinion is strengthened when a body representing it is empowered to translate such 'opinion' into authoritative decisions."[37] When it implements public policy (on health care, immigration, or taxes, for example), the US Congress transforms what it perceives to be public opinion into laws.

Although strong publics possess decision-making powers, weak publics also have power to create change. They can exert influence on people in decision-making roles. For example, if a school board is considering curriculum changes, a weak public can exert pressure on the school board members (a strong public) by participating in public hearings and making public comments. If the school board members are elected, then the weak public could exert pressure because board members might be concerned about re-election.

In the case of California's Proposition 187, a typically weak public (the electorate) was empowered to act as a strong public (the legislature) because of California's initiative system. In the initiative system, proposed laws are put to a direct vote of the people. Rhetorical scholars Marouf Hasian, Jr., and Fernando Delgado argue that the initiative system is "a means through which like-minded citizens might give voice to their policy and legislative concerns."[38] Not only can citizens form opinion, the initiative system also enabled them to pass laws.

Hybrid Publics

The immigration issue also demonstrates how debates about laws may also be debates about identity. Hasian and Delgado note that a debate that began as a general discussion of the dangers of a foreign "other" illegally immigrating to the United States "transformed into a complex debate regarding the meaning of American citizenship and the social and political power that comes from belonging to particular racial categories in the U.S."[39] This insight highlights that the public sphere may not just mediate between the state and society, it is also a sphere in which people develop understandings of their role in society. Fraser describes such publics as **hybrid publics:** *publics that do not choose between civic identity and deliberative politics, but instead recognize that both can exist in a mutually reinforcing relationship.*[40]

Rhetoric that forms identity and rhetoric that forms policy are equally important. Rhetoric exploring what it means to be a US citizen is as much a part of the public sphere as rhetoric defending a policy. Thus, rhetoric in the public sphere includes epideictic and forensic rhetoric about identity as well as deliberative rhetoric about policy. Hauser clarifies the link between rhetoric, the public sphere, and social reality when he writes: "Public spheres . . . are discursive spaces where society deliberates about normative standards and even develops new frameworks for expressing and evaluating social reality."[41]

Habermas's original formulation, in which there is only one state and one public that can speak to universal interests, and only those two interact, provides a model for understanding the public sphere, but does not describe actually existing democracies. Habermas himself admits that a society does not need a unitary public to have critical debate; that a "pluralistic" public composed of diverse publics can criticize state action, which is the public sphere's primary function.[42] How might critics understand a pluralistic conception of publics?

PUBLICS, COUNTERPUBLICS, AND TRANSNATIONAL PUBLICS

Publics are not equally powerful. A dominant public tends to emerge, one that has the strength to translate its beliefs into actions affecting even people who do not share its beliefs. Unfortunately, the power of a dominant public often masks the existence of other publics and makes it more difficult to recognize that not everyone's needs and interests are being represented. English professor Michael Warner explains: "Some publics . . . are more likely than others to stand in for *the* public, to frame their address as the universal discussion of the people."[43] Still, other publics may be active. For example, scholars argue that a black public sphere exists in the United States,[44] constituted by media, aesthetic forms, and memories that are owned by and targeted at black people. The existence of a black public sphere demonstrates that there is more than one public sphere, and that what is thought of as *the* public sphere does not represent universal human concerns.

Scholars have identified several limits to Habermas's original formulation of the public sphere: A single universal public does not explain actually existing democracies. The state is no longer the sole site of sovereign power, given the rise of transnational corporations. The economy, itself, can become a site of public contestation and action. Thus, scholars have expanded the study of *the* public to studies of publics, counterpublics, and transnational publics.

Counterpublics

A dominant public tends to focus only on the interests and needs of the dominant group, and in the process to subordinate those groups of people who are disempowered. In fourth and fifth century BCE Athens, a civilization often upheld as an ideal of deliberative democracy, the very notion of citizenship was defined by exclusion. Only adult, male, Athenian-born citizens were allowed to participate. Women, slaves, and noncitizens were excluded.[45] The groups excluded had identities, interests, and needs, but they had to find alternative locations and means to articulate them. For example, in 415 BCE, when the boldest Greek military offensive since the Trojan War was launched, statues of the god Hermes were mutilated. Classicist Eva Keuls argues that the act likely was done by the women of Athens to protest yet another war.[46]

To call attention to a multiplicity of publics, and to publics that are alternatives to the dominant public, scholars developed the concept of **counterpublics**, which Fraser defines as *"parallel discursive arenas where members of subordinated social groups invent and circulate counterdiscourse to formulate oppositional interpretations of their identities, interests, and needs."*[47] Counterpublics expand not only the space for argument, but also what counts in argument. As Fraser notes, "these counterpublics emerge in response to exclusions within dominant publics, they help expand discursive space. In principle, assumptions that were previously exempt from contestation will now have to be publicly argued out."[48] New topics are introduced to deliberation; so, too, are new tests for argument. Literary theorist Rita Felski proposes that counterpublics can challenge norms of argument and what is considered useful evidence.[49] Who can speak, what can be spoken about, and how, can all be topics of public discussion. Consequently, some issues not previously considered public can become public as a result of deliberation and argument.

To summarize, counterpublics create safe spaces in which participants: (1) develop alternative norms for public argument and what counts as evidence; (2) regenerate their energy to engage in argument in the political and public spheres; (3) enact identities through new idioms and styles; and (4) formulate oppositional interpretations of identities, interests, and needs through the creation of new language.

difficulty of translating interests, [and] detachment from healthy criticism."[54] Political scientist Jane Mansbridge agrees that if counterpublic participants speak only to each other, "they do not learn how to put what they want to say in words that others can hear and understand."[55] Thus, engaged argument with those with whom they disagree is an essential element of a healthy counterpublic. In terms of the immigration debates, Hasian and Delgado note that people must find and analyze "the bridges as well as the walls that have been built at contested borderlands."[56] Rhetors should search for places of agreement, not just places of difference.

Oscillation also has practical benefits for a counterpublic. In his study of ACT UP and its participation in congressional hearings concerning AIDS, Brouwer identifies a number of benefits. Oscillation can (1) garner national attention for a group and, thus, enhance its credibility; (2) open a forum for the repetition and recognition of the group's message, (3) push for implementation of the group's recommendations that require institutional support (the support of a strong public); and (4) enable the counterpublic to "push for access to strong publics."[57] Historically, counterpublics have used their specialized newspapers both to speak to members and to oscillate outward. For example, the National Association Opposed to Woman Suffrage's newspaper (*The Woman Patriot*) shifted from a single-issue focus against woman suffrage to a broader challenge to what it saw as emerging radical rhetoric.[58] Additional examples of oscillating counterpublic discourse include second-wave feminism's 1968 "No More Miss America" protest against the pageant, including their ten-point brochure outlining their arguments; the Civil Rights movement's 1955 Montgomery Bus Boycott and ensuing legal challenges to segregation; and the farmworkers' grape boycott and public education campaign in the late 1960s.

Counterpublic theory challenges the idea that a single, universal public sphere is an ideal toward which a diverse society should strive. Although Habermas initially bemoaned the erosion of the public sphere as a multiplicity of publics emerged, Fraser argues this multiplicity is not necessarily a bad thing. For people who are excluded from access to the dominant public sphere, articulation of their needs becomes nearly impossible; a universal public sphere intensifies the subordination of marginal groups' needs. Multiple publics are more likely to promote participation. According to Fraser, forcing all deliberation into the dominant public "will tend to operate to the advantage of dominant groups and to the disadvantage of subordinates" because "members of subordinated groups would have no arenas for deliberation among themselves about their needs, objectives, and strategies. They would have no venues in which to undertake communicative processes that were not . . . under the supervision of dominant groups."[59] Subordinated social groups need a space to develop language to articulate their identities, interests, and needs.

Counterpublics' orientations oscillate; their primary audiences shift. Counterpublics shift back and forth between the formulation of their identities, interests, and needs within the relative safety of their protected enclaves, where their primary audience is the counterpublic, and their participation in deliberation about administrative state action, where their audience is the dominant and strong public.[60]

Identity as a Public or Counterpublic. Publics not only engage in deliberative discourse about policy, they engage in discourse about civic culture—about who they are and what they need. Although identity formation is an element of all public discourse, counterpublic sphere theories clarify the importance of identity creation and self-expression to disempowered peoples and groups. Before people can participate in deliberation over public issues, they need to see themselves as capable of deliberation, their interests and needs as worthy of discussion. The focus on identity in counterpublics becomes apparent insofar as they are "directed toward an affirmation of specificity in relation to gender, race, ethnicity, age, sexual preference, and so on."[61] The specificity allows people to develop and explore their own identities and counter repressive characterizations.[62] For example, immigrant groups seek to define themselves in contrast to dominant public and media depictions of them as diseased masses and an undifferentiated flood overwhelming the United States. Otto Santa Ana, in his book about metaphors used to describe Latinos in contemporary public discourse, notes that countermetaphors emerged. Instead of a flood, immigrants were a "stream that makes the desert bloom," a flow of workers who could quench the thirst for labor, or the "lifeblood" of the California economy.[63]

Counterpublic discourse that contributes to identity creation is as important as the outward-directed rhetoric that contributes to policy making. The importance of circulating new understandings of identity has been explored most intensely by literary critic Michael Warner in his book *Publics and Counterpublics*. To say a group of people is a "public" or "counterpublic" is more than merely descriptive; it also constructs an understanding of who that group is and how to interact with it. When people identify themselves as members of a public or counterpublic and participate in it, their "identities are formed and transformed."[64] Warner's model, which focuses on the circulation of identities within public discourse, is referred to as the circulatory model of counterpublics.

The naming of a public and the construction of identity can be linked to the earlier discussions of language, persona, and audience. Naming can construct social meaning and understanding. How marginalized groups are named affects how, and whether, they participate in the dominant public. In the 1800s, women fought against being named chattel, and asserted their full humanity and right to participate in public discourse. In the 1960s, African Americans fought against racist names, and declared their interests to be public interests. In the 1980s, ACT UP worked with researchers to rename GRID (Gay Related Immune Deficiency) as AIDS, making clear that it was a public health issue. Presently, undocumented workers resist the name "illegal" because it reduces them to a single act and deflects recognition of them as contributing members of the economy.

Not only is the power of language evident in people's demand to name themselves and their identities, but also in the naming of "the public." As Warner points out, sometimes *a* public comes to be perceived as *the* public that represents "the people." However, "the people" is a rhetorical construction, an ideograph, that itself seeks to warrant the use of power. "The public" is also an ideograph. In the process of creating identification among members of "the public," divisions are also created, excluding people who are not part of the intimate public sphere of the U.S. . . . renders citizenship as a condition of social membership produced by personal acts and values, especially acts originating in or directed toward the family sphere."[75] Berlant sees the public sphere as privatized, stripped of its public orientation.

Through discourse, this privatizing of the public sphere is constructed and maintained. The claim that the family is the foundation of society is a recent, but now constant, persuasive message that transforms public issues into personal ones. As historian Stephanie Coontz points out, "Ever since the late nineteenth century, when President Theodore Roosevelt warned that the nation's future rested on 'the right kind of home life,' politicians have argued that civic virtue begins at home. As President Ronald Reagan put it in 1984: 'Strong families are the foundation of society.'"[76] Such claims shift public issues to the realm of personal action and responsibility. Social problems can now be blamed on the breakdown of the family, so that to solve them, people must turn inward to their own families.

Our point here is *not* that a rigid distinction between the personal and the public should be maintained. In fact, the second-wave feminist dictum that "the personal is political" is important. What happens in the privacy of the home has implications for the distribution of power; and acts of the state influence what happens in the home. Power dynamics affect even the most apparently personal decisions concerning marriage, children, and sexuality. The personal can, indeed, be political. This does not mean people can only attain political identity in a democracy through their private actions.

In many ways, however, politics has been reduced to the personal (in the form of purchasing decisions and family) and stripped of any concern with power or collective action in the public sphere. Crenson and Ginsberg have noted the same reversal. They argue that "What passes for citizenship today often inverts the feminist dictum that the personal is political. It has transformed the political into the personal. Political activity should feel 'empowering.' It should enhance self-esteem. It should not engender confusion, ambiguity, or frustration."[77]

Relationships among Publics

To understand how publics function, you need to consider not only their relationship to the state and economy, but also to each other. Counterpublics may exist counter to the state or the economy, but they can replicate some of the more oppressive elements of the state or economy. In other words, counterpublics are not counter to everything for which dominant society stands. Exclusions based on sex, race, class, and sexual orientation can be found in counterpublics, even as they attempt to counter other social problems.

For example, consider the emergence of the environmental movement. Early members of environmental groups came together as individuals to articulate new understandings of humans' relationship to the environment. In the 1800s, arguments were made to preserve nature. In 1864, Lincoln signed a bill granting Yosemite Valley and the Mariposa Grove of Giant Sequoias to California as an inalienable public trust. In 1872, Yellowstone was designated the country's first national park. Although new understandings of the environment were integrated into the public vocabulary repertoire, they tended to reinforce a notion that the environment was something other than where human beings lived. It was to be visited, preserved, and kept separate from human intervention. The reality is that *all* human beings live in environments.

Not all environments are the same. Some environments are less pristine and have large amounts of pollution. Polluted environments are not equally distributed. People of color and poor people are more likely to live near plants that produce toxic wastes and emissions, and toxic disposal sites tend to be sited closer to where the poor and people of color already live.[78] To describe this phenomenon, African-American civil rights leader Dr. Benjamin Chavis coined the phrase "environmental racism" in the early 1980s.[79] Preservation of pristine parks that socioeconomically privileged people could visit represented an incomplete understanding of humans' relationship to the environment. As a counter to environmental racism, most environmental groups now seek environmental justice and recognize that all of the environment must be valued.

Our point is that just because a counterpublic is *counter* does not mean it is without flaws. Privileges and ideologies weave themselves deeply into people's psyches. The process of testing assumptions is not done easily, nor without the danger of replicating some of the very inequalities people might be seeking to counter.

CYBERPUBLICS AND THE BLOGOSPHERE

"The public" is a concept central to discussions of US democracy. The tradition of public deliberation is typified by the New England town meeting, where members of a community come together to debate, face-to-face, about issues of common interest. The vitality of such public deliberation has long concerned political and communication theorists in the United States. The issues about which John Dewey wrote in 1927, in his book *The Public and Its Problems*, are issues with which US society continues to grapple. How does a group come to have an identity as a public? What role does public discourse play in democratic politics? How can citizen apathy be lessened? How can experts and the general public interact productively to resolve controversies?[80]

Dewey worried that "increasing social complexity threatened the collective perception and practical judgment of a functioning public of citizens."[81] In particular, he was concerned about the effects that technological change would have on public deliberation (in his time, this meant the emergence of the telephone, cheap reading material, movies, telegraph, railways, and newspapers). He worried that new entertainment technologies would distract people from discussing issues of public concern and change how people interacted.[82] Many people are now exploring this concern in relation to the role of digital technologies, social networking sites, and the Internet.

Although many people now cannot conceive of a world without the Internet and digital communication technologies, they really are relatively recent phenomena. Not until the late 1980s did e-mail become privatized

Think about the differences between a generation raised in the world of Web 2.0 and earlier generations. Many people in the Web 2.0 generation think little of posting their most interior thoughts on a public screen. Some people actually write journals on the web and allow others to read them, while people raised before Web 2.0 would find it the most extreme invasion of privacy for others to read their diaries. As another example, consider sexting: According to a 2008 study by the National Campaign to Prevent Teen and Unplanned Pregnancy and CosmoGirl.com, 20 percent of teens between the ages of thirteen and nineteen and 30 percent of young adults between the ages of twenty and twenty-six had posted or sent nude or semi-nude pictures of themselves.[88] Although they may think of their cell phone screens and computers as personal space, where only those to whom they send a picture can view it, the reality is that the image can be sent across all of cyberspace. A sixteen-year-old high school student found that out when an image she and a friend took of themselves ended up being so widely distributed that a print was left in her vice-principal's mailbox. Although she had deleted the image from her own phone, her friend had sent it to another friend, who sent it to a football player, who sent it to the team; then it was sent to the entire senior class.[89]

Public deliberation and civic participation do take place over the Internet. People are mobilized to support political candidates. Citizens organize themselves to protest government policy. Groups come together to articulate identities, interests, and needs. At the same time, the very boundary between public and private is challenged. Are you really engaging in political action when you "friend" a political candidate on Facebook? Are people's understandings of political participation affected by the format in which it occurs? When is expression on a blog an act of civic culture and identity formation, and when is it just the expression of an individual's interior thoughts on a screen that everyone can see? Scholars and users are just beginning to answer these questions.

Digital Participation and Access

The 2008 election campaign was the first time that more than half (55 percent) of the voting age population went online to get involved in election year politics.[90] Not only did people use the Internet to retrieve information about the candidates, they also used it to express their own political opinions. Politics on the web was not a spectator sport, but a form of public discourse in which citizens were actively engaged. According to the Pew Internet & American Life Project's survey about political participation, 18 percent of Internet users participated in an online forum where they posted their own thoughts; 45 percent went online to watch a video; one in three forwarded information to another; and almost 55 percent of people who were eighteen to twenty-four years old took part in political activities on social networking sites.

What does this information tell us about how people think about political participation? Is it only constituted by attending a rally, or can you virtually experience politics by watching a video of a rally? Is participation limited to going door to door, to brick-and-mortar homes, to leave pamphlets, or can you be a virtual campaigner by forwarding information? Does political participation matter only in relation to campaigns, or does the work of civic identity formation also count? Do you exhibit civic interest only by reading newspapers, or can you participate in opinion formation by responding to a blog? History professor Mark Poster, in his discussion of cyberdemocracy, describes how the Internet institutes "new social functions" that can only be understood if we are not tied to outdated patterns of interpretation that maintain rigid boundaries between the public and private, forms of political participation, and the role of government.[91] He explains that the Internet is challenging the ways that society approaches questions of civic participation:

> If one understands politics as the restriction or expansion of the existing executive, legislative and judicial branches of government, one will not be able even to broach the question of new types of participation in government. To ask, then, about the relation of the Internet to democracy is to challenge or to risk challenging our existing theoretical approaches to these questions.[92]

The relationship of cyberspace to counterpublics and publics complicates existing theoretical approaches. For example, in Habermas's ideal of the public, he assumes that people come together in face-to-face interactions to deliberate. Yet, in a digital world, face-to-face interaction is no longer the only means of interaction.

If you attend to Poster's admonition about an expansive understanding of participation, when you discuss cyberactivism you should think not only about participation in institutionalized politics (were you a presidential candidate's Facebook friend?) but also about broader forms of discursive action on the Net.[93] When the political functions of the Net are discussed, people tend to focus not on its interactive nature, but on its ability to transmit information.[94] Many discussions of the democratic potential of the Internet, even when they recognize its interactive nature, still limit interaction to questions concerning administration and governance, and tend to ignore the role cyberpublics can play in identity formation.[95]

Some sites and cyberactivism do challenge the limited uses of the Net that some theorists describe. In particular, several sites attempt to open space for the formation of publics and counterpublics. For example, the Institute for the Study of Civic Values focuses on neighborhood empowerment. ProtestNet is a location where activists come together to form their own media. In many ways, these sites seek to create the space for discussion of ideas, for the development of alternative validity claims, and for the development of the vocabulary with which subordinated groups can articulate their needs. In addition, a dizzying array of issue-specific websites and Facebook pages also exist.

Recent writings about citizen activism on the net include myriad parallels between cyberactivism, social movements, and counterpublics. Just as social movements seek to mobilize others of like mind, virtual communities are a way in which "the creative powers of controversy can spread beyond local communities"[96] as people form connections with those who share interests, even with people who live in other states or countries.[97]

Some analysts fear that the type of participation that occurs on the web will result in increasing fragmentation, as people are able to seek out only that information with which they most agree and to avoid any meaningful interaction with people who have different perspectives. Legal scholar Cass R. Sunstein argues most forcibly for this fear, explaining, "If people on the Internet are deliberating mostly with like-minded others, their views will not merely be reinforced; they will instead be shifted to more extreme points. . . . With the Internet, it is exceedingly easy for each of us to find like-minded individuals."[98] It appears the very ability of the Internet to assist in identity formation also enables it to participate in polarization, as differences are identified and then intensified. Instead of being a site where public deliberation can occur despite time and distance constraints, the Internet could result in polarization and lead to an erosion of a sense of common cause.

Not everyone is as pessimistic as Sunstein. Although people tend to seek reinforcement, rather than challenges, to their ideas, and the Internet may contribute to the creation of deliberative enclaves, the Internet can also be a way to open up those enclaves and allow for the development of community. For example, research indicates that homosexual youths living in rural communities once felt extremely isolated, but the Internet now provides them an opportunity to belong to a virtual community and seek social support outside of their own geographic locations.[99] Communication scholar Lincoln Dahlberg claims that "the internet is being used by many people [to] encounter difference that they would not normally encounter in everyday life."[100] Instead of functioning as an echo chamber, the Internet can provide access to information that people may not be able to access in their daily lives. When judging the Internet, we should not compare it to some ideal world of civic discourse, but to a non-Internet world. Using the 2004 presidential election as a basis for analysis, the Pew Internet & American Life Project discovered that Internet users were exposed to a wider range of information about the candidates and the political arguments than were nonusers, "including those that challenge their candidate preferences and their positions on some key issues."[101]

Not all people are able to access the Internet, however. Although it is theoretically open to all, material barriers to participation exist. Unfortunately, studies of actual usage indicate those groups most in need of an oppositional interpretation of identity are the very groups who most lack access.

A recent research finding by the Pew Internet & American Life Project confirms that nonwhite people in the United States use the Internet at significantly lower rates than white people do.[102] The digital divide is closing, with African Americans being the most active (and fastest growing) users of the mobile Internet, but the divide still exists. In addition, the way in which people use the Internet is determined by their degree of subordination. According to the National Telecommunications and Information Administration, for example, "demographic characteristics not only determine *whether* and *where* one uses the Internet. Income, education, race, and gender, among other characteristics, strongly influence what a person does online."[103] People who belong to subordinated demographic groups are more likely to use the Internet to take courses or conduct job searches. They use it as an instrument to enter the economic system of paid labor, not as a means to engage in forming public spheres.

If marginalized groups are not represented on the Net, then cyberspace cannot expand the discursive arena. Instead, in Fraser's words, it merely replicates the "modes of deliberation that mask domination"[104] as it absorbs the less powerful into a dominant cyber-we. An appearance of deliberation is created in cyberspace. A series of monologues transversing the web do not substitute for critical engagement. Inequitable Internet access should be troubling, not only because it mirrors other inequalities in society, but also because it masks the existence of those inequalities. It is difficult to recognize the absences of some groups if you cannot even identify who is present.[105]

The digital divide is even worse on a global scale, with developed countries having the infrastructure and money to provide increased access. As of 2005, over 50 percent of Internet users came from developed countries, even though those countries account for only 15 percent of the world's population.[106] Yet, people around the world have used communication technologies such as cell phones, web pages, and blogs to supplement and sustain civic engagement and political action.

Cyberpublics and the Blogosphere

Cyberpublics are a new form of activism. **Cyberpublics** are *publics formed or strengthened through the use of the Internet and social media.* The development of cyberpublics and the changing form of social activism in a digital age is made vivid by the Zapatista movement in Chiapas, Mexico, and its support of pro-democracy reforms.[107] Formed in 1983, the EZLN (Ejército Zapatista de Liberación Nacional) demanded autonomy for the indigenous people of Chiapas when increasing governmental and economic pressures threatened their communal lands, diverse local cultures, and languages. The movement expanded to cyberspace on January 1, 1994, when its supporters launched a cybercampaign using networks created during an earlier international campaign against the North American Free Trade Agreement (NAFTA), which became official on that day. The transition to cyberspace was not easy. The Zapatistas were transmitting messages from villages that did not have electricity, much less modems. Communiqués would be delivered via courier to newspapers in cities within twelve hours of creation, and be circulated internationally within twenty-four hours. Supporters would translate the messages from Spanish and send them to e-mail list subscribers on networks such as Peacenet, the Internet, and Usenet. The speed with which the world heard about this struggle by a small band of indigenous peoples, and mobilized to support it, was unique.[108]

The protest was not solely digital. Real bodies were put at risk, even as information was distributed electronically. On the same day the group's demands went digital, material bodies put themselves on the line. Elements of the EZLN seized several towns, with some reports indicating "at least 145 people died in the ensuing battle with state troops."[109] Supporters flocked to Chiapas to document and protest the Mexican government's attempts at military repression. Despite police repression, hundreds of thousands demonstrated in the streets of Mexico City and other cities and towns, eventually forcing the government to shift from overt military attacks on the EZLN to political negotiations and covert repression. Once again, human rights activists from around the world came to Chiapas to observe, report, and seek to constrain government actions.

The Mexican government sought to quash this uprising and limited press coverage by the state-controlled television network Televisa, but the world heard about it because of messages posted on web sites and sent over the Net. University of Texas economics professor Harry Cleaver explains that the pro-Zapatistas' use of electronic and computer communications made the government's efforts to isolate and silence the movement difficult. His narrative is illuminating:

> Despite its initial defeat, a key aspect of the state's war against the Zapatistas (both in Mexico and elsewhere) has been its on-going efforts to isolate them, so that they can be destroyed or forced to accept co-optation. In turn, the Zapatistas and their supporters have fought to maintain and elaborate their political connections throughout the world. This has been a war of words, images, imagination and organization in which the Zapatistas have had surprising success.
>
> Vital to this continuing struggle has been the pro-Zapatista use of computer communications. While the state has all too effectively limited mass media coverage and serious discussion of Zapatista ideas, their supporters have been able, to an astonishing degree, to circumvent and offset this blockage through the use of electronic networks in conjunction with the more familiar tactics of solidarity movements: teach-ins, articles in the alternative press, demonstrations, the occupation of Mexican government consulates and so on.[110]

Instead of having to rely on traditional commercial or state-controlled media to broadcast their message, the group was able to speak to the world directly through e-mail and then, increasingly, through dozens of transnational supporters' web pages in many languages. A small group of activists supporting indigenous Mayan farmers in Chiapas against repressive policies of the Mexican government were able to take their message global, speaking not just to the "strong public" of the Mexican government or the "weak public" of Mexican citizens, but to a "transnational public" of global citizens. The publics to which the Zapatistas spoke were far larger than those within the nation's borders, and they sustained their interest across the years. During periods of renewed military repression in early 1994, and again in early 1995, supporters demonstrated against the Mexican government's actions at Mexican embassies and consulates in over forty countries.

The early use of cyberspace to communicate with a transnational public was only the first step. The Zapatistas, with the help of supporters, used digital communication technologies to engage in a variety of protests. Early in 1994, Internet-based organizing brought together thousands of prodemocracy advocates in a Zapatista village for a National Democratic Convention to discuss how to get beyond the essentially one-party rule in Mexico. In 1995, the Zapatistas called for, and their supporters organized, a Plebiscite for Peace and Democracy that had over a million attendees. Internet technology enabled international participation. In 1996, Internet connections provided the main vehicle to organize Continental Encounters Against Neoliberalism and For Humanity, as well as an Intercontinental Encounter that brought together thousands of grassroots activists from around the world.

We can trace a direct line from the Intercontinental Encounter in 1996 in Chiapas villages and the rise of the antiglobalization/anti-WTO movement. The 1996 global meeting gave rise to People's Global Action, which organized the 1998 anti-WTO protest in Geneva and participated in the 1999 anti-WTO protest in Seattle. In addition, Indymedia, "a grassroots network committed to using media production and distribution as tools for promoting social and economic justice"[111] that began to emerge during the Zapatista support experience was fully developed "in late November of 1999, to allow participants in the anti-globalization movement to report on the protests against the WTO meeting that took place in Seattle."[112] Ultimately, Zapatistas and their supporters have used "the Internet as a means to build a global grassroots support network" not bound by time or space.[113] Since 1994, using the most basic of digital technologies (cell phones and listservs), you can find discussions of Zapatistas on blogs.[114] The EZLN has a Myspace profile. Zapatistas are on Facebook.

Supporters have sometimes acted autonomously, using cyberspace forms of protest that have generated controversy within the pro-Zapatista movement. In 1998, a small group organized a virtual sit-in against five financial institutions in Mexico. It sent e-mail instructions to supporters, calling on them to connect to the websites and hit reload several times during the hour in order to overload the site and stop all business, just as the sit-ins by US civil rights protestors sought to stop commerce at targeted businesses. These actions were controversial because many in the Zapatista support movement were afraid the state, which was much better equipped, would counterattack and shut down supporters' websites or block their listservs.

Cybercounterpublics should be able to fulfill all the functions of counterpublics, even as they face similar challenges. Cybermovements can contest existing norms and develop alternative validity claims. Just as counterpublics often renegotiate the distinctions between the public and private, so may cyber-activism. Stephen Wray, a member of the Electronic Disturbance Theatre, sees an inherent potential for cyberactivism to challenge dominant validity claims, but cautions that cyberactivism should be carefully considered because those engaging in it do not, alone, create the rhetoric about it and are not the only ones who can engage in it. He would like to see his attempts at electronic civil disobedience redefine infowar and make it a plausible form of activism, because "We need to seriously question and abandon some of the language that the state uses to demonize genuine political protest and expression."[115] Wray and the

EDT have provided software, such as FloodNet, that enables people to stage nonviolent mass protests (virtual sit-ins) in cyberspace.[116] In many ways, protest in the public sphere is being supplemented and/or replaced by protest on a public screen.

THE PUBLIC SCREEN

Historically, public sphere discourse was associated with the type of discussion that happens in a bricks-and-mortar public sphere: the town square or the town hall. Prior to the emergence of electronic mass media, such settings were the only ones in which the discourse that forms reasoned exchanges of opinion could occur. In such settings, media such as newspapers served a subsidiary role; they provided the information with which (and sometimes the medium in which) members of the public advanced their arguments.

The evolution of media such as television and the Internet challenge such a simple role for mass media in public discourse. Media no longer transmit information that is primarily verbal. We live in an age in which visuals play a dominant role; people in the United States live in a visual culture. Once critics begin to recognize the power of visuals and the places in which they appear, we need to consider whether our understanding of participation forms should expand. Instead of talking exclusively about discourse in the public sphere, do critics need to talk about verbal and visual forms of public interaction?

In the 2006 immigration protests, the rallies not only brought like-minded people together to organize and call for political action, they also functioned as a way to speak to those who were not in attendance. The rallies were planned for the congressional recess so that representatives and senators who had returned to their home states could see the masses of their constituents who attended the demonstrations,[117] but it was not necessary to be present at the rallies to see their size. Television and newspaper reports showed images of the rallies. An AP story posted on MSNBC's website included Lucas Jackson's image for Reuters News Service of a street filled with people.[118] Anti-immigration protests sought to appear on the public screen. Jim Gilchrist, the founder of the Minuteman Project and organizer of the 2006, thirteen-city tour ending in Washington, DC, maintains a web page for the group that contains a video archive of news stories and member-made videos.[119]

The massive rallies and counterrallies constituted image events that demanded media coverage. Pro-immigration rally organizers thought carefully about the images. Initially, participants waved flags from their countries of origin to demonstrate cultural pride and unity. Italian flags wave during Columbus Day celebrations and Irish flags wave during St. Patrick's Day parades; and rally participants saw flag waving as an expression of pride in the diversity of the United States. When anti-immigration groups responded to the foreign flags as unpatriotic and as proof of immigrants' inability, or unwillingness, to assimilate, rally organizers called for marchers to wave the US flag to "signify their allegiance to US cultural values and principles. Visually, rallies shifted significantly, from a profusion of colors and emblems to a more consistent red, white and blue."[120] Such a shift only matters insofar as the image could be distributed and seen.

DeLuca and Peeples offer the concept of the public screen as an alternative way to conceive of public discourse. The **public screen** is composed of *the constant circulation of symbolic action enabled by the relatively new media technologies of television, computers, photography, film, Internet, and smart phones that is "characteristic of contemporary communication."* DeLuca and Peeples encourage people to recognize "that most, and the most important, public discussions take place via 'screens'—television, computer, and the front page of the newspaper."[121] They explain, "Today's scene is predominantly a visual one. TV trades in a discourse dominated by images not words, a visual rhetoric."[122] Thus, when we study public communication, the focus should not only be on public speeches, but also on "image events," which have become "a central mode of public discourse both for conventional electoral politics and alternative grassroots politics in an era dominated by a commercial, televisual, electronic public screen."[123]

DeLuca and Peeples's point is not that the visual rhetorics of the public screen are superior to the verbal discourses of the traditional public sphere, nor that everyone should engage in image events instead of public discourse.[124] Instead, they argue that one cannot really understand the complete dynamics of contemporary public controversies unless one accounts for the role of the visual. As they explain, "the public screen is the essential supplement to the public sphere. In comparison to the rationality, embodied conversations, consensus, and civility of the public sphere, the public screen highlights dissemination, images, hypermediacy, spectacular publicity, cacophony, distractions, and dissent."[125] The public screen does not share the ideals of consensus formation and civility that typifies descriptions of the ideal public sphere, but neither does all public communication, as the confrontational rhetoric of British suffrage advocates of the 1800s and the antiwar protests of the 1960s and 1970s demonstrated. Attention to the public screen does emphasizes that public discourse, as it exists, is diffuse, messy, loud, vivid, and immediate. In many cases, it does more to generate controversy than to generate consensus.

CONCLUSION

Defining "public" is a complex process. A group of people that exists prior to a rhetor's message does not come into being as a public until it is constituted through rhetoric. Further, publics are fluid, coming into and out of existence. An understanding of the multiplicity of public spheres reveals the multifaceted relationships between the rhetor, audiences, public spheres, power, economy, and state.

Habermas's ideal public sphere is "open to all citizens," addresses "matters of general interests," and is free from coercion.[126] Although everyone should be included in public sphere deliberation, this ideal is not a reality. Not everyone is accorded access to the public sphere; not everyone's words are given the same weight as others. Power differentials matter.

When people perceive that they are outside of the dominant public and that their issues and concerns are not being addressed, they can construct counterpublic spheres in which they offer definitions of their identities and concerns that counter the dominant public sphere perspective. The Internet provides a place in which counterpublic spheres can form, as well as a space for participation in the dominant public sphere and in the strong public of the state.

The concept of the public sphere has been expanded to include the public screen, as well as visual and verbal messages, because modern media have changed the ways people communicate and obtain messages. Not all public rhetoric achieves the high ideals of reasoned face-to-face communication that theorists such as Habermas and Dewey imagined. Instead, communication on the public screen can appear emotional, other-than-rational, and disruptive. This is not necessarily a problem. Argument and controversy are signs of a healthy democratic society and central to civic engagement. Disagreement opens space for argument, challenges norms, and urges us to consider which arguments make sense.

Civic engagement occurs whenever a public sphere is brought into being through discourse. People participate in individual and collective action to develop solutions to social, economic, and political challenges in their communities, states, nation, and the world. In any democratic society, change and maintenance of social, political, and economic structures is accomplished through civic engagement, which is accomplished through rhetoric. Civic engagement is not about what people do in the public sphere, but how they interact. It is a process with many different forms, all of which involve rhetoric.

DISCUSSION QUESTIONS

1. The public sphere is not open to everyone. For example, media coverage and participation in presidential debates is limited to the "major" or "serious" candidates. Given your understanding of the public sphere, how might you explain the role (or lack thereof) of third-party candidates in elections? How can broader participation in elections be accomplished?

2. A public space open for public participation has long been a foundation for democratic societies. In the United States "public square" is the common term for the public sphere, meaning the public streets, parks, and spaces in the community. Today, with the rise of malls, the public gathering place is private property. Should malls be considered public spheres, protected for citizens to organize and persuade? Is the mall a private place or a public space?

3. Some government agencies have argued that the Internet has allowed dangerous counterpublics to organize. They argue that terrorists can also organize, and that is dangerous to society. What, if any, controls should the government have on the Internet to monitor such activity? What criteria should be used to identify a counterpublic as dangerous?

4. Identify publics to which you belong. What identifies you as a member of that public? How has your participation in that public developed your own identity?

SUGGESTED READINGS

Asen, Robert, and Daniel C. Brouwer. "Introduction: Reconfigurations of the Public Sphere." In *Counterpublics and the State*. Edited by Robert Asen and Daniel C. Brouwer, 1–32. Albany: State University of New York Press, 2001.

DeLuca, Kevin Michael, and Jennifer Peeples. "From Public Sphere to Public Screen: Democracy, Activism, and the 'Violence' of Seattle." *Critical Studies in Media Communication* 19, no. 2 (June 2002): 125–151.

Fraser, Nancy. "Rethinking the Public Sphere." In *Habermas and the Public Sphere*. Edited by Craig Calhoun, 109–137. Cambridge, MA: MIT Press, 1992.

Mansbridge, Jane. "Using Power/Fighting Power: The Polity." In *Democracy and Difference: Contesting the Boundaries of the Political*. Edited by Seyla Benhabib, 46–66. Princeton, NJ: Princeton University Press, 1996.

ENDNOTES

[1] The Sensenbrenner Bill, officially known as House Resolution 4377: Border Protection, Antiterrorism, and Illegal Immigration Control Act of 2005, passed in the House in December 2005, catalyzing the Spring 2006 protests. It did not pass in the Senate.

[2] Anne Demo, "Review Essay: Policy and Media in Immigration Studies," *Rhetoric and Public Affairs* 7, no. 2 (2002): 215–229, 216.

[3] Richard D. Pineda and Stacey K. Sowards, "Flag Waving as Visual Argument: 2006 Immigrations Demonstrations and Cultural Citizenship," *Argumentation and Advocacy* 43 (Winter and Spring 2007): 164–174; Kent A. Ono and John M. Sloop, *Shifting Borders: Rhetoric, Immigration, and California's Proposition 187* (Philadelphia: Temple University Press, 2002).

[4] Rick Klein, "After the Rallies, a Focus on Momentum; Immigration Rights Leaders Hope for Sustained Effort," *Boston Globe*, April 12, 2006, A2.

[5] Nina Bernstein, "In the Streets, Suddenly, an Immigrant Groundswell," *New York Times*, March 27, 2006, A14.

[6] Quoted in Rick Klein, "Immigrants' Voice: 'We're in the Fight'," *Boston Globe*, April 11, 2006, A1.

[7] Ralph Ranalli and Yvonne Abraham, "O'Malley Urges Policy Reform based on Respect: Immigration Backers Stream through Hub," *Boston Globe*, April 11, 2006, A22.

[8] Amanda Paulson, "Rallying Immigrants Look Ahead," *Christian Science Monitor*, May 3, 2006, 1.

[9] Wes Allison, "When Does a March Become a Movement?" *St. Petersburg Times* (Florida), April 16, 2006, 1A.

[10] Stephen Dinan, "The Washington Times," *Washington Times*, May 4, 2006, A01.

[11] Rachel L. Swarns, "Immigrants Rally in Scores of Cities for Legal Status," *New York Times*, April 11, 2006, A1.

[12] Keyonna Summers, "End of Minuteman Tour Marked by Confrontations; Demonstrators Compare Group to Klan," *Washington Times*, May 13, 2006, A09.

[13] Richard Sammon, "Immigration Bill Still a Long Shot," *Kiplinger Business Forecasts* 2006, No. 0505 (May 1, 2006), LexisNexis.

[14] Lou Dobbs, *Lou Dobbs Tonight*, April 1, 2006, http://transcripts.cnn.com/TRANSCRIPTS/0604/01/ldt.01.html (accessed February 24, 2011).

[15] Gerard A. Hauser, "Features of the Public Sphere," *Critical Studies in Mass Communication* 4, no. 4 (December 1987): 437–441, 440.

[16] James Jasinski, *Sourcebook on Rhetoric* (Thousand Oaks, CA: Sage, 2001), 474. Jürgen Habermas's writings include *The Structural Transformation of the Public Sphere: An Inquiry into a Category of Bourgeois Society*, trans. Thomas Burger (Boston: MIT Press, 1991); *Reason and the Rationalization of Society*, vol. 1, *The Theory of Communicative Action*, trans. Thomas McCarthy (Boston: Beacon, 1984); *Lifeworld and System: A Critique of Functionalist Reason*, vol. 2, *The Theory of Communicative Action*, trans. Thomas McCarthy (Boston: Beacon, 1987).

[17] Jürgen Habermas, "The Public Sphere," in *Jürgen Habermas on Society and Politics: A Reader*, ed. S. Seidman, 231–236 (Boston: Beacon, 1989), 230, italics added.

[18] Habermas, "The Public Sphere," 232.

[19] Habermas, *Structural Transformation*, 32–41.

[20] Robert Asen, "The Multiple Mr. Dewey: Multiple Publics and Permeable Borders in John Dewey's Theory of the Public Sphere," *Argument and Advocacy* 39 (Winter 2003): 174–188; Robert Asen, "A Discourse Theory of Citizenship," *Quarterly Journal of Speech* 90, no. 2 (May 2009): 189–211.

[21] Nancy Fraser, "Rethinking the Public Sphere," in *Habermas and the Public Sphere*, ed. Craig Calhoun, 109–137 (Cambridge: MIT Press, 1992), 110.

[22] Habermas, "The Public Sphere," 231.

[23] "Read Gov. Walker's Budget Repair Bill," wisconsinrapidstribune.com, February 24, 2011, http://www.wisconsinrapidstribune.com/article/20110224/WRT0101/110224063/Read-Gov-Walker-s-budget-repair-bill.

[24] Judy Keen, "Wisconsin Budget Crisis Has Folks Talking," *USA Today*, February 24, 2011, 3A.

[25] Although Habermas points to eighteenth- and early nineteenth-century Europe for an example of the emergence of a public sphere, other scholars have noted that his bourgeois public sphere was premised on exclusions based on sex and class. See Mary P. Ryan, "Gender and Public Access: Women's Politics in Nineteenth-Century America," and Geoff Eley, "Nations, Publics, and Political Cultures: Placing Habermas in the Nineteenth Century," in *Habermas and the Public Sphere*, ed. Craig Calhoun, 259–339 (Cambridge: MIT Press, 1992). Habermas recognizes such exclusion. See Jürgen Habermas, "Further Reflections on the Public Sphere," in *Habermas and the Public Sphere*, ed. Craig Calhoun, 421–461 (Cambridge: MIT Press, 1992).

[26] Melanie Loehwing and Jeff Motter, "Publics, Counterpublics, and the Promise of Democracy," *Philosophy and Rhetoric* 42, no. 3 (2009): 220–241.

[27] Fraser, "Rethinking," 110.

[28] Robert Asen and Daniel C. Brouwer, "Introduction: John Dewey and the Public Sphere," *Argumentation and Advocacy* 39, no. 3 (Winter 2003): 157–160, 10. See also John Dewey, *The Public and Its Problems* (1927; repr. Athens, OH: Swallow, 1954).

[29] Valeria Fabj and Matthew J. Sobnosky, "AIDS Activism and the Rejuvenation of the Public Sphere," *Argumentation and Advocacy* 31 (Spring 1995): 163–184.

[30] The authors thank Robert Asen for his useful distinction between universality and multiplicity.

[31] Fraser, "Rethinking," 134, italics added.

[32] Fraser, "Rethinking," 134, italics added.

[33] Ono and Sloop. See also J. David Cisneros, "Contaminated Communities: The Metaphor of 'Immigrant as Pollutant' in Media Representations of Immigration," *Rhetoric and Public Affairs* 11, no. 4 (2008): 569–602; Otto Santa Anna, *Brown Tide Rising: Metaphors of Latinos in Contemporary American Public Discourse* (Austin: University of Texas Press, 2002).

[34] Marouf Hasian, Jr., and Fernando Delgado, "The Trials and Tribulations of Racialized Critical Rhetorical Theory: Understanding the Rhetorical Ambiguities of Proposition 187," *Communication Theory* 8, no. 3 (August 1998): 245–270, 259.

[35] Matthew Webster, "The Border Crossed Us," *Nonviolent Migration*, http://nonviolentmigration.wordpress.com/2007/10/19/the-border-crossed-us (accessed October 6, 2009) and Rubén Martínez, "Fighting 187: The Different Opposition Strategies," *NACLA: Report of the Americas* 29, no. 3 (November/December 1995): 29–34, 30.

[36] Fraser, "Rethinking," 134.

[37] Fraser, "Rethinking," 134–135.

[38] Hasian and Delgado, "Trials," 254.

[39] Hasian and Delgado, "Trials," 262.

[40] Fraser, "Rethinking," 136.

[41] Hauser, "Features," 439.

[42] Habermas, "Further Reflections," 438.

[43] Michael Warner, *Publics and Counterpublics* (New York: Zone, 2002), 117.

[44] The Black Public Sphere Collective, ed., *The Black Public Sphere* (Chicago: University of Chicago Press, 1995).

[45] George A. Kennedy, *Classical Rhetoric and Its Christian and Secular Tradition from Ancient to Modern Times*, 2nd ed. (Chapel Hill: University of North Carolina Press, 1999): 20.

[46] Eva C. Keuls, *The Reign of the Phallus* (New York: Harper and Row, 1985), 391.

[47] Fraser, "Rethinking," 123, italics added.

[48] Fraser, "Rethinking," 124.

[49] Rita Felski, *Beyond Feminist Aesthetics* (Cambridge, MA: Harvard University Press, 1989), 12.

[50] Catharine A. MacKinnon, *Women's Lives, Men's Laws* (Cambridge, MA: Harvard University Press, 2005), 111.

[51] Catherine Squires, "The Black Press and the State: Attracting Unwanted (?) Attention," in *Counterpublics and the State*, ed. Robert Asen and Daniel C. Brouwer, 111–136 (Albany: State University of New York Press, 2001), 132, n. 1, italics added. In addition to discussing enclaved and oscillating publics, Squires offers two additional levels of distinction: a counterpublic "engages in mass actions to assert its needs . . . utilizing disruptive social movement tactics to make demands on the state," and parallel publics "work in conjunction with other [publics] on equal footing." For our purposes, her discussion of oscillation and enclaved publics is the most useful.

[52] bell hooks does not capitalize her name. Her birth name is Gloria Jean Watkins. She chose the name of bell hooks in remembrance of her lineage (she took her great-grandmother's name), as well as to distinguish her voice from Gloria Watkins's. The pseudonym and the lower-case letters signify the importance of her ideas and writing instead of her socially constructed identity.

[53] bell hooks, *Talking Back: Thinking Feminist, Thinking Black* (Boston: South End, 1989), 29.

54 Robert Asen and Daniel C. Brouwer, "Introduction: Reconfigurations of the Public Sphere," in *Counterpublics and the State*, ed. Robert Asen and Daniel C. Brouwer, 1–32 (Albany: State University of New York Press, 2001), 8.

55 Jane Mansbridge, "Using Power/Fighting Power: The Polity," in *Democracy and Difference: Contesting the Boundaries of the Political*, ed. Seyla Benhabib, 46–66 (Princeton, NJ: Princeton University Press, 1996), 58.

56 Hasian and Delgado, "Trials," 259.

57 Daniel C. Brouwer, "ACT-ing UP in Congressional Hearings," in *Counterpublics and the State*, ed. Robert Asen and Daniel C. Brouwer, 87–110 (Albany: State University of New York Press, 2001), 132, n. 1.

58 Kristy Maddux, "When Patriots Protest: The Anti-Suffrage Discursive Transformation of 1917," *Rhetoric and Public Affairs* 7, no. 3 (Fall 2004): 283–310.

59 Fraser, "Rethinking," 99–100.

60 Asen and Brouwer, "Introduction," 20.

61 Felski, *Beyond*, 166.

62 Lisa A. Flores, "Creating Discursive Space through a Rhetoric of Difference: Chicana Feminists Craft a Homeland," *Quarterly Journal of Speech* 82 (1996): 142–156.

63 Santa Ana, *Brown*, 298–299.

64 Warner, *Publics*, 57.

65 Nancy Fraser, "Transnationalizing the Public Sphere: On the Legitimacy and Efficacy of Public Opinion in a Post-Westphalian World," *Theory, Culture and Society* 24, no. 4 (2007): 7–30, 16.

66 Fraser, "Transnationalizing," 19.

67 Kevin Michael DeLuca and Jennifer Peeples, "From Public Sphere to Public Screen: Democracy, Activism, and the 'Violence' of Seattle," *Critical Studies in Media Communication* 19, no. 2 (June 2002): 126.

68 Asen and Brouwer, "Introduction," 16.

69 Dana Cloud, presentation at the National Communication Association preconference "Connection and Action in Public Sphere Studies: Conversations about What We Do and Why We Do It," Chicago, November 15, 2006.

70 Apple, R. W., Jr., "A Nation Challenged: News Analysis: Nature of Foe is Obstacle in Appealing for Sacrifice" [Electronic version], *New York Times*, October 15, 2001, B1; Matthew A. Crenson and Benjamin Ginsberg, *Downsizing Democracy: How America Sidelined Its Citizens and Privatized Its Public* (Baltimore: Johns Hopkins University Press, 2002); Liz Kowalczyk, "Patriotic Purchasing Americans Are Being Urged to Spend, But Analysts Doubt the Strategy Will Have an Impact in the Long Run," *Boston Globe*, September 28, 2001, C1.

71 Crenson and Ginsberg, *Downsizing*, 9 and 2.

72 Lauren Berlant, *The Queen of American Goes to Washington City: Essays on Sex and Citizenship* (Durham, NC: Duke University Press, 1997), 5.

73 Berlant, *Queen*, 3.

74 Berlant, *Queen*, 3.

75 Berlant, *Queen*, 5.

76 Stephanie Coontz, *The Way We Never Were: American Families and the Nostalgia Trap* (New York: Basic Books, 1992), 94.

77 Crenson and Ginsberg, *Downsizing*, 7.

78 Clifford Rechtschaffen, Eileen Gauna, and Catherine O'Neill, *Environmental Justice: Law, Policy & Regulation*, 2nd ed. (Durham, NC: Carolina Academic Press, 2009), esp. excerpt from Vicki Been.

[79] Benjamin Chavis, "Concerning the Historical Evolution of the 'Environmental Justice Movement' and the Definition of the Term: 'Environmental Racism,'" September 4, 2009, http://www.drbenjaminchavis.com/pages/landing ?Concerning-the-Historical-Evolution-of-t=1&blockID=73318&feedID=3359 (accessed June 27, 2011).

[80] Asen and Brouwer, "Introduction."

[81] Robert Asen and Daniel C. Brouwer, "Introduction: John Dewey and the Public Sphere," *Argumentation and Advocacy* 39, no. 3 (Winter 2003): 157–160, 1.

[82] Dewey, *The Public*, 30.

[83] Pew Internet & American Life Project, "Adults on Social Network Sites, 2005–2009," October 8, 2009, http://www.pewinternet.org/Infographics /Growth-in-Adult-SNS-Use-20052009.aspx (accessed October 14, 2009); John Horrigan, "Wireless Internet Use," July 22, 2009, http://www.pewinternet.org/Reports/2009/12-Wireless-Internet-Use.aspx (accessed October 14, 2009).

[84] Bob Simon, "How a Slap Sparked Tunisia's Revolution," *60 Minutes*, February 20, 2011, http://www.cbsnews.com/stories/2011/02/20/60minutes/main20033404.shtml (accessed February 24, 2011).

[85] Hillary Clinton, "Internet Rights and Wrongs: Choices and Challenges in a Networked World," February 15, 2011, http://www.state.gov/secretary/rm/2011/02/156619.htm (accessed February 22, 2011).

[86] Interestingly, one of the most public places on the University of Northern Iowa's campus, the student union, has a policy prohibiting public speaking. Maucker Union's "Policies and Procedures" clarify: "In an effort to promote a comfortable, student centered, educationally focused community . . . agents of any cause, organization or product are prohibited from active solicitation within Maucker Union. This includes activities such as public speaking . . . ." http://www.uni.edu/maucker/policies/section-0500.shtml (accessed October 7, 2009).

[87] Vivian Sobchack, "Democratic Franchise and the Electronic Frontier," in *Cyberfutures: Culture and Politics on the Information Superhighway*, 77–89, ed. Ziauddin Sardar and Jerome R. Ravetz, (New York: New York University Press, 1996), 82.

[88] The National Campaign to Prevent Teen and Unplanned Pregnancy, *Sex and Tech: Results from a Survey of Teens and Young Adults*, 2008, http://www.thenationalcampaign.org/sextech/PDF/SexTech_Summary.pdf (accessed October 5, 2009).

[89] Chana Joffe-Walt, "'Sexting': A Disturbing New Teen Trend?" *All Things Considered*, March 11, 2009, http://www.npr.org/templates/story/story.php?storyId=101735230 (accessed October 5, 2009).

[90] Aaron Smith, "The Internet's Role in Campaign 2008," Pew Internet & American Life Project, April 15, 2009, http://www.pewinternet.org/Reports/2009 /6—The-Internets-Role-in-Campaign-2008.aspx (accessed October 14, 2009).

[91] Mark Poster, "Cyber Democracy: The Internet and the Public Sphere," in *The Information Subject: Mark Poster Essays*, ed. Stanley Aronowitz, 95–116 (Amsterdam: G + B Arts International, 2001), 96.

[92] Mark Poster, "The Internet and the Public Sphere," in *Reading Digital Culture*, ed. David Trend, 259–280 (Malden, MA: Blackwell, 2001), 260.

[93] Brenda Chan, "Imagining the Homeland: The Internet and Diasporic Discourse of Nationalism," *Journal of Communication Inquiry* 29, no. 4 (October 2005): 336–368; Peter Dahlgren, "The Internet, Public Spheres, and Political Communication: Dispersion and Deliberation," *Political Communication* 22, no. 2 (April/June 2005): 147–162.

[94] Wendy M. Grossman, *Net.wars* (New York: New York University Press, 1997).

[95] See, for example, Graeme Browning, *Electronic Democracy: Using the Internet to Influence American Politics* (Wilton, CT: Pemberton, 1996; Lawrence K. Grossman, *The Electronic Republic: Reshaping Democracy in the Information Age* (New York: Viking, 1995); Kevin A. Hill and John E. Hughes, *Cyberpolitics: Citizen Activism in the Age of the Internet* (Lanham, MD: Rowman and Littlefield, 1998); Jay Kinney, "Is There a New Political Paradigm Lurking in Cyberspace?" in *Cyberfutures: Culture and Politics on the Information Superhighway*, ed. Ziauddin Sardar and Jerome R. Ravetz, 138–153 (New York: New York University Press, 1996).

[96] Patty Riley, James Klumpp, and Thomas Hollihan, "Democratizing the Lifeworld of the 21st Century: Evaluating New Democratic Sites for Argument," in *Argument and Values*, ed. Sally Jackson, 254–260 (Annandale, VA: National Communication Association, 1995), 259.

[97] Patty Riley, Thomas Hollihan, and James Klumpp, "The Dark Side of Community and Democracy: Militias, Patriots and Angry White Guys," in *Argument in a Time of Change: Definitions, Frameworks, and Critiques*, ed. James F. Klumpp, 202–207 (Annandale, VA: National Communication Association, 1997), 205.

[98] Cass R. Sunstein, *Going to Extremes: How Like Minds Unite and Divide* (New York: Oxford University Press, 2009): 81.

[99] Christopher J. Stapel, *No Longer Alone: A Resource Manual for Rural Sexual Minority Youth and the Adults Who Serve Them* [pamphlet], National Youth Advocacy Coalition, http://www.nyacyouth.org/docs/ruralyouth/NoLongerAlone.pdf (accessed October 14, 2009).

[100] Lincoln Dahlberg, "Rethinking the Fragmentation of the Cyberpublic: From Consensus to Contestation," *New Media and Society* 9, no. 5 (2007): 827–847, 830.

[101] John Horrigan, Kelly Garrett, and Paul Resnick, *The Internet and Democratic Debate*, Pew Internet & American Life Project, 2004, http://www.pewinternet.org/Reports /2004/The-Internet-and-Democratic-Debate.aspx (accessed October 9, 2009).

[102] Susannah Fox and Gretchen Livingston, "Latinos Online," *Pew Internet and American Life Project*, http://www.pewinternet.org/pdfs/Latinos_Online_March_14_2007.pdf (accessed April 5, 2007).

[103] Commerce Department, *Falling through the Net: Part II: Internet Access and Usage*, http://www.ntia.doc.gov/ntiahome/fttn99/part2.html (accessed January 15, 2007).

[104] Fraser, "Rethinking," 123.

[105] Catherine Helen Palczewski, "Cyber-Movements, New Social Movements, and Counterpublics," in *Counterpublics and the State*, ed. Robert Asen and Daniel C. Brouwer, 161–210 (Albany: State University of New York Press, 2001), 171–172.

[106] World Summit on the Information Society, "The Digital Divide at a Glance," last updated 2005, http://www.itu.int/wsis/tunis/newsroom/stats/index.html (accessed October 14, 2009).

[107] For more information, see *Zapatistas in Cyberspace*, a website maintained by University of Texas associate professor Harry M. Cleaver, Jr., http://www.eco.utexas.edu/faculty/Cleaver/zapsincyber.html. We are particularly

thankful to Professor Cleaver for his expert feedback on this section's discussion of the events in Chiapas.

[108] Harry M. Cleaver, Jr., "The Chiapas Uprising and the Future of Class Struggle in the New World Order," uploaded February 14, 1994, http://www.eco.utexas.edu/facstaff/Cleaver/chiapasuprising.html (accessed October 7, 2009).

[109] Donna Kowal, "Digitizing and Globalizing Indigenous Voices: The Zapatista Movement," in *Critical Perspectives on the Internet*, ed. Greg Elmer, 105–126, (Lanham, MD: Rowman and Littlefield, 2002), 111.

[110] Harry Cleaver, "The Zapatistas and the Electronic Fabric of Struggle" (uploaded November 1995), http://www.eco.utexas.edu/faculty/Cleaver/zaps.html (accessed October 7, 2009).

[111] "Mission Statement," indymedia.us, http://indymedia.us/en/static/mission.shtml (accessed January 26, 2011).

[112] Indybay, "Indymedia and Indybay History," http://www.indybay.org/newsitems/2005/03/11/17262451.php (accessed January 26, 2011).

[113] Jill Lane, "Digital Zapatistas," *The Drama Review* 47, no. 2 (2003): 129–144, 135.

[114] Jesus Barraza, "Celebrating 15 years of Zapatista Struggle," (posted January 5, 2009) http://www.justseeds.org/blog/2009/01/celebrating_15_years_of_zapati.html (accessed October 7, 2009). Postings also have appeared on the *De Tod@s Para Tod@s* blog (see for instance, http://detodos-paratodos.blogspot.com/2010/05 /april-2010-chiapaszapatista-news.html), *the new internationalist* blog (see for instance, http://www.newint.org/blog/majority/2008/06/09/zapatistas-threatened), and *The Frugal Traveler* (see for instance, http://frugaltraveler.blogs.nytimes.com/2008/12/09/in-the-village-of-the-zapatistas) (accessed August 10, 2011).

[115] Stephen Wray, quoted in B. Paquin, "Hacktivism: Attack of the E-Guerillas!" *The Straits Times* (Singapore), December 13, 1998, 32–33, http://www.lexis-nexis.com (accessed February 13, 1999).

[116] Jill Lane, "Digital Zapatistas," *The Drama Review* 47, no. 2 (Summer 2003): 129–144.

[117] Pineda and Sowards, "Flag Waving," 164.

[118] Associated Press, "Immigration Issue Draws Thousands into Streets," http://www.msnbc.msn.com/id/11442705/ (accessed October 29, 2009). Image RTR1CZPR on the Reuters website.

[119] http://www.minutemanproject.com/immigration-topics/archive.asp (accessed October 12, 2011).

[120] Pineda and Sowards, "Flag Waving," 172.

[121] DeLuca and Peeples, "From Public," 129, 131, italics added.

[122] DeLuca and Peeples, "From Public," 132.

[123] DeLuca and Peeples, "From Public," 144.

[124] DeLuca and Peeples, "From Public," 147.

[125] DeLuca and Peeples, "From Public," 145.

[126] Habermas, "The Public Sphere," 231.

Credits and Acknowledgments

Grateful acknowledgment is made for permission to use the following:

Excerpts on pages 21, 76, and 121 from Barry Schwartz, "The Social Context of Commemoration: A Study of Collective Memory." From SOCIAL FORCES vol. 61. Copyright © 1982 by the University of North Carolina Press. Used by permission of the publisher. www.uncpress.unc.edu

Text on page 48 of "Million Voices for Darfur" postcard, 2006, reproduced with permission of the Save Darfur Coalition.

Excerpt on page 37 from Edward Sapir, "The Status of Linguistics as a Science," *Language* 5, no. 4 (1929). Language by LINGUISTIC SOCIETY OF AMERICA. Copyright 1929 Reproduced with permission of LINGUISTIC SOCIETY OF AMERICA in the format Textbook via Copyright Clearance Center.

The description on pages 40–41 of "fetus" and "baby" as illustrations of terministic screens, adapted from Victoria DeFrancisco and Catherine H. Palczewski, *Communicating Gender Diversity*, 2007. Used with permission of Sage Publications, Inc.

Excerpt on page 45 from George Lakoff, "Framing the Dems," *The American Prospect*, vol. 14, no. 8, September 2003, reproduced by permission *The American Prospect*.

Excerpts on pages 45 and 46 from Riikka Kuusisto, "Heroic Tale, Game, and Business Deal? Western Metaphors in Action in Kosovo," *Quarterly Journal of Speech* 88, no. 1, February 2002, copyright © National Communication Association reprinted by permission of (Taylor & Francis Ltd., http://www.tandf.co.uk/journals) on behalf of National Communication Association.

Excerpts on pages 76–77 from Paul Watson, "One Day on the Water with Bob Hunter," Sea Shepherd Conservation Society webpage, reproduced with permission of Sea Shepherd Conservation Society.

Excerpts on pages 89–90 and 100 from Mark Jenkins, "Who Murdered the Virunga Gorillas," *National Geographic* 214, no. 1, July 2008, Mark (Wyoming) Jenkins/ National Geographic Stock. Reproduced with permission of the National Geographic Society.

Excerpt on page 90 from Chris Falzon, letter to the editor, *National Geographic* 214, no. 5, November 2008, reproduced with permission of Chris Falzon.

Excerpt on page 90 from Bryan Berry, letter to the editor, *National Geographic* 214, no. 5, November 2008, reproduced with permission of Bryan Berry.

Excerpts on page 91 from John Dewey, "Creative Democracy," *1939–1941/Essays, Reviews, and Miscellany*, vol. 14, *John Dewey: The Later Works, 1925–1953*, 1988, reproduced with permission of Southern Illinois University Press.

Excerpt on pages 92–93 from transcript of Newt Gingrich, "Stop Imperial Judges . . . Support Proposition 8," 2008, reproduced with permission of Newt Gingrich.

Excerpt on page 93 from *"Reneging on a right,"* the *Los Angeles Times Editorial Staff*, August 08, 2008. Copyright © 2008, Los Angeles Times. Reprinted with Permission.

Definition on page 102 of "Truthiness," Merriam-Webster's Words of the Year 2006. By permission. From *Merriam-Webster Online* © 2011 by Merriam-Webster, Incorporated (www.Merriam-Webster.com).

Index

About the Authors

Catherine Helen Palczewski is professor of communication studies, former director of debate, and an affiliate faculty member in Women's and Gender Studies at the University of Northern Iowa. She received her BS, MA, and PhD from Northwestern University. She teaches courses in rhetorical theory, the rhetoric of social protest, rhetorical criticism, argumentation, gender in communication, and political communication. She coedits *Argumentation and Advocacy*. She has published essays in that journal, as well as in the *Quarterly Journal of Speech, Communication Studies, NWSA Journal*, and the *Southern Communication Journal*. She has also published numerous book chapters. She has served on the editorial boards of the *Quarterly Journal of Speech, Argumentation and Advocacy, Women's Studies in Communication, Communication Studies, Controversia, Communication Monographs*, and the *Southern Communication Journal*. She has received the Francine Merritt Award for Outstanding Contributions to the Lives of Women in Communication, the Iowa Regents Award for Faculty Excellence, the University of Northern Iowa College of Humanities and Fine Arts Faculty Excellence Award, the George Ziegelmueller Outstanding Debate Educator Award, and the Rohrer Award for the Outstanding Publication in Argumentation. In 2001, she was the keynote speaker at the AFA/NCA Summer Conference on Argumentation, a conference she will direct in 2013.

Richard Ice is professor of communication and academic dean at the College of St. Benedict and St. John's University. He received his AB from Wabash College. He received his MA and PhD from the University of Iowa. He teaches courses in rhetorical analysis, classical rhetoric, freedom of speech, public address, group communication, and organizational communication. He has published essays in *Management Communication Quarterly* and *Communication Quarterly*, as well as several book chapters. He has received the St. John's University Robert L. Spaeth Teacher of Distinction Award and the College of St. Benedict / St. John's University Academic Advisor Award.

John Fritch is professor of communication studies and associate dean of the College of Humanities, Arts and Sciences at the University of Northern Iowa. He received his BA from the University of Nebraska–Lincoln. His MA and PhD are from the University of Kansas. He teaches courses in rhetorical theory, language and communication, and ethics. He coedits *Argumentation and Advocacy*. He has published essays in that journal, as well as in the *Southern Journal of Forensics*, several editions of the published papers of the biannual NCA/AFA conference on argumentation, and *A Century of Transformation: Studies in Honor of the 100th Anniversary of the Eastern Communication Association*. Formerly, he was the director of forensics at Southwest Missouri State University. Currently, he is the director of the National Debate Tournament. He has received the Donn W. Parson Young Educator Award, the Outstanding Teaching Award from the College of Arts and Letters at Missouri State University, and the Outstanding Graduate Faculty Member in Communication Studies Award at Missouri State. He was recognized as a Centennial Scholar by the Eastern Communication Association.